D0072309

Critical Essays on T. S. Eliot:
The Sweeney Motif

Kinley E. Roby

G. K. Hall & Co. • Boston, Massachusetts

1985

Published by G. K. Hall & Co.
A publishing subsidiary of ITT

Library of Congress Cataloging in Publication Data

Main entry under title:

Critical essays on T.S. Eliot.

(Critical essays on American literature)
Bibliography: p.
Includes index.
1. Eliot, T.S. (Thomas Stearns), 1888–1965 — Criticism and interpre-
tation — Addresses, essays, lectures. 2. Eliot, T.S. (Thomas Stearns),
1888–1965 — Characters — Sweeney — Addresses, essays, lectures. 3.
Sweeney (Fictitious character) — Addresses, essays on lectures. I. Roby,
Kinley E. II. Series.
PS3509.L43Z655   1985   821'.912   84-22441
ISBN 0-8161-8689-8

CRITICAL ESSAYS ON AMERICAN LITERATURE

This series seeks to anthologize the most important criticism on a wide variety of topics and writers in American literature. Our readers will find in various volumes not only a generous selection of reprinted articles and reviews but original essays, bibliographies, manuscript sections, and other materials brought to public attention for the first time. This volume on the Sweeney motif in the poetry and plays of T. S. Eliot, edited by Kinley E. Roby, is a welcome addition to our list. There are reprinted reviews and articles by many leading critics of modern literature, including D. E. S. Maxwell, Katherine Worth, Nevil Coghill, Marjorie J. Lightfoot, Jane Worthington, and Jerome Meckier, among others. In addition to an extensive introduction by Professor Roby, there are original essays by Carol H. Smith, Jonathan Morse, and Nancy D. Hargrove. We are confident that this volume will make a permanent and significant contribution to American literary study.

James Nagel, GENERAL EDITOR

Northeastern University

CONTENTS

INTRODUCTION

1

In 1973 A. Walton Litz was able to write that the time had come for "placing" T. S. Eliot.[1] Robert Adams in the same volume speaks of "precipitating" Eliot.[2] Northrop Frye, ten years earlier, could affirm with little fear of contradiction that "a thorough knowledge of Eliot is compulsory for anyone interested in contemporary literature," which is a way of saying that the writer's place and value has been established.[3] To carry the case back a little further, Dame Helen Gardner concluded in 1949 that Eliot had "created the taste by which he is enjoyed," taking us into that period in which Gardner, F. R. Leavis, Cleanth Brooks, F. O. Matthiessen, and a few others could rejoice in having established Eliot's reputation.[4] It was another twenty years before their assessments were significantly adjusted by a new generation of Eliot scholars. Further major modifications in the amended outlines of critical assessment must await the availability of biographical material currently being withheld.

In the scholarship that has developed around Eliot's work, the poet of *The Waste Land* and *Four Quartets*, the critic of *The Sacred Wood*, and the dramatist of *Murder in the Cathedral* and *The Family Reunion* are most thoroughly "precipitated." Less well understood is the writer of the quatrain poems, composed between 1914 and 1922, the year *The Waste Land* was published, and the complex character of Sweeney, who first appears in these poems. In dealing with Sweeney, scholars have too frequently dismissed him as a South Boston pugilist; a parodic version of Sweeney Todd, the Demon Barber of Fleet Street, who cut his patrons' throats and smuggled them next door to be made into meat pies; or as a decayed version of the classic hero, the modern world's disgraceful entry in the lists of mythical heroes, a man without culture, traditions, ideals, or moral vision.

Had these limited interpretations been exhaustive, Sweeney could hardly be said to embody a major idea in Eliot's work. Yet he does embody such an idea; and although the idea and its attendant emotions seem to have had more force in Eliot's thinking in the years before 1927, the year of the poet's announced religious conversion, than in the following years, they are never entirely absent from Eliot's work. They change with time but remain pervasively present. Eliot's shifting attitude toward the Sweeney material is a bellwether of attendant changes in his poetry as a whole.

Critics have been slow to respond to the Sweeney motif in Eliot's work. Early evidence of any response is scarce. As Mildred Martin makes clear in her *A Half-Century of Eliot Criticism*, there are only a handful of responses to Eliot's poetry in the period before 1922, when *The Waste Land* began to attract the critics' serious attention.[5] In fact it is probably fair to say that until the publication of *The Waste Land*, critics were more interested in *The Sacred Wood* (1920) than in either *Prufrock And Other Observations* (1917) or *Poems* (1920). *Poems* contains the first appearance of Sweeney as a named character, although he had been adumbrated in the earlier Prufrock volume. Among the reviewers and commentators who responded to Eliot's poetry in this early period were Conrad Aiken, Babette Deutsch, Marianne Moore, Ford Madox Ford, Louis Untermeyer, Mark Van Doren, May Sinclair, and, of course, Ezra Pound. These writers were, for the most part, supportive of what Eliot was attempting as an innovator, but none found Sweeney particularly interesting. Of their number, perhaps only Pound understood the significance of what Eliot was attempting in Modernist terms. The rest, for the most part, saw Eliot as an antiromantic, an Imagist, an imitator of Laforgue and Browning, and even as a literary joker.

Publication of *The Waste Land* focused attention on Eliot, and in 1922 in two ground-breaking essays, "The Rag-bag of the Soul," and "The Poetry of Drouth," Edmund Wilson began the task of placing Eliot in his time and evaluating the influences behind his poetry.[6] It was an intellectual exercise that would be repeated with increasing frequency into the 1960s, when the flood of Eliot criticism finally began to abate somewhat. In 1931 in *Axel's Castle*, Wilson devotes a chapter to Eliot's poetry and criticism, giving some attention to Sweeney. Speaking of "that dark rankling of passions inhibited" which Wilson saw as a principal subject in Eliot's poetry, he goes on to draw a comparison between Eliot and Henry James. "The fear of life, in James," Wilson writes, "is closely bound up with the fear of vulgarity." Wilson wrote that "Eliot, too, fears vulgarity — which he embodies in the symbolic figure of 'Apeneck Sweeney' — at the same time that he is fascinated by it."[7]

By identifying Sweeney as a symbolic figure in Eliot's poetry, Wilson became one of the first major critics to recognize Sweeney's importance, while at the same time failing to grasp the character's complexity, reducing him, as he does, to an embodiment of vulgarity. Nevertheless, Wilson touches on a very important feature of Eliot's persona in the early poems, his ambivalence towards vulgarity, especially when it manifests itself in overt female sexuality in, for example, Grishkin and her "promise of pneumatic bliss." Wilson also recognizes the power Sweeney possesses to remain in the reader's memory, ascribing that trait to Eliot's "essentially Dramatic" imagination. Prufrock and Sweeney have become, Wilson suggests, "characters as none of the personages of Pound, Valéry, or Yeats is — they have become a part of our modern mythology."[8] In thirteen brief years Eliot had come from obscurity to center stage, chiefly because of *The Waste Land*, and with the blessings of such critics as Wilson, Allen Tate, Richard Aldington, I. A. Richards, and others. He was not, however, without his detractors, most influential of whom were Gertrude Stein, Louis Untermeyer, Edwin Muir, J. Middleton Murry, and Clement Wood, who in "The Tower of Drivel," labeled *The Waste Land* "a farrago of nonsense."

By 1929 essays on Eliot were beginning to appear in collections of essays and in single works of some length, such as George Williamson's thirty-seven-page monograph, *The Talent of T. S. Eliot*, no. 32 in the University of Washington Chapbooks series. The criticism of Eliot in this period tends to concentrate on the influence behind Eliot, on the relationship of his practice as a poet and his critical declarations, and on his position as a humanist. Henry Seidel Canby, for instance, called Eliot a genuine humanist, while R. P. Blackmur in the same year thought Eliot an enemy of humanism.[9] Some of the critics were still struggling to understand *The Waste Land*; but the best of them, such as I. A. Richards, had begun to grasp that Eliot had found a new way of writing poetry and that poetry had received a wound from which it would not soon recover. Serious attention to Sweeney, however, was still missing.

F. R. Leavis's *New Bearings in English Poetry* (1932) and its influential chapter on Eliot may be said to mark an early stabilizing of Eliot's reputation as a poet. It also marks the beginning of serious effort to understand what Eliot was attempting in such poems as "Sweeney among the Nightingales," through the poet's use of quotation and allusion. Having dismissed as "too simple an account" the suggestion that Eliot was by means of the technique condemning the present by "the standards of an ideal past," Leavis somewhat tentatively offers the explanation that what is going on in "Sweeney among the Nightingales" and similar poems "has a closer bearing upon the sense of stale disillusion."[10] He then adds that by 1920 Eliot's achievement was such that "English poetry had made a new start."

With the publication of F. O. Matthiessen's *The Achievement of T. S. Eliot* (1935), the first stage of Eliot criticism is brought to maturity. Matthiessen identifies Prufrock and Sweeney as the most convincingly definite characters in modern poetry and sees them as "so widely pervasive elements in modern city life that they can stand alone almost as symbols."[11] Matthiessen contents himself, as many critics were to continue to do for another twenty years, with seeing Sweeney as exclusively "apeneck" and urban. Matthiessen's major contribution is the particular attention he gives to the Sweeney poems, treating them seriously, although still rather superficially. Slightly more than two decades later, George Williamson's *A Reader's Guide to T. S. Eliot* (1955) and Grover Smith's *T. S. Eliot's Poetry and Plays: A Study of Sources and Meaning* (1956) would carry forward the work begun by Leavis and Matthiessen and continued by Helen Gardner, among others, of chasing down the allusions and quotations in the quatrain poems and allowing the task of assessing the function of these neglected poems to progress.

It is probably due to the slowness of the critical response to Eliot's Sweeney material that important steps toward understanding the significance of them did not begin to appear until the 1950s. Even here much of the critical energy was expended in attempting to develop compelling readings of such individual poems as "Sweeney Erect" and "Sweeney among the Nightingales." In fact, the present collection represents the first effort to bring the criticism together in such a way as to demonstrate the power and the importance of the Sweeney material in the Eliot canon. The essays written specifically for this volume offer the first comprehensive examination of the Sweeney motif in T. S. Eliot's poetry. While the critics represented here do not always agree on such specific issues as who kills whom in *Sweeney Agonistes*, they are increasingly united as they approach the present in the conviction that Sweeney is a vital force that cannot be ignored if the reader hopes to understand the full implications of Eliot's poetry.

2

Over the period of some thirty years during which Eliot developed the Sweeney motif in his poetry, he was consciously manipulating the material as a part of a general attempt to unify his work. Elizabeth Schneider's assertion that Eliot made a conscious effort "to unify the whole body of his poetry and plays . . ." appears to be borne out by the ways in which he handles Sweeney and that constellation of images, ideas, and language patterns that grew up around him over the years.[12] The Sweeney materials provide a surprisingly clear record of Eliot's development as a poet and are especially useful in tracing the evolution of Eliot's thinking. They are, in addition, important bridges linking various stages in the poet's work and helping readers to follow the shifting technical and conceptual developments in his writing.

Sweeney appears named in four poems and a fragmentary play: "Mr. Eliot's Sunday Morning Service," "Sweeney Erect," "Sweeney among the Nightingales," *The Waste Land*, and *Sweeney Agonistes: Fragments of An Aristophanic Melodrama*. These poems were written and published between roughly 1917 and 1932. The 1917 date is somewhat in doubt because the first poem in which Sweeney is named was not published until 1918, although Pound, whom Eliot met in 1914–15, began at once urging him to give up the religious verse he was writing and return to the kind of writing he had done in "Prufrock." In 1918 Pound made the announcement that Eliot was at work on "new and diverting verses."[13] Eliot may, of course, have been writing the poems slightly earlier than 1918 although probably not much before 1917, or the world would have heard sooner from Pound. "The Love Song of J. Alfred Prufrock," "Mr. Apollinax," and "Preludes" were written in 1910–11, and the character of Sweeney, who appears named for the first time in "Sweeney among the Nightingales" and "Mr. Eliot's Sunday Morning Service," surfaces in these earlier pieces only as gestures and anonymous figures.

In "Mr. Apollinax," written at least in part as a humorous tribute to Bertrand Russell's visit to Harvard in 1914, while Eliot was still a graduate student there, Eliot speaks of "Priapus in the shrubbery / Gaping at the lady in the swing."[14] Along with the echoes of Fragonard there is in the lines an evocation of echoes of the god of sensual pleasure manifesting himself briefly among his nonadmirers, Mrs. Phlaccus and the Channing-Cheetah's. Although Eliot has not fully worked out in "Mr. Apollinax," what he wants to do with Priapus / Sweeney, his introduction of the god is not simply paradoxical, comic, or parodic, but is rather expressive of the demonic power of the sexual being, even its demonic attractiveness.

In "Preludes" proto-Sweeney is even less clearly defined but still present. The lines "short square fingers stuffing pipes" and "Wipe your hand across your mouth, and laugh" contrast sharply with "The notion of some infinitely gentle / Infinitely suffering thing," which may be Christ's sacrifice, reproduced in the martyrdoms of the saints, and go beyond simply realistic descriptions of actions observed.[15]

The "lonely men in shirt-sleeves, leaning out of windows" in "The Love Song of J. Alfred Prufrock" are less clearly Sweeney figures, but they do offer a contrast to Prufrock.[16] They are not, apparently, tempted or even inclined to ask that "overwhelming question," toward which Prufrock feels himself propelled and from which he recoils in fear. Although they are lonely, they are not engaged in foolish, fruitless activity but instead, like the man in *Sweeney Agonistes* who has killed a woman, they only wait. To ascribe hopelessness to the men or sordidness to their lives is to bring into the poem qualities not actually given them by Eliot. They anticipate, for example, the "Silent man" in "Sweeney among the Nightingales" who also leans in a window and watches.[17]

Another poem in which the Sweeney idea is anticipated is "The Hippopotamus," first published in *The Little Review* in 1917.[18] The poem is an early example of Eliot's using naive imagery for ironic effect. The contrast between the hippopotamus and the "True Church" is an obvious and at least partially comic element in the poem; but the comic aspects of the poem can be misleading, because as Lyndall Gordon has pointed out, Eliot had learned from his study of Laforgue "to dramatise his most serious ideas as irrational, even ridiculous emotions."[19] Although heavily masked, "The Hippopotamus" does represent a deeply felt emotion in Eliot.

The picture of the hippopotamus taking wing, "Ascending from the damp savannas," surrounded by "quiring angels" is certainly amusing.[20] The joke, however, has a serious intent, as does Sweeney. Eliot confronts in the hippopotamus less the issue of the Church's failure than the full meaning of Christ's sacrifice, the full meaning of redemption. Also buried in the poem is the figure of St. Augustine, Bishop of Hippo; and here are found together, more explicitly than in the other published poems of this period, Sweeney and the saint, antiphonic voices of alternating appeal and revulsion.

There is, however, an unpublished poem of this early period, "The Love Song of Saint Sebastian," written in Germany in July 1914, that is one of three poems concerned with martyrdom done in the same year. (The other two are "The Burnt Dancer" and "The Death of Saint Narcissus," in which Sweeney and the saint are enclosed within a single character.)[21] In Gordon's opinion the poem expresses the Sweeney-saint antithesis in terms that carry the "debate" "beyond the possibility of resolution."[22] It is probably dangerous to deal with the two extremes represented by the action of the saint in the poem exclusively as ideas, because they are, more accurately stated, emotional states.

In that poem Sebastian seeks to ingratiate himself with a beautiful woman, before whom he whips himself almost to the point of death. She then accepts his suit. In a swift reversal of behavior, Sebastian strangles the woman "with sinister fondness."[23] The poem can be regarded as a confrontation between asceticism and sensual indulgence, and there is also something of the medieval *debat* about it. Perhaps of greater interest are the dual impulses, one toward renunciation of the flesh and the other toward complete indulgence, which the poem presents. It is probably accurate to say that it is from the sensual impulse that the character of Sweeney emerges.

However, to say, as Gordon does, that "the brute Sweeney" emerges from the "instinctual side of Sebastian, wielding his towel . . ." is to insist on too much and too little.[24] Sweeney, as Eliot develops him, certainly is instinctual man, if by that Gordon means sensual man, but he is not brutal, although he may seem brutish. There is an unfortunate knee-jerk response in Eliot scholarship that encourages thinking about Sweeney to stop at his ape neck. Even in the quatrain poems, Sweeney is a more complex construct than is implied by the term "brute Sweeney." Sebastian does murder his lady; and someone in *Sweeney Agonistes*, possibly Sweeney himself, has killed or intends to kill a woman. These two killings, however, are not simple homicides. Too much has been made of the *News of The World* aspect of the dead woman in the bathtub, preserved in lysol, and too little of Sweeney's efforts to convey a sense of what the experience meant to the murderer or, for that matter, just what was killed.

3

Following the publication of "The Hippopotamus" in 1917, "Sweeney among the Nightingales" and "Mr. Eliot's Sunday Morning Service" appeared in the *Little Review* in September 1918, and "Sweeney Erect" in *Art And Letters* in the summer of 1919. These and other poems appeared in a volume called *Poems*, published in 1919 by Virginia and Leonard Woolf at the Hogarth Press. Although not published in the United States, the contents of *Poems*, with minor variations, were to appear again the following year in two further volumes, *Ara Vos Prec* and *Poems*, the latter brought out in the United States by Alfred A. Knopf.[25]

"Fragment of a Prologue," the first part of what was eventually to become *Sweeney Agonistes*, appeared in the *Criterion* in 1926.[26] "Fragment of an Agon" appeared in the *Criterion* in January 1927.[27] Both pieces were published in 1932 by Faber & Faber under the title, *Sweeney Agonistes: Fragments of An Aristophanic Melodrama.* The publication of this fragmentary work, which has been produced from time to time as a play but was finally designated by its author an uncompleted poem, brings to an end the appearance of Sweeney as a named character in Eliot's work. After 1932 Sweeney disperses into the poetry and plays as the debate of body and soul moves toward resolution.

It is generally recognized and has been extensively explored by Gordon especially that between the composition of "Prufrock" in 1910–11 and the major composition of *The Waste Land* in 1921, Eliot passed through a sequence of personal experiences that profoundly modified his thinking and created the forms his poetry would take. It was in this period and in particular in the seven years from 1914 to 1921 that the idea of Sweeney gradually took shape in Eliot's mind, providing him with a character in whom he could express at least a part of the emotional conflict for which he would not find a personal or artistic resolution until his conversion in 1927. The artistic solution, perhaps never complete, was at least partially reached with the publication of *Sweeney Agonistes* in 1932 and "East Coker" on Good Friday 1940.

There are three other fragments, assembled under the title "Doris's Dream Songs," which have a peripheral importance to the Sweeney materials. These poems or parts of poems appeared in *Chapbook* in 1924 and consist of I: "Eyes that last I saw in tears"; II: "The wind sprang up at four o'clock"; and III: "This is the dead land."[28] The third poem was to become Part III of "The Hollow Men." The poems are of interest because a character named Doris appears with Sweeney in "Sweeney Erect" and *Sweeney Agonistes.* In the earlier poem she comes "padding" into the action bearing "sal volatile / And a glass of brandy neat." In the later poem she seeks her future in a card reading and tries to avoid paying her debt to Pereira. Sweeney attempts to explain to her what life is but fails. In a less pronounced way than with Sweeney, Doris has animal associations; but more importantly she is locked to the earth and seems to be linked in Eliot's vision with "death's other kingdom" and, unlike Sweeney, has no hope of escape from it. She embodies a cluster of feelings and ideas deserving of more thorough study than she has yet received.

Neither space nor occasion permit a detailed account of Eliot's life between 1910 and 1921, but a full understanding of Sweeney is impossible without having in mind at least an outline of Eliot's life in this period. In

1910 he took his M.A. *in absentia* from Harvard and departed for France for a year of living abroad.[29] He had by this time read Arthur Symons' *The Symbolist Movement in Literature* (1899) and absorbed the poetry of Jules Laforgue. He had also read Baudelaire and had discovered that he shared with both of these writers "a powerful sense of evil and a passionate antagonism toward society. . . ."[30]

Before leaving Harvard he had familiarized himself not only with Cambridge society but with the seamier life exhibited in the back streets of Boston. In his unpublished "Caprices in North Cambridge," written in 1909, he describes the debris and litter fouling the streets, and his mind came "to rest with a curious repose on vacant lots. . . . It was his first image of a waste land, a scene he was to make his own."[31]

He had begun that fascination with the urban scene and in particular the more sordid aspects of its people and its scenes which would find its ultimate expression in *The Waste Land*. To complicate his already complex responses to the life he was observing with such a mixture of horror and attraction, Eliot had a religious experience in June of 1910. While walking he suddenly felt that the street before him divided and time ceased to exist. He recorded the event in an unpublished poem, "Silence," in which he sets forth more lucidly than perhaps elsewhere in his published work that bright, eternal moment outside of time in which the Absolute draws near.[32]

It is probably still generally assumed that Eliot's religious conversion occurred in the second half of the 1920s and that whatever convulsions he underwent to arrive at his famous declaration of faith had occurred around the time of his public statement of conviction. Such a perception requires modification. The struggle actually goes back to his undergraduate years at Harvard, a time when he was becoming increasingly estranged from his Unitarian past. In 1910 he wrote a series of poems recording his failures of faith, and in the 1920s poems he rejects the blandness, rationalism, respectability, absence of religious instinct, denial of the traditions of formal Christianity which had characterized his experience of the Unitarian faith or branch of "decayed Protestantism" as he characterized it.[33]

He felt that while he had been rigorously schooled in the proprieties of behavior, he had not been taught the realities of good and evil. His grandfather, William Greenleaf Eliot, had been "the standard of conduct" to which he was expected to adjust his own life. This standard had consisted of such austerities of self-denial that he was left "permanently scarred by an inability to enjoy even harmless pleasures."[34] As for headier pleasures, they were absolutely forbidden. Eliot's father regarded sex as "nastiness" and syphilis as God's punishment for indulging in it. He also expressed the hope that a cure for the disease would never be found.[35] T. S. Matthews suggests that Eliot was burdened with a morbid sense of guilt growing out of masturbation and that very early in his life "sex and sin became the same thing."[36]

Connected with these proscriptions against sexual indulgence is Eliot's longstanding detestation of women. Matthews points out that Eliot never succeeded in expressing sexual desire for a woman in his poetry, as, for example, Yeats did. Gordon suggests that his "characteristic irritability" with women is a result of his own sense of inhibition and an equally strong sense of "having dared too little" with them.[37] Predictably and regrettably, he took his mother's poetry, in which she appeals to her readers to "loose the spirit from its mesh, / From the poor vesture of the flesh," literally. Wedding her exhortation to his father's jeremiad, he began a long-lasting quarrel with the world of sense, especially as that world was embodied in women. Only with the hyacinth girl in the garden, a nonsexual figure who probably brings together Matilda from Dante and the figure of Jean Verdenal, is there a sense of the longing for some kind of closer attachment.[38]

This revulsion against sex, against the world of sense, broadened at Harvard to a horror of the "commercial city" and against its inhabitants, against the pragmatism advocated by William James because it made man the measure of things, against the hopefulness of his mother's poetry, and against the temporal world as a whole. This last opposition came from Eliot's almost unbearable sense of time's passing, which, understandably, drove him to seek for some means of transcending time.[39]

What is aimed at in the preceding paragraphs is not an attempt to "account" for Eliot's poetry in the period between 1910 and 1921 through a selective resorting to biographical material. A study of Eliot's poetry does not end with the biographical elements revealed, but it begins there. Eliot made his life the subject of his poetry. Everything he wrote between 1909 and 1921 draws its substance from tensions, unresolved conflicts, and persistent obsessions present in his life. When he began to write the quatrain poems and to develop the character of Sweeney, he did so principally because he could draw closer to the more pressing and immediately personal issues only through "brief autobiographical fragments and poems" which he suppressed until their inclusion in *The Waste Land*. In 1914, when he met Ezra Pound, he was writing religious poetry; and it was Pound who directed his attention back toward social satire.[40]

Pound's encouragement helped Eliot to break free from the block that had prevented him from writing poetry he was willing to publish. To express what happened in another way, Pound helped Eliot to discover a way to approach personal issues and yet remain sufficiently distant to prevent the encounter from crippling his ability to express himself. By 1914 he had come to distrust his own religious intuitions and had arrived at an impasse in his efforts to express those intuitions. As he wrote to Conrad Aiken, "I know the kind of verse I want, and I know this isn't it."[41]

In struggling with the division of body and soul, which had come increasingly to stand as absolute choices, Eliot had left himself no hope of reconciling the demands of the two positions. As in the poem about St. Sebastian, the flesh and the spirit stood locked in irreconcilable conflict, a tradition in American literature that goes back to Anne Bradstreet, Edward Taylor, and the Puritan poets. What the quatrain poems permitted was access to a form of "middle ground" through the adaptation of Laforgian irony and distance and the formalities of the verse forms which Eliot employs in the poems. The poems written between 1917 and 1919 are regarded by Gordon as "a digression from his poetic career."[42] While they may appear to be a digression, they are not so in reality.

[The creation of Sweeney as the embodiment of the flesh in the body / spirit debate gave Eliot a means of discussing a very important personal emotional issue that he had since "Prufrock" been unable to express to his own satisfaction either because he dreaded revealing his own feelings or because he could not find a poetic vehicle capable of expressing those feelings. His dissatisfaction is made clear in his letter to Conrad Aiken mentioned earlier. It is important that Eliot did not abandon Sweeney when with the publication of *The Waste Land* he overcame his dread of self-revelation and solved the problem of finding an adequate poetic form in which to express himself. Sweeney appears in *The Waste Land* and several years after the publication of the poem is made the protagonist of the fragmentary poetic drama *Sweeney Agonistes*. Sweeney provided Eliot with a versatile and compelling means of dealing with one of those "overwhelming questions" that haunted the poet's life.]

Excessive solemnity in dealing with Sweeney runs the risk of masking the comic elements present in the materials. Gordon has already pointed out a "comic repertoire" in the poems—Prufrock, Sweeney, the hippo, and so on.[43] She has also suggested that these figures may have a connection with some traditional figures in the pantheon of American humor. The ignorant, often drunken Irishman of story and stage is an obvious example. The Aunt Polly–like, antifeminist figures of Aunt Helen, Cousin Nancy and the Jamesian parody of the lady in "Portrait of A Lady" are others. Prufrock has an ancestor in Ichabod Crane. Gerontion, "An old man in a draughty house / Under a windy knob," is a grotesque figure, whose prototypes are common in New England and Western folk humor. Mrs. Turner and Mrs. Porter and all their sisters and all their daughters are the ribald tale and raunchy ballad-women of the male subculture which, however protected by his sisters and mother, Eliot would have known.

Eliot's use of comic characters and parodic material may have been a consequence of his having imitated Laforgue.[44] Laforgue's devices of splitting his persona between a "mocking commentator and droll sufferer" and employing comic masks for speakers of serious ideas does have a parallel in Eliot's practice of linking serious ideas to ludicrous, grotesque, or outrageous characters, settings, and situations. The hippo entering heaven, the epileptic on the bed, Sweeney in his bath are examples. Eliot may have had the connection made between serious message and comic messenger by Laforgue, but the traditions of rural American humor would have provided him with equally compelling examples of exaggeration, startling comparisons, understatement, ironic observation, and deceptive simplicity, of the sophisticate, the self-righteous, the self-important laid by the heels. Eliot's methods in the 1920s poems may owe more to his American inheritance than has yet been acknowledged.

The comic elements in the Sweeney material are an escape for Eliot from the emotional conflicts in his life that gave rise to the poetry. They are occasions distancing the poet from his material, freeing him, no doubt imperfectly and only temporarily, from the painful divisions of his mind on the issues of religious faith, belief, and commitment, which had been obsessing him since Harvard and perhaps earlier. After his disastrous marriage in 1915 to Vivienne Haigh-Wood, he could add the terrors of failed sexuality and emotional incompatibility with his wife to the list of his anguishings. His almost instantly failed relationship with Vivienne illustrates the absence of a middle ground in Eliot's thinking about emotionally charged issues. Unable to live with Vivienne, driven to nervous collapse by the pressures of her near madness, he could not divorce her, although to live with her was destroying him. He endured years of suffering before he found the courage to live apart from her.

The quatrain poems provided Eliot with an escape mechanism, first through their humor and then more directly through the escape motif, which is everywhere present in them. Gordon has noted in other of Eliot's poems and plays "Fantasies of a man's escape from a constraining tie. . . ."[45] In the Sweeney material Sweeney is nearly always seen escaping, an aspect of his characterization that makes it unlikely that he is murdered in "Sweeney among the Nightingales." From Mr. Apollinax onward the Sweeney figure is shown either entirely outside of controlling mechanisms present elsewhere in the work or declining to enter the baited trap that would imprison him. Mrs. Phlaccus and Professor and Mrs. Cheetah cannot encompass Mr. Apollinax, and in *Sweeney Agonistes* the man who murders the woman gets so far beyond the constraining bonds of ordinary humanity that "Death or life or life or death" no longer applied to him.

The hippopotamus in the poem of the same name ascends from the damp savannas surrounded by angels, leaving the True Church earthbound. Washed as white as snow, the hippo gains the ultimate freedom. In "Mr. Eliot's Sunday Morning Service" Sweeney in his bath avoids making Origen's mistake, is not controversial, and does not walk the avenue of penitence. The water of Christ's baptism sloshes around Sweeney's hams as he shifts in the tub, free as the sable presbyters and masters of the subtle schools are not. There is, of course, an apparent contradiction in Sweeney's escape as there is in the hippo's apotheosis; but the escape is nonetheless real.

Sweeney's laughter in "Sweeney among the Nightingales" signals his escape from whatever stratagems the person in the Spanish cape and Rachel *née* Rabinovitch have concocted for his overthrow. The host, the man in brown, and Sweeney all appear to have escaped the gins constructed by the two women and seem not about to repeat the tragedy of Procne, Philomela, and King Tereus, whose story is adumbrated in the reference to the nightingales in the last two stanzas of the poem.

His escape in "Sweeney Erect" is more complicated and perhaps more clearly indicative of Eliot's interest in keeping Sweeney free, whatever the exact meaning this freedom had for Eliot. Through its epigraph and other references the poem introduces the themes of deception, abandonment, and betrayal. Debased, rendered comic or sordid, the themes appear to be worked out in Sweeney's "abandonment" of the epileptic screaming in the bed and his "betrayal" of Mrs. Turner's principles. Mrs. Turner's principles, however, are distinctly suspect, and the epileptic's condition is not susceptible to treatment. Doris's ministrations will prove futile. Sweeney stands clear of the woman with the falling sickness and will escape from Mrs. Turner's house.

The pattern of escape is not, however, sustained in *The Waste Land*. Here Sweeney comes to Mrs. Porter in the spring with the inevitability of April. It is possible that Sweeney's entrapment in *The Waste Land* is a consequence of the poem's having been constructed principally from a set of materials that developed parallel to but separate from the quatrain poems. These fragments, which Eliot composed from at least as early as 1911 onwards, come at the emotional and the expressive problems with which Eliot was struggling from a different angle from the one employed in the quatrain poems. After the publication of *The Waste Land*, however, the two positions merge increasingly into a single, steadily intensifying vision, culminating in the *Four Quartets*.

Elizabeth Schneider has drawn attention to the solitary nature of Gerontion and Prufrock.[46] In *The Waste Land* Sweeney is also a solitary, who is social only under the compelling sexual imperative of spring. In the other poems and especially in *Sweeney Agonistes* his solitariness exists in a social context. Least perhaps in "Mr. Eliot's Sunday Morning Service" and most clearly so in *Sweeney Agonistes*, Sweeney's significance is intensified by the relationship between himself and the other characters in the poems. What separates Sweeney from the other characters is not so much a physical distance as a distinction between what is true for Sweeney and what is true for the others. This truth is with the passage of time increasingly a specifically spiritual truth.

In "Mr. Eliot's Sunday Morning Service" Sweeney sits in his bath, assured, secure, in Christ's baptism and His sacrifice. The elaborations of the Church, whether in textual exegesis, doctrine, or ritual, are impotent (emasculated Origen) to alter the fact of Christ's sacrifice, which includes Sweeney in its grace. In this poem Sweeney sits apart and serves as one of the poles of dramatic tension in the poem with Christ as the other. In "Sweeney among the Nightingales" Sweeney is involved in the poem's action. He frustrates an attempted seduction and, by implication, avoids the consequences that destroy Agamemnon, who takes Cassandra into his bed and dies for it, completing another episode in the bloody history of the house of Atreus. In "Sweeney among the Nightingales" the history of the house of

Atreus may express human history before Christ's intervention. Sweeney stands aside. He has access to truth through the gate of horn and does not fall in with the women's plans or eat the suspect fruit.

In the poem Sweeney's animal characteristics, his ape neck, striped jaw, hanging arms, are transcended by his ability to resist temptation, to guard truth. This ability sets him apart in his action from the two women, who seem still linked to the violent and fallen world of the bloody wood. Sweeney's distinctiveness is presented even more forcefully in "Sweeney Erect." The title of the poem carries the ambivalences that are central to Eliot's perception of Sweeney in the period of the poem's construction. There is the sexual inuendo of *erect*, the adjective bearing simultaneously, however, the meaning "upright," thus emphasizing both his human identity and moral straightness.

In the action of the poem, which in its epigraph and in its events deals with betrayal, Sweeney is paired with Theseus, who abandons Ariadne. There is much to be said about this pairing, but for now it is enough to say that Eliot neatly subverts the mocking irony implicit in the pairing by making Sweeney a true "hero." Sweeney's heroism consists of his "abandonment" of the epileptic and his "betrayal" of those conventional virtues, exemplified by Doris and the ladies of the corridor, led by Mrs. Turner. As in the two poems discussed above but with increased emphasis, Sweeney stands apart from the temptations offered by a lower order of social behavior and acts instead according to the imperative of a higher order, the nature of which the poems implicitly define as the one made available through Christ's sacrifice.

Eliot's interest in Sweeney as a pilgrim figure deepened with time, as *Sweeney Agonistes* demonstrates. The verse play deals with man's attempt to find truth. At least truth is what concerns Sweeney. The epigraphs introduce Orestes, who broke the curse on the house of Atreus, and St. John of the Cross, who sought God through Christ, who had broken the curse of original sin. Sweeney tells a story, having badly disappointed Doris with his reduction of life on the Paradise Isle to birth, and copulation, and death, and then thoroughly frightened her by telling her that life is death.

Sweeney's story is that of the man who murders a woman and keeps her in his bath, a macabre baptism, with Lysol rather than God's grace serving as the preserving agent. At one level the tale is simply a horrific *News of the World* story about a bizarre killing. At another level it is about renunciation and suffering for a spiritual purpose. The torments of Orestes, inflicted on him by the Furies, for having murdered his mother bring him at last to Athens and deliverance at the hands of the gods. St. John's passage through the dark night of his soul searching brings him to God. Sweeney may have passed the same way. He clearly has knowledge that the rest of the people in Doris and Dusty's flat do not have. For one thing, he remembers his own birth and tells Doris that he has no desire to be born again; once is enough. His pilgrim character is most specifically set forth in *Sweeney Agonistes*. He is contrasted with the other characters in the drama by his awareness and, again, by his action.

In 1940 Eliot published, on Good Friday, the second of the *Four Quartets*, "East Coker." Eliot's ancestor, Andrew Eliot, had migrated from here in 1677. In section 1 of the poem, Eliot finds Sweeney and Doris in a midnight field, celebrating a wedding: "On a summer midnight, you can hear the music / Of the weak pipe and the little drum / And see them dancing around the bonfire. . . . Two and two, necessary conjunction. . . . Lifting heavy feet in clumsy shoes. . . . The time of coupling of man and woman / And that of beasts."[47] Sweeney as well as Eliot has found his way home. I do not mean that Eliot necessarily thought of these ghostly dancers as Sweeney and Doris. There is no evidence to support such an assertion. What does happen, however, in "East Coker" is that the debate of body and soul is resolved by the discovery that there is no debate. Sweeney's pilgrimage (or is it Eliot's?) ends at East Coker in "A dignified and commodious sacrament."

It is Dame Helen Gardner's assessment of the development of Eliot's poetry that up to *The Waste Land* he is basically working to put new content into old forms "and to revive the forms by returning to older handlings of them."[48] Eliot was not finally satisfied with the method; and after experimenting with the quatrain, abandoned his efforts and turned to the verse form used in "Gerontion." In 1912 Robert Bridges had written in a *Times Literary Supplement* review that English syllabic verse was in a "stage of artistic exhaustion."[49] Eliot seems not to have shared Bridges' view but, nonetheless, abandoned it for a form with greater flexibility.

What Eliot is seeking to do in the 1920s poems is to create a wholly modern world while, at the same time, employing an archaic verse form with a specialized traditional subject matter, that is to say the ballad form, and to bend it into a new use. The ballad traditionally has been a form of narrative poetry whose subject matter is passion, violence, betrayal, and death, often occurring all together as in "The Three Ravens." Eliot's quatrain poems deal with the same subjects, although generally masked and globalized. Eliot's method is to exploit the cultural and poetical traditions behind the ballad while at the same time adapting these conventions of form and belief to his own uses.

The traditional ballad was addressed to an audience that shared a common understanding of the conventions of love and honor that were central to the subject matter and the form. The audience was also thoroughly familiar with the ironic subversions of the chivalric code and courtly love which lay behind the action of the poems. What Eliot seeks to do in his adaptations is to create a commonality of understanding in an audience that, as Dame Gardner notes in speaking of the *Four Quartets*, has no such shared understanding.[50] Eliot, of course, replaces the conventional secular love of the ballad with divine love; or, more accurately, he uses secular love as a means of revealing the horror of life without access to divine love.

A further complication that Eliot makes in the form is the addition of allusions, chiefly literary, and using them not in traditional ways but in new ways. As Stanley Sultan points out in *"Ulysses," "The Waste Land" And Modernism*, literary allusion was, prior to the modernists' modifications in the practice, primarily for decorative or illustrative purposes, functioning to "enhance an already coherent and complete literal discourse or action. . . ."[51] With both James Joyce and Eliot, the method underwent a significant change. Joyce referred to this change as "a way of working," and Eliot in reviewing *Ulysses* describes the method as "a way of . . . giving a shape and a significance to the immense panorama of futility and anarchy which is contemporary history" and so a means for "making the modern world possible for art."[52] In the same review he credits Yeats with being the first "contemporary" to be conscious of the need for such a method.

Sultan suggests that what Eliot means by the phrase "making the modern world possible for art" is that the method would enable the artist to assert a "continuity in art, culture and society at a time of acute confrontation with the very opposite," a way of linking present human experience with the past.[53] The reading public was generally familiar with the traditional method of employing allusion for either a decorative or a single, illustrative purpose, or even as a structural device. Sultan suggests Dante's *Commedia*, Herbert's *The Temple*, Dryden's *Absalom And Achitophel*, and Voltaire's *Candide* as examples of the traditional way of working with allusion.[54]

What Eliot does in *The Waste Land* in a most pronounced way and what he also does in several of the earlier poems is to remove the coherent and complete literal discourse and proceed by a method of substituting the allusive referents in the discourse for the literal discourse, with the result that what Sultan calls "sense and integrity" in the poems "depend upon contributions made by various objects of allusion."[55] The working of the method, everywhere apparent in the poems, is particularly evident in "Sweeney among the Nightingales," a poem in which the meanings can be derived only by dealing with the allusions as substitute structures for literal statements. The method places the reader in a new relationship with the poetry. This new relationship allows Eliot to generate meanings not available to him through the received traditions of poetic discourse. Why the new relationship between reader and poem still generates so much uneasiness in a large class of readers should soon become clear.

"Sweeney among the Nightingales" remains impenetrable to a conventional, premodernist reading. It is, presumably, a narrative poem, constructed in the recognizable form of a ballad, employing a conventional four line stanza rhyming *a b c b* but lacking a refrain. So far, so good. Ease of mind, however, vanishes with a moment's reflection on the title. Titles such as "Barbara Allen," "Sir Patrick Spens," "Lord Randall," and the like present no problems. They are straightforward signifiers, even when, as in the case of "The Three Ravens" they introduce a deeply ironic poem.

"Sweeney among the Nightingales" is not so simple. The "Nightingales" in the title not only introduce the birds but also the London prostitutes of Eliot's time, who went by the name, and the story of Philomela, who was turned by the gods into a nightingale in order to bring to an end the terrible chain of events that began with her rape by her brother-in-law King Tereus who cut out her tongue and imprisoned her to prevent her telling her sister Procne what had happened. No one is likely to be so misguided as to see these references as decorations; and if in some way they are present to enhance the discourse, they are disturbingly contradictory and ambiguous. The reader is almost certain to ask what these elements mean.

The answer, of course, is that Eliot has expressed his intention as well as his meaning in the dual references present in the title. What these meanings are cannot be satisfactorily determined, however, until the rest of the poem is dealt with. The epigraph contains a further classical reference, this time to the Greek play *Agamemnon*. The Greek line translates, "A deep, a mortal blow," and is spoken by Agamemnon after he has been stabbed by his wife, Clytemnestra, for having brought home his concubine Cassandra, who had predicted the tragedy but had not been believed. There is also a second excised epigraph, a quotation from *The Raigne of King Edward III*: "Why should I speak of the nightingale? The nightingale sings of adulterous wrongs." Now the reader is even more puzzled. Why a reference to the hero Agamemnon? Surely Eliot cannot intend a comparison between the Greek king and the person described in the poem's first stanza.

The answer is both yes and no. No, the epigraph will not reveal its functions if it is regarded as decoration or illustration of the discourse. Yes, it does carry meaning and does "make sense," not as an adjunct to the poem but as an integral part of the poem. After the first stanza with its feral imagery of ape, zebra, and giraffe and its bit of narrative, placing Sweeney in a sitting position, laughing with spread knees, the poem veers violently away toward seemingly unconnected references to Marlowe's *Doctor Faustus* in "The Circles of the stormy moon"; a newspaper report on South American shipping in "the River Plate"; an unspecified battle, with death and a scavenger above it, in "Death and the Raven drift above"; and the gate of true dreams and a reference to the *Aeneid* in "And Sweeney guards the hornéd gate."

By this point in the poem it is clear that a conventional reading will only result in defeat for the interpreter. The reader will have to make up his mind to begin to read the poem in some other way or dismiss it as gibberish. Because there is almost no narrative to work with and what there is is incomplete and possibly inconsistent, the reader is thrown back on the allusions. These increase to include *The Song of Solomon* in stanza six with its lines, "Rachel *née* Rabinovitch / Tears at the grapes with murderous paws"; the nightingales again in stanza nine and Agamemnon in ten.

All of the allusions in the poem are a part of the poem in a way that, say, Auden's allusion to Brueghel's *Icarus* in "Musée des Beaux Arts" is not. In Auden's poem the painting illustrates a meaning Auden is developing within the poem from other materials of discourse. In "Sweeney among the Nightingales" the referents of the allusions form the discourse itself, along with the nonallusive language in stanza four, for example. By understanding the role of the allusions, the reader can try once again to "make sense" of what he has read. At once the poem ceases to be simply a sordid story about an Irishman named Sweeney, who declines to be seduced by two whores in what appears to be a café while the host talks with an unidentified person at the door. The word *host*, of course, suggests the event in the mass in which the bread and wine become the flesh and blood of Christ, who may be the "someone indistinct" in the ninth stanza.

The personae of the poem are now seen as expanding to include Sweeney, Agamemnon, King Tereus, Philomela, Procne, Clytemnestra, Cassandra, Orion, the Pleiades, Rachel and the lady in the Spanish cape, the host, Christ, and the sisters of the Convent of the Sacred Heart, plus all of those involved in reading the *Times*' bulletins on shipping to and from South America. To the expanded list of characters must also be added all of the events with which these individuals are associated. The poem explodes outward from Sweeney to become a reading of the events of human history up to the present moment, which finds Sweeney declining the whores' gambit. The presence of Christ in the poem, conversing with the host, does not change the bloody events of human history but offers those involved in them, in this case Sweeney, an escape through grace from the endless repetition of lust, violence, and death. Sweeney declines the gambit, an indication of his escape, perhaps, from the fate of Agamemnon in the bloody wood.

No doubt, many critics will find the conclusion that Sweeney is "saved" an unwarranted forcing of the poem. David Ward is much less sanguine about Sweeney's prospects, although he does find Sweeney at the center of these poems in which he bears a principal role and that his presence suggests that he is "the essential subject of the incredible theological drama . . ." being playing out there. In his discussion of "Mr. Eliot's Sunday Morning Service" Ward concludes that Sweeney "at the end of the poem, in his baptismal bath, is in a bizarre way the imitation of Christ . . .," a reading arrived at by Ward's arguing persuasively that the painting in the poem "symbolizes the whole pattern of doctrine." Christ's feet are in the water; he is the baptised God, "half in, half out of this world" and "Christ links the timeless world and the waters of time."[56] Whatever reading of the poems one prefers, it is to be arrived at by employing a version of these techniques. One must respond to the allusions. To a degree, as Adams has suggested, the reader is called upon to make his own poem from the materials provided by the poet.[57]

Earlier, however, Ward, speaking for an important segment of critical opinion, expresses the opinion that the quatrain poems as a group are deeply divided against themselves and that they split over Eliot's perception of humanity's double nature. He sees the quatrain poems dealing with the double nature of humanity. He speaks of their "edgy comedy" and "almost neurotic love of witty concealment and evasion," a set of factors that make the poems impossible to "understand completely."[58] He also finds in the poems an expression of Eliot's personal stress, which finds expression in the "kind of over-clever play which often is the signal of a delicate and very active mind driven close to desperation by unresolved conflicts."[59]

Ward also finds the quatrain poems "more purely metaphysical in their natures than most of the poems of Donne, Marvell or Herbert. . . ."[60] In them Eliot expresses an overriding metaphysical anxiety which "controls the whole world of poetic feeling," keeping the poems "imprisoned in terrible doubt and uncertainty."[61] Ward is convinced that the degree of doubt and uncertainty expressed is so intense that the poems give voice to what amounts to "a metaphysical and therefore a personal sickness. . . ."[62] Unfortunately, the biographical information that would help to determine the exact nature and extent of Eliot's mental and emotional stress at the time of the poems' composition remains concealed and suppressed and is likely to continue to be so for a considerable time into the future. In fact there seems to be a stiffening of resolve on the part of those in possession of the material to stifle efforts to gain access to such information.

Ward finds the quatrain poems flawed. He finds them "slightly hysterical, overly clever, melodramatically vague in their disgust with the world" and "the poet of the quatrains after a time . . . a somewhat tired and tiring clown whose personal problems . . . do not engage our interest for very long."[63] The harshness of Ward's judgment should, perhaps, be tempered by remembering that Eliot's set of emotional and spiritual problems, about which he could not then bring himself to speak directly and for which he could discover no solutions or resolutions, could, in all probability, be best and perhaps only addressed through the oblique and ironic utterances that characterize the quatrain poems. These utterances at once mask the truth and yet allow it to be addressed, the distance provided by the irony holding the awful power of the felt emotions in check while at the same time acknowledging them.

Dame Gardner's view of the poems is in marked contrast to Ward's final assessment of them. She praises the "oblique manner" of the quatrain poems and their "highly passionate and dramatic style, which constantly escapes from the regions of wit, irony and sensibility into a dramatic intensity of feeling."[64] In particular she finds them successful in their "complex rather mannered sophistication, their power of phrasing. . . ."[65] Singling out the quatrain poems from among his earlier work, she argues that Eliot handled the verse form "with the greatest brilliance and confidence. . . ."[66]

From the very outset, of course, critical opinion has been divided on the subject of the poetry. In 1916 Arthur Waugh attacked Eliot in the pages of the *Quarterly Review*,[67] and in December of the following year May Sinclair defended him against the *Quarterly Review* attacks.[68] Although critics have drawn more closely together over the years in their favorable opinion of his work, Eliot's reputation is not beyond question as Graham Hough makes clear in "Reflections on A Literary Revolution."[69] And there remains Professor Bateson's damning conclusion that Eliot's "plagiarisms" from earlier authors are unjustified and represent "the magpie-instinct" for other authors' imagery or phraseology.[70]

4

Dame Gardner refers to a consciousness of the "abyss" unifying Eliot's poetry. The nature of this abyss and an understanding of what it was for Eliot is a critical component in any effort to understand what his poetry, at any stage of his development, is really about. He speaks of it very directly in his essay on Matthew Arnold in *The Use of Poetry And The Use of Criticism*.[71] Having faulted Arnold for suggesting that "it is of advantage to a poet to deal with a beautiful world," Eliot counters by saying that the "essential advantage for a poet is not, to have a beautiful world with which to deal: it is to be able to see beneath both beauty and ugliness; to see the boredom, and the horror, and the glory." There is very little beauty in the Sweeney poems of a conventionally "pretty" sort. Beauties of language, of course, abound, of invention, and of execution; and there is plenty of horror, in and out of Mrs. Turner's "boarding house." The glory, if it exists anywhere, lies in the representations of Christ's presence in these fallen worlds of the quatrain poems. In "Mr. Eliot's Sunday Morning Service" and again in "Sweeney among the Nightingales" the references to Christ go far toward redeeming what appear to be not only fallen but also lost worlds. Commenting on the passage in "Arnold," Dame Gardner finds the movement in Eliot's poetry up to *The Waste Land* is "from . . . boredom to something that might be called terror, alternating with . . . horror . . . in which boredom is swallowed up."[72]

The abyss is also present in the unrelieved harshness of Eliot's view of these imagined worlds and the absence in them of any middle ground on which the reader might find a space in which to rest. Between the hippopotamus's "damp savannas" and the heaven toward which he is rising, there is only thin air. In "Mr. Eliot's Sunday Morning Service" there is heaven behind Christ's head, the desert surrounding his feet, the "avenue of penitence" and Sweeney's bath. Even the garden wall offers no release from extremes. The absence of available intellectual and spiritual halfway houses in the poetry suggests a matching absence of their emotional equivalents in Eliot's perception of the world. Lydall Gordon has had something to say about Eliot's spiritual rigidity and the pain it caused him.[73] Even in "Modern Education And The Classics," written in 1932, he was still compelled to assert a destructive dualism. "There are only two finally tenable hypotheses about life," he writes, "the Catholic and the materialistic."[74] Frye comments on the assertion and especially on what follows in the essay to the effect that Eliot insists that what is neither Catholic nor materialistic "forms a series of queasy transitional hesitations, each worse than the one before it."[75]

Published in the *Egoist* in 1919, "Tradition and the Individual Talent" displays another aspect of Eliot's rigidity of mind.[76] In a by-now famous or, perhaps, infamous line in the essay, Eliot asserts that poetry "is not an expression of personality, but an escape from personality." Probably at least wholly or partially composed in 1917, the essay is a parallel and nonpoetic expression of the ideas with which he was working in the Sweeney poems. In it Eliot reveals something of his state of mind in the period when he writes, after having made his point about poetry and personality. "But, of course, only those who have personality and emotions know what it means to want to escape from these things."[77]

The essay reveals more than Eliot's pain and the rigidity of mind that is so much a part of the pain. It shows Eliot struggling to express his conviction that "the whole of literature of Europe from Homer and within it the whole of the literature of his own country has a simultaneous existence and composes a simultaneous order."[78] In the Sweeney poems, past and present, as has already been pointed out, exist together. Sweeney and Agamemnon share a "simultaneous existence." He also asserts that "the past should be altered by the present as much as the present is directed by the past."[79] It is in relation to this "conception of poetry as a living whole of all the poetry that was ever written," that the reader of the 1920s poems should approach Eliot's use of allusions. At the center of it lies Eliot's belief that a "historical sense" is "indispensable" to the poet and that it is a proper response to this "sense" that makes him, in the best meaning of the word, traditional.

Schneider has carried the relationship between Eliot's quatrain poems and the essay even further and has found the relationship to be very plain. "The importance of tradition, recognition of the past as constituting all but the whole of the present, finds objective proof in the poems, each a small package of pieces from the past yet each more contemporary than last week's news."[80] Perhaps it is worth laboring the obvious to confirm Schneider's point by calling attention, for the purpose of furnishing an example, to "Sweeney among the Nightingales." In the poem "all but the whole of the present" read as the poem itself is made up of allusions to events and objects in a literary past, while the subject of the poem is a contemporary event, Sweeney's temptation. The other Sweeney poems are structured in a roughly similar fashion.

Eliot rapidly abandoned his position regarding poetry's being an escape from personality. In 1927 in "Shakespeare and the Stoicism of Seneca" he wrote, "Shakespeare, too, was occupied with the struggle—which alone constitutes life for a poet—to transmute his personal and private agonies into something rich and strange, something universal and impersonal. The rage of Dante against Florence, or Pistoia, or what not, the deep surge of Shakespeare's general cynicism and disillusionment, are merely gigantic attempts to metamorphose private failures and disappointments. The great poet, in writing himself, writes his time."[81] For further evidence in Eliot's later prose of his retreat from his position in "Tradition and the Individual Talent," see Elizabeth Schneider's very helpful discussion.

What can be said, of course, is that having found a way to give expression to his personal feelings in a more direct fashion than he was doing in the Sweeney poems, Eliot found it necessary to bring his critical theories up to date with his practice. After *The Waste Land* it was inevitable that "Shakespeare and the Stoicism of Seneca" should link the poet's experience with the experience of his time and his need to give expression to it. The great change wrought in Eliot's style by what he accomplished in *The Waste Land* also made it inevitable that *Sweeney Agonistes* would be structurally different from the Sweeney poems that precede it.

Sweeney Agonistes was published in England in 1932 by Faber & Faber under the title of *Sweeney Agonistes: Fragments of an Aristophanic Melodrama*. It was published in the United States four years later in *Collected Poems* and then in 1954 in *Twenty-four One-act Plays, Selected by John Hampden*.[82] A note on page [346] asserts that, "The author wishes to point out that *Sweeney Agonistes* is not a one-act play and was never designed as such. . . ." The note concludes with Eliot's observation that the work is made up of "two fragments" and that "as the author has abandoned any intention of completing them, these two fragmentary scenes have frequently been produced as a one-act play."[83] The fragments to which Eliot refers are "Fragment of a Prologue," which as noted above first appeared in *Criterion*, and "Fragment of an Agon," which was also published in *Criterion* under the somewhat burdensome title of " 'Fragment of an Agon' from *Wanna Go Home, Baby?*"

Eliot's note in John Hampden's collection is misleading, most obviously, perhaps, because he allowed the "fragment" to be included in the collection and because twenty years earlier he had been thinking of *Sweeney Agonistes* as a play. In the spring of 1933 Hallie Flanagan, who was teaching at Vassar, wrote to Eliot, asking for permission to stage *Sweeney Agonistes* in May of that year in the Vassar Experimental Theatre. Eliot responded favorably to her request and closed with the promise that he would be at Vassar in May to help with the production if it were at all possible. Flanagan prints Eliot's letter in *Dynamo*, giving a very interesting glance at Eliot's attitude towards his own first effort at poetic drama. By the time he came to write the note for Hampden's volume, he may have forgotten his letter to Flanagan, in which he makes it abundantly clear that he regarded *Sweeney Agonistes* as a play.

"I have no objection to your doing *Sweeney*," he writes, "what there is of him, though I cannot imagine what anybody can do without me there to direct it."[84] Eliot goes on to give detailed instructions for staging the play, including such intriguing details as making the action as "stylized" as Noh drama after the manner Yeats describes in the preface and notes to *The Hawk's Well*, placing masks on the players, and accompanying the entire play with "light drum taps." Eliot follows these instructions with a new scene for the play involving an old gentleman dressed in an evening suit, who is Time. Sweeney puts several puzzling questions to him, which he answers in equally puzzling responses, and the play ends. Schneider regards this new ending as "a jocular burial of a hopelessly fake start, which clearly had no future of the sort he had projected."[85] This additional scene has not been incorporated in further printings or reprintings of the piece in either the *Collected Works* or in other places. Eliot did, in fact, see the Vassar production and stayed on at the college to discuss his poetry with the students. One of the questions he was asked produced an answer that bears on the question of how to deal with his poetry. " 'My poetry is simple and straight-forward,' he declared; and when the audience laughed he looked pained. 'It is dubious whether the purpose of poetry is to communicate anyway. Poetry ought simply to record the fusion of a number of experiences.' "[86]

Eliot began working on "Fragment of a Prologue" in 1924. In September of that year, he went to see Arnold Bennett at the Reform Club, to solicit a response from Bennett to Virginia Woolf's recent article in the *Criterion*, in which she had responded to a piece Bennett had written a year earlier for *Cassell's Weekly*. Bennett agreed, and the conversation shifted finally to Eliot's interest in dramatic writing. He told Bennett he "didn't mind" what he said about not understanding *The Waste Land* "as he had definitely given up that form of writing. . . ."[87] Eliot told Bennett that he wished "to write a drama of modern life (furnished flat sort of people) in a rhythmic prose 'perhaps with certain things in it accentuated by drum-beats.' And he wanted my advice. We arranged that he should do the scenario and some sample pages of dialogue."[88] Bennett does not mention again these tentative plans to help Eliot with his play, although he does say that he began but failed to finish a response to Virginia Woolf's critical attack on his method of delineating character.

Eliot did, however, write the play, at least what he regarded as a fragmentary version of it and which appears increasingly with the passage of time to be, in fact, a finished work. It is about contemporary life, and it does take "furnished flat sort of people" for its characters but does so not as the realists did or would do again in the 1950s. Through the characters of Sweeney and Doris, the play is linked with the pre–*Waste Land* period and in the form of its verse is clearly a post–*Waste Land* production. As Dame Gardner has pointed out, the themes of the play are boredom and horror, or, more specifically, "the boredom and horror that lie beneath the commonplace and the ugly."[89] She adds that "the theme of Mr. Eliot's early verse finds supreme expression in *The Waste Land*, to which *Sweeney Agonistes* appears a rather sterile appendix."[90]

Dame Gardner's analysis of the work leaves out of consideration one very important aspect of the play that is not either repetitive or sterile. The play develops Sweeney as a questing figure and moves the argument of *The Waste Land* beyond the place to which Tiresias carries it — give, sympathize, control — to a place where the mystery is seen and found to be incommunicable — "I gotta use words when I talk to you. / But if you understand or if you don't / That's nothing to me and nothing to you. . . ."[91] Robert Langbaum finds in *The Waste Land* a quest for "personal order that leads to cultural order and cultural order that leads to personal order. . . ."[92] In *Sweeney Agonistes* the search for cultural and personal orders is supplanted by a search for spiritual order, which is adumbrated in the epigraphs.

The first epigraph is taken from one of Orestes' speeches in the *Choephori*, the second play in Aeschylus' trilogy dramatizing the murder of Agamemnon by Clytemnestra; her murder by Orestes, committed to avenge his father's death; and Orestes' pursuit by and eventual deliverance from the Furies, who are unleashed by his act of matricide. The idea of the Furies tormenting men for their sins attracted Eliot; and he uses the device more extensively in *The Family Reunion*, where they appear, more or less unsatisfactorily, depending on the production, to torment Harry. It is important to keep in mind that their appearance in the works named is a prelude to purgation. In Orestes' case he is forgiven for having murdered his mother, thus breaking the curse on his father's house. In Harry's case, by accepting the punishment the Furies bring, he can expiate his crime. In *Sweeney Agonistes*, perhaps Sweeney, perhaps the man "who once did a girl in" are by implication involved in some sort of expiation leading to deliverance.

The second epigraph comes from *The Ascent of Mount Carmel* by St. John of the Cross, in which St. John is, among other things, attempting to explain what happens in the dark night of the soul, that portion of the spiritual journey toward the direct experience of God, in which the person making the quest dies to the world of ordinary experience without yet having been born to the new world of enlightened experience. One of the things, as the quotation suggests, that has to occur is the seeker's casting off of all of his attachments by means of which he has, heretofore, defined himself, known himself to be real. The relationship of the epigraph to the action of *Sweeney Agonistes* is most directly seen in Sweeney's account of the man who "did a girl in" and his efforts to explain what the man went through while the corpse floated in the bathtub and he took in the milk. What both Sweeney and St. John struggle with is the task of attempting to put into words experience that cannot be adequately described and can really only be experienced.

The significance of the dead girl is that she is the embodiment of "the love of created beings," which the man in his pilgrimage, in his entrance into the dark night of the soul, has cast off. She is preserved in the bathtub because although she is dead to him, he cannot yet rid himself of her because he is still in that state of spiritual paralysis in which he can only take in the milk and pay the rent, that is, endure and suffer. It is no wonder that Doris, Dusty, and the rest do not understand what Sweeney is trying to tell them. There is, in fact, some doubt whether Sweeney is really talking to them or whether they provide him with a convenient occasion for thinking out loud thoughts that are profoundly absorbing and important to him.

Frye further expands the function of the epigraphs by saying that they describe "the two extremes of existence, heaven and hell . . ."[93] in the play, providing the frames within which "Sweeney works out his own versions of the two inner worlds."[94] Frye sees these "versions" as represented in the "crocodile isle" and in the girl in the bathtub. Frye feels sure that Sweeney is not "haunted by furies . . . and his troubled vision is something much more than a song for simians."[95] Schneider, less generously, dismisses the entire effort, epigraphs and play, as conveying "by technical means . . . his own disgust, relieved by amusement, at the human world of Sweeneys and Dorisses and Dusties."[96]

In 1933 in the conclusion to *The Use of Poetry and the Use of Criticism*, Eliot refers obliquely to *Sweeney Agonistes* in the course of discussing the "question of obscurity" in poetry, a discussion which quickly leads him to another and for him more pressing question, the challenge and difficulty of writing for "a large and miscellaneous" audience. He makes the point that he regards the theater as "the ideal medium for poetry" and that ideal poetic vehicle would address simultaneously several levels of understanding likely to be represented in the audience. He then mentions having "once designed, and drafted a couple of scenes, of a verse play."[97] The play was, of course, *Sweeney Agonistes*. Having said that he intended to have a protagonist "whose sensibility and intelligence should be on the plane of the most sensitive and intelligent members of the audience," Eliot adds that what this character says is to be understood by only "a small number of the audience" and that the remainder of the audience would not be expected to understand any more of what was being said than the "other characters in the play."[98]

It is clear from the conclusion that Eliot was eager to place himself before a large audience, that he thought there was a "direct social utility," as he expresses it, in so doing, and that he thought the theater the best place in which to do it. *Sweeney Agonistes* is, obviously, an attempt to make the transition from verse to verse drama, an attempt that was continued with critically and commercially greater success with the plays that followed *Sweeney Agonistes*. Eliot's achievement in *Sweeney Agonistes* should not, however, be undervalued. The two fragments bring together several of the poet's interests—in verse drama, in developing a verse form flexible enough to meet the various demands of dramatic expression, continuing the development of Sweeney as an emergent character, and attempting to create poetry of some social value. Eliot carefully avoids saying exactly what the nature of this social value is, contenting himself with the assertion that it is not to "meddle with the tasks of the theologian, the preacher, the economist, the sociologist or anybody else. . . ."[99]

What has seemed to interest the critics most about the play is the form of Eliot's verse. Dame Gardner has written that in *Sweeney Agonistes* Eliot had stopped trying to put new content into old verse forms "for the opposite method of finding what is the verse form for the new content."[100] It is frequently noted that the rhythms of jazz lie behind the staccato rhythms of the play, and Dame Gardner goes so far as to say that this basic drumbeat "is the base on which Mr. Eliot has built his new style."[101] In "The Music of Poetry," delivered at Glasgow University in 1942, Eliot says that "Every revolution in poetry is apt to be, and sometimes to announce itself to be, a return to common speech."[102] A few lines later he adds that the "music of poetry, then, must be a music latent in the common speech of its time."[103] It is safe to assume that in *Sweeney Agonistes* Eliot was striving to capture the rhythms of the common speech of his time. Of this effort Dame Gardner goes further and adds that the beginning he made in *Sweeney Agonistes* in developing "the primitive elements of his art" would lead him in the *Four Quartets* back to "the medieval tradition of accentuated verse."[104]

Sweeney Agonistes is a transitional work of great importance. It continues several of the concerns that had been present in the early poetry. It shows Eliot seeking new settings in which to place Sweeney, perhaps to continue the debate of the body and the soul. If this latter point is, however, valid, it is only valid in terms of the meaning of Eliot's conversion.[105] *Sweeney Agonistes* should be seen in terms of its subject matter and argument as Christian in a sense that *The Waste Land* is not. In it Eliot should be seen struggling to find a way of expressing the Incarnation as a fact of Sweeney's world. Robert Adams has written that it was a struggle that ultimately defeated Eliot, that the Incarnation remained for him "a bright light, an abstraction, a principle," but that he "never worked out the stylistic or human implications" of it.[106]

It is possible to argue that Eliot was more successful than Adams is willing to admit. *Sweeney Agonistes* is optimistic in a way that *The Waste Land* is not. In his tale of the man who did the girl in, he reminds his listeners of the outcome of the actions in the two epigraphs. Orestes found deliverance and St. John found God. Perhaps the man in Sweeney's story will be equally successful in his quest. Sweeney, the man in the play who knows more than the others, will become Agatha in *The Family Reunion* and Julia and Harcourt-Reilly in *The Cocktail Party*, while the "ape neck" part of him will dissolve in the redeemed dancing rustic figures in "East Coker." The possibility of grace, the resolution of conflict between flesh and spirit seem to have been achieved. These promises are the Incarnation at work in

Eliot's poetry from *Sweeney Agonistes* onward and represent a culmination of the evolution of the ideas treated in the Sweeney material and mark the comedic end of Sweeney's pilgrimage.

Kinley E. Roby
Northeastern University

Notes

1. A. Walton Litz, "*The Waste Land* Fifty Years After," in *Eliot in His Time: Essays on The Occasion of the Fiftieth Anniversary of The Waste Land* (Princeton: Princeton University Press, 1973), p. 4.

2. Robert Adams, "Precipitating Eliot," in *Eliot in His Time: Essays on The Occasion of The Fiftieth Anniversary of The Waste Land*, ed. A. Walton Litz (Princeton: Princeton University Press, 1973), p. 134.

3. Northrop Frye, *T. S. Eliot: An Introduction* (Chicago: University of Chicago Press, 1963), p. 5.

4. Helen Gardner, *The Art of T. S. Eliot* (Boston: Faber & Faber, 1979), p. 1.

5. Mildred Martin, *A Half-Century of Eliot Criticism: An Annotated Bibliography of Books and Articles in English, 1916–1965* (Lewisburg: Bucknell University, 1973), pp. 19–22.

6. Edmund Wilson, "The Rag-Bag of The Soul," *New York Evening Post Literary Review*, pp. 237–38; and "The Poetry of Drouth," *Dial*, 73 (1922), 611–16.

7. Edmund Wilson, *Axel's Castle: A Study in the Imaginative Literature of 1870–1930* (New York: Charles Scribner's Sons, 1931), p. 102.

8. *Axel's Castle*, p. 113.

9. Henry Seidel Canby, "New Humanists," *Saturday Review*, 6 (1930), 749–51; and R. P. Blackmur, "The Discipline of Humanism," *The Critique of Humanism*, ed. C. Hartley Grattan (New York: Brewer and Warren, 1930), p. 251.

10. F. R. Leavis, *New Bearings in English Poetry: A Study of the Contemporary Situation* (Ann Arbor: Univ. of Michigan, 1964), p. 88.

11. F. O. Matthiessen, *The Achievement of T. S. Eliot: An Essay on the Nature of Poetry* (New York: Oxford Univ., 1947), p. 104.

12. Elizabeth Schneider, *T. S. Eliot: The Pattern in the Carpet* (Berkeley: University of California Press, 1975), p. 5.

13. Gordon, p. 69.

14. T. S. Eliot, *Complete Poems and Plays 1909–1950* (New York: Harcourt, Brace and World, 1952), p. 18.

15. *Complete Poems and Plays*, p. 13.

16. *Complete Poems and Plays*, p. 5.

17. *Complete Poems and Plays*, p. 36.

18. T. S. Eliot, "The Hippopotamus," *Little Review*, 4, No. 3 (1917), 8–11.

19. Gordon, p. 29.

20. *Complete Poems and Plays*, p. 30.

21. Gordon, p. 58.

22. Gordon, p. 61.

23. Gordon, pp. 61–62.

24. Gordon, p. 62.

25. Donald Gallup, *T. S. Eliot: A Bibliography* (London: Faber & Faber, Ltd., 1970), pp. 25–27. Gallup's discussion of the error in the original title, *Ara Vus Prec*, makes the issues clear. The title should have read *Ara Vos Prec* and is now generally referred to by the correct spelling.

26. T. S. Eliot, "Fragment of a Prologue," *Criterion*, 4, No. 4 (1926), 713–18.

27. T. S. Eliot, "Fragment of An Agon," *Criterion*, 5, No. 1 (1927), 74–80.

28. T. S. Eliot, "Doris's Dream Songs," *Chapbook*, 39 (Nov. 1924), 36–37.

29. T. S. Matthews, *Great Tom Notes Toward the Definition of T. S. Eliot* (New York: Harper & Row, 1974), p. 32.

30. Gordon, p. 30.

31. Gordon, p. 19.

32. Gordon, p. 35.

33. Gordon, pp. 12–13.

34. Gordon, p. 8.

35. Gordon, p. 27.

36. Matthews, *Great Tom*, p. 22.

37. Gordon, p. 27.

38. Matthews, *Great Tom*, p. 33. For a further discussion of this point, see Northrop Frye, *T. S. Eliot*, pp. 53–54. For a provocative discussion of Jean Verdenal's relationship to Eliot and Eliot's poetry, see John Peter, "A New Interpretation of *The Waste Land*," *Essays in Criticism*, 2 (1952), 242–66, and the reprinting with "Postscript" in the same journal in the April issue 1969. For an evaluation of Peter's seriously neglected interpretation and for additional supporting material, see James E. Miller, Jr., *T. S. Eliot's Personal Waste Land: Exorcism of the Demons* (University Park: Pennsylvania State University Press, 1977), pp. 7–16.

39. Gordon, p. 25.

40. Gordon, p. 69.

41. Gordon, pp. 61–62.

42. Gordon, p. 90.

43. Gordon, pp. 31–32.

44. Gordon, pp. 31–32.

45. Gordon, p. 123.

46. Schneider, *T. S. Eliot*, p. 45.

47. *Complete Poems and Plays*, p. 123–24.

48. Gardner, *The Art of T. S. Eliot*, p. 22.

49. Robert Bridges, *Collected Essays and Papers* (London: Oxford Univ. 1927–36), 2–3, no. 13, p. 36.

50. Gardner, *The Art of T. S. Eliot*, p. 57.

51. Stanley Sultan, *"Ulysses," "The Waste Land" and Modernism* (Port Washington: Kennikat Press, 1977), p. 32.

52. T. S. Eliot, " 'Ulysses,' Order and Myth," *Dial*, 75, No. 5 (1923), [480]–83.

53. " 'Ulysses,' Order And Myth," p. 33.

54. " 'Ulysses,' Order and Myth," p. 32.

55. " 'Ulysses,' Order and Myth," p. 32.

56. David Ward, *T. S. Eliot between Two Worlds: A Reading of T. S. Eliot's Poetry And Plays* (Boston: Routledge & Kegan Paul, 1973), p. 34.

57. Adams, "Precipitating Eliot," p. 139.

58. Ward, *T. S. Eliot*, p. 29.

59. Ward, *T. S. Eliot*, pp. 31–32.

60. Ward, pp. 31–32.

61. Ward, pp. 31–32.

62. Ward, p, 32.

63. Ward, pp. 41–42.

64. Gardner, *The Art of T. S. Eliot*, pp. 70–71.

65. Gardner, p. 84.

66. Gardner, pp. 18–19.

67. Arthur Waugh, "The New Poetry," *Quarterly Review*, 226 (Oct. 1916), 386.

68. May Sinclair, "Prufrock And Other Observations: A Criticism," *Little Review*, 4 (Dec. 1917), 8–14.

69. Graham Hough, "Reflections on A Literary Revolution," *Image and Experience* (London: Duckworth, 1960), pp. 23.

70. F. W. Bateson, "The Poetry of Learning," *Eliot in Perspective: A Symposium*, ed. Graham Martin (New York: Humanities Press, 1970), p. 39.

71. T. S. Eliot. "Matthew Arnold," *The Use of Poetry and The Use of Criticism Studies in the Relation of Criticism to Poetry in England* (Boston: Faber & Faber, 1980), p. 106.

72. Gardner, *The Art of T. S. Eliot*, p. 79.

73. Gordon, p. 24.

74. T. S. Eliot, "Modern Education And The Classics," *Selected Essays* (New York: Harcourt Brace & World, 1964), p. 458.

75. Frye, *T. S. Eliot*, p. 8.

76. T. S. Eliot, "Tradition And The Individual Talent," *Egoist*, 6, No. 4 (1919), 54–55. Also in *Selected Essays*, pp. 3–11.

77. Eliot, *Selected Essays*, p. 11.

78. Eliot, p. 4.

79. Eliot, p. 5.

80. Schneider, *T. S. Eliot*, p. 40.

81. Eliot, "Shakespeare And The Stoicism of Seneca," *Selected Essays*, p. 117.

82. T. S. Eliot, *Sweeney Agonistes: Fragments of An Aristophanic Melodrama* in *Twenty-four One-act Plays, Selected by John Hampden*, ed. John Hampden, Revised edition (London: John M. Dent & Sons, Ltd., [1954], pp. [345]–56.

83. John Hampden, *Twenty-four One-act Plays*, p. [346].

84. Hallie Flanagan, *Dynamo* (New York: Duell, Sloan and Pearce, 1943), pp. 82–83.

85. Schneider, *T. S. Eliot*, p. 98.

86. Flanagan, *Dynamo*, p. 84.

87. Arnold Bennett, *The Journal of Arnold Bennett*, ed. Newman Flower (New York: The Garden City Publishing Co., 1933), p. 786.

88. Bennett, *The Journal*, pp. 786–87.

89. Gardner, *The Art of T. S. Eliot*, p. 129.

90. Gardner, 131–32.

91. *Complete Poetry and Plays*, p. 84.

92. Robert Langbaum, "New Modes of Characterization in *The Waste Land*," *Eliot in His Time*, p. 118.

93. Frye, *T. S. Eliot*, p. 58.

94. Frye, p. 58.

95. Frye, p. 58.

96. Schneider, *T. S. Eliot*, p. 98.

97. Eliot, *The Use of Poetry*, p. 153.

98. *The Use of Poetry*, p. 153.

99. *The Use of Poetry*, p. 154.

100. Gardner, *The Art of T. S. Eliot*, pp. 25–26.

101. Gardner, p. 27.

102. T. S. Eliot, "The Music of Poetry," *On Poetry and Poets* (New York: Farrar, Straus & Giroux, 1967), p. 23.

103. "The Music of Poetry."

104. Gardner, *The Art Of T. S. Eliot*, p. 27.

105. John D. Margolis, *T. S. Eliot's Intellectual Development* (Chicago: University of Chicago Press, 1972), p. 104.

106. Adams, "Precipitating Eliot," pp. 150–51.

"Mr. Eliot's Sunday Morning Service"

Mr. Eliot's Sunday Morning Parody Anselm Atkins*

"In the beginning was the Word" opens the Prologue of the fourth gospel. The line occurs twice in T.S. Eliot's "Mr. Eliot's Sunday Morning Service." His poem, like the Prologue, is an elaboration of those words. But not only does the content of the poem parody the Prologue. Its diction parodies the verbosity of the theologian Origen, the commentator on the Prologue whom Eliot holds up for explicit ridicule.

As critics have already noticed, Eliot's poem hinges on the contrast between the "Word" of God (Christ) and the words of His "sapient sutlers." The Word of God is Christ the Logos; the sapient sutlers are Origen, the church's first systematic theologian, and all his tribe. Christ, though simple and earthly, is fecund and lifegiving, but the word of the over-wise followers is complicated, hard to comprehend, and sterile. Origen's word is doubly sterile in comparison with the Word, for Origen, in a fit of youthful (and later-regretted) zeal, made himself all too literally a "eunuch for the kingdom of heaven." The contrast between the Word of the Father and Origen's word does not, however, exhaust Eliot's irony. There is in the poem a third word which, like Origen's, and in mock imitation of his, is contrasted with the Word. That other word, which seems to have escaped everyone's attention, is the word of Eliot himself, the word of his poem-prologue.

According to the fourth gospel, there was a Word "in the beginning." There is also a "word" *in the beginning of Eliot's poem:* the octo-syllabic "polyphiloprogenitive." Here is a word that *is* a word, a *one word* that stands for all human words. The function of "polyphiloprogenitive" as verbosity-incarnate is further emphasized by a classical structural device used in the first two stanzas. The repetition of the line "In the beginning was the Word" (which is otherwise hard to account for) makes a *chiasm* which serves to put Eliot's word in the same formal position as Origen's with respect to the divine Word. . . . Just as in the second stanza the line "In the beginning" looks forward to Origen for its point of contrast, so in the first stanza that same line looks backward to Eliot's awkward coinage. There is thus established a *coincidentia oppositorum* between Eliot's word and the

*Reprinted, with permission, from *Renascence*, 21 (1967), 43–54.

Word of the Prologue, as well as a playfully deliberate identification of Eliot himself with Origen.

The equation of Eliot with Origen is strengthened by Eliot's use, throughout the poem, of pedantic words. His language is as recondite as Origen's: "polyprimoprogenitive," "superfetation," "sapient," "mensual," "enervate," "pustular," "piaculative," "staminate," "pistilate," and "epicene." Eliot and Origen are both "polymath," and each is equally distant from the Logos and equally irrelevant to the fleshy Sweeney lolling in his bathwater. Eliot makes fun of Origen both by imitating his verbosity and by setting his sterility (and that of the whole brood of theologians) in contrast to the true spiritual fecundity made available to the world through the events proclaimed in the fourth gospel's Prologue. Eliot thus creates a parody *of* the language of Origen, as well as a parody *in* the language of Origen *of the Prologue*. In both parodies the bad reflection is only upon Origen.

Eliot's first long word launches his Prologue-parody. Having uttered this initial "word," he proceeds, following the fourth gospel's Prologue step by step. The "superfetation of Tò ἕν" in the second stanza recalls the opening verses of the fourth gospel: "and the word was God. The same was in the beginning with God" (John 1:1-2). The Tò ἕν is the Father, the neo-Platonic One from whom the Logos emanates. But "superfetation" suggests too much fecundity—and so applies more directly to the endless theological commentaries on the Joannine words. In the Word, moreover, was "life" (John 1:4). The theologians, Eliot ironically implies, are incapable of imparting life to mankind by their excogitations. Like the worker bees in the seventh (and possibly the first) stanza, theologians—especially Origen—are "epicene" and "enervate." Instead of begetting spiritual sons after the manner of the Father of the Logos, they are "progenitive" only of words and professional theological replacements.

John 1:6-8 introduces John the Baptist, who bore witness to and baptized Jesus at the River Jordan. Although the fourth gospel, unlike the three synoptics, does not explicitly mention Christ's baptism by John, it does narrate the accompanying events. The scene the evangelist has in mind is that described in the earlier gospels. Now, this is the very scene rendered by the Umbrian painter as described by Eliot in stanzas three and four. And the evangelist does refer to the descent of the Spirit "like a dove" (John 1:32-34), a detail which Eliot has included in his poem. There is, then, a definite correspondence between stanzas three and four, and the opening scenes of the fourth gospel. Eliot's main point here is that Christ's "unoffending feet" "still shine" through the water, although the drabness of the wilderness background presses in around him as if to smother the Light of the World. Eliot's theme is the same as the evangelist's: "And the light shineth in darkness; and the darkness comprehended [or, captured, overcame] it not" (John 1:5).

The next two stanzas, five and six, can be understood as another version of the gospel's thematic contrast between "Christ the Light" and darkness, parodied already in the two preceding stanzas. The baptism administered by John the Baptist at the Jordan demanded repentance. The "presbysters approach / The avenue of penitance," their River Jordan, but fruitlessly; for they are "sable," dark: their inner darkness and professional dullness neither comprehend nor express (though they cannot finally stifle) the spiritual life-bearing Word. Even the devout "under the penitential gates" are "dim," for Christ alone is lightsome.

The flower-pollenating bees on the next lines allude to the Word as the principle of spiritual fecundity. According to the Prologue, those who are "sons God" are "born, not of blood, nor of the will of the flesh, nor of the will of man, but of God" (John 1:13). Their rebirth is entirely spiritual, non-fleshy — in other words, asexual, like the worker bees themselves. The neuter workers have no sex-life of their own, yet they are spiritual mediators among stamens and pistils, rendering the flowers fertile by their distribution of pollen. In this they resemble the Word of the Prologue, who, himself celibate, effected a spiritual reconciliation between God and man, a marriage of heaven and earth.

The last graphic image in Eliot's "prologue" is Sweeney shifting "from ham to ham" in his bath. "And," says the evangelist, "the Word was made flesh, and dwelt among us, and we beheld his glory" (John 1:14). Sweeney, in all his Sunday-morning glory, splashes in the tub, exposed to the eye of the reader. His final neo-Platonic emanation, the Word has become incarnate in Sweeney's pink ham-flesh — as humiliating a comedown for the Word as His descent into the confines of Origen's 5000 tomes.

The closing words, "the masters of the subtle schools / Are controversial, polymath," comment on the entire poem. Eliot's poem-prologue has been a parody of lifeless, wordy theology. The spiritual message of that theology, in contrast to the fourth gospel's Prologue, is nil. The last words are thus a dismissal of the theology and its hucksters. Those words also give the reason, or perhaps the excuse, which the ordinary man of limited religious sensibility (the Sweeney-type) would offer for his lack of interest in traditional theology and institutional Christianity. The masters are too remote; there is no use trying to follow them. (Sweeney's excuse is valid, of course, only to the extent that the young Eliot's critique of Origen and his theological heirs is valid.) In another sense, Eliot himself, the poet who has contrived the parody, is (as we saw) subtle and polymath like Origen. The meaning of his prologue may be lost on the casual reader who, like Sweeney, would prefer some more accessible literature instead of Eliot's remote quatrains. Yet Eliot surely foresaw and took mischievous delight in the bewildering effect his poem would have on the reader. The last two lines, then, reflect not only Sweeney's disinterest in theology but also the sentiments of the overwhelmed reader confronted with Eliot's own pedantic and obscure "word," the poem. The reader, a victim of "Young Possum's" craft, finds himself identified at last with Sweeney, and Eliot-Origen has the last laugh on both.

Christians and Jews in "Mr. Eliot's Sunday Morning Service"

George Monteiro*

In "Mr. Eliot's Sunday Morning Service," according to Hugh Kenner, through juxtapositioning and intercutting, we encounter four ways in which Christ has been perceived historically: "the Christ of Greek theologians and the patristic controversialists"; "the Christ of Pre-Raphaelite iconography"; the Christ of "the nonconformist Christians"; and the Christ of "ape-neck Sweeney." These four "Christs," through Eliot's poetic method of "sudden juxtapositions," continues Kenner, are presented in a satiric medium finely tuned to twentieth-century usage.[1]

Implicit in Kenner's commentary is the notion that the poem is one of Eliot's earliest satires on the way in which historical Christianity has progressively decayed. Nowhere, however, does Kenner account for the "semitic" element introduced into this satire on Christianity by the poem's epigraph, a line from Christopher Marlowe's play *The Jew of Malta*, and which carries over into the first verse line of the poem, the single word— "polyphiloprogenitive."

If the "semitic" element in Eliot's poem is underplayed in the verse-body of the poem, it is explicit in its epigraph. In Marlowe's play the line is spoken by the servant Ithamore to his master Barabas the Jew: "*Look, look, master; here come two religious caterpillars.*" The line epitomizes the scene in which Barabas and Ithamore, who have themselves poisoned a convent of nuns, are seen railing at ecclesiastics. But the body of Eliot's poem does not take up the "semitic" aspect of the subject evoked by his Marlovian epigraph. Actually Eliot's use of the epigraph suggests the idea that Christianity, from the Greek theologians to the loutish Irish Catholics (typified by Sweeney) has been marked by as much religiosity and cupidity as the semitic religions of old. What Ithamore says to his master in the play is ironically most appropriate not to the Jews but to the Christians whose collective actions substantiate the irony of "Mr. Eliot's Sunday Morning Service."

Were it stripped of its epigraph, Eliot's poem might appear, if only superficially, to be devoid of semitic reference. Yet the case is more apparent than real. As a satire on the decay of Christianity, the poem first suggests its main point in the way Marlowe's anti-semitism leaches onto the opening of the poem proper. The first line of the poem immediately following the "semitic" epigraph is the single word "*Polyphiloprogenitive.*" Adhering to Eliot's use of this term is its association with the Jew. "Among the distinguishing mental and moral traits of the Jews," reads one encyclopedia account at the turn of the century, are "a strong family sense and *philoprogenitiveness.*"[2]

Love of generation, meaning both love of progency and, above all,

*Reprinted, with permission, from *T.S. Eliot Review*, 3 (1976), 20–22.

love of the sexual act itself, links the Jews of the epigraph to the Greek theologians of Eliot's poem, for their task, according to Strauss' *New Life of
Jesus*, was "to assimilate" Jesus "to the *philoprogenitive* Gods of the
heathen."[3]

If the Jew is *philoprogenitive*, the decadent Christian has gone him one
better, implies Eliot; he is poly*philoprogenitive*. In this poem those Christians who are wont to revile Jews become themselves the object of satire. To
attack decadent Christians Eliot turns back upon them their own anti-semitism. The emergence of ape-neck Sweeney as the poem comes to closure
rounds out Eliot's manipulation of the Christian's own prejudice against
himself — opening with anti-semitism and concluding with anti-Irish-Cath-
olic sentiments — prejudices which, oddly, the poet himself shared.

Finally, however, we must heed the satiric hint provided by the poem's
title. If Sweeney spends his Sunday morning in his bath, shifting from ham
to ham, Mr. Eliot spends his own Sunday morning supercilliously and
smugly appropriating the aberrations of *other* Christians.

Notes

1. *The Invisible Poet: T. S. Eliot* (New York: McDowell, Obolensky, 1959), pp. 87–88.

2. *New International Encyclopedia* (New York, 1902; 2nd ed., 1921), XII, p. 678; italics
added.

3. David Friedrich Strauss, *A New Life of Jesus* (London and Edinburgh: Williams and
Norgate, 1865), II, 41; italics added.

"Mr. Eliot's Sunday Morning Service"

Ernest Schanzer*

The perusal of the recent correspondence in *Essays in Criticism* about
the meaning of "The Cooking Egg" has left us sadder and wiser men. For it
startlingly revealed the complete lack of agreement among trained critics
about even the most general meaning of one of Mr. Eliot's less difficult
poems. While divided on whether to blame the poet or his critics for this
breakdown in communication, most of us are probably agreed on the usefulness of such an occasional co-operative attempt at elucidation. I propose
to take what seems to me a much more difficult poem from the same collection as "The Cooking Egg," "Mr. Eliot's Sunday Morning Service," hoping
that some of its perplexities may be resolved by means of a similar discussion.

The poem's setting is indicated by its title. It is Sunday morning and a

*Reprinted, with permission, from *Essays in Criticism*, 5 (1955), 153–58.

service is in progress in what must be either a High Anglican or a Roman Catholic church, for religious paintings are found within its walls. The poem's outward unity is supplied by the wandering eye and mind of Mr. Eliot. While he sits in the church his eye strays along the stained glass windows depicting various early Church Fathers, among them presumably Origen, so that the figures appear to drift past him in procession. . . . They make him reflect on the ironic contrast between the Word of God and the wordiness of the controversialists of the early Church. "In the beginning was the Word," the poet comments sarcastically. At the very beginning of our Church history came the copious flow of words from the pens of the learned theologians, the "sapient sutlers," with a pun on "sutlers" and the ironic implication that "the hungry sheep look up and are not fed." For instead of feeding the army of the Church Militant with the Word of God the sutlers provide an abundant diet of subtle, abstract, and barren arguments. . . . The wordiness of some of the early theologians is described as a "superfetation," a second conception, of God, following upon the initial conception of the Word of God (the repetition of the last line of the preceding stanza is probably meant to underline this). Eliot chooses Origen as representative of this group of theologians. For not only was he one of the most voluminous of all the Church Fathers (St. Epiphanius in an exaggerated estimate puts the number of his writings at 6000), but he was particularly famed for his lengthy commentaries on the Scriptures. His comments on St. John's "In the beginning was the Word" alone "furnished material for a whole roll" (*Catholic Encyclopaedia*). In the spectacle of Wordiness commenting on the silent Word the ironic contrast is crystallized for us. Origen is also chosen because, as the word "enervate" reminds us, he committed self-castration as a youth of seventeen. We have thus the further contrast between his verbal fertility and his sexual sterility, a contrast which is also enforced by the poet's use of words of primarily sexual connotation, such as "superfetation" and "polyphiloprogenitive," in a non-sexual context. The essential sterility of Alexandrian theology is thus suggested to us. The poem's rather ludicrous opening word with its suggestion of both the prolificity and the prolixity of the writings of the Alexandrian school at once sets the tone of the whole poem and adumbrates its main satiric theme: the remoteness of the Alexandrian theology from simple Christian sentiment and belief.

In the third stanza the poet turns from the wordiness of Origen to the Word become Flesh, the Logos in its illuminative and redemptive activity. His eyes wander from the stained glass figures of the early Fathers to an Umbrian painting of the Baptism of Christ. . . . With its "Wasteland" symbolism and its sensuous simplicity the description admirably suggests the feeling of primitive Christianity as well as of primitive Italian painting, and as a contrast to what precedes it needs no comment, except for the reminder that Origen was famous for his voluminous speculations on the nature of the Trinity.

An interval of time seems indicated by the dotted line which divides the poem into two halves of equal length. The poet's eye now fastens on the officiating priests and on members of the congregation. [Here Schanzer quotes stanza five.]

The next, grammatically incomplete stanza appears to contain the description of another religious painting that has caught the poet's eye. It depicts the tortures of purgatory.

> Under the penitential gates
> Sustained by staring Seraphim
> Where the souls of the devout
> Burn invisible and dim.

Eliot's choice of Seraphim for its guardian angels may be due to their association with purgation of sins through the Seraph that in Isaiah's vision touches his lips with a live coal, and perhaps also to the fact that, according to the *Encyclopedia Britannica*, representations of such figures as the Seraphim seen by Isaiah "were to be found at the entrance to oriental temples, where they served as guardians of the gate." But it may well be that in his choice of Seraphim Eliot was also guided by memories of Dante, who in the *Convivio* declares that the Seraphim are supreme in their comprehension of God the Father ("li serafini che veggiono più della prima Cagione, che alcun' altra natura." *Conv.* II, 6). The Seraphim with their intuitive understanding of God may thus be seen as providing a further contrast to the Alexandrian theologians with their elaborate and arduous reasoning about His nature. The description of the Seraphim as "staring," though perhaps entirely due to some pictorial impression, may also owe something to memories of the lines in the *Paradiso* in which the Seraph is described as

> quell' alma nel ciel che più si schiara,
> Quel serafin che 'n Dio più l'occhio ha fisso. (XXI, 91–2)

It is of course possible to interpret the sixth stanza as describing the continued approach of the presbyters through the chancel arch into the nave. But though this makes better syntactic sense it seems to me to raise more difficulties than it solves; above all it leaves the last two lines of the stanza excessively obscure. As I see it stanzas 5 and 6 stand in clear contrast to each other. The true purgation of sinful man in purgatorial flames, as depicted in the religious painting, is contrasted with the easy penance by means of 'piaculative pence' of the modern churchgoer. Yet the very fact that two such utterly divergent interpretations of stanza 6 should be conceivable points to one of the serious flaws in the poem.

The poet's eye next drifts through the open window out into the churchyard. . . . The blest office of the epicene bees is here contrasted with the office of the epicene priests which, to the poet, lacks the blessing of fruitfulness. The quotation from "The Jew of Malta," "Look, look, master, here comes two religious caterpillars," which forms the poem's epigraph, being clearly inapplicable to the "sapient sutlers," who are marked by excessive industry rather than sluggishness, seems intended for application to the sable presbyters. While the sapient sutlers fail in their function by providing a barren fare of words, the sable presbyters fail more completely still, and merely feed themselves. They possess not even the industry which links the Alexandrian Fathers with the bees, while both are sterile, incapable of fertilizing and feeding the life of the spirit.

The poem's unity of setting is abandoned in the last stanza, where Eliot introduces his Irish-American voluptuary and vulgarian, Sweeney. . . . The description of Sweeney in his bath helps to knit up the poem by providing a threefold contrast by means of surface parallels with other parts of the poem: that between Sweeney and the masters of the subtle school, stirring the waters of controversy, and shifting their argumentative positions; that between Sweeney's "hams" in the bath-water and Christ's "unoffending feet" in the river Jordan; and that between Sweeney's voluptuous wallowing in his hot bath and the tortures of the elect in the flames of purgatory.

The poem is clearly carefully constructed. Its final two lines closely correspond to the two opening lines. At the centre of the poem are two religious paintings, suggesting the true Christianity from which both the Alexandrian Fathers and the modern priests and congregation seem to the poet to have strayed. The poem is held together by a series of simple contrasts, or by surface parallels with underlying oppositions. The first four stanzas seem to me an unqualified success. But with the introduction of the sable presbyters and the theme of purgation the satiric focus of the poem is dispersed, much to the detriment of its unity and the bewilderment of the reader. There seems to be an insufficient connection between the satire directed against the sable presbyters, which, much as in "The Hippopotamus," appears to be essentially an attack on the church of the Laodiceans, and that directed against the Alexandrian Fathers, and the stitching together of the two themes by means of the references of the last two stanzas seems to me insufficient to overcome the poem's lack of thematic unity. The abandonment of the unity of setting by the introduction of Sweeney in the last stanza, whatever the compensations it brings with it, still further lessens the coherence of what has always seemed to me one of Mr. Eliot's most bewildering and most fascinating poems.

T.S. Eliot's Painter of the Umbrian School

Floyd C. Watkins*

"Mr. Eliot's Sunday Morning Service" is a poem of many diverse parts: the first stanza apparently establishes a religious service as the setting and as the general context for what at first seem to be rambling thoughts and digressions in the rest of the poem; the second stanza reflects upon the origins of Christianity, "the Word" and the early Church Fathers; an Umbrian painting is the topic in stanzas three and four; the last four stanzas of the poem consider, in sequence, the church service again, a scene in purgatory, the symbolic busy-work of bees just outside the church window, the ubiquitous Sweeney in his bath, and the controversial "masters of the subtle schools." The poem is an especially happy hunting ground for mythologizers and allusion-hunters. Several critics have discussed the "painter of the Umbrian school," but no one, I believe, has identified the particular painting which Eliot had in mind. Grover Smith, Jr., has cautiously stated that "The style of painting Eliot had in mind might be typified by Perugino's 'Baptism of Christ' (Foligno)."[1]

Eliot describes the Umbrian painting in meticulous detail [here Watkins quotes stanzas three and four].

I have found three paintings of the baptism of Christ by members of the Umbrian school: Perino painted the "Baptism of Christ" in the Logge of the Vatican; a fresco of the baptism in the Sistine Chapel "was for long attributed without question to Perugino";[2] and Piero della Francesca painted "The Baptism of Christ." The works of Perino and Perugino do not conform to the description in "Mr. Eliot's Sunday Morning Service." Frescoes are not painted upon gesso; and Perino's "Baptism" has no suggestion of the dove or the Paraclete.

Francesca's painting of the baptism is a gesso panel, and since 1861 it has been owned by the National Gallery, London, where Eliot must have seen it many times. Indeed, Francesca was something of a discovery for the intellectuals in the period after 1915; he influenced the Cubists and one phase of the work of Picasso.

Although Francesca drew no nimbus of halo in his painting, the vessel which contains the holy water of baptism may serve symbolically as a halo. Or perhaps Eliot's poem suggests that Christ himself may be spoken of in the figure of a nimbus: "A painter . . . / Designed . . . / The nimbus of the Baptized God." Francesca portrayed Christ's feet clearly through the water; the surface of the water strikes both legs precisely at the ankle. The painting, therefore, may have provided the inspiration for the most beautiful and striking image in the poem:

> But through the water pale and thin
> Still shine the unoffending feet. . . .

*Reprinted, with permission, from *Notes and Queries*, 36 (1964), 72–75.

The wilderness in the painting "is cracked and browned," and sparse plants and sand at the edge of the water of the river seem to suggest a wilderness or even a desert place. Eliot's "cracked" possibly refers to the deterioration of the materials of the painting, but it seems most likely to describe the bursting of the soil by the seeds which herald "the future of the world, in eternal youth and perennial spring. . . ."[3] The wilderness, "cracked and browned," might thus suggest the waste land of the world without Christ, the promise of rebirth, and perhaps even the sterility ("browned") of the failure to realize the meaning of rebirth. The painter did "set" the Paraclete, the Holy Spirit, above the head of Christ in the form of a dove. But there is no representation of God the Father in the painting. Possibly He is an addition by Eliot, or He may be suggested by the thick-foliaged tree just above the head of Christ, or He may also be embodied in the symbol of the dove (in Matthew 3:16–17 "the Spirit of God" descends like a dove, and "a voice from heaven" speaks).

Francesca's painting of "The Baptism of Christ" may contribute more to the reading of the poem than the fact of a source for the imagery. If Eliot interpreted the painting as Bernard Berenson does, it may substantially reinforce the theme of "Mr. Eliot's Sunday Morning Service." Eliot emphasizes the "ironic contrast between the Word of God and the wordiness of the controversialists of the early Church."[4] "Superfetation of τὸ ἕν" suggests "the effort to fertilize 'the one' by a fresh begetting; to make of the Word a Queen bee mated with numerous drones. . . ."[5] The futility and sterility of prolific words is symbolized by the "enervate Origen," the self-castrated and heretical Church Father, who was reported by St. Epiphanius to have written six thousand treatises.[6] Like Origen and the writers of pedantic theology, "The Baptism of Christ" perhaps suggests the sterile incomprehension of the Word. Piero della Francesca, Bernard Berenson has written, "seems to have been opposed to the manifestation of feeling, and ready to go to any length to avoid it."[7] But Christ, the truth of the Word, emerges despite the austerity of the painter. Though "The wilderness is cracked and browned" and the water is "pale and thin," through the water "Still shine the unoffending feet. . . ." They shine. They do not offend as the words do. They are the Word.

Perhaps one should protest that it is excessive preciosity and obscurity for the poet to rely so heavily upon an unidentified painting. On the other hand, Eliot gave rather definite clues, and no doubt he expected those who read the poem well also to know the painting. At any rate, reading the poem with Francesca's painting as the background makes the imagery clear and the theme striking.

Notes

1. Grover Smith, Jr., *T. S. Eliot's Poetry and Plays* (Chicago, 1956), p. 304. (Professor Thomas B. Brumbaugh has kindly given me much helpful advice about the writing of this note.)

2. Evelyn March Phillipps, *The Frescoes in the Sistine Chapel* (London, 1901), p. 16.

3. Lionello Venturi, *Piero della Francesca*, trans. James Emmons, *The Taste of Our Time*, collection planned and directed by Albert Skira (Geneva, 1954), p. 36.

4. Ernest Schanzer, " 'Mr. Eliot's Sunday Morning Service,' " *Essays in Criticism*, V, 153 (1955).

5. Elizabeth Drew, *T. S. Eliot: The Design of His Poetry* (New York, 1949), p. 38.

6. Schanzer, p. 154.

7. Bernard Berenson, *Piero della Francesca: Or the Ineloquent in Art* (New York, 1954), p. 3.

[From *T. S. Eliot: The Design of His Poetry*]

Elizabeth Drew*

Some of the juxtapositions are comparatively simple: the more or less innocent materialism of the secular world, compared with the hypocritical materialism of the "True Church" in "The Hippopotamus"; the romantic and classical symbols of lustful passions beside the sordid scene in the rooming house of "Sweeney Erect"; the childish day-dreams of dazzling successes compared with the actuality of the stale and unsavoury emotional present in *A Cooking Egg*. The present, indeed is uniformly stale and unsavoury in all these poems, as it is in the earlier ones, but interwoven with it is the continuous reminder of times when it was not so, and of works of the creative imagination in art and thought which have embodied a different reality and pictured a different vision. And the dramatic interplay and organization of these antagonisms becomes increasingly intricate and concentrated in its suggestions.

Sometimes indeed, too much so, as in "Mr. Eliot's Sunday Morning Service," where by the time the reader has finished with the Encyclopedia Britannica and the Oxford English Dictionary he has not much heart for the intellectual *tour-de-force* of the use of the material in the poem. Like "The Hippopotamus" it is a satire on the decay of religion, but a very much more complex one. On the one side, or in the centre rather, there is the basic Christian concept, "In the beginning was the Word," twice stated; also two verses describing an Italian painting [here Drew quotes stanzas three and four of the poem]. The lines are full of implications; of the creative mystery of the Logos; of the rich symbolic content of the sacrament of baptism and the doctrine of the Trinity; of the simple humanity of the still-shining figure, still reminding man in the modern "wilderness" of the redemption of his "offences"; and of the whole "design" which the painter has "set" on his ground. In ironic contrast Eliot sets various symbols of degradation and ugliness and a complicated parallel between the sterility of the worker-bees

*Reprinted by permission of the publishers from *T. S. Eliot: The Design of His Poetry*. Charles Scribner, 1949.

and that of the "Word" of sectarian theological argument. The "superfetation of τὸ ἔν," that is, the effort to fertilize "the one" by a fresh begetting; to make of the Word a Queen bee mated with numerous drones, inevitably produces a swarm of neuter religions, symbolized by the heretical Origen, the self-made eunuch. The sterile "masters of the subtle schools" who think themselves "sapient sutlers of the Lord" (servers or food-bringers) are barren. Not only as barren as the bees, but as barren in meaning to common humanity as the appalling polysyllables and learned terms with which the poem is loaded. The only area in it where this "neuter" use of the "word" is not used is in the two verses describing the painting.

The neuter worker-bees, also "sapient sutlers," at least fertilize the flowers as their "hairy bellies" gather the pollen, and so may be said to perform a "blest office" in the scheme of nature; but the same cannot be said of the "blest office" of the church service, or of "the sapient sutlers of the Lord" who are the clergy and congregation. The "sable presbyters" move up the aisle like the "religious caterpillars" in the epigraph, who were more interested in getting the Jew of Malta's "piaculative pence" than in saving his soul. The black gowns and red, spotty faces and the "dim souls" of the devout congregation all contrast with the shiny halo and the pale thin water and "unoffending feet."

The final degrading "offence" is the contrast of Sweeney wallowing in his bath with the figure of the Baptized God; with the further irony that there is a parallel between the movement of his body, shifting from ham to ham and stirring the water, and the "controversial" antics of the learned theologians.

"Sweeney Erect"

Emerson's "Self-Reliance," Sweeney, and Prufrock

Robert G. Cook*

> Upon the glazen shelves kept watch
> Matthew and Waldo, guardians of the faith,
> The army of unalterable law.
> ("Cousin Nancy")

F. O. Matthiessen has recorded both Eliot's "sustained distaste for Emerson" and the fact that Eliot is deeply indebted to the whole New England tradition of which Emerson is a part.[1] Emerson's faith in the infinite capacity of the human soul must have seemed naive to Eliot; his tendency to deny the normal bonds of community, friendship, and family in favor of a mystical oneness of all things must have been uncongenial; his scorn for history and the great literature of the past was in direct contradiction to Eliot's own views as expressed in "Tradition and the Individual Talent"; and above all, his ignorance of human sin and evil (e.g., his conversion of evil into good in "Compensation") must have seemed downright perverse.[2] Nonetheless, as Perry Miller has shown,[3] Emerson is very much a child of New England and the Puritan mentality which also shaped Eliot. Though Emerson's individualism is opposed to the Puritan concern for the body politic, and though his lack of a sense of evil made possible a direct approach to nature unavailable to Puritans,[4] he shares with them a deep moral concern and a relentless search into the depth of the human soul.

There is a congenial similarity between Eliot's theory of impersonality and Emerson's distrust of the purely subjective, so skillfully described by Matthiessen.[5] Both men explored thoroughly their own consciousnesses, but in a way totally different from the "romantic cultivation of the ego"; their interest was in general truth, not self-consciousness or self-advancement. To this end the entire soul, and not just the intellect, was to be fully explored. Both men scorned "the dry intellectualized distrusting of the emotions, which Emerson recognized as the worst blight that had been left by waning Puritanism."[6]

And yet even on the matter of self-consciousness and intellect versus emotion the two men are worlds apart, as this note will demonstrate by

*Reprinted, with permission, from *American Literature*, 42, (1970), 223–26.

43

pointing out a relation to Emerson's "Self-Reliance" that has not been suggested before. Eliot knew this essay well and probably had it in the front of his mind when he wrote: "Neither Emerson nor any of the others was a real observer of the moral life. . . . It [Hawthorne's observation of the moral life] will always be of use; the essays of Emerson are already an encumbrance."[7]

A parenthetic stanza in "Sweeney Erect" contains this direct mention:

> (The lengthened shadow of a man
> Is history, said Emerson
> Who had not seen the silhouette
> Of Sweeney straddled in the sun.)

The reference is to the following passage in "Self-Reliance":

> Every true man is a cause, a country, and an age; requires infinite spaces and numbers and time fully to accomplish his design; — and posterity seem to follow his steps as a train of clients. A man Caesar is born, and for ages after we have a Roman Empire. Christ is born, and millions of minds so grow and cleave to his genius that he is confounded with virtue and the possible of man. An institution is the lengthened shadow of one man; as Monachism, of the Hermit Antony; the Reformation, of Luther; Quakerism, of Fox; Methodism, of Wesley; Abolition, of Clarkson. Scipio, Milton called "the height of Rome"; and all history resolves itself very easily into the biography of a few stout and earnest persons.[8]

Eliot's change of the word "institution" to "history" is justifiable, for Emerson is here supporting the so-called great men theory of history, a theory which must have seemed as preposterous to Eliot as it did to Tolstoy. Tolstoy attacked the theory by deliberately assigning "great men," most notably Napoleon, a small significance in determining historical events. "The life of the nations is not contained in the lives of a few men, for the connexion between those men and the nations has not been found."[9] For Tolstoy the independence of the individual personality was severely limited; historical events are the doings of *all* the participants. Perhaps Eliot's attack on the great men theory in "Sweeney Erect" is in line with these ideas: Emerson spoke of his Luthers and Caesars, not realizing that the Sweeneys too cast their shadows.

If Sweeney is Eliot's animal-man, a Caliban whose consciousness does not extend beyond "birth, and copulation, and death" and the immediate satisfaction of basic desires, Prufrock is his opposite. The two men may be regarded as two halves of a dissociated sensibility, the sensuous and the intellectual, each isolated from its natural partner. Two years before his well-known remarks on the unified sensibility of "The Metaphysical Poets" appeared in *TLS*, Eliot expressed the same idea with his New England forebears in mind: "It is probable that men ripen best through experiences which are at once sensuous and intellectual; certainly many men will admit that their keenest ideas have come to them with the quality of a sense-perception; and that their keenest sensuous experience has been 'as if the body thought.' "[10] Prufrock is, in one sense, the extreme of the man who has not ripened in this way. His problem is an excess of consciousness—to put it more accurately, an unhealthy self-consciousness. Sweeney carries lack of inhibition to the "healthy" extreme of unreflective direct action; Prufrock carries self-consciousness to the pathological extreme of paranoic inaction and paralysis.

It is likely that Prufrock, no less than Sweeney, was affected by Eliot's reading of "Self-Reliance," for in that essay there are a striking number of passages that virtually define Prufrock's character. Immediately following the "great men" passage quoted above, for example, we read:

> Let a man then know his worth, and keep things under his feet. Let him not peep or steal, or skulk up and down with the air of a charity-boy, a bastard, or an interloper in the world which exists for him. But the man in the street, finding no worth in himself which corresponds to the force which built a tower or sculptured a marble god, feels poor when he looks on these. To him a palace, a statue, or a costly book have an alien and forbidding air, much like a gay equipage, and seem to say like that, "Who are you, Sir?" (pp. 61–62)

One of the main purposes of Emerson's essay is to overcome, in this fashion, the intimidations of "the man in the street." Eliot's Prufrock may be seen as a caricature of this man, an antitype to Emerson's self-reliant man, a totally un-self-reliant man. Prufrock constantly feels that he is being asked: "Who are you, Sir?"

Early in the essay Emerson points to the "nonchalance of boys who are sure of a dinner" as an example of natural self-trust and lack of self-consciousness. In contrast,

> the man is as it were clapped into jail by his consciousness. As soon as he has once acted or spoken with *éclat* he is a committed person, watched by the sympathy or the hatred of hundreds, whose affections must now enter into his account. There is no Lethe for this. Ah, that he could pass again into his neutrality! Who can thus avoid all pledges and, having observed, observe again from the same unaffected, unbiased, unbribable unaffrighted innocence, — must always be formidable. He would utter opinions on all passing affairs, which being seen to be not private but necessary, would sink like darts into the ear of men and put them in fear. (p. 49)

Prufrock, clapped into jail by his consciousness, has an *excessive* fear of expressing himself (("Shall I say, I have gone at dusk through narrow streets . . . ?"). For him there is no Lethe which would free him from abnormal concern for the opinions of others; he desires an even stronger Lethe, total inconspicuousness and oblivion ("I should have been a pair of ragged claws / Scuttling across the floors of silent seas"). At the same time, he longs, like a

self-reliant man, to utter opinions which would sink like darts into the ear
of men and put them in fear ("I am Lazarus, come from the dead . . .").

Where Emerson teaches "What I must do is all that concerns me, not
what the people think" (p. 53), Prufrock is paralyzed by his fears of what
people think. Where Emerson teaches that "the great man is he who in the
midst of the crowd keeps with perfect sweetness the independence of solitude" (p. 54), Prufrock is "pinned and wriggling on the wall." Prufrock is
incapable of regarding the faces he has known with Emerson's equanimity:
"the sour faces of the multitude, like their sweet faces, have no deep cause,
but are put on and off as the wind blows and a newspaper directs" (p. 56).

One reason Prufrock does not speak out is his fear of being misunderstood: "Would it have been worthwhile. . . . " In this too, Prufrock has not
profited from the teaching of Emerson: "Is it so bad then to be misunderstood? Pythagoras was misunderstood, and Socrates, and Jesus, and Luther,
and Copernicus, and Galileo, and Newton, and every pure and wise spirit
that ever took flesh. To be great is to be misunderstood" (pp. 57–58).

One of the symptoms of Prufrock's paranoia is his lack of a sense of
proportion, his inability to distinguish between great and small, with the
result that everything takes on exaggerated importance. In the timorous
formula "Do I dare?" eating a peach becomes tantamount to disturbing the
universe. The phrase "eternal Footman" expresses his undifferentiated fear
of an ordinary servant and the eternal God. Emerson's self-reliant man goes
to the opposite extreme and fears nobody, not even the great: "Let us never
bow and apologize more. A great man is coming to eat at my house. I do not
wish to please him; I wish that he should wish to please me" (p. 60). As far as
God is concerned, the self-reliant man need not fear Him, for in fact He is
present within the self-reliant man:

> Let us affront and reprimand the smooth mediocrity and squalid content-
> ment of the times, and hurl in the face of custom and trade and office, the
> fact which is the upshot of all history, that there is a great responsible
> Thinker and Actor working wherever a man works; that a true man be-
> longs to no other time or place, but is the centre of things. Where he is,
> there is nature. He measures you and all men and all events. (pp. 60–61)

On all these counts, basic both to Emerson's essay and to Eliot's portrayal, it is clear that Prufrock is the very opposite of the man Emerson envi-
sions. In fact, he is remarkably like the man Emerson is preaching against:
"The sinew and heart of man seem to be drawn out, and we are become
timorous, desponding whimperers. We are afraid of truth, afraid of fortune, afraid of death, and afraid of each other" (p. 75). "Fear" is also the
key word for Prufrock: "And in short, I was afraid."

It seems then that in both "Sweeney Erect" and "The Love Song of J.
Alfred Prufrock" Eliot is giving the lie to Emerson's "Self-Reliance." Just as
Emerson's view of the role of great men in the shaping of history did not
take into account the massive force of such men as Sweeney, neither did his

idealized notion of the self-reliant man take into account the plain fact that the adult consciousness is circumscribed. Eliot is of course dealing in extremes, but he seems to be saying that if you look for a human shadow, the odds are that it will be thrown by a Sweeney. Ask for an adult sensibility and you are more likely to find a Prufrock than an Emersonian nonconformist. These are Eliot's realistic responses to Emerson's idealistic proposals.

Notes

1. *The Achievement of T. S. Eliot* (3rd ed., New York, 1958), p. 8. See also p. 144: Throughout his life Eliot has been in reaction against the centrifugal individualism which characterized the America into which he was born. His deep-seated desire to link himself with a living tradition grew directly out of his revulsion against the lawless exploitation by which late nineteenth-century American individuals made any coherent society impossible. He was equally dissatisfied with the undefined spirituality of Emerson or Arnold: neither "Self-Reliance" nor "The Buried Life" was adequate.

2. For a good account of Emerson's optimistic view of human nature, see Matthiessen's *American Renaissance* (New York, 1941), pp. 179–184.

3. "Jonathan Edwards to Emerson," *New England Quarterly*, XIII (Dec., 1940), 589–617; reprinted in *Errand into the Wilderness* (New York, 1964).

4. The ecstasy and the vision which Calvinists knew only in the moment of vocation, the passing of which left them agonizingly aware of depravity and sin, could become the permanent joy of those who had put aside the conception of depravity, and the moments between could be filled no longer with self-accusation but with praise and wonder. Unitarianism had stripped off the dogmas, and Emerson was free to celebrate purely and simply the presence of God in the soul and in nature, the pure metaphysical essence of the New England tradition. (*Errand into the Wilderness*, p. 198)

5. *American Renaissance*, pp. 8–9.

6. Matthiessen, *The Achievement of T. S. Eliot*, p. 106.

7. From a review of the second volume of *The Cambridge History of American Literature* which appeared in the *Athenaeum*, No. 4643 (April 25, 1919), p. 237; quoted in Matthiessen, *The Achievement of T. S. Eliot*, p. 24.

8. *Essays, First Series* (Boston, 1903), p. 61. Subsequent references are in parentheses.

9. *War and Peace*, Epilogue II (trans. Louise and Ayhner Maude).

10. "A Sceptical Patrician," a review of *The Educational of Henry Adams*, *Athenaeum*, No. 4647 (May 23, 1919), p. 362. In this review Eliot describes "the Boston doubt" as a lack of capacity for passionate absorption and mentions as an example Emerson's declining to administer the Communion "because (in his own words) it did not interest him."

Some Psychological Patterns in the Poetry of T. S. Eliot

Marie Baldridge*

In "Sweeney Erect," Eliot describes with symbols out of classical literature the desolate atmosphere of the brothel, Mrs. Turner's, where Sweeney has lodged for the night. Here Eliot gains the effect through irony, the piquancy of which covers the unpleasantness, and makes the poetic concoction palatable. Here, and in many other poems, the poet displays a concern with the parts of the body. When he deals with the physical aspects of love, he avoids tenderness for, understanding of, or identification with, the partner of the love act; he emphasizes only the ugly and disgusting. In his descriptions of lust there are many images of the parts of the body. In the following quotation from "Sweeney Erect," note the contrast of the epic grandeur and the ugliness [here Baldridge quotes the first four stanzas of the poem]. This is a scene complementary to the one described by Tiresias in "The Waste Land" and it is viewed with all the fascination of the voyeur.

The excitement brings to the epileptic woman an attack, and Sweeney, who "Tests the razor on his leg / Waiting until the shriek subsides." The reader is assured not only of Sweeney's virility but also of his cruelty. Though he is burly and gross and sexually predatory, he is cruel, and hence is related to Prufrock, who says, "There will be time to murder and create." The Sweeney type of man is but an extension of Prufrock—he is Prufrock successful but still unsatisfied. The thoughts of both men are distorted and cruel. There is no surprise when Sweeney says, as he moves through "Sweeney Agonistes, Fragments of an Aristophanic Melodrama," "I knew a man once did a girl in. . . ." Sweeney thinks that he is speaking for all men, "Any man has to, needs to, wants to, do a girl in." Actually he is speaking for the Harrys, as well as for the Sweeneys, both of whom have murdered a woman. Neither has any feeling of guilt for his crime; both feel a sense of relief. When Swarts asks, "What did he do?/ All that time, what do?" Sweeney replies, "What did he do! what did he do?/ That don't apply. . . . We all gotta do what we gotta do—" Sweeney is undoubtedly a madman and a necrophile. Though he is licentious, he is unsatisfied. He is introduced as a foil for Prufrock. Similar in *Crime and Punishment*, there is a foil for Raskolnikov in the character of Svidrigailov, who lives licentiously, murders a servant, a young girl, and his wife. Later he has hallucinations of the dead, who accuse him in much the same way that the Eumenides pursue Harry to torment him for the murder of his wife. To relieve himself of the sense of guilt, Svidrigailov commits suicide. If "Sweeney Agonistes" were a completed poem, Sweeney's only logical release would be through suicide.

The relation between Sweeney and Harry is established by the poet

*Reprinted, with permission, from *Psychoanalysis: Journal of Psychoanalytical Psychology*, 3 (1954), 37–39.

himself in the quotation about the Furies, which follows the title "Sweeney Agonistes":

> ORESTES: You don't see them you don't — but *I* see them: they are hunting me down, I must move on. — *Choephoroi.*

This quotation is followed by a second one which describes the thematic development of Eliot's poetry, the need to escape from physical lust into Divine Love.

> Hence the soul cannot be possessed of the divine union, until it has divested itself of the love of created beings. — *St. John of the Cross.*

Prufrock and Sweeney are parts of one psychological pattern: they have failed in the emotional integration of the physical and the spiritual aspects of instinctual desire, are disposed to cruelty, and are in need of religion and salvation to relieve them of the guilt brought on by their murderous impulses.

"Sweeney Erect" and the Emersonian Hero

Charles Peake*

So much of the critical energy applied to the poetry of T. S. Eliot has been expended on the identification of sources, references and echoes, and on the explication of their function in the poems, that it is remarkable that one of his few explicit literary references has provoked little or no discussion of its relevance to the poem in which it appears.

In the seventh verse of "Sweeney Erect" Eliot parenthetically observes,

> (The lengthened shadow of a man
> Is history, said Emerson
> Who had not seen the silhouette
> Of Sweeney straddled in the sun.)

Although the reference to Ariadne at the beginning of the poem has led to its being interpreted in terms of the fertility myth, and a doubtful source for the description of Sweeney's bedmate has been found in Shelley's *The Triumph of Life*, no-one seems to have turned to the context of the Emerson reference for light on the poem. Yet this context appears to be closely connected to the thought of the poem, to have influenced the vocabulary and phrasing, and to have suggested the title.

The allusion is generally said to be to the famous essay "Self-Reliance," which is the second essay in Emerson's first series. But Eliot is not quoting precisely; what Emerson in fact said was that "an institution is the lengthened

*Reprinted, with permission, from *Neophilologus*, 44 (1960), 54–61.

shadow of one man", though he added that "all history resolves itself very easily into the biography of a few stout and earnest persons". But it is very possible that Eliot's emendation of Emerson's assertion was intended to
recall, as well as "Self-Reliance," the essay immediately preceding it — "History." Certainly these two essays together provide a very adequate commentary on "Sweeney Erect": or perhaps it would be more correct to say that
"Sweeney Erect" can be read as a conscious and ironic commentary on the
matter and manner of the two essays.

The gist of the first essay is that history, being merely the record of the
universal mind, can be understood only by those who interpret it in terms of
their own personal, even trivial, experiences: "If the whole of history is in
one man, it is all to be explained from individual experience."[1] But it is the
converse of this theory — that our individual experiences are to be interpreted in terms of history or myth — that is most relevant to "Sweeney
Erect": "The student is to read history actively and not passively; to esteem
his own life the text, and books the commentary . . . I have no expectation
that any man will read history aright, who thinks that what was done in a
remote age, by men whose names have resounded far, has any deeper sense
than what he is doing to-day."

After giving some examples "such as fall within the scope of every
man's observation, of trivial facts which go to illustrate great and conspicu-
ous facts," Emerson proceeds to explain the fascination for all men of Ancient Greece:

> This period draws us because we are Greeks. It is a state through
> which every man in some sort passes. The Grecian state is the era of the
> bodily nature, the perfection of the senses, — of the spiritual nature un-
> folded in strict unity with the body. In it existed those human forms
> which supplied the sculptor with his models of Hercules, Phoebus, and
> Jove; not like the forms abounding in the streets of modern cities, wherein
> the face is a confused blur of features, but composed of incorrupt, sharply
> defined and symmetrical features, whose eyesockets are so formed that it
> would be impossible for such eyes to squint, and take furtive glances on
> this side and on that, but they must turn the whole head.
>
> The manners of that period are plain and fierce. The reverence ex-
> hibited is for personal qualities, courage, address, self-command, justice,
> strength, swiftness, a loud voice, a broad chest. Luxury is not known, nor
> elegance. A sparse population and want make every man his own valet,
> cook, butcher, and soldier; and the habit of supplying his own needs edu-
> cates the body to wonderful performances.

It is not only history and the Greeks that supply parallels for our own
individual experiences. Quite early in his essay Emerson asserts that poetic
myths are no less than immortal signs made out of historical fact, and later
he develops this assertion:

> The advancing man discovers how deep a property he hath in all
> literature, — in all fable as well as in all history. He finds that the poet was

no odd fellow who described strange and impossible situations, but that universal man wrote by his pen a confession true for one and true for all. His own secret biography he finds in lines wonderfully intelligible to him, yet dotted down before he was born. One after another he comes up in his private adventures with every fable of Aesop, of Homer, of Hafiz, of Ariosto, of Chaucer, of Scott, and verifies them with his own head and hands.

The beautiful fables of the Greeks, being proper creations of the Imagination and not of the Fancy, are universal verities.

And Emerson illustrates his argument by showing how the stories of Prometheus, Apollo, Antaeus, Orpheus, Proteus, and Tantalus relate to the lives of all men.

It will be seen that some of these ideas are not essentially alien to Eliot's own attitude towards history and literature, although he would almost certainly dislike the somewhat brash and egocentric individualism of their tone and context in Emerson's essay. In "Sweeney Erect" he seems to have used the procedures recommended in "History" to provide an ironical setting for his satire of the Emersonian hero as depicted in "Self-Reliance."

Eliot's modern scene is of a deserted female lamenting the departure of her lover. The poet follows the Emersonian prescription. It does not matter that the theatre is a room in a boarding-house (perhaps a whore-house), that the laments are hysterical and grotesque, that the lover is Sweeney — after all, "we are Greeks." This biographical episode has been "dotted down" in "the beautiful fables of the Greeks." The type of the deserted female is, of course, Ariadne deserted on Naxos by Theseus. In Beaumont and Fletcher's *The Maid's Tragedy* (II, 2) the forsaken Aspatia had made a similar identification and had presented herself as a model for her maid's needlework picture of Ariadne on Naxos; and Eliot, to make his point clear, uses part of Aspatia's speech as an epigraph. It is a stock comparison; Thackeray, for instance, used it concerning Fanny Bolton in *Pendennis* (Ch. 55).

Eliot, however, wants as much to draw attention to the differences between his modern woman and her classical counterpart as to indicate a resemblance; or, rather, the resemblance is noted only to emphasise the differences. He therefore describes Ariadne in a style which is poetical, rhetorical and elevated, in order to make the shift to the modern hysteric the more violent. . . . As Aspatia, in the lines quoted in the epigraph, had made the landscape background for Ariadne a reflection of her own wretchedness, so Eliot's landscape reflects certain features of the Sweeney situation; like a rock, the bold, broad-bottomed Sweeney faces the yelping seas of tears of the hysterical woman; her knotted hair is an ugly echo of the tangles of Ariadne's hair. (Although in one place the woman is referred to as "the epileptic on the bed," I take it that the term is used descriptively, and that "the ladies of the corridor" are right in attributing the uproar to hysteria. All the circumstances confirm their diagnosis, and Doris's remedies seem better suited for a hysteric than an epileptic.) Even in this anthropo-morphic treatment of landscape Eliot may have had "History" in mind: Emerson declares, "Nature is full of a sublime family-likeness throughout her works. She delights in startling us with resemblances in the most unex-pected quarters. I have seen the head of an old sachem of the forest, which at once reminded the eye of a bald mountain summit, and the furrows of the brow suggested the strata of the rock." The step to seeing Sweeney as a bold anfractuous rock is an easy one.

In the third verse Eliot makes a skilful transition from the heroic Greek sea-scape to the modern bedroom. The poetical language is maintained for our first glimpse of Sweeney and his bedmate — "Morning stirs the feet and hands" — and an aside suggests a comparison with Nausicaa and Poly-pheme. The reason for this unlikely pairing is, I suppose, that Eliot wished to recall ironically two of the most famous dawn-awakenings in the *Odyssey*, and at the same time smooth his transition to modern sordidness by a suggested resemblance between Sweeney and the brutal Polypheme. The hint is reinforced by the emergence of Sweeney from the bed-clothes with a "gesture of orang-outang." This animal image and the even more brutal pic-ture of the woman which follows may also owe something to "History." Emerson seems uncertain whether to welcome or deplore human animality. In one place he writes: "In man we still trace the rudiments or hints of all that we esteem badges of servitude in the lower races, yet in him they en-hance his nobleness and grace." But later he changes his tune: "The transmi-gration of souls: that too is no fable. I would it were; but men and women are only half human. Every animal of the barn-yard, the field and the for-est, of the earth and of the waters that are under the earth, has contrived to get a footing, and to leave the print of its features and form in some one or other of these upright, heaven-facing speakers." Perhaps Emerson's belief in the "nobleness and grace" with which the rudiments of the lower races manifest themselves in man accounts for the delightful blend of the formal and the savage in "Gesture of orang-outang," and very probably part of the significance of the title of the poem is that Sweeney is an "upright, heaven-facing" ape.

Eliot seems also to have "History" in mind in his description of the hys-terical woman. There is no need to turn to *The Triumph of Life* (lines 182–8) for the source of "This withered root of knots of hair," although it is just possible that Shelley's image of the figure like "an old root" influenced Eliot.[2] A more meaningful comparison can be made with a sentence in "History": "A man is a bundle of relations, a knot of roots, whose flower and fruitage is the world." It is quite in keeping with the whole relationship of the poem to Emerson's essays that this hysterical creature should be de-scribed in a mocking inversion of Emerson's phrase; especially as the im-plied comparison of the screaming face, the features of which are mere gashes in a withered surface, to the beautiful Greek Ariadne is also reminis-cent of the passage, quoted above, where Emerson compared the "confused blur of features" of many modern faces with the "incorrupt, sharply-defined and symmetrical features" of the Greeks, placing particular emphasis on the formation of the eye-sockets.

The scene is now set for the appearance of the Emersonian hero "addressed full length to shave," and the Emerson references shift from "History" to "Self-Reliance." But both essays contribute to Sweeney. He, too, has traces of the Greek about him, though for the most part they are degenerate. The "broad chest" of the Greek is humbly echoed in Sweeney's broad bottom; his overall pinkness reflects the Greeks' perfect physical health; their "address" is perhaps present in the curiously formal verb "addressed"; and like them Sweeney is "his own valet." The "self-command" he exhibits in a difficult situation is worthy of a Greek, but more importantly it is worthy of the hero or great man described in "Self-Reliance": "The great man is he who in the midst of the crowd keeps with perfect sweetness the independence of solitude." Sweeney is as far above the emotions which might trouble an ordinary man in his circumstances as he is above the complaints and moral disapproval of the women in the corridor. He feels no tie of intimacy with or responsibility for the hysteric; he is quite unafraid; he has no urge to relieve the woman's condition, whether it be hysteria or epilepsy; he has no charitable thought. Imperturbably he lathers his face, tests the razor on his leg while he waits for the shriek to subside, and with philosophic calm recognises the generic cause underlying the particular phenomenon — it is all a matter of "the female temperament." Both his imperturbability and his grasp of generality are thoroughly characteristic of the Emersonian hero: "At times the whole world seems to be in conspiracy to importune you with emphatic trifles. Friend, client, child, sickness, fear, want, charity, all knock at once at thy closet-door and say, 'Come out unto us'. — Do not spill thy soul; do not all descend; keep thy state; stay at home in thine own heaven; come not for a moment into their facts, into their hubbub of conflicting appearances, but let in the light of thy law on their confusion." Other passages in "History" and "Self-Reliance" show how surely Sweeney seizes upon the kind of general law which helps the great man to remain calm amid the "hubbub of conflicting appearances": "The progress of the intellect consists in the clearer vision of causes, which over-looks surface-differences. . . . Genius detects . . . through countless individuals the fixed species." ("History") The soul is raised over passion. It seeth identity and eternal causation . . . Prayer is the contemplation of the facts of life from the highest point of view." ("Self-Reliance").

But, as Emerson knew, the world (represented here by "the ladies of the corridor") does not appreciate self-reliant heroism: "For nonconformity the world whips you with its displeasure . . . It is easy enough for a firm man who knows the world to brook the rage of the cultivated classes. Their rage is decorous and prudent; for they are timid, as being very vulnerable themselves. But when to their feminine rage the indignation of the people is added . . . it needs the habit of magnanimity and religion to treat it godlike as a trifle of no concernment." Whether or not the ladies who deprecate the goings-on in Sweeney's bedroom are cultivated, they are certainly anxious with their talk of "principles" and "taste" to pretend to cultivation, and their indignation is not only "decorous and prudent" but symptomatic of their own vulnerability:

> The ladies of the corridor
>   Find themselves involved, disgraced,
> Call witness to their principles
>   And deprecate the lack of taste
>
> Observing that hysteria
>   Might easily be misunderstood.

In these last two lines occurs another of those verbal echoes which confirm that it was not only in the parenthetical seventh verse that Eliot had Emerson's essays in mind. The great soul, declares Emerson, must not bother about consistency: "Ah, then, exclaim the aged ladies, you shall be sure to be misunderstood. Misunderstood! It is a right fool's word. Is it so bad then to be misunderstood? Pythagoras was misunderstood, and Socrates, and Jesus, and Luther, and Copernicus, and Galileo, and Newton, and every pure and wise spirit that ever took flesh. To be great is to be misunderstood." The worldly Mrs. Turner, while presumably sharing the offended principles and taste of the other ladies, adds a more material note — "It does the house no sort of good." She clearly, as landlady or madam, has some property-interest threatened by the situation, and she too, has her place in the unheroic world which Emerson contrasts with his hero: "And so the reliance on Property, including the reliance on governments which protect it, is the want of self-reliance. Men have looked away from themselves and at things so long, that they have come to esteem what they call the soul's progress, namely, the religious, learned, and civil institutions, as guards of property, and they deprecate assaults on these, because they feel them to be assaults on property." "Deprecate" is a common enough word, but when one considers the other verbal coincidences, its appearance in "Sweeney Erect" may seem not merely accidental. In any case, the way in which Mrs. Turner expresses the economic roots of her moral indignation is a good illustration of Emerson's observation.

The last verse introduces us to Doris, bringing relief to the sufferer in the form of sal volatile, "And a glass of brandy neat." She completes the pattern of the poem by recalling the myth with which it began. If the hysteric is Ariadne, Doris with her brandy is the hand-maiden and herald of the consoling Bacchus. But she may also play a part in Eliot's satirical commentary on "Self-Reliance." Without any overt praise, Eliot makes us approve of Doris. While Sweeney is occupied with being imperturbable and the ladies with calling witness to their principles, Doris hastens, "towelled from the bath," to bring what assistance and consolation she can. Emerson, however, seems to disapprove of such weak sympathy: "Our sympathy is just as base. We come to them who weep foolishly, and sit down and cry for company, instead of imparting to them truth and health in rough electric shocks, putting them once more in communication with the soul."

Earlier I have suggested that part of the implications of the title of the poem is that Sweeney is an erect ape; but the choice of the word "erect" (and I fail to see that the sexual connotation has much significance here) seems to have been suggested by the culminating passage of "Self-Reliance," where Emerson sums up his message: "He who knows that power is in the soul, that he is weak only because he has looked for good out of him and elsewhere, and so perceiving, throws himself unhesitatingly on his thought, instantly rights himself, stands in the erect position, commands his limbs, works miracles." This is the Emersonian hero, and this, I have tried to show, is Sweeney.

It requires little knowledge of Eliot's thought to perceive that at any time in his poetic career he would have found Emerson's creed wrong-headed, offensive, and dangerous, and it is not difficult to find evidence of this dislike. For instance, in a review of the *Cambridge History of American Literature,* written in the same year as "Sweeney Erect," Eliot remarked that "Neither Emerson nor any of the others was a real observer of the moral life";[3] and the late F. O. Matthiessen has reported a conversation with the poet in which the latter spoke of "his sustained distaste for Emerson."[4] It is interesting that Matthiessen associated this distaste with "Self-Reliance," the tenets of which, he said, "led logically to an inhuman extreme of individualism."[5]

In tracing the relationship of Eliot's poem to the two essays of Emerson, I have possibly strained a connection here and there, although I have tried not to be too ingenious. It is not altogether inconceivable that Eliot wrote the poem fresh from a re-reading of Emerson's essays, and that the echoes and similarities were, apart from the seventh verse, unconscious. It is not altogether inconceivable; though the extent and nature of the parallels make it seem highly improbable. However this may be, that the poem as a whole is very intimately related to the two essays taken together seems to me incontrovertible. Moreover it seems to me equally certain that the poem gains in significance and satirical point from a recognition of the extent and nature of the references to Emerson. Eliot is not merely contrasting a sordid modern scene with the glory that was Greece; but as in "Mr. Eliot's Sunday Morning Service" (a poem written in the same year) he presents a satirical picture of one aspect of modern life and at the same time exposes the false ideas which are part cause and part consequence of it. Emerson's two essays advocated and were expressions of that very state of anthropocentric, individualistic, self-sufficient blindness, without faith, humility or obedience, which Eliot saw as the fundamental cause of the spiritual barrenness of his times. Like Fielding in *Jonathan Wild* he reveals the inadequacy and folly of a current conception of "greatness" by giving it an exaggerated exemplification in contemporary terms.

The question of how far Eliot was justified in expecting his readers to recognise recondite allusions hardly arises here. The two essays were among the most famous of Emerson's productions, and were almost certainly more familiar to the readers of 1919 than they are to those of to-day. The detailed references and echoes were perhaps for the delectation of the poet himself and for such of his readers as knew Emerson's essays well or were prepared to follow up the hint given in the seventh verse. For the rest, who were satisfied with a more general apprehension of the poem's meaning, the gist of the satire was sufficiently clear. If, as Emerson put it, "An institution is the lengthened shadow of one man; as, the Reformation, of Luther; Quakerism, of Fox; Methodism, of Wesley; Abolition, of Clarkson," what sort of world, what sort of institution, what sort of history would be the shadow thrown by the Emersonian hero, Sweeney, the type of modern man? It is a question not unlike the question put by Yeats at about the same time in a very different poetic vein, but with a similar horror at the anarchy of modern life—"And what rough beast, its hour come round at last, / Slouches towards Bethlehem to be born?"

Notes

1. All quotations are from the Everyman edition of the *Essays* (Dent: 1906), a representative popular edition of the early part of the century.

2. Grover Smith, *T. S. Eliot's Poetry and Plays* (University of Chicago Press, 1956), p. 48.

3. *Athenaeum*, 25 April 1919.

4. *The Achievement of T. S. Eliot* (London: Oxford University Press: 1947), p. 8.

5. *Ibid.*, p. 144.

The Poetry of T. S. Eliot   D. E. S. Maxwell*

In "Prufrock and other Observations" to a limited extent, more apparently in *Poems 1920*, are dispersed the themes which are developed and organised to achieve their greatest impact in *The Waste Land*. Some of these anticipations have already been indicated. Before it can be properly seen how *The Waste Land* uses its material, however, it is necessary to examine the more tentative grouping of themes in the second volume of poems. This volume contains the seeds not only of *The Waste Land* but also of the transition poems leading to *Four Quartets*. An examination of it is therefore essential to detailed interpretation of *The Waste Land*, and to an understanding of Eliot's poetic development.

*Reproduced by permission of the publishers from *The Poetry of T.S. Eliot:* Routledge & Kegan Paul (1966).

Perhaps the clearest allusion in "Prufrock and other Observations" to the fertility motif is in "Mr. Apollinax":

> I thought of Fragilion, that shy figure among the birch trees,
> And of Priapus in the shrubbery
> Gaping at the lady in the swing.

A parallel reference in *Poems 1920* occurs in "Sweeney Erect," where Ariadne replaces Priapus:

> Display me Aeolus above
> Reviewing the insurgent gales
> Which tangle Ariadne's hair
> And swell with haste the perjured sails.

The intricately devised opening stanzas lead from a description of the Grecian islands to Greek mythology. The link is Aeolus, whose winds disturb the seas and Ariadne's hair. The reference to Ariadne is the first key to the poem's theme. She is the goddess of vegetation, personification of Spring and returning life, symbol of fertility. On this level of interpretation a contrast is immediately suggested with "this withered root of knots of hair," associated with Sweeney and his bed-fellow. Theirs is a mating that has denied the aim of reproduction, a sterile coupling in a brothel. The contrast, then, is between this and the cycle of death and rebirth in the Ariadne fertility myth. Once this is seen the essence of the poem is revealed. Yet there is a further complexity in the classical allusions.

Ariadne, before her rebirth and marriage with Dionysus, is abandoned by Theseus and her love betrayed: as love is betrayed by Sweeney too, though in a different way. As additional emphasis, the winds that "tangle Ariadne's hair" also "swell with haste the perjured sails." In Eliot's elaborately concise poetry there is no place for merely decorative phrasing, and as this last line must have a meaning, it is most likely that it refers to the sails of the ship bearing Isolde to the dying Tristan[1]: again a betrayal.[2] This is particularly interesting in its anticipation of the use made of this legend in *The Waste Land*. Time is telescoped to include at the same instant Sweeney, Ariadne, Tristan and Isolde, connected by what might seem to be the superficially descriptive opening stanzas.

What is suggested is not a bare and simple contrast. Always love has been betrayed and fertility denied; always the hope of rebirth is offered. But the rebirth demands sacrifice, suffering, and a life conditioned by principles far different from those to which "the ladies of the corridor" call witness. In this way from the suffering of Philomel came rebirth and the "inviolable voice" of the nightingale. (See *The Waste Land*, ll. 97–103.) There is no indication here, however, that the offer of rebirth is acceptable to the contemporary world. It accepts living death, and the only remedies produced by Doris are sal-volatile and neat brandy. This poem illustrates well the obliquity of Eliot's poetry, the layers of meaning that can lie behind a single line.

A comparison between the openings of 'Sweeney Erect" and "L'Allegro," which have a certain similarity of pattern, emphasises the peculiarity of Eliot's method. All we need to know of the classical figures to whom Milton alludes is given within the poem. It is sufficient to know that Cerberus is associated with "blackest midnight," that Venus is lovely, that Zephyr and Aurora can be fitly mentioned with "frolic" and "playing." Milton's method, then, is quite direct. The classical figures, summoned to provide a suitable parentage for Euphrosyne, have their characteristics and function straightforwardly allotted to them. The pattern is similar to that of "Sweeney Erect": a picture of desolation, reinforced by classical memories is followed in Milton by a charming evocation of lightness and joy, in Eliot by a reminder that his desolate background contained the beauty and fertility of Ariadne — as Sweeney's does not. There the similarity ends. For the success of Eliot's method depends on the reader's recognising that Ariadne is not to be looked on as representing merely a picture of jolly, flower-bedecked Spring. No direct indication is given within the poem that this Ariadne has the deep religious significance that she had for her original devotees. Yet when what is implied in the relations between the figures of the opening stanzas and those of the body of the poem is considered, the reader must come to see that it is this aspect of the myth that is significant in the context.

This is not a contrast between a good and a bad technique, but between two entirely different methods in use at widely separated times. The poets of the decadent romantic school continued to use the direct expansive method with diminished technical skill, and on subjects already sadly overworked. Eliot's bare and restrained utterance forges by its reticence a more powerful relationship between the classical and the modern scene than could have resulted from an elaboration of the opening verses. A selective elaboration comes at the proper point, where knowledge cannot be assumed, to create in a few lines a vivid picture of the sordid:

> This withered root of knots of hair
>   Slitted below and gashed with eyes,
> This oval O cropped out with teeth.[3]

The variation of the "o" and "i" sounds, the impact of "gashed" and "cropped" support more precisely the visual picture. Elaboration of the earlier part could serve only to unbalance the structure. Comparison between Milton's and Eliot's lines reveals very clearly the distinction between Eliot's methods and those of an earlier tradition.

Closely connected with *The Waste Land* is "Sweeney among the Nightingales," again concerned with the fertility theme. . . . Orion, seen at midnight, heralded the vintage season in the Egyptian calendar, but the natural order is destroyed by Sweeney and his associates. The waiter brings them "hothouse grapes" to be torn by Rachel's "murderous paws." The function of Orion is negatived, and this is but one aspect of the distortion of fertility and the natural order. The verse quoted suggests what is perhaps the primary significance of the Dog symbol in "The Burial of the Dead." In this context the Dog is obviously Sirius, the Dog star, which for the Egyptians foretold the coming of the fertilising floods of the Nile. Stetson — and Sweeney — would not welcome this returned fertility, with its attendant disruption of the settled way. In *The Golden Bough* Frazer tells how Isis and Osiris were also connected in Egyptian mythology with the rising of the waters. Effigies of the god, made of corn, were buried to symbolise the death of the corn god. From this burial ensued the new harvest: hence from the death of Osiris came the deliverance of the people. With this ritual should be compared the burial performed by Stetson, which can symbolise only the attempt to forget a spiritual failure. Not, as with Osiris, a bringing of life by the burial of the material body. From Stetson's ritual can come no resurrection. Frazer points out the similarity between the Osiris and Dionysus legends: so we return to the Ariadne allusion in "Sweeney Erect."

Egyptian ritual, described in Frazer's work, that has a relevance to "Sweeney among the Nightingales" is the practice whereby images of Adonis and Aphrodite were displayed on couches, and beside them were placed ripe fruits of all kinds.[4] A debased version of this is represented by the fortuitous offering of, " . . . oranges / Bananas figs and hothouse grapes:" by the waiter. These allusions are an early use of the fertility myths as symbols of the poems' significance. Orion and the Dog are veiled; the fertilising floods are far distant, and the life-giving water is diminished in the "shrunken seas." The horned gate guarded by Sweeney is possibly that of *The Spanish Tragedy*, guarded by Pluto, king of the Underworld, "Where dreams have passage in the silent night" (I, i, ll. 75–82). This is the atmosphere of the trance-like cities of *The Waste Land*.

The opening stanzas of this poem have the same function as those of "Sweeney Erect." They evoke an atmosphere — one of foreboding, and some impending disaster — and elucidate in their indirect way the fertility theme at the core of the poem. Here the loss of fertility is again associated with the idea of infidelity and betrayal. The major parallelism is to the story of Agamemnon. Aegistheus, who had seduced Clytaemnestra during Agamemnon's absence, plots with her to kill Agamemnon on his return. Agamemnon's dying words form the epigraph to Eliot's poem. In "Sweeney" there is again a plot: that of Rachel and the lady in the cape against the man with heavy eyes. This is in keeping with the feeling of foreboding aroused in the opening verses, but the real betrayal lies deeper in the relations between the men and women in the poem. It is the same betrayal that occupies Eliot in "Sweeney Erect": the degradation of love to an animal-like mechanical relationship. By this Sweeney too — and it is part of the condemnation that he does not realise it — has been "struck a mortal blow within." Of this there is more to be said. But first may be mentioned Eliot's inevitable association of the nightingale in some way with misfortune.

On its first publication in *Ara Vos Prec*, "Sweeney among the Nightin-

gales" bore this *1st publication* additional epigraph: "Why should I speak of the Nightingale? The Nightingale sings of adulterous wrong." Within the narrow limits
of his verse-form Eliot achieves, at the culmination of this poem, the tremendous effect of:

> The nightingales are singing near
> The Convent of the Sacred Heart.
>
> And sang within the bloody wood
> When Agamemnon cried aloud;
> And let their liquid siftings fall
> To stain the stiff dishonoured shroud.

The nightingales sing at betrayal and death, at the decay of fertility, as they
did when Agamemnon was killed. Harry in *The Family Reunion* says of the
Eumenides: "In Italy, from behind the nightingales' thicket, / The eyes
stared at me and corrupted that song." For Harry, the birds accompany the
agents of retribution.

At the end of the Sweeney poem, it is the nightingales that link the
betrayal of Agamemnon, of Sweeney's activities, and apparently of the
Convent too, for there also fertility is denied. This association probably has
its source, as has been suggested, in the original Philomel legend. This involves a betrayal, and gives a further meaning to the proximity of the nightingales to the brothel. They sang as retribution followed Harry, as the
women of the brothel plotted, and the song itself was born of Philomel's
suffering. This use of the nightingale is a deliberate break with the romantic
conception of the bird as being associated entirely with beauty, and a vague
feeling of nostalgia — desire to be elsewhere. Of this break the mention of
the birds' "liquid siftings" — excrement, and not the birds' song — is a detail.
Similarly the "golden grin" of verse eight is intended not to evoke a pleasur-
able upsurge of romantic feeling — Housman's "hearts of gold" — but to describe the gleaming of gold-filled teeth. Frank Wilson in his book on Eliot
produces from the lines a similar misinterpretation: "There is a sinister suggestiveness, almost a furtive beauty, in the scene, for all is illuminated by
the eerie light of impending disaster, just as the weird light in Grendel's
mother's cavern shone upon her fight with Beowulf: 'Branches of wistaria /
Circumscribe a golden grin' " (Frank Wilson: *Six Essays on the Development of T. S. Eliot*, p. 18). With these lines, however, a diversion can be
offered. Looking on to the gardens of Merton College, Oxford, where Eliot
spent a year of post-graduate study, is a window surrounded by wistaria. It
is pleasant to think of the poet's seeing through this window, one day, the
flash of teeth, and focusing the incident with sharp clarity and intensity,
years later, in a poem. No doubt part of the fascination lies in the minute
relevance of Eliot's biography to his poetry, in the infrequency with which
we can divert ourselves with such imaginings.

It is difficult not to think that the close relationship between brothel,
convent, and the death of Agamemnon implies that the convent also repre-

sents a distortion of values.[5] Withdrawal from the world is not an effective means of coping with the world's distress. Collingwood, in a perceptive note on this passage, sees the relationship between the three strands of the poem,[6] but he errs, I think, in supposing that Sweeney also sees the connexion between them, in his drunken reverie: Sweeney never heard of Agamemnon. Castigation of established religious practices is not a novelty in these poems. Here, the implied condemnation of the convent, and in "The Hippopotamus" the more general gibes at ". . . the True Church, . . . below / Wrapt in the old miasmal mist."

This is not atheism, nor a condemnation of objective religious values and morals. It is an expression of dissatisfaction with the negative attitude to life which Eliot saw operative in the established religions almost as much as in the lives of the Sweeneys of this world. On the one hand we have a negative attitude to evil, on the other an equally negative attitude to good:

> The hippo's feeble steps may err
> In compassing material ends,
> While the True Church need never stir
> To gather in its dividends.

Such an attitude is a weakening, a vulgarisation of the churches' task. Broadly speaking, it is particular instances of the general process of vulgarisation that occupy Eliot in these poems.

Notes

1. This is purely conjectural. There is nothing in the legends alluded to, nor in their organization within the poem, to enable us to say with any assurance that this connection is in fact intended. It must be accounted a failure in the poem that, if this is the meaning of the line — and no other suggests itself — its unravelling has been left so haphazardly to chance association of ideas. Eliot's normal practice produces so closely-knit a pattern of mood and idea that elucidation presents no insurmountable difficulty. Here, however, the concise development is so rapid as to defeat its own purpose.

2. The epigraph is from a speech by Aspatia, the betrayed maiden, in Act II, scene ii of Beaumont and Fletcher's *The Maid's Tragedy*. In it she suggests a fitting background for her portrait.

3. A strong theoretical force is infused in these lines. One may compare John of Gaunt's, "This royal throne of kings, this sceptured isle. / This earth of majesty, this seat of Mars." Eliot's own comments on the rhetoric make it quite clear that he does not think it necessarily a vice; see his essay "Rhetoric and Poetic Drama," *Selected Essays*, p. 37.

4. *The Golden Bough*, Vol. 2: Chapter 4.

5. The Puritan tradition in Eliot's New England background had not at this time been replaced by his later religious preferences. Even his Anglo-Catholicism, as will be shown, bears the signs of his upbringing. It is fair to assume, then, that he speaks at least partially from his own experience when, in *Notes towards the Definition of Culture*, he discusses the Puritan attitude to the life of the religious celibate: ". . . just as a culture which is only accessible to the few is now deprecated, as was the enclosed and contemplative life condemned by extreme Protestantism, and celibacy regarded with almost as much abhorrence as perversion" (p. 33).

6. R. Collingwood: *Principles of Art*, p. 110.

"Sweeney among the Nightingales"

A Freudian Dream Analysis of "Sweeney Among the Nightingales"

George Whiteside[*]

"Sweeney Among the Nightingales" defies a conventional analysis in a way and to a degree that no other of T. S. Eliot's poems does. I suggest, therefore, that we try a dream analysis. It seems to me that the poem succeeds by getting readers to enter into a nightmare, wherein one is moved, one is frightened, without in the least knowing why. It is the purpose of this paper to examine the way in which this nightmare has its effect.

We may begin by comparing Sweeney in this poem to his appearance in "Mr. Eliot's Sunday Morning Service" and "Sweeney Erect," the two other poems in which he appears. The title of the latter, echoing "Pithecanthropus Erectus," implies that Sweeney is an apeman, and when he stretches in bed this is called "Gesture of orang-outang." Yet in fact he is depicted as an ordinary man in the bathroom: "Broadbottomed, pink from nape to base," he "wipes the suds around his face," shaving. And in "Mr. Eliot's Sunday Morning Service," too, he is a man in the bathroom, "shift-[ing] from ham to ham" while lying in the tub. However, among the nightingales Sweeney is different. His skin is not pink but hairy, so that although he is clean-shaven, his beard is like "Zebra stripes" of five-o'clock shadow that swell into "giraffe" spots when he laughs. And he is truly an apeman in appearance, with the neck of an ape, arms hanging down like an ape's, and the sitting posture of an ape. In this poem we are dealing not with an ordinary human but with a humanoid whose strangeness befits a dream rather than reality.

After the first quatrain of the poem shows us Sweeney, the second sets the scene. It is on the Rio Plata, which separates Argentina from Uruguay. Montevideo, Uruguay is on the northern bank of this river, and from there one would see the moon move "westward toward" the river, so the scene is set in that city. We should note, however, that a reader is not likely to discover this without the help of a geographical atlas. As described, the scene is just of a broad, flat (plata) river near the sea, with a haloed moon "Slid-[ing]" above: an elemental vista. More often than not in dreams, the setting appears thus elemental and strange, and only later does the dreamer recog-

[*]Reprinted, with permission, from *Yeats-Eliot Review*, 5 (1978), 14–17.

nize what particular place it is. This setting arouses fear, perhaps agoraphobia. Ill omen ("the Raven") and "Death" "drift above" the place. The moon is "stormy." No friendly stars twinkle in the sky, for the stars ("Gloomy Orion and the Dog" star, Sirius) are "veiled" by thin clouds. Finally, the whole atmosphere is unnaturally quietened. There is no noise of surf, for the "seas" are "hushed."

This silencing, this hushing of normal sounds, is a feature of many dreams. In them, events more often than not happen silently, and if there is some sound — the tick of a clock, for instance — it will stand out unnaturally in the surrounding silence. In the dream scene of this poem there is no sound at first. When Sweeney laughs, for instance, we do not hear his laughter but only see his face contort into a rictus. When the woman "in the Spanish cape" falls off his knees onto the floor, it is like a pratfall in a silent film. And the "gap[ing]" mouth of the "silent man" near the window gives forth no sound. So also we see Rachel "Tear" at the grapes, but no word describes the noise of eating.

In this place there is a waiter (line 19), the "host" (line 33), and "someone indistinct" with whom he talks. These three are peripheral figures in the scene. Aside from them, there are only four principal characters whom I have named: Sweeney, the "silent man," Rachel, and the "person in the Spanish cape": two men and two women. The women may be prostitutes. In the title of the poem Eliot perhaps hinted that they seemed so to him, for as Grover Smith has noted in *T.S. Eliot's Poetry and Plays*, "nightingales" in French is a slang term for whores and Eliot would have been likely to have had it in mind. "Sweeney Among the Whores" would then be the title of this picture, this scene that we are given. It is not a brothel scene, however, for there is a "host" here, not a madam. Interestingly, the setting of "Sweeney Erect" is more clearly a brothel, with its "Mrs. Turner," yet her "house" lacks the heavily sexual atmosphere of this place. The "host" who owns this place may be, symbolically, paternal.

The women here, Rachel and the one in the cape, "Are suspect, thought to be in league," presumably against Sweeney and the silent man. It is a case of the women menacing the men. And the men are both sitting in the same defenseless posture: Sweeney "spreads his knees / Letting his arms hang down . . . ," and the "silent man in mocha brown / Sprawls. . . ." In this posture, with their legs spread and semi-supine, they are vulnerable to castration, and I suggest that the threat or menace is that the women will castrate them. Sweeney is oblivious of this danger and does not move. It is the "silent man" who "suspect[s]" that the women are "in league." When he becomes suspicious, he "Contracts and concentrates, withdraws"; he "Declines the gambit" (the women's sexual offer) and "Leaves the room. . . ." Sweeney is then left alone with the caped woman and "Rachel *née* Rabinovitch," who "Tears at the grapes with murderous paws."

Her name suggests a rabid animal. In particular, with letters transposed it sounds like "Raven-a-bitch": a bitch dog with ravenous hunger.

This bitch is eating from a plate of "oranges / Bananas figs and hothouse grapes," and a moment's reflection on dream symbolism makes us realize that here we probably have woman's belly and vulva (oranges and figs) next to male's phallus and testicles (bananas and grapes). The grapes then are symbolically testicles, and Rachel *née* Rabinovitch is a bitch "Tear[ing]" hungrily at male testicles: an image of a female castrator.

Sweeney is an apeman, presumably with raw sexual drive, yet he is utterly relaxed in posture and unaggressive throughout. It is the "silent man" who is sexually aggressive. And his very form itself, indeed, is a strange dream image of a penis: "mocha brown" in color, "Sprawl[ed]," it is a "vertebrate" that suddenly "Contracts and concentrates." His "heavy eyes" image slumbrous sexual power, and his gold teeth, gleaming in the darkness, bespeak sadistic oral aggression. Symbolically, it seems clear, he represents the active sexual desire of the dreamer whereas Sweeney represents the dreamer's sexual vulnerability. As to the two women, the "person in the Spanish cape" is the only one of them whose body is shown: she is the one who seductively approaches Sweeney; her cape, a sort of dress open in front, images female receptivity. In short, in an odd symbolic way she is the sexually alluring woman. Rachel, in contrast, pays no heed to the men; she is solely a picture of sadistic oral aggression.

What we have, then, are the dreamer's sexual desire (the "silent man") and the female object of that desire (the woman in the cape) plus the dreamer's fear of being castrated (Sweeney in danger) as punishment for that desire (Rachel menacing punishment). The dream censor does not allow the dreamer to be wholly aware of his desire, and so the silent man and caped woman are not named, and she is not even called female. But the dreamer *is* aware of his fear: Sweeney and Rachel are named. This, of course, is the typical situation in a nightmare. Typically a dreamer knows that he is afraid but does not know why the fear arose. To know that would be to know the forbidden wish that the dream is fulfilling in symbolic form.

Let us look at the four characters in another way. Two of them are aggressive. One of these, the "silent vertebrate," is not a human figure really so much as a phallus in appearance, a phallus at first inactive and then active. After this "vertebrate" has withdrawn, it "reappears," "leaning in" the window, where "Branches of wistaria / Circumscribe" it. This is a vivid image of sexual penetration, the window with its border of wistaria representing a woman's vulva, with its pubic hair "Circumscrib[ing]" the entered phallus. And this phallus ends in a "golden grin": in gleaming teeth. This silent man is phallic, yet ultimately he is an expression of oral sadism. He is an image for the dreamer's sexual impulse, yet ultimately that is an impulse to bite. Naturally, then, by the *lex talionis*, the dreamer fears being bitten; he fears oral-sadistic retaliation; and so it is Rachel's aggressive eating which frightens him. She too is not a human figure really but a representation in quasi-animal form of "murderous" orality.

The other two characters are passive; they are not drives on the move.

Their bodies, therefore, are not imagings of phallic and oral motions. Even so, they too are subhuman figures. Sweeney is a caricature of human maleness, and one which exaggerates brute virility. The "person in the Spanish cape" is a caricature of human femaleness. However, instead of exaggerating, the dreamer's mind minimizes her seductive femaleness, making her less than a woman, in fact desexualizing her into a "person" of mechanical, farcical movements. Evidently the dreamer feels his maleness vividly, in the figure of Sweeney, all the more so for feeling the terrible threat to it; but female allure is something that his mind will not allow him to feel vividly.

The movement of events is this poem is typical of a nightmare's. First we are shown the passive male and female, Sweeney and the caped woman, and while they hold the stage, nothing happens. Thus, like most nightmares this one starts with a long stretch of merely forboding aimlessness. The fruits, symbolic male and female pudenda, are then brought in, and at this point the male sexual drive, the "silent vertebrate," suddenly becomes active and the feared female retaliation for it — Rachel tearing at the grapes — begins as well. The nightmare has come alive; the desire — and consequent fear — are now aroused. What happens next is interesting. To allay the fear, the dreamer denies to himself that he feels desire. Thus his mind imagines the opposite of his impulse; it imagines that the "vertebrate" "Contracts and concentrates, withdraws" when in fact it is becoming erect and preparing to enter. Because of this denial, when the "vertebrate" does enter the symbolic window later, its action is a shock. This experience of shock in a nightmare occurs because denial and disguise suddenly cease to avail. This usually happens in the moment before waking. We wake, of course, to avoid facing the dream's meaning.

Like many dreams, this one is silent until the moment before waking, whereupon an alarming sound suddenly fills the air. It is the singing of nightingales "near / The Convent of the Sacred Heart. . . ." What has happened is that suddenly, in the dream, the appearance of things has changed. Up to this point, the dreamer has felt aroused in a promiscuous sensual milieu. But once the "vertebrate" "lean[s] in" the window, the scene shifts without warning to nightingales near a convent. That is, once he achieves symbolic sexual penetration, things change in a way to make him feel caught guilty in the act. Philomel the nightingale sang after being ravished, but she, like the nuns in the convent, was a maiden. Whores, we have seen, are called "nightingales," perhaps sarcastically to express the sense that they are the opposite of maidens protesting ravishment. That the luring whores of this dream should give way suddenly to protesting nightingales, that the place the dreamer thought sensual should turn into a convent, therefore comes as a shock. It is as though an intimate boudoir changed abruptly to a bank with ringing burglar alarm. The singing has the effect of such an alarm, suddenly bespeaking the guilty act that the "vertebrate" has performed.

The final quatrain of the poem is Eliot's interpretation of the dream, for the dream itself ends at line 36. We recall that the dreamer's two feelings were male desire and fear of alluring females' retaliation for it. The nightingales' song is protest against violent male desire, as Philomel sang to protest Tereus' rape of her, in Ovid's *Metamorphoses*. And Agamemnon's loud cry came as Clytemnestra stabbed him after having lured him in, in Aeschylus' *Agamemnon*. (The words he cried are the epigraph of this poem, which translates, "Ay me! I am smitten deep with a mortal blow!") We have, then, the voice of females harmed by male desire and then the voice of a man harmed by an alluring female's retaliation. Thus, in this quatrain Eliot is saying that desirous men do violence to women (the nightingales sing of that), and women retaliate by doing violence to men (Agamemnon cries that aloud). Clearly, he interprets the dream to mean that sex is a violent business. And it is a business in which women will besmirch a man, as the fantastic final image of the nightingales / defecating on Agamemnon's shroud makes clear. Those last two lines paint an appalling symbolic picture; a man dead in his shroud, with birds that should be lovely circling over befouling him. So ends a man among nightingales.

There remains only one line to comment on: we are told that "Sweeney guards the horned gate." In book VI of the *Aeneid*, dreams that bespeak truth to the mind are said to come into it through a "gate of horn." That Sweeney "guards" the horned gate suggests that he keeps a truth-telling dream from entering his mind. This implies that there is such a dream and that it tells the truth that Sweeney is in danger. Of course, this dream could be of something other than the scene that he is in. However, Eliot may be hinting that the dream is of this scene, in other words, that Sweeney is dreaming what is happening to him and will not admit the truth that the dream tells.

I take this hint and suppose the poem to be Sweeney's dream. It seems to me that we cannot understand it otherwise. Sweeney's "spread . . . knees," the cape of the woman, the plate of fruits, Rachel's transposed name, the wistaria-bordered window — these things make no sense whatever together until seen as Freudian dream symbols, and then they make perfect sense. Surely that is no accident.

Pattern and Value in "Sweeney among the Nightingales"

John Ower*

In a recent article in PMLA,[1] William V. Spanos has argued that the attempt of the New Critics to "spatialize" Eliot's poetry, to regard it as "an art of stasis to be perceived simultaneously in aesthetic contemplation," has

*Reprinted, with permission, from *Renascence*, 23 (1971), 151–58.

resulted in an unnecessary vitiation of the poet's reputation in the existentialist, time-oriented Sixties. The new critical emphasis upon the "spatial form" of Eliot's poems has given the impression that an essentialist perspective governs his aesthetic, and this has rendered his work uncongenial to an age that tends to perceive human experience in terms of relativities, paradoxes and ambiguities. In opposition to this point of view, Spanos brilliantly analyzes Eliot's "Sweeney Agonistes" in terms of its "radically existential, that is, time-defined nature," and one can only conclude that his essay has provided a fruitful and necessary supplement to earlier approaches. Nonetheless, it must always remain debatable whether a poet infatuated with Dante, who so elaborately spatialized his moral and spiritual vision, could have ever abjured system-building aspirations in either his artistic or his religious endeavours. The following paper is intended at least in part to serve as a counter-demonstration to Professor Spanos' thesis. By analyzing another of the Sweeney poems in as diagrammatic a fashion as its text will allow, I hope to suggest that relatively early in his artistic career, Eliot had already succeeded in creating through the medium of poetic mythology an absolute, fundamentally atemporal ordering of experience which transcended the spiritually perplexed milieu out of which his early poetry grew. Eliot's system-building involves the compression into "Sweeney among the Nightingales" of no less than four different planes of human existence. Together, these form a complex "spatial" patterning of history in accordance with a scale of moral and spiritual values, and this transcends the existential drama of man as a being radically conditioned by time, and ultimately faced with absurdity and annihilation.

The highest of the four spiritual planes which Eliot introduces into "Sweeney among the Nightingales" may easily be passed over or underestimated simply because it is ironically the least emphasized. This capstone of Eliot's pyramidal hierarchy is the Catholic Christianity of the "Convent of the Sacred Heart," which is significantly mentioned only once, and in the second-last stanza of his poem. Although Christianity emerges as the key element in Eliot's spiritual and historical system in "Sweeney among the Nightingales," the moral and cultural values which he attaches to it are only allowed to appear implicitly, and by way of contrast with lower levels of experience. Eliot's technique of indirection with regard to Christianity, together with his scant and tardy mention of its existence, suggests ironically that the most immediately significant fact about the contemporary Church is its withdrawal from the modern world into a state of self-contained isolation. This retreat is aptly figured by the tree-screened convent which, if not completely turned inward upon itself, is at least comfortably distant from the unsavoury farce of vulgarity and depravity which is being enacted at the café. Judging from Eliot's wicked little satire "The Hippopotamus," published the year before "Sweeney . . ." was composed,[2] the poet already attaches enough importance to Christianity to satirize the inaction of the present-day Church as a grossly culpable dereliction of essential spiritual duties.

Because of the defection of the Church, God is dead as an influence on the denizens of Sweeney's cafe, who of course form a microcosm of the "ménagerie infâme" of the modern world. The spiritual and moral vacuum which has been left at the centre of contemporary life has produced in Sweeney's circle a half-ironic, half-pathetic combination of hopeless degradation and hopeless romanticism. Any participation in a truly vital religious tradition has long since been abandoned. We may suppose that the Boston Irishman Sweeney was at least baptized a Catholic, and he might even have a relative cloistered in the "Convent of the Sacred Heart." Yet his brief but indelible portrait suggests, as Edith Sitwell has put it, "man part braying beast, part worm, part ape, or . . . but the worm turned vertebrate."[3] Equally sordid and tragic is the degeneration of Judaism which is implied in the figure of "Rachel *née* Rabinovitch." The ancient religion of the Chosen People, at one time noble enough to be the progenitor of Christianity, has now in Eliot's opinion sunken into a crass materialism and a superficial internationalism which are well epitomized by the witch-like figure tearing at exotic fruits with her "murderous paws."

The vital spiritual role which has lately been abdicated by Christianity is ironically defined only in connection with the second level of experience which Eliot introduces into his poem: the pagan naturalism of the Heroic and Classical Ages of ancient Greece. The essential qualities of Greek culture are deftly evoked by Eliot through four brief but pregnant references: to the "hornèd gate" of the Underworld from which dreams were supposed to arise, and to the stories of Philomela, Orion, and Agamemnon. The latter tales of evil, violence, and suffering suggest a world which in psychological terms is elemental or archetypal, and in the context of Christian theology, fallen. Pagan man is tragic and in need of redemption, his plight being deeply rooted in the irrationality and egocentric savagery of his deepest instincts and passions. As Eliot suggests through his reference to a "daemonic, chthonic" Underworld, these violent psychic energies are all the more difficult to control because they originate in the hidden yet intensely potent dream-world of the unconscious mind, the sphere of Freud's *Id* and *Libido*, and of the Jungian archetypes. The intuitive recognition by the Greeks of the unconscious and its awesome power finds symbolic expression not only in their Underworld, but also in the bone-chilling stories which, like those of Orion, Philomela, and Agamemnon, are embodied in their myths, epic legends, and tragic dramas. However, such tales do not have only a psychological significance. In the *Bacchae* of Euripides, perhaps the most powerful dramatic expression of the sensibility of Classical Greece, the human unconscious is linked with the terribly paradoxical energy of a Dionysian life-force which is "the supreme artist, amoral, recklessly creating and destroying . . . ridding himself . . . of his internal contradictions."[4] If Eliot recognizes this connection, then he would see Pagan man as ineluctably bound through his elemental psychic drives to a fallen nature of paradox and ambiguity, of ungovernable appetite, violence and death.

Although the world to which the stories of Orion, Agamemnon, and Philomela belong is essentially fallen and tragic, there are certain of its features which do foreshadow the redemption of humanity through Christ. As they are presented to us in the Greek myths, legends, and tragedies, man's basic passions such as *hubris* and lust have not only a terrible potential for destruction, but also a size and power which lend them a certain majesty. Pagan man can at least rise to the heroic, whose two poles of exalted action and sublime suffering are embodied respectively in the literary forms of epic and tragic drama. Moreover, the evil and suffering of his fallen condition are mysteriously capable of a self-transcending transformation to an immortal beauty and joy. In the metamorphosis of Orion into a heavenly constellation, and of Philomela into the eponymous ancestor of the melodious nightingale, tragedy becomes a divine comedy which anticipates the Redemption of man.[5]

Eliot thus seems to be continuing the Renaissance tradition of allegorizing Classical literary documents such as Ovid's *Metamorphoses* in Christian theological terms. This is particularly apparent in his treatment of Agamemnon, who is associated with a "bloody wood" which recalls the sacred groves of the ancient fertility cults, and especially the wood at Nemi whose sinister cult forms the point of departure for *The Golden Bough*.[6] Murder in a dark wood is of course an ironic antitype to love in a Paradisal garden, and the fertility religions on one level provide us with an appropriate image of the fate of fallen man in a fallen world. However, Eliot would also have been familiar with Gilbert Murray's identification of the *Pathos* of the hero of the Greek tragedy with that of the dying and reviving fertility god,[7] and this once again paves the way for a conversion of the tragedy of the Fall into the divine comedy of Redemption. The suffering and death of the god, ritually lamented by his worshippers, is only the prelude to his joyous resurrection. There is thus a close parallel between the death and revival of the fertility god, and the Passion and Resurrection of Christ, through which were achieved the Redemption of man. This suggests that the nature-cults and their lineal descendents the mystery religions, were providential foreshadowings which prepared the essentially negative sensibility of Paganism for the faith, hope, and charity of the Christian religion. On one level, the "bloody wood" of fallen nature in which Agamemnon is murdered is identical with Gerontion's "wrath-bearing tree," but this is after all the tree of knowledge of good as well as of evil, and looks forward to the Cross upon which Christ suffered His terrible yet redemptive Passion.

Of equal importance to a practising poet like Eliot would be the fact that in Classical tragedy the theological and ritualistic drama of fall and redemption embodied in the story of Agamemnon finds expression in a consummately developed literary form. The connection between the religious

ritual of antiquity and its various art forms was the subject of detailed inves-
tigations by Weston, Cornford, Murray and Harrison.[8] Any of these might
have suggested to Eliot that behind the Aristotelian notion of the cathartic
effect of tragedy, there lay the fundamentally religious conception of an exorcism of the destructive daemons of the unconscious mind, which in turn
foreshadowed Christ's salvation of "natural" man from the savagery of his
uncontrollable obsessions. In the historical schema which Eliot is developing in "Sweeney among the Nightingales," Greek civilization thus represents a more rudimentary level of moral and spiritual attainment than
Christianity, but one whose art and religion nonetheless foreshadow it. On
one plane, it exemplifies the sinfulness and sorrow of the "Old Adam" or
natural man who was born of the Fall. On another, it looks forward to the
grace-transfigured, spiritually self-controlled Christian of St. Paul's
Epistles.

The civilization of ancient Greece is elaborately parodied in "Sweeney
among the Nightingales" by the third cultural plane of Nineteenth Century
Romanticism.[9] Although Romanticism is one step down the spiritual ladder
from Classical Paganism, and two beneath Christianity, it is ironically
brought much more into the foreground than either. This inversion of perspective whereby a geometrically increasing prominence is given to progressively lower levels on Eliot's moral and cultural scale is of course one of
his more subtle ways of indicating the degeneracy of the modern world.

Romanticism is represented in "Sweeney among the Nightingales" primarily as an attempt on the part of contemporary man to extricate himself
from the emptiness and sordidness into which he has been plunged by the
decline of Christianity as a vital influence upon his life. Several characteristic forms of Romantic escapism appear in Eliot's poem. In Stanzas two and
three, Sweeney lapses momentarily into a daydream, whose exotic if som-
bre stage properties recall simultaneously the Georgian flirtation with far-
away places and strange-sounding names and also the strain of morbid and
gloomy brooding which runs through Romanticism from the "Graveyard"
poets to its decadence. Just as the distant in time and place seems to Sweeney exciting and elevated because of its remoteness from his squalid surroundings, to the drunken lady of Stanzas three and four attempts to add a
dash of intrigue to her Lesbian attraction with a "Spanish cape," and "Rachel née Rabinovitch" titillates her jaded palate with exotic fruits.

The distancing involved in Romantic exoticism has a corollary which
was particularly deplored by Eliot, Hulme, and Pound. This is a mistiness
and vagueness intended to suggest the transfiguration of the physical world
by a spiritual presence, but which too often results in a mere fogging of
reality. The sentimental and rhetorical blurring of bad Romanticism of the
hard, sharp contours of the empirical is suggested in Stanzas eight and nine
of Eliot's poem, in which objects become progressively fuzzier and more
ethereal in direct proportion to their distance from the poet's camera-eye,
which ironically seems to have a very short focal-length indeed. Thus, the

face of the "silent vertebrate in brown" suddenly seems to take on an aura of loveliness when framed outside of the café by a circlet of wistaria blossoms. However Eliot's use in this connection of the term "circumscribes," which implies a sharp visual definition, hints that the phrase "golden grin" could as easily refer to a mouth crammed with gold fillings[10] as to a face suffused with sunlight. The poet's eye suddenly cuts through the Romantic haze to focus with devastating precision upon the immediate realities of the situation.

The Romantic dissolution of the outlines of the external world is paralleled by its exaltation of emotion over reason, a tendency which finds its paramount expression in the deification of sexual passion. This Romantic cult of love also comes in for some sharp satirical digs in "Sweeney among the Nightingales." The great surrender to the divine blur of desire is effectively parodied by the drunken lust of the "person in the Spanish cape" who attempts to seduce Sweeney, while her "league" with "Rachel née Rabinovitch" suggests the degeneration of Romantic eroticism into the Decadent interest in sexual perversion.[11]

There are several references which imply that in the context of the historical and spiritual schema which Eliot is promulgating in "Sweeney among the Nightingales," Romanticism represents an attempt to escape the contemporary decadence by a return to Pagan naturalism. To the sentimentalizing eye of the Romantic, the Classical age appears to be a prelapsarian "state of nature," in which a spiritually inspired innocence raises man to a heroic or even a divine stature. Thus, Sweeney's daydream, which significantly incorporates the Classical myths of Orion and the Underworld, involves his magnification to heroic proportions. Similarly, the apotheosis which was paradoxically possible for Ancient man seems to be repeated in the case of the "silent vertebrate in brown." Taken at its Romantic valuation, his "golden grin" with its aureole of blossoms evokes the sun-gods and vegetation-spirits of the Pagan nature-cults. The earth-goddess of these religions may also be suggested, albeit with an unmistakable note of irony, by "Rachel née Rabinovitch," who in gobbling her exotic fruits could represent an ingenious parodic reversal of the icon of Ceres with her overflowing cornucopia. The attempted seduction of Sweeney by Rachel's drunken lover likewise constitutes an obvious burlesque of the Bacchic revels and sacred sexual orgies which accompanied the ancient fertility rites.

Eliot's treatment in parodic terms of the Romantic endeavour to recreate the Pagan sensibility suggests that modern man's attempts to transcend his debased existence are doomed, if not to self-evident failure, then at least to a sentimental unreality. In the first place, as the poet implies ironically in his reference to Rachel's grapes, Romanticism is a "hothouse" growth, totally unsuited to the harsh spiritual climate of the contemporary world. The bursting of the Romantic bubble by the rough edges of modern man's degradation and savagery is beautifully encapsulated in the rude interruption of Sweeney's dream. This epitomizes the way in which the "fair luminous cloud" of the exotic and misty is dispelled in "Sweeney among the Nightingales" by its abrupt juxtaposition with the crassness and immorality of the present age [here Ower quotes stanzas three and four of the poem]. The Romanticism is a sentimental evasion not merely of the degenerate state of the contemporary world, but of the whole of the fallen nature of reality, is made apparent in stanza ten, which suddenly undercuts the progressive etherealization of stanzas eight and nine. This deflation is ironically accomplished by a reference to the tragic savagery of the Paganism which Romanticism so naively idealizes and attempts to emulate:

> The nightingales are singing near
> The Convent of the Sacred Heart,
>
> And sang within the bloody wood
> When Agamemnon cried aloud,
> And let their liquid siftings fall
> To stain the stiff dishonoured shroud.

Eliot's point about the exemplary nature of Paganism as an expression of the fallen state of both man and the world is clinched with the phrase "liquid siftings," in which a bad Romantic poeticism for bird-song is ironically applied instead to the nightingale's excrement. Bird-song is of course from Wordsworth to Bridges a stock Romantic symbol of the joyousness and beauty of a spiritually inspired nature, but Eliot is implying that the natural world is fallen and therefore also has a terrible aspect of cruelty, squalor, and indifference. This dark face of nature, together with pagan man's tragic involvement in its savagery, is clearly recognized by Euripides in the *Bacchae*, but not by a diluted late Romanticism.

The lowest and at the same time the most prominent of the four levels of value which are treated in "Sweeney among the Nightingales" is the sordid contemporary reality which undercuts the Romantic dream. Modern man's gross materialism and spiritual degeneracy are figured primarily in terms of a psychic lapse from full civilized humanity into the fallen physical nature of egocentric and destructive appetite. The animality of the inmates of Eliot's café is immediately impressed upon the reader by the unforgettable portrait of Sweeney with which his poem opens: "Apeneck Sweeney spreads his knees. . . ." Just as Sweeney has atavistically descended to the level of the savage wildlife of Africa, so Rachel, who "Tears at the grapes with murderous paws," could as well be a tigress rending the bloody meat of her kill. Eliot's sketch of the "silent man in mocha brown" suggests a still lower form of life which is barely "vertebrate," let alone human. This fecal creature, who "Contracts and concentrates," has the slowness and shapelessness of an amoeba.[12] In the "fatigue" which quickly overpowers his sexual desire, as well as in the sketch of the drunken woman sprawled and yawning upon the floor, we see modern man sinking beneath even the feral energy and appetite of the animal. His ultimate condition is closer to a vege-

table passiveness, or to the amorphous deadness of mud. The implicit identification of the "vertebrate" and Rachel with the vegetation-spirit and the
earth-mother thus in the last analysis suggests not apotheosis, but rather
contemporary man's assimilation into the lowest levels of physical existence.

The patrons of Sweeney's cafe do not simply lapse into nature, but also
pervert it, and they are accordingly decadents rather than honest-to-good-
ness Pagans. This is perhaps the most significant of the ways in which the
pseudo-sophistication of the modern world falls beneath the tragic magnifi-
cence of Greece. The ancient Greek may have been a "natural man" in the
Christian sense of the term, and hence a prey to savage passions. However,
his elemental drives had at least an awe-inspiring directness and energy.
Moreover, there existed through the medium of art and culture the possibility of an upward metamorphosis of his dark and disordered emotion into
transcendent spirituality. In contrast to "The glory that was Greece," modern man's debased substitute for a civilization either panders to his lapse
into nature, or else helps to give it a perverted twist. Thus the café, traditionally a place of cultivated recreation and artistic discussion, is in "Sweeney among the Nightingales" little better than a brothel. Moreover, the
appetites of its denizens appear in jaded or distorted forms, and are titil-
lated only by the artificial or the unnatural. It requires hot-house fruit to
trigger Rachel's pampered if ravenous appetite, and her lady-love can be
aroused to a normal concupiscence only by drunkenness. Lacking such a
stimulus, the lust of the "vertebrate in brown" loses its battle with his consti-
tutional inertia. Far from representing an advance upon Pagan antiquity
either spiritually or culturally, the contemporary world parodies it upon a
lower level. Historically, it represents both a degeneration into something
weaker and smaller, and a retrogression to a level more primitive and incho-
ate. Spiritually, far from looking beyond fallen nature towards Christian
redemption, it involves a wholesale perversion of the natural order whose
end result is the disintegration of both body and soul.

It is undoubtedly possible to view "Sweeney among the Nightingales,"
along with Eliot's other poetry, from a purely existentialist perspective. In
fact, such an approach probably cannot be left unexplored without doing a
great disservice to his complex and prophetic art. Nevertheless, it is hoped
that the present essay has suggested that the New Critics were not fundamentally wrong in reading Eliot as they did, and that the central impetus of
his art may yet be found to consist in an attempt to evolve a static, transcen-
dental scale of spiritual values.

Notes

1. William V. Spanos, " 'Wanna Go Home, Baby?': *Sweeney Agonistes* as Drama of the
Absurd," *PMLA*, Vol. 85, No. 1 (January, 1970), pp. 8–20.

2. See B. C. Southam, *A Guide to the Selected Poems of T. S. Eliot* (New York, 1968), pp. 59 and 64.

3. Edith Sitwell, *Aspects of Modern Poetry* (London, 1934), p. 109.

4. Friedrich Nietzche, *The Birth of Tragedy*, trans. Francis Goffling (New York, 1956), p. 9.

5. See Elizabeth Drew, *T. S. Eliot: the Design of his Poetry* (London, 1954), p. 66.

6. For a discussion of the significance of Agamemnon in these terms, see Drew, *op. cit.*, pp. 65–66.

7. For a summary of Murray's position, see F. M. Cornford, *The Origin of Attic Comedy* (New York, 1961), p. 14.

8. See Jane Allen Harrison, *Ancient Art and Ritual* (New York, 1913); Harrison, *Themis* (Cambridge, 1912); Jessie Weston, *From Ritual to Romance* (Cambridge, 1920) and Cornford, *op. cit.*

9. For some of Eliot's anti-Romantic references, see D. E. S. Maxwell, *The Poetry of T. S. Eliot* (London, 1966), pp. 85–86.

10. Maxwell, *op. cit.*, p. 86.

11. See Mario Praz, *The Romantic Agony* (London, 1951).

12. Drew, *op. cit.*, p. 67.

Sweeney among the Nightingales   P. G. Mudford*

The version of "Sweeney among the Nightingales" in Eliot's *Poems* (1919) and *Ara vos Prec* (1920) was preceded by two quotations: ὦμοι πέπληγμαι καιρίαν πληγὴν ἔσω, and "Why should I speak of the Nightingale? The Nightingale sings of adulterate wrong.' The second (from the anonymous *Edward III*, II: 109–10) did not appear either in *The Little Review* for September 1918, where the poem was first printed, or in the *Collected Poems*, 1909–25. But together they associate the title of the poem with the *Agamemnon* and the tale of Tereus and Philomela in Book VI of Ovid's *Metamorphoses*, as well as providing a sign-post to the landscape of the poem, which Eliot may well have felt to be necessary after its first appearance. No doubt the obvious weakness of the second quotation in comparison to Agamemnon's single line played some part in its disappearance; and anyway after *The Waste Land* the association of nightingales, in Eliot's mind, with the *Metamorphoses* needed no underlining. The point, though, is worth raising, I think, because the second quotation does have its uses in interpreting a poem which continues to raise difficulties. Hugh Kenner, for example, writing in *The Invisible Poet*, remarks, "Sweeney among the Nightingales . . . is deliberately involved in Eliot's besetting vice, a never wholly penetrable ambiguity about what is supposed to be happening."[1] Grover Smith comments, "In plot, setting and characters this poem is opacity itself," an opacity that he goes on to thicken by telling us that the nightin-

*Reprinted, with permission, from *Essays in Criticism*, 19 (1969), 285–91.

gales migrated into Eliot's concluding stanzas from the grove of the Furies ("bloody wood") in Sophocles's *Oedipus at Colonus*, and then continues, "Eliot really brought in the Nightingales from Sophocles by mistake."[2] This kind of truffle-hunting attitude towards literary criticism, which ends in displaying the truffle and destroying the poem, really will not do.[3]

While Grover Smith and Kenner both charge Eliot with violations of poetic decency, F. R. Leavis confines himself to an admission that the problem is of a subtler kind, involving something possibly recondite that it may be necessary to struggle with a bit to gain a glimpse of: "In 'Sweeney among the Nightingales' . . . the contrast is clearly something more than that between the sordid incident in a modern brothel and the murder of Agamemnon."[4] I wish here to suggest by means of an interpretation of the poem what this something more may conceivably involve; and in doing so to indicate a way of avoiding the flight in which Professors Kenner and Grover Smith have taken refuge.[5]

The line from the *Agamemnon*, which stands at the head of the poem, conveys the power of its feeling, to a considerable degree, from the emphasis which falls on the adverbial ἔσω, at the end of the line. And one does not need either to be a Greek scholar, or to turn up the various translations of this line, to respond to its ambiguity: Agamemnon has been struck down within the palace; he has also been struck down within the House of Atreus, by his own wife, in fulfilment of the doom that has fallen upon it. And this gives us a clue to the kind of relationship that we may expect between Sweeney and his nightingales. At the same time it suggests an important difference: the murder of Agamemnon violated a rigid bond between husband and wife which the more flexible associations of Sweeney do not seem to include. The signficance of this last point I hope to make clear when I come to discuss the last six lines of the poem.

The poem begins with Apeneck Sweeney alone; and he at once confronts the reader with the question of how he is intended to be taken. The problem becomes more pressing when the first two verses have made apparent the remoteness of the Sweeney from that of "Sweeney Erect," behind whom the figure of the Boston pugilist, Steve O'Donnell, is easily and closely felt. The Sweeney of this poem embodies a different kind of force which is suggested by the central metaphor that the first verse contains. His nickname, Apeneck, is taken up in the simian suggestiveness of "letting his arms hang down to laugh," and is extended in the metaphorical use made of the "zebra" and "giraffe." By means of these animal metaphors Sweeney is identified in name, personality, and appearance with the instinctive "primitive" man; and Sweeney's landscape or environment, typified in the next verse, is conveyed in images appropriate to a figure of that imaginative level, ritualistic and hierarchical. . . .

The moon, death, and the river of silver, named after Spanish fantasies of fabulous wealth in the South American continent, are at the same time richly suggestive and naturally associated; and they form an appropriately numinous landscape for the Sweeney of the first four lines. One important problem, however, remains: the significance of the fact that Sweeney guards the hornéd gate? It means literally, of course, that he guards the gate through which true dreams pass; and the rest of the poem may most easily be taken, I think, as an amplification of what it means to say that Sweeney guards this particular gate. On a tiny scale, it will be seen, the structure of the poem can be compared to the circles of descent in Dante's *Inferno*. Sweeney represents a personification of the animal instinct inside us; and this ritualistic figure is established in the first two verses. In the third, we pass through the horned gate to get a glimpse of his soul within the house. And what we find there, as in the descent of Dante's *Inferno*, is not something radically different, but the projection of a more complex darkness, through the harmonisation of landscape with the emotions of particular individuals.

On the other side of the gate, the landscape, appropriately, does not change much at first; as the moon is stormy outside, so here the stars are veiled (a fact that sets off an echo of Macbeth's "Stars hide your fires, let not your light see my black and deep desires") and the seas are shrunk. Here, though, a reduction in "poetic" intensity occurs; the focus of the poem turns from the numinous landscape to the more active social world of people, but people whose primary purpose is still to amplify the significance of Sweeney as guardian of the gate.

It is at this point that Eliot's comment upon the poem, quoted by F. O. Matthiessen, becomes useful: "All that I consciously set out to create in 'Sweeney among the Nightingales' was 'a sense of foreboding.'"[6] By means of the shadowy silent figures who surround Sweeney, Eliot fulfils his conscious intention: the person in the Spanish cape thought to be in league with Rachel *née* Rabinovitch of the murderous paws, the silent vertebrate in brown, the indistinct figure with the host by the door, and the man with the heavy eyes and a golden grin (who suggests in a menacing way the daylight crime that is anticipated and unprevented) accumulate the atmosphere that Eliot aims at — and in close imaginative consistency with the kind of figure that we know Sweeney to be. The eye of the poem moves — and I think this is all that needs to be said abut these central verses — between these shadowy figures, as the visual eye moves through the prisons of Piranesi — with similarly disturbing effects. It is an environment in which things (the various fruits and the wistaria), not people, possess an overabundant clarity that once again recalls the ambiguity of objects in dreams. And this physical clarity contrasts effectively with the psychological shadows in the behaviour of people.

But the sense of foreboding is not consummated in any act of violence, because the poem is not concerned with an event, but a state (another way of explaining why the last eight verses are an amplification); and this state is summed up and commented on in those six lines of very remarkable intensity with which the poem ends. . . .

The nightingales that sing near the convent of the sacred heart remind us both of the nightingales that hover near Sweeney physically and of Philomela who sings of her violation — and was referred to in the abandoned quotation. But stating this does not account for the kind of effect that these lines achieve. In one sense they can, no doubt, not be interpreted, except in different terms by psychology; but they can be illuminated by comparison with passages whose intensity is of a similiar kind. And one of these occurs, I think, in the *Agamemnon*, not very far from the line which Eliot quotes.

After Clytemnestra has led her husband away to be killed in his bath, Cassandra is left outside with the Chorus, and she sees, as in a hallucination, what is happening within. At this point the Chorus compare her, in her prophetic lamentation, to Philomela, in a passage that I quote here from Louis MacNiece's translation:

> You are mad, mad, carried away by the god,
> Raising the dirge, the tuneless
> Tune, for yourself. Like the tawny
> Unsatisfied singer from her luckless heart
> Lamenting 'Itys, Itys', the nightingale
> Lamenting a life luxuriant with grief.[7]

The Chorus, by its association of the prophetess carried away by the god, with the nightingale luxuriant with grief, underlines the intense communication between the mind of Cassandra and the events that are taking place inside the palace. She has become for them, as for us, a figure of horror, as well as a provider of information. In short, she simultaneously symbolises the murder by her immersion in it, and proclaims it. So here, in Eliot's poem, the nightingales of Sweeney's landscape proclaim a threat that is all too near the convent of his sacred heart, and at the same time symbolise its nature, through their mythological role as birds luxuriant with grief at the knowledge of a desecration performed.

But Eliot communicates an important difference (which I mentioned earlier) between the crimes of which these nightingales know, and that against Agamemnon: the voice of Philomela recalling an incestuous violation has become liquid excreta falling upon the stiff dishonoured shroud. And this underlines a degradation in the historical process, a dissolving of the clear definitions in human relationships which gave to the crimes of Tereus and Clytemnestra a part in the pattern of sacred events. The stiff dishonoured shroud acts as a metaphor for the violation that exists in Sweeney's dream-world (one might compare the "corpse in the garden" of *The Waste Land*); and the liquid excreta that fall upon it not only provide a comment upon its dishonour, but communicate the poem's grasp of that area of the mind where the sacred and the profane touch each other closely — in a form that would now find plenty of corroboration in the annals of psychoanalysis and criminal pathology.

Any whole response to the poem demands, then, a recognition of the different levels of intensity that the verse achieves: the first ten and the last six lines are remarkable for their appeal to what W. H. Auden has defined as the primary imagination: "The concern of the Primary Imagination, its only concern, is with sacred beings and sacred events. . . . The response of the imagination to such a presence or significance is a passion of awe."[8] Apeneck himself, and the nightingales, like Cassandra in that particular scene of the *Agamemnon*, seem to demand that we respond to them as Sacred Beings of this sort. And one of the weaknesses in the poem is perhaps that the transitions in it involve the leaping of imaginative gulfs that are more personal than the brilliant surface of the poem at first suggests. The achieved objectivity was not — and could not be — at the beginning of the twentieth century of the same order as Eliot's poetic forebears had achieved in the seventeenth. And this no doubt was one of the things to which he was pointing, in his now largely discredited dictum about the "dissociation of sensibility." Nevertheless, the power and the suggestiveness of the poem is extraordinary; it succeeds in making concrete that area of the mind where the sacred and profane are uneasy companions of everyday affairs; and communicates how the appearance of this conflict is transformed by the social context into which it erupts. What in the world of Greek tragedy meant the fall of a royal house had become by the end of the First World War a chimerical and pervasive darkness that menaced a man from within.

Notes

1. Kenner, Hugh: *The Invisible Poet*, London, 1960, p. 79.

2. Grover Smith, J.: *T. S. Eliot's Poetry and Plays*, Chicago, 1956, pp. 45–46.

3. Eliot stated in a letter to the *Sunday Times* of April 6, 1958 that "the wood I had in mind was the grove of the Furies at Colonus; I called it 'bloody' because of the blood of Agamemnon in Argos." This remark not only shows up the confusion in Grover Smith's argument, but makes clear his failure to consider (before condemning the poem) what Eliot had said much earlier about poetic borrowing — i.e. that good poets make what they borrow into something better, or *at least something different.*

4. Leavis, F. R.: *New Bearings in English Poetry* (new edition), 1954, p. 88.

5. The view I am putting forward here is not inconsistent, I think, with admitting that the "feeling" of the poem has the directness of something seen in a music-hall or a "saloon." But one can get no further along those lines.

6. Matthiesen, F. O.: *The Achievement of T. S. Eliot*, 1958, p. 129.

7. Aeschylus: *Agamemnon*, translated by Louis MacNeice, 1936, pp. 51–52.

8. Auden, W. H.: *The Dyer's Hand*, 1963, pp. 54–55.

Eliot's "Sweeney Among the Nightingales" and *The Song of Solomon*

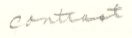

Frederick L. Gwynn*

The Aeschylean background of Eliot's poem is well known: the two epigraphs (reduced to one in 1920) and the last two stanzas set up a relationship between Agamemnon and Sweeney. The poet probably intends this relationship both as contrast (between the rich tragic myth of the ancients and the inane machinations of the moderns) and as equation (of ancient mortal man with modern mortal man).

On the level of contrast, there are also echoes of the Old Testament: as "The Convent of the Sacred Heart" calls up Christian tradition, so may "Rachel" betoken Hebrew tradition, with the beautiful wife of Israel and mother of Joseph now merely the gluttonous and conspiratorial daughter of Rabinovitch. [1] More specifically, there are reminiscences of *The Song of Solomon*, whose often quoted second chapter in the Authorized Version breathes an ecstatic and idyllic love in sharp antithesis to the apathetic sexual intrigue of "Sweeney Among the Nightingales."

Eliot's poem takes place in some kind of café and *Solomon* (2) has a background of "the banqueting house" (2/4); but "Death and the Raven[2] drift above" Sweeney, whereas for the girl of *Solomon* "his banner over me was love" (2/4). Eliot's "silent man" first "Sprawls at the window-sill and gapes" and then appears "Outside the window, leaning in," circumscribed by "Branches of wistaria" — just as the male beloved of *Solomon* "looketh forth [in] at the windows, shewing himself through the lattice" (2/9). (The wistaria-vines, by the way, match the grape-vines of *Solomon* 2/13, 15, and 7/12 that "give a good smell.") But the silent man has "heavy eyes," and his mouth is "a golden grin" of false teeth, whereas the man in *Solomon* has "eyes of doves" (5/12), and "His hands are as *gold* rings. . . . His *mouth* is most sweet: yea, he is altogether lovely" (5/14 — 16; my italics).[3]

It would be fanciful to balance the animals of "Sweeney" (ape, zebras, giraffe, dog) with those of *Solomon*, (goat, horse, deer, fox, sheep, lion, leopard), but we may note the animalism of both poems. And is Rachel, who "Tears at the grapes with murderous paws," very far away from "the little foxes, that spoil the vines" (2/15)? Furthermore, both poems are full of "all manner of pleasant fruit" (7/13), with the figs and grapes mentioned in one verse of *Solomon* (2/13) turning up in a single line of "Sweeney" (20). The significant differences are that *Solomon's* animals are symbols of beauty and value, "Sweeney's" of regression: the Hebrew fruit is freshly "green" and "tender," whereas Eliot's is "hothouse" and brought in by a waiter. And where the Shulamite girl murmurs, "Stay me with flagons, comfort me with apples: for I am sick of [overwhelmed by] love" (2/15),

*Reprinted, with permission, from *MLN*, 68 (1953), 25–27.

Eliot's tawdry women overturn their coffee-cups and tear at grapes, for they are sick of love to the point of boredom.

Finally, it is the nightingales who give the modern poem its ironic title, its poignant conclusion, and indeed, its point — the persistence of meaningful beauty in the face of materialism. But where the tragic song of nightingales is heard in Eliot and Aeschylus, it is the ecstatic "voice of the turtle" (dove) in the vernal "time of the singing of birds" that is heard in *Solomon* (2), the Hebrew motif of sexual purity[4] contrasting notably with the Greek reminiscence of sexual violence and infidelity.

To summarize: Eliot's overt use of Aeschylus is plainly the most important referential element in "Sweeney Among the Nightingales." But there are unconscious echoes, verbal and conceptual, of *The Song of Solomon*, whose sweet youthful passion provides additional ironical comment on the gross and comatose world of Sweeney.

Notes

1. Eliot may have been contrasting his Rachel with Dante's (*Inferno*, *II*, 102, IV, 60), who, according to Charles Eliot Norton's note (which Eliot probably read), was "the type of the contemplative life, that life in which the soul withdraw[s] itself from earthly concerns. . . ." It is also possible that Eliot's circles of the stormy moon" owes something to Virgil's mention, a few lines earlier (II, 78), of the "heaven which has the smallest circles" — i.e., that of the moon.

There may be another contrast, between the nightingales who "sang within the bloody wood" and the Harpies who "make lament on the strange trees" (*Inferno*, XIII, 15), trees that become bloody when Dante breaks off branches (XIII, 22–45).

2. Cf. "his head is . . . black as a raven" in *Solomon* 5/11.

3. *Solomon* emphasizes the fineness of its golden items (1/10, 11; 3/10, 5/11, 14, 15), in contrast to the flashy display of gold teeth in "Sweeney."

The End of Sweeney   James Davidson*

> . . . the modern world seems capable only of the low dream.

Although the brilliant, fourth-dimensional backdrop of T. S. Eliot's "Sweeney among the Nightingales" has given rise to critical variety, on the fundamental dramatic issue, the fate of Sweeney, there is a general accord. Sweeney, most of his critics say, is going to be assassinated.[1] This view seems to have originated with F. O. Matthiessen in 1935, who earlier had enjoyed the friendship of Eliot during his lecture-visit in America. Matthiessen's interpretation, based upon a remark offered by Eliot, has been the guiding star of much subsequent criticism:

*Reprinted, with permission, from *College English*, 27 (1966), 400–403.

Eliot once remarked that all he consciously set out to create in "Sweeney among the Nightingales" was a sense of foreboding. Yet the very exactitude with which he has built up his impression by means of the close details of his night-town scene, as well as by the way he underlines his effect through a reference both in the epigraph and in the final stanza to another scene of foreboding that ended in the murder of Agamemnon, inevitably causes his delineation to take on wider implications. The sharp contrast that seems at first simply to be mocking a debased present as it juxtaposes Sweeney with the hero of antiquity, ends in establishing also an undercurrent of moving drama: for a sympathetic feeling for Sweeney is set up by the realization that he is a man as well as Agamemnon, and that his plotted death is therefore likewise a human tragedy.[2]

In this attractive and apparently obvious reading, now so respectable that writers barely mention it in passing, Matthiessen appears to assume that Eliot intended the assassination of Sweeney, when he "consciously set out to create . . . a sense of forboding." But foreboding is not an accomplished fact. It can take many paths, or none at all; a foreboding could, ironically, fail to come off. Eliot's comments, like his notes for *The Waste Land*, are sometimes as cryptic as the material they are about.

The poem itself does not tell us that Sweeney is to die. All we know for certain is that he has some difficulty and leaves the cafe. The fact that Agamemnon is evoked twice, once in the epigraph and once at the end of the poem, does not necessarily indicate that Sweeney is to be slain, any more than it shows that he has an unfaithful wife. Nor does the poem furnish reasons for Sweeney's death. The two women and even the host with his "indistinct" companion are not agents of doom. It is only when we assume the dire fate of Sweeney that they can seem so.

Sweeney's drama, as pictured by Matthiessen and later writers, unfolds somewhat as follows. Sweeney, in a low-life cafe, is enjoying himself in a coarse, animalistic, somewhat inebriated fashion. He is unaware that a trap is being set for him, baited with a woman of the streets. But Sweeney rejects her advances, perhaps becoming aware of his danger. When another woman, Rachel, takes over, Sweeney, now thoroughly alarmed, cannily refuses to respond and departs with feigned casualness. The host gives orders to yet another person, who will presumably follow Sweeney and do him in. Sweeney's fate may be thus postponed, but, like Agamemnon's, not avoided.

The essential inadequacy of this interpretation is that it does not properly consider the tone. It pictures Sweeney as tragic, whereas fundamentally he is comic. Although he and his companions are empty and sordid, they are also funny, much in the aimless manner of Falstaff and his companions. Moreover, Sweeney is a member of the lower class, and hence his role is restricted in a Shakespearean sense. He may be funny, crude, and possibly pathetic, but never tragic; he has no high estate to fall from. In a timeless sense, he and Agamemnon are in the same play, but their parts must not be confused. Together they furnish one another an enlightening contrast, but not a parallel.

And so the night scene—not a dangerous intrigue, not a low-gear tragedy, but a broad burlesque—would go as follows: Sweeney, out for an evening on the town, is enjoying himself with some cronies in a cheap cafe. Like the animals he is linked with—ape, zebra, giraffe—he is a harmless oddity, in a human zoo. A woman of the streets, synchronizing her boldest advance with what appears to be Sweeney's happiest mood, finds nevertheless that Sweeney's lap is unyielding. She flops gracelessly and ridiculously to a heap on the floor.

Where she leaves off, her professional sister, Rachel, another "type" Sweeney might find more to his taste, takes over. She contrasts with her Biblical namesake in the same manner that Sweeney contrasts with Agamemnon. The Rachel of Genesis persisted heroically in the face of misfortune. First she was bypassed in marriage by Jacob, who really loved her and had worked hard for her but who was tricked by her father into marrying her older sister, Leah. Finally when Jacob obtained her as his second wife, she was unable to bear and had to undergo the humiliation of watching her sister have children. But she endured, and eventually was rewarded with two sons, Joseph and Benjamin; and after her death, such an outstanding figure had she become, she was alleged by Jewish tradition to have risen from her grave to intercede with God in behalf of her "children," the tribes of Israelites descended from her, marching along the road to captivity. How different is the case with Eliot's Rachel, who although a wife is given only her maiden name, a further indication of her purposeless and sterile drifting. Tearing at the grapes, she makes a ridiculous contrast with the Rachel of Dante's dream, engaged in beatific contemplation (*Purgatory*, Canto XXVII).

Thus the hothouse fruit—the tasteless, artificial, commercial variety—of adultery is offered to Sweeney. And adultery is the theme of the second epigraph to the poem, discarded in the 1920 edition: "Why should I speak of the nightingale? The nightingale sings of adulterous wrong." The connection with Clytemnestra and Aegisthus, or with Agamemnon and Cassandra, is obvious. Again, the poem furnishes an absurd contrast. Sweeney is *not* adulterous with Rachel, for the most humdrum of reasons. It is not that he scents a dangerous plot, it is certainly not that he detects an immorality, but simply that he is tired. He has finally indulged too many times and paid out too much money in fruitless union, and tonight he decides to forego it.

The classical background, the cosmic foil against which Sweeney and his friends perform, clearly delineates them and heightens both the comedy and irony of the drama. The foreboding that Eliot spoke of emerges from this background, but even apart from Agamemnon and the bloody wood, the atmosphere is electrically dismal, with its light overcast that causes moon and stars, along with their forecast of the future, to appear fuzzy. The feeling is reminiscent of *Moby Dick,* particularly Chapter 51, "The Spirit-Spout," in which the *Pequod* is cruising along the "Plate," an expanse of sea near the estuary of the Rio de la Plata in South America. (The Rio, or the River Plate, would be westward from here, where the moon is situated in Eliot's poem.) At the conclusion of the novel another sailing vessel, the *Rachel,* is looking for her children, some lost crew members including a son of the captain. Eliot's Rachel, on the other hand, is not looking for hers, for she is unaware that she needs them; *i.e.,* a significantly productive life.

The foreboding in *Moby Dick* and "Sweeney" is real, but in Sweeney's drama it is in terms of contrast with the comedy, where it becomes a mock foreboding, a foreboding of nothing. Eliot makes it perfectly clear that such is the case. The "lady in the Spanish cape" might seem momentarily exotic and dangerous, until we see her slumped on the floor, yawning and tugging on a stocking. Her Spanish cape is a comic investiture of false dignity. If the alternative proposed by Sweeney's critics be true, that this unfortunate lady is betraying Sweeney to his death, she must go down in literary history as the blowziest *femme fatale* of all time. Rachel "née Rabinovitch" is better coordinated, perhaps less drunk. There is a seriousness about her not found in her nameless colleague. However, her tearing at the grapes "with murderous paws" is not a harbinger of doom, but a wry symbol of her emptiness.

The protagonist drifts through these scenes almost in a trance because he is spiritually numb, drugged by self-gratification. Ironically, he is at the same time unable to perceive that a different kind of dreaming, an imaginative awareness, could point the way out of his difficulty. Through the window at which he sprawls can be seen the stars and planets which, although they measure the fate of man, are yet indications of the heights to which he can aspire. Sweeney is posted fairly near the door where he can look over the entering and exiting clientele, and where also he "guards the horned gate" against entry by real dreams[3] – again ironically, comically, for this dense cipher has no inkling of the stuff that dreams are made on.

When Sweeney "declines the gambit," he is not afraid for his life, but simply wishes to avoid one more fatiguing game of chess of the manipulative sort that Lil and her husband play in *The Waste Land.* How different is the chess played by Ferdinand and Miranda near the end of *The Tempest.* In a game that was traditionally one of the few social interchanges of medieval times permitted young lovers, they enact symbolically their unselfish feelings in anticipation of their life ahead. Sweeney and his companions, on the other hand, are interested only in winning a personal advantage; and, moreover, they do not have enough intelligence and perception to win even this trifling prize. The temptation scene having come to its pointless conclusion, Sweeney departs, pausing to grin in the window on his way up the street.

Sweeney is comic, partly by contrast with the tragic figure of Agamemnon. He seems even more absurd when he is subtly juxtaposed with the

Greek hero. But "Sweeney among the Nightingales" is not a frivolous poem; it is a poem of high seriousness, higher actually because of its comedy, because of the "alliance of levity and seriousness (by which the seriousness is intensified)" that Eliot speaks of in his essay on Andrew Marvell.[4] Here is the culminating irony: if it is ridiculous that anyone should wish to kill Sweeney, it is at the same time even worse than if someone did, because Sweeney would be invested thereby with a dignity that in reality he will never know. Agamemnon died a dirty death, but it emphasized his importance. Not so with Sweeney. The horrible and funny truth is that Sweeney is just not worth killing.

Sweeney is, in fact, already dead, one of the crowd flowing over London Bridge. He is devoid of the spiritual vitality which constitutes the only significant life. And in this sense, finally, he does have a kinship with Agamemnon. Although in an earthly way they are far apart, both are given the wherewithal to express man's divinity. Each fails the trust, each is a spiritual loss, a loss which remains constant, whether it is found in the active life of Agamemnon, or in the contemplative, sensitive existence of Prufrock, or in the unconsciousness of Sweeney.

Notes

1. See Roy P. Basler, "Eliot's 'Sweeney among the Nightingales,' " *Explicator*, 2 (December 1943), item 18; Charles C. Walcutt, "Eliot's 'Sweeney among the Nightingales,' " *Explicator*, 2 (April 1944), item 48; George Williamson, *A Reader's Guide to T. S. Eliot*, pp. 97–99; Jane Worthington, "The Epigraphs to the Poetry of T. S. Eliot," *American Literature*, 21 (March 1949), 13. This is a sampling; other writers state or imply the same thought. An outstanding exception is Elizabeth Drew (*T. S. Eliot: The Design of His Poetry*, p. 42), who feels not that Sweeney is to be killed, but that "It is everything that Agamemnon and his story (and myth in general) stands for that has been killed by Sweeney and his like."

2. F. O. Matthiessen, *The Achievement of T. S. Eliot* (Boston, 1935), pp. 129–130. In the 1959 edition, this passage is slightly altered.

3. The best interpretation of this variously explicated image still seems to be that it derives from Homer and Vergil, according to whom there are twin gates from which dreams emerge: real dreams, visions of truth, from the gate of horn, and false dreams from the gate of ivory. See Walcutt; Leo Kirschbaum, "Eliot's 'Sweeney among the Nightingales,' " *Explicator*, 2 (December 1943), item 18; and for a counter-interpretation, Elizabeth Rudisill Homann, "Eliot's 'Sweeney among the Nightingales,' " *Explicator*, 17 (February 1959), item 34.

4. *Selected Essays* (New York, 1950), p. 255.

Sweeney Agonistes: Fragments of an Aristophanic Melodrama

Sweeney and the Jazz Age

From the time of T. S. Eliot's first publication of two dramatic fragments in the *New Criterion* in 1926 and 1927, *Sweeney Agonistes* has puzzled and fascinated Eliot's readers. The epigraphs from St. John of the Cross and the *Choephoroi* of Aeschylus suggested the theme of mystical purgation, yet on the surface the jazz rhythms and party world of Sweeney and Doris seemed to belie a spiritual theme. Were the "fragments" to be part of a longer drama? If so, was the poet of *The Waste Land* experimenting with a new kind of dramatic form, when he had said so often that the contemporary age was too formless to produce poetic drama? With hindsight, after Eliot's celebrated conversion to Anglo-Catholicism and his long line of religious plays from *Murder in the Cathedral* to *The Elder Statesman*, it is possible to see the fragmentary *Sweeney Agonistes* as one of Eliot's first attempts to portray in dramatic form the role of the penitent on the mystic path. But why did Eliot choose jazz rhythms and the party world of the 1920s for his dramatic experiment with this theme and why did he make Sweeney, his representative of the natural man in earlier poems, his hero? In order to understand these unlikely juxtapositions of theme, setting and hero it is necessary to understand something about Eliot's interest in jazz and the English music-hall in the 1920s and the connections he saw between jazz rhythms and the origins of classical drama.

In 1920 in *The Possibility of a Poetic Drama*, Eliot had examined what he considered to be the multiple failures of modern drama; in his judgment both ordinary social comedy and poetic dramas which attempted to imitate Greek or Elizabethan models failed by artistic standards:

> Possibly the majority of attempts to confect a poetic drama have begun at the wrong end. They have aimed at the small public which wants "poetry." . . . The Elizabethan drama was aimed at a public which wanted *entertainment* of a crude sort, but would *stand* a good deal of poetry; our problem should be to take a form of entertainment, and subject it to the process which would leave it as a form of art. Perhaps the music-hall comedian is the best material.[1]

*This essay was written specifically for publication in this volume and is included here by permission of the author. © Carol H. Smith, 1984.

It is clear from these remarks that while Eliot was concerned with artistic form and indeed insisted that any new kind of poetic drama must be subjected "to the process which would leave it a form of art," he was also impatient with attempts to create a poetic drama for the elite, "the small public which wants 'poetry.' "[2] Probably because of the model of Shakespeare and the Elizabethan theater, he envisioned a popular art that would have something for everyone. Its poetry might be concealed in the popular forms of dance and patter with which the music-hall comedian entertained his audiences. There is ample evidence in Eliot's writings on drama during this period that he was aware of the realistic difficulties of creating such a new popular dramatic form; he comments in this same essay on the formlessness of the contemporary age and on the fact that no one poet could accomplish the whole task of inventing a form, creating a taste for it, and perfecting it as well. Nevertheless, Eliot seemed convinced that a new poetic drama must be created and that existing attempts were doomed to failure.

It is interesting to trace Eliot's attempts to solve this problem in his writings of this period. In "The Beating of a Drum" (1923), he comments that "the *nature* of the finished product . . . is essentially present in the crude forerunner" and urges others interested in drama to avoid the work of literary critics and to study instead the work of the Cambridge School of Classical Anthropology. These theorists, Gilbert Murray, Francis M. Cornford, and Jane Ellen Harrison, found the origins of classical drama to be in ancient ritual, especially in the primitive celebrations marking the cycles of the earth's growth. Eliot cites in particular the ideas about comedy suggested by Cornford and Murray, that "the comic element, or the antecedent of the comic, is perhaps present, together with the tragic, in all savage or primitive art." Comedy and tragedy as separate forms are "late and perhaps impermanent abstractions." Beneath these forms lies the one essential ingredient of drama—rhythm:

> The essentials of drama were, as we might expect, given by Aristotle: "poetry, music, and dancing constitute in Aristotle a group by themselves, their common element being imitation by means of rhythm— rhythm which admits of being applied to words, sounds, and the movements of the body," . . . It is the rhythm, so utterly absent from modern drama, either verse or prose, and which interpreters of Shakespeare do their best to suppress, which makes Massine and Charlie Chaplin the great actors that they are, and which makes the juggling of Rastelli more cathartic than a performance of "A Doll's House."
>
> The drama was originally ritual; and ritual, consisting of a set of repeated movements, is essentially a dance. . . . It is . . . possible to assert that primitive man acted in a certain way and then found a reason for it. An unoccupied person, finding a drum, may be seized with a desire to beat it. . . . The reason may be the long continued drought. The next generation or the next civilization will find a more plausible reason for beating a drum. Shakespeare and Racine—or rather the developments

which led up to them — each found his own reasons. The reasons may be divided into tragedy and comedy. We still have similar reasons, but we have lost the drum.[3]

Eliot's endorsement of rhythm explains a great deal about his own program for reforming poetic drama during these years and his ideas about drama in general. The "comic element" in primitive ritual that Cornford and Murray found to be the source of all later drama clearly suggested to Eliot the acting of Massine and Chaplin and even the juggling of Rastelli. While, according to Eliot, all sense of rhythm was lost in "artistic" imitations of Athenian or Elizabethan plays, it could be discovered alive and well in the popular entertainment of the day — in the music-hall and in jazz. It is also clear that Eliot is extending the usual meaning of rhythm to include the ordered relationship of parts to the whole that is implied in Aristotle's discussion of rhythm and catharsis. A new poetic drama might attempt to combine the comic effects of music-hall patters and the rhythmic effects of dance and ritual in a satisfying and ordered whole.

Eliot's interest in the English music-hall is indicated in another essay written in the same year. Writing in memory of Marie Lloyd (1923), he praises another aspect of the art of vaudeville performers: the social bond that existed between the performers and their audience. "The working man who went to the music-hall and saw Marie Lloyd and joined in the chorus was himself performing part of the act; he was engaged in that collaboration of the audience with the artist which is necessary in all art and most obviously in dramatic art."[4] Eliot's sense of social mission is strongly reflected in these sentiments. He asserts that unless a new form of drama is developed to rescue the public from "the cheap and rapid-breeding cinema," all communal dramatic art will disappear.

The first draft of *Sweeney Agonistes* was completed the next year. Arnold Bennett recorded in his journal of 10 September 1924 that Eliot had visited him and asked his help in writing a play: "He had definitely given up that form of writing [poetry like *The Waste Land*] and was now centred on dramatic writing. He wanted to write a drama of modern life (furnished flat sort of people) in a rhythmic prose perhaps with certain things in it accentuated by drum-beats. And he wanted my advice. We arranged that he should do the scenario and some sample pages of dialogue."[5]

We can conclude from this information that Eliot had more than one reason for his use of a new kind of rhythm in this work. As we have seen, jazz syncopation seemed linked to the comic origins of religious ritual. Moreover, it seemed appropriate to the "drama of modern life" with "furnished flat sort of people." Startled as Bennett seems to have been by Eliot's plan to use drum-beats, it was consistent with Eliot's search for a new rhythm for a new drama.

In his introduction to his mother's poetic drama, *Savonarola*, published in 1926, the same year Eliot first published "Fragments of a Prologue" in the *New Criterion*, he commented on this need for new verse forms for drama: "The next form of drama will have to be a verse drama but in new verse forms. Perhaps the conditions of modern life (think how large a part is now played in our sensory life by the internal combustion engine!) have altered our perception of rhythms. At any rate, the recognized forms of speech-verse are not as efficient as they should be; probably a new form will be devised out of colloquial speech."[6]

Eliot's wish to capture colloquial speech in machine-like rhythms is itself a telling commentary on his attitude toward modern life. Such a verse style would go a long way toward controlling the content of the new drama and would impose a context for the modern hero which would evoke the brittle and mechanical aspects of modern experience. We get some sense of the stylization of modern life that Eliot intended from his instruction to Hallie Flanagan, who presented the fragments at Vassar in 1933: "Diction should not have too much expression. I had intended the whole play to be accompanied by light drum taps to accentuate the beats (esp. the chorus, which ought to have a noise like a street drill)."[7]

It might have been this modern setting which first suggested to Eliot that Sweeney might be the hero of his experimental drama. Eliot's readers were already familiar with the character of Sweeney, who had been used in several contexts to suggest man at his most elemental level. The origins of this character are unclear, although it has been suggested by Conrad Aiken that Eliot used as his model a Boston Irishman who gave him boxing lessons.[8] One suggested source that is consistent with the themes of *Sweeney Agonistes* is the fictional Sweeney Todd, Demon Barber of Fleet Street, created by T. P. Prest in the 1840s. This villain butchered his customers and turned them into veal, which he supplied to the pie shop next door for meat pies.[9] In *Sweeney Agonistes*, Sweeney threatens to turn Doris into "A nice little, white little, missionary stew."

In Eliot's earlier poems he had placed the character of Sweeney in juxtaposition with traditional heroes or myths to make an ironical statement about the decay of values in the modern world. "Mr. Eliot's Sunday Morning Service" (1918), for example, offers a complex theological criticism of doctrinal proliferation and confusion in the modern church, as well as the church's tendency to ignore the physical needs of modern man through its historically sterile doctrines, such as those rejecting bodily resurrection announced by "enervate Origen," who castrated himself in the service of the Lord. Although there are still remnants of the true meaning of the Word (in the mural of the Baptized God), the modern presbyters, "the sapient sutlers of the Lord," have nothing to offer the natural man. In a poem filled with ironic juxtaposition, Sweeney's appearance at the end of the poem provides the commentary on the church's failure, for Sweeney's baptism on Sunday morning is at home in his own bathtub:

> Sweeney shifts from ham to ham
> Stirring the waters in his bath

> The masters of the subtle schools
> Are controversial, polymath.

It is important to recognize that Eliot's criticism is leveled against the church, not against Sweeney. It is against the standard of Sweeney's needs that the church is found wanting, for, though he represents unregenerate man, his salvation is the mission of the church. Eliot has consistently seen in Sweeney man's plight in the face of his natural needs and appetites; even in this early poem he represents both man's resistance to the world of the spirit and his spiritual needs.

In "Sweeney Erect" (1919), Sweeney provides the ironic commentary on Emerson's view that history is the lengthened shadow of a man. Eliot implies that Emerson's idealism could not survive in the face of Sweeney and his kind. As the double meaning of the title suggests, Sweeney is not far from the animal state both in his level of development and in his sexuality. He complacently shaves while a prostitute writhes in an epileptic seizure, upsetting the ladies of the house. The poem contains a series of parallels to mythology and literature; the epileptic is compared to the young princess Nausicaa in the *Odyssey*, who falls in love with the shipwrecked Odysseus, while Sweeney is compared to Polyphemus, the Cyclops. In the epigraph from *The Maid's Tragedy*, another maid's tragic tale is announced. Aspatia, whose handmaidens are weaving a tapestry showing the story of Ariadne, tells them that she herself could be the model for the scene of sexual betrayal. The effect is to give a kind of endless regression of the mythical method; each heroine is weighed in the scale of the previous myth, but only the reader is aware of these rich and tragic relationships. There is nothing in the modern situation to grant dignity or beauty to these parallel events.

In "Sweeney among the Nightingales" (1918), Eliot again uses the "mythical method" in his juxtaposition of Sweeney's and Agamemnon's plight, as the epigraph makes clear. While there is an ironical contrast between the threat to "apeneck" Sweeney in a modern roadhouse or café and King Agamemnon's homecoming, they also share the same fate of death at the hands of lecherous women. As we have seen in the other Sweeney poems, the difference is that Sweeney is not aware of the significance of his fate. As ape man, he is awakened to danger as an animal might be. The poem is filled with allusions to lechery and blood guilt but they are placed to separate the modern situation from its ancient meanings, rather than to show their continuity:

> Gloomy Orion and the Dog
> Are veiled; and hushed the shrunken seas;
> The person in the Spanish cape
> Tries to sit on Sweeney's knees

Eliot carried many of the elements of the mood of this poem into *Sweeney Agonistes*. The atmosphere of foreboding, the theme of lechery and the danger of sexual impulses toward women, even the bath imagery which connects the murder of Agamemnon with Sweeney's plotted bloodbath, are all exploited in the rhythms of jazz in Eliot's first experimental play.

In *The Waste Land*, Sweeney again makes a brief appearance as part of Eliot's parody of Marvell's "To His Coy Mistress":

> But at my back from time to time I hear
> The sound of horns and motors, which shall bring
> Sweeney to Mrs. Porter in the spring.

Here, in the richly allusive context of Buddha's "Fire Sermon," Spencer's "Prothalamian," *The Tempest*, and Verlaine, this parody both undercuts its source and echoes the message of Buddha, that moral regeneration in the modern world can only come from conceiving an aversion to the lusts of the flesh. This is also the major theme of *Sweeney Agonistes*, as one of its epigraphs, from St. John of the Cross, indicates: "Hence the soul cannot be possessed of the divine union, until it has divested itself of the love of created beings." Sweeney inhabits a world where the entrapment of "the love of created beings" takes the form of prostitution. As the context of the passage shows, not only is Sweeney trapped in his world because he cannot see beyond it, but his experience of sexual love is a parody of "the love of created beings," which in Marvell's world is threatened only by time; for "Time's winged chariot" which forces the lovers to hurry their courtship clearly places the love of man and woman in the context of God's love for man and of eternity. Sweeney's spring renewal brings only a motor trip to Mrs. Porter.

Despite the jazz-age atmosphere and the party setting, the character of Sweeney is significantly different in *Sweeney Agonistes*. He is no longer "apeneck Sweeney," the man unaware, "shifting from ham to ham" in his Sunday morning bath. Sweeney is now portrayed as natural man experiencing the agony of human depravity and guilt. Whereas before he represented the unaware, physical man unconscious of all but his body's needs, now Sweeney is man suffering from an awareness of his lustful nature. The play's epigraphs from the *Choephoroi* and from St. John of the Cross describe the purgation of sin and the dangers of secular love for the penitent who seeks unity with spirit. Although the play exists only in trial fragments, it is clear that Sweeney's identification with Milton's Samson, also betrayed by a woman, and the atmosphere of threat and danger in the fortune-telling scene are intended to prepare us for a Sweeney who is natural man in a new sense; he reflects the horror of awakening to spiritual meaning in a world blind to such truth. Just as Eliot used Sweeney for purposes of parody in *The Waste Land*, *Sweeney Agonistes* is a new kind of parodic representation of the wisdom of St. John of the Cross, for Sweeney's tale of a murderer who immerses his victim's body in a lysol bath is a tale of crime and punishment.

Readers of Eliot's earlier Sweeney poems might well be puzzled by the choice of Sweeney to portray spiritual suffering and the Christian path. It is possible that the murderer's experience suggested to Eliot both a realistic example of spiritual suffering and a metaphor for the need to sever human bonds in order to pursue the spiritual life. Sweeney's nature as physical man may have recommended him as a candidate for the role of teller of a tale of violence and even for the role of the murderer himself, for there are hints that Sweeney is talking about himself. We know that Eliot's own spiritual and psychological suffering was intense during the period that he drafted these fragments and that since his college years he had suffered intense conflict about his own spiritual commitment. Lyndall Gordon in *Eliot's Early Years* describes the disturbing religious episodes which Eliot experienced during his Harvard years and which he later documented in two religious poems. "The Love Song of Saint Sebastian" and "The Death of Saint Narcissus" were written in Germany in 1914 or 1915 and parts of these poems became the earliest visionary fragments of *The Waste Land* manuscript.[10] It is possible to see resemblances between these poems and *Sweeney Agonistes*.

The idea for the first of these two poems came to Eliot from 15th century paintings of Saint Sebastian he saw in Italy and Belgium in the summer of 1914. In the legend associated with Saint Sebastian, he does not die from the arrows that pierce his flesh, but is rescued by a woman who nurses him in her lodgings. "The Love Song of Saint Sebastian" describes two fantasies of violence. In the first the saint's martyrdom is self-inflicted and an attempt to exhibit his suffering to his rescuer. Saint Sebastian flogs his body at the foot of a lady's stair while she watches in a white gown. She pities him, calls him to her bed and he dies between her breasts.[11] In the second fantasy the lover's role is reversed; while bending her head beneath his knees, he strangles his beloved with a towel. This second episode seems a clear model for *Sweeney Agonistes* for the saintly self-punisher is transformed into a violent, instinctual man who strangles his lover as the world dissolves in heat or ice. In this early poem Eliot seems to be dramatizing the violent oppositions in the saint's nature, the narcissistic fervor of self-inflicted suffering and the opposite but complementary destruction of others who might threaten his spiritual commitment. In this presentation of the saint's agony, both sides of his nature threaten to destroy him.

In "The Death of Saint Narcissus," a similar commentary is made on the psychology of the saint. Narcissis, powerfully captivated by the exquisiteness of his own beauty, is punished by being burnt dry in the desert. The impulse of Narcissus to retire from the world in order to experience a purified sense of godhead is countered by the innate nature of man's self-worship. In both poems the mystical imagery of hot and cold, fire and ice, is used to convey the forces of purgation which must destroy what is human and impure in the saint's nature before spiritual rebirth is possible. Eliot has consistently used this imagery throughout his career, in, for example, Harry's description in *The Family Reunion* of his purgatorial suffering in "the heat of the sun and the icy vigil," and in the water and fire imagery of *Four Quartets*, especially in the wounded surgeon stanzas of "East Coker":

> The chill ascends from feet to knees,
> The fever sings in mental wires.
> If to be warmed, then I must freeze
> And quake in frigid purgatorial fires
> Of which the flame is roses, and the smoke is briars.

As Gordon has shown, Eliot's interest in the ascetic experience of saints dates back to his college years. During his last years at Harvard he made a study of the lives of saints and mystics, including St. Theresa, Dame Julian of Norwich, Mme. Guyon, Walter Hilton, St. John of the Cross, Jacob Bohme, and St. Bernard. He also studied closely Evelyn Underhill's *Mysticism*, noting the phases in the progress of a religious life (awakening, unworthiness, mortification of the senses, and illumination), as well as the dangers of the disease of doubt, which leads to paralysis and delusional insanity. He also noted Underhill's warning that visions through the senses are often a delusion and he kept this skepticism about visionary experience all his life. The ambivalence towards Saint Sebastian and Saint Narcissus in Eliot's poems demonstrates both his attraction to asceticism and his suspicion of the vanity and self-deception that might be present in the saint's experience. All of Eliot's later heroes who are attracted to the saint's path are equally suspicious of their own motives, as can be seen in Thomas in *Murder in the Cathedral*, Harry in *The Family Reunion*, and Celia in *The Cocktail Party*.

The second epigraph to *Sweeney Agonistes* suggests another aspect of the saint's experience which had long fascinated Eliot—the relentless pursuit of the unwilling penitent by spiritual agents determined to drive him to God:

> ORESTES: You don't see them, you don't—but *I* see them: they are hunting me down, I must move on. — *Choephoroi*

These lines describe Orestes' first awareness of the Furies, who pursue him after his murder of his mother and her lover. Like the caution of St. John of the Cross, the passage expresses the painful purgation necessary before blood guilt can be assuaged, whether that guilt is the result of matricide and murder or the saint's acknowledgment of his depravity. Eliot paraphrased these lines in *The Family Reunion* when Harry sees his pursuing spirits.

Despite (or perhaps because of) the violence of Eliot's conception of the spiritual life, his decision to choose Sweeney as its representative shows that he conceived this experimental drama to be comic in his special sense of that term. Eliot's conviction that the new drama must reflect popular culture made Sweeney an appropriate choice, for despite the horror of the metaphor he had chosen for purgation—the murderer's act of immersing his mistress's body in a lysol bath—the comic surface of the music-hall skit satisfied the ritual conditions which Cornford had found to underlie both comedy and tragedy; it combined a comic surface with the celebration of death and rebirth. Eliot may have meant to convey this idea by the play's subtitle: *Fragments of an Aristophanic Melodrama*. It is clear from a number of his comments about drama during this period that he found tragedy unsatisfactory: "To those who have experienced the full horror of life, tragedy is still inadequate. . . . In the end, horror and laughter may be one—only when horror and laughter have become as horrible and laughable as they can be . . . then only do you perceive the aim of the comic and the tragic dramatists is the same: they are equally serious [for] there is potential comedy in Sophocles and potential tragedy in Aristophanes, and otherwise they would not be such good tragedians or comedians as they are."[12]

At the same time, he was aware of the difficulties involved in juxtaposing the ascetic penitent and the flat characters intended to be caricatures of the party world of the jazz age. Later, in *The Use of Poetry and the Use of Criticism*, Eliot described *Sweeney Agonistes* as a dramatic experiment that attempted to reproduce in a modern verse play the various levels of significance that Shakespeare's theater included:

> In a play of Shakespeare you get several levels of significance. For the simplest auditors there is the plot, for the more thoughtful the character and conflict of character, for the more literary the words and phrasing, for the more musically sensitive the rhythm, and for auditors of greater sensitiveness and understanding a meaning which reveals itself gradually. . . . I may make my meaning a little clearer by a simple instance. I once designed, and drafted a couple of scenes, of a verse play. My intention was to have one character whose sensibility and intelligence should be on the plane of the most sensitive and intelligent members of the audience; his speeches should be addressed to them as much as to the other personages in the play — or rather, should be addressed to the latter who were to be material, literal-minded and visionless, with the consciousness of being overheard by the former. There was to be an understanding between this protagonist and a small number of the audience, while the rest of the audience would share the responses of the other characters in the play. Perhaps this is all too deliberate, but one must experiment as one can.[13]

Unlikely as Sweeney is as a representative of spiritual insight, Eliot must have been appealed to by the implication that the saint's experience is always separate from and misunderstood by the world of ordinary humanity.

The first fragment of *Sweeney Agonistes*, "Fragment of a Prologue," is probably intended to correspond to what Cornford described as the first part of the ritual drama—the procession of the worshippers of Phales which was the preparation for the ritual sacrifice.[14] Doris and Dusty, two London prostitutes, and their guests, "Loot" Sam Wauchope, "Cap" Horsfall, and Klipstein and Krumpacker, American businessmen visiting London, seem appropriate phallic representatives, and the blood sacrifice which Sweeney describes in the second fragment is foreshadowed here by a series of ominous signs of violence and death. The scene opens with Doris and Dusty discussing whether or not to invite Pereira, who "pays the rent," to the party to be held that evening. Doris objects that although he pays the rent: "He's no gentleman, Pereira: / You can't trust him!" Dusty agrees and adds: "And *if* you can't trust him — / Then you never know what he's going to do." Both girls panic when the telephone rings, for they know that Pereira is on the other end of the line. In order to get rid of their unwanted caller, Dusty tells him that Doris has "a terrible chill," and that she "just hates having the doctor," both echoes of the imagery Cornford discusses in his treatment of the cook-doctor.[15] Even Pereira's name is significant; Pereira is a medicine made from the bark of a Brazilian tree and used to treat fever. Pereira's insistent pursuit of Dusty and Doris suggests his identity as the first in a long line of spiritual pursuers in Eliot's plays who, like the Eumenides who hunt down Orestes, are viewed negatively by those who cannot accept the agony of purgation.

The second sign of the painful agon to come is the fortune-telling scene, a device which Eliot had used before in *The Waste Land*, citing there Jessie Weston's work on the Arthurian romances as his source. Dusty and Doris anxiously "cut the cards for tonight," reading in the king of clubs, the four of diamonds, and the queen of hearts violence against women; as Doris says, "We're all hearts." When they turn up the two of spades, the Coffin card, they are terrified, especially Doris, who is convinced that it is meant for her because she "dreamt of weddings all last night."[16] The knave of hearts introduces the arrival of the party guests. The rest of the fragment presents the superficial party chatter stylized into the rhythms of a vaudeville patter.

In the second scene, "Fragment of an Agon," Sweeney joins the party and in his dialogue with Doris reveals himself as both the agent of violence and one who has come back from another world, like Lazarus, to tell all. Like the hero of classical comedy, he hides his wisdom in feigned stupidity and outwits his antagonist by a debate which is won by wit and ironic abuse. When Sweeney threatens to carry Doris off to a cannibal isle where he will be the cannibal, she answers that she will be the missionary and convert him. Sweeney retorts: "I'll convert *you*! / Into a stew. / A nice little, white little, missionary stew." Although Doris does not understand his meaning, Sweeney tells her that life without spiritual rebirth is like:

> You see this egg
> You see this egg
> Well that's life on a crocodile isle.
> There's no telephones
> There's no gramophones
> There's no motor cars
> · · · · · · · · · ·
> Nothing at all but three things
> · · · · · · · · · ·

> Birth, and copulation, and
> death.

When Doris says, "I'd be bored," Sweeney agrees for fundamentally life in the party world of the jazz age is a crocodile isle. Sweeney adds that he has been born and once is enough. When Doris cries out that she would just as soon be dead, Sweeney tells his purgatorial tale:

> That's what life is. . . .
>
> . . . .
>   Life is death.
>
> . . . .
> I knew a man once did a girl in
> Any man might do a girl in
> Any man has to, needs to, wants to
> Once in a lifetime, do a girl in.
> Well he kept her there in a bath
> With a gallon of lysol in a bath.

Sweeney's tale is both a grotesque version of the epigraph from St. John of the Cross and a violent expression of the murderous rage that may be engendered in the name of love between man and woman. Despite its stylized setting, the revulsion revealed in this violent picture expresses, more clearly than anything Eliot has written, his state of mind and the state of his painful marriage during the years before his separation and conversion.[17] It expresses Eliot's sense of the futility of human relationships, the isolation of every human creature, and the resultant horror of life stripped of all illusion. As an enactment of Christian mysticism, it refers to the idea that the distance between the creator and the creature is irrecoverable unless the creature is purged of all human affections, since they represent dependence on the senses and make demands which cut man off from his first duty, complete attention to God's love. Thus the beloved's murder represents a brutal cleansing of human desire and an abandonment of the old life of "birth and copulation and death." Doris' terror in the face of such a threat is captured in her refrain: "A woman runs a terrible risk."

Encouraged by Swarts and Snow, entertainers brought in to provide the jazz songs and dance routines popular at parties in the twenties, Sweeney continues his story, emphasizing the failure of words to capture the murderer's horror and guilt:

> He didn't know if he was alive
>   and the girl was dead
> He didn't know if the girl was alive
>   and he was dead
> He didn't know if they both were alive
>   or both were dead
>
> . . . .
> I gotta use words when I talk to you

> But if you understand or if you dont
> That's nothing to me and nothing to you

The play ends with a final song sung by the "full chorus." It describes a nightmare, perhaps of the murderer, who dreams he is pursued, first by the "hoo-ha's" and then by the hangman. This song is followed by a hoo-ha chant and by ominous rhythmic knocks upon the door. The hoo-has serve the same function as the Furies in their pursuit of Orestes, as the epigraph from Aeschylus suggests. In ending the play with the fear of the hangman's knock upon the door, Eliot has combined the murderer's fear of discovery and punishment with the hanged god allusion cited by Jessie Weston and Frazer and described by Eliot in the notes to *The Waste Land.* Just as a murderer awaits the hangman who will mete out punishment for his crime, so the supplicant awaits the "hanged man" who will mete out purgatorial justice.

What Eliot expresses in this fragmentary play is both the agony of the saint and the private anguish and rage of the man trapped in a world of demanding relationships with women ("Any man might do a girl in," "A woman runs a terrible risk.") It is significant that Eliot saw these themes as related and chose to merge them in his first experiment in a new form of drama. The common ingredient is human isolation, both in emotional and in spiritual terms. Eliot never again expressed the mood of anxiety and isolation so directly, nor so clearly identified the spiritual and the sexual, although several of the later plays hint at this identification. In Sweeney's story of violence and horror, sexual love leads to spiritual purgation, and yet this theme is by definition incommunicable to a world terrified of death and unaware of anything beyond it. Eliot's dramatic mission was clearly a drama of the impossible—communicating to the unenlightened by the sheer force of the dramatic form and its primitive rhythm. In giving to Sweeney the vision of spiritual enlightenment, Eliot made a daring choice, for he selected a character plucked out of the very world predisposed to reject his message. The implication is that sexual love is the ground of human suffering and that "any man" can know the murderer's spiritual agony. In Sweeney's tale of love and murder, Eliot came closer to the human heart than was perhaps comfortable for him; only the stylized jazz surface and syncopated rhythms stood between his experience and his audience. The play was never finished, but its precarious method became the model for all of Eliot's later dramatic works.

Notes

1. T. S. Eliot, *The Sacred Wood: Essays on Poetry and Criticism* (London: Methuen & Co., 1928), p. 52.

2. Eliot may have been thinking of Yeats's plays for dancers. We know that Pound took Eliot to see *At the Hawk's Well* in 1916. While he may have been impressed with Yeats's use of

masks and musical instruments, in Eliot's statements on drama during these years he consistently rejected the model of a drawing room theater for a specialized audience of poetry lovers.

3. T. S. Eliot, "The Beating of a Drum," *The Nation and the Athenaeum*, xxxiv (October 6, 1923), 12.

4. T. S. Eliot, *Selected Essays* (New York: Harcourt, Brace & Co., 1950), p. 407.

5. Newman Flower, ed., *The Journals of Arnold Bennett*, vol. 3, *1921–28* (London: Cassell & Co., 1933), p. 52.

6. T. S. Eliot, Introduction to *Savonarola: A Dramatic Poem by Charlotte Eliot* (London: R. Cobden-Sanderson, [1926]), p. xi.

7. Hallie Flanagan, *Dynamo* (New York: Duell, Sloan and Pearce, 1943), p. 82.

8. Conrad Aiken, "King Bolo and Others," *T. S. Eliot: A Symposium*, ed. Richard March and Tambimuttu (London: Editions Poetry London, 1948), p. 21.

9. Grover Smith, *T. S. Eliot's Poetry and Plays* (Chicago: University of Chicago Press, 1950), pp. 44–45.

10. Lyndall Gordon, *Eliot's Early Years* (Oxford: Oxford University Press, 1977), pp. 58–59.

11. The rescuing lady in white figures in "Ash Wednesday."

12. T. S. Eliot, "Shakespearian Criticism: I. From Dryden to Coleridge," *A Companion to Shakespeare Studies*, ed. Harley Granville-Barker and G. B. Harrison (Cambridge: Cambridge University Press, 1934), pp. 287–99.

13. T. S. Eliot, *The Use of Poetry and the Use of Criticism* (Cambridge: Harvard University Press, 1933), pp. 146–47.

14. There is clear evidence for this source in a letter that Eliot wrote to Hallie Flanagan, who presented *Sweeny Agonistes* at Vassar in 1933. He told her that the action should be stylized as in the Noh drama, the characters should wear masks, and the whole play should be "accompanied by light drum taps to accentuate the beats (esp. the chorus, which ought to have a noise like a street drill)." He noted that in the second fragment the characters should be in a shabby flat, seated at a refectory table, with Sweeney in the middle scrambling eggs in a chafing dish. He urged her to consult Cornford's *Origin of Attic Comedy* "which is important to read before you do the play." Cornford describes the buffoon-cook or doctor as roles played by the hero of the ritual drama. The egg is a traditional symbol of elemental life and rebirth, as in the Easter egg. Eliot uses the device of the buffoon-cook scrambling eggs later in *The Cocktail Party* when Alex insists on making Edward's supper of "half-a-dozen eggs" in Act 1, Scene 1. Eliot included in his letter an unpublished ending for the second scene, which gives a dialogue between Father Time and Sweeney. Sweeney questions the old man in riddles and he is answered in equally cryptic responses. See Hallie Flanagan, *Dynamo*, pp. 82–83.

15. The doctor figure with spiritual associations recurs in several of Eliot's plays, most notably *The Family Reunion, The Cocktail Party*, and *The Elder Statesman*.

16. The coffin and the dream of weddings are symbols drawn from Cornford's discussion of the ritual scenes of death and resurrection. See Francis M. Cornford, *The Origin of Attic Comedy* (London: Edward Arnold, 1914), pp. 70–104.

17. Gordon, *Eliot's Early Years*, pp. 95–140.

Mr. Eliot's Agon

Sears Jayne*

Most of the poems of T. S. Eliot require elucidation, and most of them have long since attracted the detailed analysis which they require. But one of the longest, the 379-line poem entitled *Sweeney Agonistes*, remains almost completely neglected.[1] There are two reasons for this neglect. One is that the work is in dramatic form; although it was published as a poem, critics have usually tried to discuss it in connection with Eliot's plays,[2] and in this context have had, of course, to dismiss it as merely an early and unsuccessful experiment. The other and more important reason is that Mr. Eliot himself calls it an "unfinished" work, and critics have therefore felt that the elucidation which it needs is hardly worth the trouble.[3]

But *Sweeney Agonistes* is worth the trouble if one regards it as a poem instead of as a play, and if one takes into account a basic principle of Eliot's poetry, which is that the integrity of the poem is less important to Eliot than the integrity of the verse-blocks of which the poem is built. Seen from this point of view, *Sweeney Agonistes* is at least as "finished" as most of Eliot's poems, and it has a special interest for the critic in that it is the only poem in which Eliot takes as his central theme the irony of his own situation as a poet in the modern world.

A first step toward understanding any Eliot poem is to adopt Eliot's view of poetic integrity and concentrate on verse-blocks rather than on whole poems; perhaps the best way to appreciate how little Eliot worries about poem-integrity is to review the publishing history of such a poem as "Doris's Dream Songs,"[4] but the publishing history of *Sweeney Agonistes* itself illustrates the principle very effectively.

The first appearance of any part of *Sweeney Agonistes* in print was the publication in the *Criterion* for October, 1926, of a block of verse entitled simply "Fragment of a Prologue." At the head of this block were published two epigraphs:

> ORESTES: You don't see them, you don't — but I see them: they are hunting me down, I must move on. — *Choephoroi.*
>
> Hence the soul cannot be possessed of the divine union until it has divested itself of the love of created beings. — *St. John of the Cross.*[5]

At the end of the block was printed the phrase, "to be continued." In the next issue of the *Criterion* (January, 1927) appeared another block of verse entitled: *Fragment of an Agon* (From *Wanna Go Home, Baby?*) At the head of this block were again printed the same two epigraphs.

From these facts and from Mr. Eliot's own remarks we may conclude that by 1927 Mr. Eliot had completed at least these two blocks of a poetic drama possibly entitled *Wanna Go Home, Baby?*[6] but decided to publish them separately, joined only by the fact that they had the two epigraphs in

*Reprinted, with permission, from *Philological Quarterly*, 34 (1955), 395–414.

common. Yet he evidently thought the two completed blocks had a certain integrity of their own, for he republished them in 1932 as a single work in a separate volume entitled: *Sweeney Agonistes: Fragments of an Aristophanic Melodrama*. In this edition of the work there was no mention of *Wanna Go Home, Baby?* and the two epigraphs were printed only once, at the head of the whole work.

The change in the title of the work reflects Mr. Eliot's own change of plans and is worth looking into. In its original form *Sweeney Agonistes* came before the public as two fragments of an uncompleted play, but the reader was provided with three keys to the meaning of the fragments: the title of the play and two epigraphs. The title *Wanna Go Home, Baby?* implied that the language of the play was to be that of the London pub in the 1920's; the first epigraph, from Aeschylus, suggested that the form of the work was to be that of a Greek tragedy; the second epigraph, from St. John of the Cross, showed that the ideological import of the work was to be religious. One may reasonably infer that *Wanna Go Home, Baby?* was originally planned as an ambitious attempt to combine in one work a music-hall melodrama, a Greek tragedy, and a theological poem, thus satisfying auditors of every degree of intelligence and sensitivity.

In the new version of the work the two epigraphs were retained, suggesting that the reminiscences of Greek drama and the theological meaning were still to be noticed; but the title was changed to *Sweeney Agonistes*, suggesting that although the work seems to be in dialogue form, it is now not to be conceived of as a play for the stage, but rather as a dramatic poem, like Milton's *Samson Agonistes*, combining, as Milton does, the Christian tradition with the Greek, but using the language of Sweeney. The new title also suggested that, though the original play was to deal primarily with a decision put to a woman, the fragments as they stand deal mainly with a problem facing a man. The reader gathers that in the apparently ignoble, pagan, and Aristophanic figures of Mr. Eliot's poem there is intended some element of the noble, the religious and the tragic in Samson; the work is meant to have tragic overtones, but Mr. Eliot specifically removes it from the realm of tragedy by labelling it part of "an Aristophanic melodrama"; melodrama differs from tragedy in that the protagonist's career curves up at the end rather than down, though the tragic emotions may be played upon in both. *Wanna Go Home, Baby?* is to be associated rather with a work like *Alcestis* of Euripides than with the *Agamemnon* of Aeschylus, and its humor is to be associated with that of Aristophanes, a vigorous and satirical criticism of contemporary life, with a heavy emphasis upon sex.

By giving the two fragments a title of their own, and separate publication as well, Mr. Eliot had done everything he could to launch *Sweeney Agonistes* upon an independent career, but he apparently still did not feel that the fragments could really stand alone, for when he gathered his poems together for the *Collected Poems* volume in 1936, he placed *Sweeney*

Agonistes in a section entitled "Unfinished Poems,"[7] and in that state it remains today.[8]

On the other hand, though *Wanna Go Home, Baby?* was never finished (except insofar as *The Cocktail Party* may be regarded as the completed work), the fragments themselves have been given a very high polish indeed. To cite only one example of the care which Mr. Eliot has lavished on the poem, we may notice the pair of characters called *Snow* and *Swarts*. In the original blocking Mr. Eliot must have had in mind two characters called *Black* and *White*, signifying their opposition. The names *Black* and *White*, however, would have been too obvious and literal for the more sensitive members of his audience and he therefore tried to think of other names which would get the idea across to the thoughtful reader and yet remain innocuous to the casual one. For *White* he chose *Snow*, which makes a better last name than *Sheet*, for example; in casting around for a name which might alliterate with *Snow* (for closer parallelism) he went to the German *Schwartz*. This, however, was too uncolloquial, so he changed it to *Swarts*.

The names *Snow* and *Swarts*, like the "hot gates" in "Gerontion," warn us that the poem must be loaded with meanings which Mr. Eliot has concealed for the greater pleasure of the "most sensitive and intelligent members" of his audience. In addition to one set of meanings which come through on the level of the least educated reader of the poem, *Sweeney Agonistes* has other and more complex meanings which are available in part only, and then only to the scholar.

What those more complex meanings are, scholars have not agreed. Miss Helen Gardner says that the theme of the poem is "the boredom and horror that lie beneath the commonplace and the ugly."[9] A more common view is that expressed by Mr. T. H. Thompson, who sees the poem as one more vignette from the life of the same apeneck Sweeney who appears in four other poems of Eliot. Mr. Thompson pursues the life of Sweeney as a detective story through the five poems and concludes that *Sweeney Agonistes* is simply the story of Sweeney's confession of the murder of Ariadne Porter.[10]

Professor Matthiessen emphasized the treatment of levels of communication in the poem; Mr. Rossell Robbins thinks that *Sweeney Agonistes* is about the Christian sense of sin. Professor Williamson says that the "serious import" of the work was concealed by the original title, *"Wanna Go Home, Baby?"* The only other person who professes to have found a serious meaning in the poem is Mr. Nevill Coghill, who was apparently discouraged from publishing his views by personal assurances from Mr. Eliot himself that any view of the work is a satisfactory view.[11]

Myself:
> I had no idea the play meant what he (Mr. Doone) made of it . . . that everyone is a Crippen (i.e., a murderer). I was astonished.

Mr. Eliot:
> So was I.

Myself:

Then you had meant something very different when you wrote it?

Mr. Eliot:

Very different indeed.

Myself:

Yet you accept Mr. Doone's production?

Mr. Eliot:

Certainly.

Myself:

But . . . but . . . can the play mean something you didn't intend it to mean, you didn't know it meant?

Mr. Eliot:

Obviously it does.

Myself:

But can it then also mean what you *did* intend?

Mr. Eliot:

I hope so . . . yes, I think so.

Myself:

But if the two meanings are contradictory, is not one right and the other wrong? Must not the author be right?

Mr. Eliot:

Not necessarily, do you think? Why is either wrong?

Though Mr. Eliot generously allows any interpretation of the poem, he admits that he did intend at least one particular meaning, and he has told us something about that meaning in *The Use of Poetry and the Use of Criticism* (London, 1933), p. 153:

> The ideal medium for poetry, to my mind, and the most direct means of social "usefulness" for poetry, is the theatre. . . . For the simplest auditors there is the plot, for the more thoughtful the character and conflict of character, for the more literary the words and phrasing, for the more musically sensitive the rhythm, and for auditors of greater sensitiveness and understanding a meaning which reveals itself gradually. . . . I once designed, and drafted a couple of scenes, of a verse play. My intention was to have one character whose sensibility and intelligence should be on the plane of the most sensitive and intelligent members of the audience; his speeches should be addressed to them as much as to the other personages in the play—or rather, should be addressed to the latter, who were to be material, literal-minded and visionless, with the consciousness of being overheard by the former. There was to be an understanding between this protagonist and a small number of the audience, while the rest of the audience would share the responses of the other characters in the play.

The "protagonist" is, of course, Sweeney; we shall return to him shortly, but first we must consider another aspect of Mr. Eliot's intention which is shown in his lecture on *Poetry and Drama* (Harvard University Press, 1951), p. 31: ". . . people are prepared to put up with verse from the lips of personages dressed in the fashion of some distant age; they should be made to hear it from people dressed like ourselves, living in houses and apartments like ours, and using telephones and motor cars and radio sets. . . . What we have to do is to bring poetry into the world in which the audience lives and to which it returns when it leaves the theatre."

The world to which the audience of *Wanna Go Home, Baby?* would have returned was the London of the shell-shocked era (after World War I), but it is that London seen in a particular way, through the eyes of a sensationalist press. The view of humanity which we see in *Sweeney Agonistes* is exactly the view one gets in reading *News of the World,* a Sunday weekly which has built up the largest circulation in the world (more than eight million) by shrewdly catering to popular taste. In the early twenties *News of the World* specialized in lurid accounts of current British crimes, described in the fullest possible detail; in addition, it printed each week the words and music of a popular song. The general impression which the *News* gives of life in the period of *Wanna Go Home, Baby?* is that all human activity is based on three fundamental appetites: the desires for music, drink, and sex. All three desires are of central importance in *Sweeney Agonistes* and are expressed there in terms unmistakably dated in the first quarter of the twentieth century.

The rhythms of the songs in *Sweeney Agonistes* are unmistakably jazz-rhythms, and their syncopated beat carries over into the speeches of Sweeney as well. The song entitled "Under the Bamboo Tree," which is sung in the poem by Wauchope and Horsfall, is based on a song by Bob Cole and J. Rosamond Johnson first published in London in 1905; Mr. Eliot's tune is obviously different, but he has borrowed from the original song the title and the last two lines of the chorus: "One live as two, two live as one, / Under the bamboo tree."

In the same year (1905) was published a book entitled *Intemperance* and a pamphlet entitled *Intemperance as a Hindrance to Spiritual Life,* both by Bishop Henry Horace Pereira (1845–1926). Pereira, who had been Honorary Chaplain to Queen Victoria, was the leader of the Temperance movement in England. He died in January, 1926, and was remembered by a long obituary and some correspondence in the *Times*; when the "Fragment of a Prologue" first appeared in October of the same year, many of its British readers must have seen in the Pereira of the poem the nemesis of the drunken pub-keeper Sweeney, dispensing booze and hard-boiled eggs to himself as well as to his customers.

Music and drink, however, were much less important in the original design of *Wanna Go Home, Baby?* than sex. Not only the implication of the title, but the entire plot was to be based upon sex. As Mr. Eliot has said, he thinks it is the plot which the least educated members of the audience concentrate upon, and he accordingly selected the kind of plot which the uneducated man could most easily follow: the sex-murder in which the motive is jealousy. Though Mr. Eliot's technique of adaptation is too free to permit the identification of a particular crime of the time as the source of that in

Wanna Go Home, Baby? the best way to understand what he had in mind is to read some of the numerous accounts of sex-motivated murders in *News of the World*; it is almost certainly such a model which produces in *Sweeney Agonistes* details like the gallon of Lysol, Doris's superstitious reference to the old proverb "After a dream of a wedding comes a corpse," and the shouts of the arriving visitors, "We'll be right up," heard by the neighbors a few hours before the murder.

That it is a murder we know because the card-drawing of the Prologue explains most of the Doris plot for us. The plot was to run something like this:

> A stupid and grossly materialistic girl, living in a cheap London flat provided for her by a man whose attentions she despises (Pereira), invites two other men (Wauchope-Horsfall and Snow-Swarts) to an evening card party. On the very evening of the party she once more refuses to see Pereira, feigning physical illness. The party is marked by an atmosphere of foreboding and distrust, and the friends go out to a nearby pub for drinks. The foreboding pursues them even there and is only increased by a story which the pub-keeper (Sweeney) tells about a girl who was murdered. Suddenly there is a mysterious knocking at the pub door, which turns out to be no one; this unnerves everyone, and one by one the girl's friends find excuses to leave until only the pub-keeper is left to ask, "Wanna go home, baby?" He takes her home, and she is later found murdered in the bathtub; he himself is also later found mysteriously murdered.

This is the part of the story which we know about from the Prologue. The two fragments of the play which we have are: the scene in Doris's apartment in which the party is planned, Doris's future is told in the cards, and the first guests arrive; and the scene in the pub preceding the knocking at the door, a scene which is also a prophecy of Doris's death. The motives of Sweeney and Pereira, the position of Doris, and the conversation of the guests any reader of *News of the World* would have understood. A reader of Greek tragedy would have understood a good deal more, for Mr. Eliot has carefully coordinated parts of the popular plot with episodes and techniques from Greek tragedy. He did not take his plot as a whole from Greek tragedy because of his interest in reproducing the world of the audience, but the dramatic irony and sense of foreboding which pervades any play in which the audience can foresee the protagonist's death derive in *Sweeney Agonistes* from Greek tragedy, and many aspects of particular Greek plays are reflected in the poem; the most influential plays are the *Choephoroi* and *Agamemnon* of Aeschylus and the *Alcestis* of Euripides.

We immediately suspect the influence of the *Choephoroi*, of course, because of the epigraph from that play which identifies Orestes with Sweeney in his awareness of danger which is invisible to others. Sweeney himself reinforces this association with his talk of the confusion between life and death, reminding us of the fact that the characters in the *Choephoroi* could not tell whether Orestes was alive or dead. We are reminded of Orestes again, in his relation to Pylades, by the two travelling merchants, Klipstein and Krumpacker; this association is especially clear in the scene in which Dusty (like Clytemnestra) greets them on their arrival. Sweeney, like Orestes, once in his lifetime "did a girl in," and Sweeney was pursued for it (by Pereira) as Orestes was by the Furies, but there is no parallel in the *Choephoroi* for the Doris plot.

We are reminded of the *Agamemnon* by the similarity between the clairvoyance of Sweeney and that of Cassandra; Sweeney went home with Doris, and Cassandra went home with Agamemnon, and Agamemnon, like Doris, was killed in his own bath.

Much more interesting is the influence of the *Alcestis*, from which Mr. Eliot borrowed his technique for beginning the play. The *Alcestis* begins with a dialogue between Apollo and Death in which the plot of the play is explained; thus the audience is equipped for its proper enjoyment of dramatic irony and the closing of the jaws of fate. In Mr. Eliot's play the opening scene is between Doris and Death, and the card-drawing serves the same function exactly, that of explaining the events to come to the more intelligent auditors of the play. The division of the choruses into half chorus and full chorus in the *Alcestis* is also imitated by Mr. Eliot in the songs of the Agon. The drunken Sweeney escorting Doris back to her home parallels the similar, but different, service rendered Alcestis by the drunken Heracles, and the implications of Alcestis's position as a sacrifice for Admetus are suggested in the Christ-associations of Sweeney, which we shall examine shortly.

Such are the principal external materials bearing on Mr. Eliot's poem. If we recall that in *The Waste Land* Mr. Eliot had employed the fresh, if rather esoteric, medium of the Fisher-King legend to give a new vitality to the Christian view of life and death, we may conjecture, I think, that *Wanna Go Home, Baby?* was an abortive attempt to do the same thing, using Greek tragedy and *News of the World* instead of Miss Weston's book as his parallel image. It is easy to imagine why *Wanna Go Home, Baby?* was dropped once Mr. Eliot hit upon Miss Weston's book; the Fisher-King was a more dignified, more ambivalent, and much less dated image than the sordid factual story of a London murder. Once *The Waste Land* was finished, there was no point in returning to *Wanna Go Home, Baby?* for Eliot's aim of exploring the paradoxical relations between modern life and physical and spiritual death had been accomplished. One further reason for Eliot's abandonment of the original play may be revealed in the fact that the work so accurately represents the average American's reaction to British life. The play may originally have been projected as a satire not merely on modern life in general, but on British modern life in particular. If so, Eliot's acceptance of British citizenship would explain his loss of interest in the work, and the sense of *agon* in the poem.

Thus far we have been considering mainly the external bases for an interpretation of the poem, and these have led us not so much to the poem as to the unfinished play from which the poem was salvaged. We must now turn to the poem itself. We notice first that there are two fragments and two epigraphs, and we have already suggested that there were probably meant to be two plots in the original play. The entire poem is built on dualism. All of the characters appear in pairs, and in every case the dualism means something beyond the literal level: Doris and Dusty are life and death, Swarts and Snow are black and white, Wauchope and Horsfall are soul and body; and in almost every case "two live as one." Much of the difficulty of the poem lies in the fact that this dualism splits the two fragments beyond reunion; the Sweeney plot, to which the Agon belongs, is never developed, though the Doris plot is laid out in full detail, and though Mr. Eliot has gone to some pains to tie the fragments together (e.g., the knocking at the door), the Prologue is not really a prologue to the Agon, but to *Wanna Go Home, Baby?* and the two fragments were never really welded into a whole by the clever title, *Sweeney Agonistes*.

But to return to the epigraphs, we have noticed that there are two, and that one is Hellenic and the other Hebraic. In general, the second epigraph seems to refer to the first fragment (the rejection of Pereira by Doris) and the first epigraph seems to refer to the second fragment (the superior foresight of Sweeney), but in a way each of the epigraphs applies to the other fragment as well.

In both fragments we see groups of people who are beset by the same two difficulties: (1) they do not understand each other and feel pursued by an invisible force, and (2) they are too engrossed in life as a sexual experience to understand the real (ie., spiritual) meaning of life. In the Prologue Dusty understands the cards, but Doris doesn't, and Doris is pursued by Pereira, an invisible force which she rejects in favor of a "created being." In the Agon Sweeney feels the futility of trying to make other people understand what he understands, which is that they will all be pursued by death so long as they continue to be interested only in sex. With these general clues, provided by the epigraphs, we must now proceed to a detailed analysis of the poem.

The Fragment of a Prologue is blocked out in three sections. The first section, through line 63, is a conversation between two women, interrupted by a telephone call. The second section, through line 141, duplicates the first except that the events take place in the guise of playing cards; the cards also point forward to the action of section three. The third section gives the arrival and preliminary chit-chat of several more characters.

The two women, Doris and Dusty, are talking in the first section about a mysterious person named Pereira, who pays Doris's rent but is no gentleman and is accordingly refused when he telephones to make a date with her. Dusty acts as intermediary on the telephone. Eliot forces us to inquire into the meaning of this incident by giving his characters puzzling names, by repeating ominously the phrase "That's Pereira," and finally by putting into Doris's mouth the very questions which he wants us to ask, "Wonder what that means?" and "What does that mean?" Some of the answers to Doris's questions are given in section two by Dusty, using a common symbol of double meaning in everyday experience: the playing card.

The first card drawn, Dusty tells us, represents Pereira. The second card represents several things, and Dusty leaves it to us to pick which of the three possible meanings the card can have. The most obvious is the meaning of a "party," representing the card party which Doris is planning. The third card again is explained by Dusty as "news of an absent friend"; this clearly refers to the telephone call of Pereira. The Queen of Hearts, misunderstood by Doris, is correctly explained by Dusty as representing Doris herself, the object of Pereira's attentions. The next card means "estrangement," which refers to Doris's rejection of Pereira's attentions. The last card is the coffin, but its significance to the action in section one is not immediately clear; when Doris says "I'd like to know about that coffin," Dusty replies only, "Well, it needn't be yours," which is to say that Doris is not dead yet, and has some choice in the matter.

Up to now, Doris has been drawing, but she is so disturbed by the drawing of the coffin card that she asks Dusty to "break the spell" and draw herself. Dusty then draws the Knave of Spades and the Knave of Hearts, which refer to the two pairs of men who are to arrive in the following section of the Prologue. Again, Eliot makes it impossible to miss his meaning; Dusty says several times that "cards are queer," and asks "isn't that a coincidence?" and Doris discovers for us that the Knave of Hearts *is* Sam Wauchope. Finally, Doris ends with the problem which Eliot is unwilling for us to escape, "I'd like to know about that coffin."

The playing cards have therefore shown us that the people in the Prologue have more than a superficial meaning, and we must now attempt to learn what that meaning is. Remembering Swarts and Snow, we turn to the names of the people, Doris, Dusty, and Pereira. *Doris* is related to the Greek word for *gift*; in *Doris Dorance* Eliot has repudiated the root, as it were, to keep us alert. *Doris* is the *give* of "What the Thunder Said." All the associations of *Dusty*, on the other hand, such as "dust to dust" and "lighted fools the way to dusty death," relate to death, and this is not surprising since a coffin has been mentioned; Dusty must therefore be death.

Pereira, who is never seen, but controls all the action, we associate, as we have seen, with the religious point of the second epigraph. The marked repetition of the phrase "That's Pereira" suggests that Pereira represents some invisible, pursuing Fate like that which Orestes sees in the epigraph. Since Pereira is "First" (compare Dusty's "First is" with the "Thine is" of *The Hollow Men*), is the King (of Clubs), and pays the rent (for Doris), he must be the same person who paid the rent for Gerontion, that is, God. (The basic irony of the original title, *Wanna Go Home, Baby?* is the familiar Eliot observation that no rented house belongs to anyone as a home, but neither do our bodies belong to us as houses for the soul.) God, then, invites Doris to the divine union mentioned in the epigraph; pleading physical illness, Doris puts him off until Monday, the day after the Sabbath, in order to have the weekend free for "created beings"; in so doing she has chosen spiritual death (this is why she draws the coffin card). Eliot is saying that to live is to divest oneself of the love of created beings and *give* oneself up to the divine union; to refuse God's invitation is to die spiritually.

Doris's objection to Pereira is that you can't trust him, and Dusty points out that to be unable to trust someone means only to be unable to predict what he is going to do, and that Doris has labelled Pereira as no gentleman simply because she can't tell what he is going to do. Eliot's point is that belief in God requires faith, a willingness to believe what is unknown. Doris refuses Pereira, although he "pays the rent," that is, gives her life. It is significant that Sam, who is dead, is acceptable to both girls: Doris says "I like Sam," and Death says with great point, "*I* like Sam." And we recall the peculiar emphasis of Dusty's remark, "It's funny how I draw court cards." That is, although Doris draws the cards for section one, those cards tell the story of her life and death, and as soon as she has drawn the coffin (i.e., died), she cannot draw any more but has to leave it to Dusty to go on; it is Death herself who draws the cards representing Sam and Horsfall (the Knave of Hearts) and Klipstein and Krumpacker (the Knave of Spades).[12]

The connection between the second epigraph and the Prologue is now obvious: Doris has refused the divine union because of her preference for Sam, and has consequently died. The connection between the first epigraph and the Prologue becomes clear when we realize that Dusty, like Orestes, has understood all this, while Doris, who is the one being pursued by Pereira, has not. The first epigraph is also central to section three of the Prologue, to which we now turn.

The surface action here is the "party" referred to in section one; the guests whom Doris was expecting turn out to be Sam Wauchope and Captain Horsfall, who have brought with them a couple of Americans whom they met in France during World War I; we see only the beginning of the party, the introductions, and a brief discussion of how the Americans like London. The card-drawing, however, has taught us to suspect the easy naturalness of the party conversation, and we begin immediately to search out the significance of the two pairs of visitors.

The differences within each pair are most directly apparent in the contrasting names. Wauchope and Horsfall belong together because Horsfall is a Captain and Wauchope is a "Loot" (Lieut.). They have both been in the Canadian Army, but they were of different rank. It is significant that although Horsfall had the superior rank, it is Wauchope who does all the talking. Horsfall, in fact, never says a word in this scene. Wauchope's name, suggesting Wanhope, the medieval sin of faithlessness, and also suggesting the Watch and Pray of Matthew 26:41,[13] refers to peculiarly spiritual and passive conditions, whereas Horsfall's name (from Horseplay and Pratfall) refers to peculiarly physical and active conditions; between them they represent modern man, composed of both body and soul, but honoring the body above the soul, and essentially dead because without faith. The fact that Wauchope and Horsfall are dead is verified by the last speech of Krumpacker.

> Specially when you got a real live Britisher
> A guy like Sam to show you around.
> Sam of course is at *home* in London,
> And he's promised to show us around.

Here it becomes evident that the "coffin" referred to in the cards is London. It is for this reason that Wauchope, being dead, is "at *home* in London" because he is a *"real live* Britisher*"* (he is actually a Canadian, of course). Wauchope, then, is apparently dead, and Horsfall, who says not a word, must be dead, too. Wauchope and Horsfall, so closely related, yet so different, seem to represent the soul and body of a person "living" in London, but actually, from Eliot's point of view, dead, for the same reasons that the Hollow Men are hollow, and that life is death in the Waste Land. The ironic equivalence between life and death is brought out here in the fact that the two soldiers who have been engaged in killing are now engaged in loving and are so represented in the cards by the Knave of Hearts. The coffin, incidentally, also represents the death of Doris; on the popular level this would mean her murder. On the religious level, it would mean her choice of "life" in contemporary London and consequent spiritual death.

Klipstein and Krumpacker seem to represent a more obvious pair of people, two typical American businessmen. But Eliot goes to great pains to show that their apparent similarity is only superficial. He carefully constructs their opening conversation to reveal a widening divergence between their points of view:

WAUCHOPE: . . . Meet Mr. Klipstein. Meet Mr. Krumpacker.

KLIPSTEIN: How do you do.

KRUMPACKER: How do you do.

KLIPSTEIN: I'm very pleased to make your acquaintance.

KRUMPACKER: Extremely pleased to become acquainted.

Wauchope has introduced them in exactly the same terms. They have both said "How do you do" in exactly the same terms. In their next remarks they both say the same thing, but in a slightly different way. From this point on, their points of view diverge more and more widely. When Krumpacker says "We were all in the war together," Klipstein says "Yes, we did our bit," apparently agreeing with Krumpacker, but actually not understanding him and going off on a different tack altogether, as is pointed out in his mention of the Germans, whereas Krumpacker's memories are of the French; at one point each of them answers a question put to the other one. Klipstein is a thin, wiry Jew whose only interest is in money and the power that money brings; in name and character he reminds us of Dante's "Trimmers." Krumpacker is a fat, expansive, cigar-smoking industrialist whose major interest in life is good living: food, drink, and sex. Klipstein fails to remember the name of either Doris or Dusty, whereas Krumpacker remembers Miss Dorrance's name quite well. Klipstein and Krumpacker represent two different aspects of vulgar American vitality being introduced to the dead in London. The most important thing about the two Americans, however, is not their vitality, but the fact that they understand neither each other nor their English friends.

To summarize, the point of the Prologue is the point made in the two epigraphs; though it seems like two points rather than one, it really is one. Eliot has shown us a woman rejecting God (and life) for man (and death); as Orestes in the epigraph points out, she does not recognize in her party guests the furies who are bringing her death; she does not see them, but we do because we are outside their deadly conversation and can see to what degree they are out of communication with each other and, therefore, dead.

The basic view of the Prologue, which is pro-God and anti-man, is perhaps not so interesting to most modern readers as is Eliot's amazing skill in demonstrating the many levels and degrees of human understanding. We see here people who lie and people who tell the truth, people who understand and people who don't, people who pretend to understand and people who understand only in certain terms, people who lie unconsciously, and people who lie and tell the truth at the same time, people who talk in symbols and people who talk in clichés, people who chatter, and people who don't talk at all, people who communicate only indirectly, and people who communicate in person. And finally, in addition to all of the concrete illustrations of the problem, Mr. Eliot gives us an explicit discussion of it which throws at least as much light on his own poetry as upon the particular poem at hand:

> DORIS: Or it might be you
> We're all hearts. You can't be sure.
> It just depends on what comes next.
> You've got to *think* when you read the cards,
> It's not a thing that anyone can do. . . .

When Eliot says, "You've got to *think* when you read the cards," he probably means "You've got to *think* if you expect to understand life," but he might just as well mean "You've got to think if you expect to understand poetry." Similarly the other comments of Doris and Dusty apply specifically to the problem of poetic communication as well as to human communication in general.

This is the meaning which Mr. Eliot thought worth salvaging in the two fragments as they stand, and the meaning to which he applied the title *Sweeney Agonistes*. If the Prologue is our chief clue to the meaning of the projected play, our best clue to the meaning of *Sweeney Agonistes* is the Agon, to which we now turn.

In the Agon Mr. Eliot shows us a man who has the powers which Orestes and Christ had in common of foreseeing their own fate, but being unable to escape it. That we are to associate Sweeney with Christ in this idiom of the street, is shown by several lines in the poem. In the Prologue Dusty suggests that the King of Clubs (i.e., God) may be identified in a way with Sweeney (i.e, Christ). In the Agon Sweeney's threat that he will eat Doris reminds us of the figure of Christ the tiger in "Gerontion." Moreover, Sweeney's remark:

> I've been born and once is enough.
> You don't remember, but I remember,
> Once is enough.

obviously refers to the fact that modern civilization has forgotten the sacrifice of Christ, and also to the Magi's remembrance of the strange identity of birth and death at the nativity. One atonement, in Sweeney's language, should have been "enough."

But Sweeney also has a good deal of the poet about him. He alone perceives the truth about the modern situation and tries hopelessly to communicate to his fellows that the life they are living, on a human plane of sex and misunderstanding, is death. Mr. Eliot explores Sweeney's difficulties with a subtlety born of personal experience. Sweeney, the poet-philosopher, is in a real sense Eliot himself agonizing with the problem of communicating an idea.

The scene in Sweeney's pub opens with a conversation between Doris and Sweeney on the subject of sex. Sweeney drunkenly tries to explain to Doris in terms of the life-symbols of egg, water, tree, and island, that life among human beings amounts to nothing more than a sexual relation between man (Sweeney) and woman (Doris) and that in this sexual relation human beings do not really generate life (the egg) but spiritual death; they kill each other (spiritually) and are therefore cannibals. Doris fails to understand Sweeney because she takes his symbols of cannibal and egg literally. Sweeney is talking poetry and Doris is hearing prose; just as Doris failed to understand the card symbols in the Prologue, she fails to understand the poetic symbols in Sweeney's remarks. It is only when Sweeney relapses into prose and says that life is only birth, copulation, and death that Doris understands him a little and says that she'd be bored.

Sweeney is assisted in his struggle by the Greek chorus of the other six men in the company. With Snow and Swarts acting as accompaniment, that is to say, pointing up the opposition between members of each pair, Wauchope and Horsfall sing a suggestive song employing the same symbols which Sweeney has introduced and pointing out that life on the purely sexual level involves no value judgments whatever; there are no values; there is only sex. After Doris rejects this life, without understanding why, Klipstein and Krumpacker sing another song, this time without any symbolism, saying directly what they mean and ending with a suggestion of the monotony of the purely sexual life. With the help of this literal approach, Doris finally comes to the judgment that the kind of life they have described is not for her, and says, with unconscious irony, that she'd just as soon be dead. This identification between the purely sexual life and death is exactly what Sweeney had been trying to get at all along with his cannibal symbol, and he now resumes the conversation.

Doris's jump from death to the symbol in the form of the coffin card does not mean, however, that she is ready to follow Sweeney's symbolical language; it merely reminds us that it is in terms of the symbolism that we are to follow Sweeney ourselves. With brief interruptions from Swarts and Snow, illustrating their polarity as black and white, Sweeney then tells his story of the man with the well-filled bathtub. In the course of telling the story, Sweeney has a great deal of difficulty in getting across his point of the identity of life and death; the difficulty is illustrated in the irony of Snow's insistence that they are all "very interested" in what Sweeney is saying; like readers of Eliot's poetry, they are all very interested, even though they do not understand what he is talking about; Sweeney's difficulties are illustrated again in the reactions of the two girls to his remark that the man came to see him sometimes and had a drink to cheer himself up. Doris can't understand why Sweeney would want to try to cheer up a man who had a dead woman in his bathtub, whereas Dusty, who understands who the man is, can't understand why Sweeney should have tried to cheer up a dead man. Sweeney admits defeat and says in a line which is the key to the meaning of the whole poem and rings with the complaint of the poet himself: "But I've gotta use words when I talk to you." The stupidity of Sweeney's audience is the stupidity of the average human being.

From this point on Sweeney falls back on explicit statement to point out the meaning of his story, which is that there is no difference between life and death. His final failure to communicate the idea, however, even though stated so explicitly, is shown in his allusion to the fact that "someone's gotta pay the rent." Doris, delighted to understand something of what Sweeney has said, and thinking of Pereira in the Prologue, says brightly, "I know who," but she obviously does not understand the meaning of the rent in Sweeney's or Eliot's sense.

Sweeney has failed to communicate his idea to Doris, but the four men who knocked at the end of the prologue now understand, as the chorus in the *Agamemnon* understands, the feeling if not the meaning of the situation; and they now sing a final foreboding chorus. Swarts and Snow are silent this time, suggesting that there is no argument possible about the view expressed in this song, that modern life is a nightmare in which it is impossible to distinguish between being alive and being dead.

The knock of Pereira upon the door at the conclusion of the nightmare echoes exactly the knock of the dead Wauchope upon the door of Doris, emphasizing the irony of the fact that even the poetic Sweeney, who understands what fate lies in store for him, does nothing to avoid it, but goes on living the kind of life that he knows means death for himself as well as for others.

In the completed play, we may conjecture, Sweeney's death at the hands of Pereira would have represented God's "killing" of Christ, but we hardly have enough of the play to venture so far. What we can say with assurance is that *Sweeney Agonistes* deals, as *The Waste Land* does, with the essential similarity of life to death in modern British life; if the poem dealt only with this, we might not look at it twice. What makes it worth reading even in its "unfinished" state is the fact that it deals subtly and personally with an aspect of the modern disease with which Mr. Eliot is intimately familiar: the difficulty of communication among human beings, and especially of poetic communication. It is Mr. Eliot himself who complains in the poem that he's "gotta use words" when he talks to us; the struggle which is the subject of the poem is the poet's own struggle; it is Sweeney's voice and Sweeney's vocabulary which we hear, but it is Mr. Eliot's Agon.

Notes

1. Though neglected by critics of poetry, the work had been often performed: e.g., at Vassar (1933), in London (1935), and at Wesleyan University (1952).

2. See, for example, Helen Gardner (*Art of T. S. Eliot*, London, 1949, p. 132) and F. O. Matthiessen (*Achievement of T. S. Eliot*, London, 1935, pp. 156–59).

3. Russell Robbins (*The T. S. Eliot Myth*, New York, 1951, p. 98) admits that the poem *needs* elucidation, but the only serious attempt to explicate it heretofore has been George Williamson's (*Reader's Guide to T. S. Eliot*, New York, 1953, pp. 191–95).

4. This poem first appeared in *The Chapbook* in 1924: Eliot later used one block of the poem for Section III of *The Hollow Men*, and another block he republished in 1936 as a separate poem entitled, "Eyes that last I saw in tears."

5. The first epigraph is from Aeschylus, *Choephoroi*, ll. 1061–2. The second is from St. John's *Ascent of Carmel*, I. v, 2 (in the translation of David Lewis [London, 1906] p. 22); both are paraphrases. St. John of the Cross was a particularly appropriate author for the purposes of this poem because he wrote a good deal of theological verse. Mr. Eliot paraphrases the same work of St. John (I, xiii) in "East Coker." For a fuller discussion of Mr. Eliot's interest in St. John, see Raymond Preston, *The Four Quartets Rehearsed* (London, 1946).

6. Note that the Americans, Klipstein and Krumpacker, sing in the Agon: "And we won't go home when it rains."

7. The only change made in the poem between 1932 and 1936 was the omission of one line, assigned to Wauchope in the early version of the Prologue:

1932	1936
WAUCHOPE: We'll be right up.	WAUCHOPE: We'll be right up.
DUSTY: All right, come up.	DUSTY: All right, come up.
WAUCHOPE: We'll be right up.	
DUSTY (To Doris): Cards are queer.	DUSTY (To Doris): Cards are queer.
DORIS: I'd like to know about that coffin.	DORIS: I'd like to know about that coffin.

8. No change was made in the 1941 *Later Poems (1925-1935)* or the 1952 *Collected Poems and Plays* editions. The pirated reprinting of the two fragments in *Two Worlds Monthly* II (1927), 143–46, and III (1927), 149–52 reproduced the *Criterion* form of the work, and is inconsequential so far as the history of the text is concerned.

9. *Art of T. S. Eliot*, p. 129.

10. This interpretation first appeared in "The Bloody Wood," *London Mercury*, XXIX (1934), 233–390, and is reprinted in Leonard Unger, *T. S. Eliot* (New York, 1948), pp. 161–69. It is borrowed, almost verbatim, in the Italian dissertation of Silvio Policardi, *La Poesia di T. S. Eliot* (Venice, 1949), pp. 129–38.

11. "Sweeney Agonistes," in the anthology of Richard March and Tambimuttu, *T. S. Eliot* (London, 1948), p. 86.

12. A few words should be said about the Knave of Spades. Dusty, whose insights are to be trusted more than Doris's, suggests that the Knave of Spades represents either Swarts or Snow, but she also goes on to say that you shouldn't expect too literal a meaning in the cards. The Knave of Hearts is certainly Sam, but the Knave of Spades apparently represents in a general way the dead society with which Doris has cast her lot. The knocking on the door at the end of section two of the Prologue seems like the proper ending of the fragment. The scene which follows, showing the arrival of some of the guests, ends like a prologue ("He's promised to show us around"), but looks in other respects like a third fragment, glued to the preceding scene by chronology only. In any case the "Prologue" must have been a continuous part of the first act of the projected play, and Snow and Swarts must have been scheduled to put in an appearance soon after the arrival of Klipstein and Krumpacker, who, in the truncated poem, ought really to be the ones represented by the Knave of Spades.

13. There are two modern British writers by this name who may have some connection with Eliot's character. They are: Major R. S. Wauchope, author of *Buddhist Cave Temples of India* (Calcutta, 1935) and O. S. Wauchope, author of *Deviation into Sense, the Nature of Explanation* (London, 1948). The latter work was published by Faber and Faber, the company of which Eliot is a director.

14. Doris's comment that "You've got to know what you want to know" reflects the point made of the Knight's career in *The Waste Land*, that you have to know what question to ask, but it also reflects one problem in reading Eliot's verse; you have to know what to look for in order to find the meaning he hides in his puzzle poems.

Sweeney Agonistes (An Anecdote or Two)

Nevill Coghill*

One morning Mr Wystan Auden, then an undergraduate at Christ Church, blew in to Exeter College for his tutorial hour with me, saying:

"I have torn up all my poems."

"Indeed! Why?"

"Because they were no good. Based on Wordsworth. No good nowadays."

"Oh . . . ?"

*Reprinted by permission of the publisher of *T. S. Eliot: A Symposium*, edited by Richard March and Tambimuttu, Chicago, Henry Regnery Co., 1949.

"You ought to read Eliot. I've been reading Eliot. I now see the way I want to write. I've written two new poems this week. Listen!"

He recited them.

I was brought up to demand a logical as well as a sensual meaning in poetry, so his recitation was completely incomprehensible to me, though I was struck by some of the images that had a sudden but seemingly irrelevant force. I can still remember one of a man by a gate looking into a field, though its "meaning," in a context unintelligible to me, escaped. I complained of this, and Auden explained with clarity and pity that to "understand" a poem was not a logical process, but a receiving, as a unity, a pattern of co-ordinated images that had sprung from a free association of sub-conscious ideas, private to himself. He again recommended the works of Mr Eliot.

All this was towards 1926–7. I had of course already made some tentative soundings in Mr Eliot's poetry and decided it was too deep for me, or else one of us was off the track of poetry. Perhaps he was a fad or fashion; if only my more advanced pupils would stop talking about him, there was a chance he might blow over . . . Or must I swot him up? It was that morning's tutorial hour that convinced me I must. "Auden," I thought, "is in the imperative."

It was at first very hard for me to adjust myself to Mr Eliot's apparently formless verses and (as I thought) Bloomsbury idiom. This of course will now seem derisory. I persevered and understanding began to dawn with pleasure, and pleasure to intensify into delight.

I was still for a long while perplexed as to the tone of voice required for certain phrases; in *Prufrock*, for instance. Was it right for ladies to come and go, talking of Michelangelo? If not, why not? What were the dangers of eating a peach? Was the "music from a farther room" a room in Bloomsbury or in some more heavenly mansion? When I asked these questions, the adherents of Eliot looked at me (how rightly) with compassion and turned kindly to subjects within my capacity.

But slowly, over about two years, I think, the poems, at my invitation, invaded me. The first to make a full conquest was *Sweeney Agonistes*. I was at once moved by the quick, pert, rhymes and rhythms, and the sense of how extremely effective they would be on the stage. And there was that palmary jazz-lyric *Under the Bamboo*. Although, as yet, I had absolutely no notion what the "fragments" of *Sweeney Agonistes* as a whole portended, I could feel that they were portentous.

In the end, however, my eye fell on the title-page, and there lay the two little latch-keys left by Mr Eliot for those who wish to enter his intention: a quotation from Aeschylus, countered by one from St John of the Cross. I fitted the keys to the poem. In a moment it seemed to be unlocked.

I now entered the vision; it appeared to be about a normal man of violence, the natural Orestes, the man who cuts his way out of a problem. His natural motives of horror and disgust have their natural expression in murder. But in an obliquity no less natural, instead of plucking out his own eye to enter the Kingdom of Heaven, he tries to pluck out what his eye has seen; and this is murder, the wrong kind of surgery, wrong and useless for (as in the case of Orestes) it brings retribution. KNOCK, KNOCK, KNOCK.

The true solution of Sweeney's predicament, which he neither knew nor took, was not natural but supernatural, namely to divest himself of the love of created beings. (St. John of the Cross.)

I had got this far in fathoming the governing idea of these fragments — how impressive they now seemed! — when a production of them in London was announced by Mr Rupert Doone. I rushed up to see it. About thirty of us were gathered round an almost empty room without a stage, but the almost fabulous figures of Lady Ottoline Morrell, Mr Aldous Huxley and Mr Eliot himself were pointed out to me in a whisper that deserved one. The play began.

It was performed with an exquisite blend of violence and restraint. The cool, rich, level voice of Mr Doone as Snow saying, "Let Mr Sweeney continue his story," sent a shudder down my back. He offered an almost entirely different interpretation of the play to that I had worked out. As he presented it, it was a study in the psychology of a Crippen; he made it seem that we were all Crippens at heart and that nothing was so true as that:

> Any man might do a girl in
> Any man has to, needs to, wants to
> Once in a lifetime, do a girl in.

And this necessity led to nightmare and to the police. KNOCK, KNOCK, KNOCK. But it remained a necessity.

I went away overwhelmed and bewildered, yet reassured of the greatness of the play in this admirable production.

It must have been a little later that I came upon *Marina*, which of all Mr Eliot's poems I find the most revealing. It created for me a unification of all his work into which the later *Four Quartets* have easily fitted. Whether this unity I seem to perceive is the same sort of unity as Mr Eliot sees in and beyond them I do not know. I hope so. The governing idea (for me) is that of rebirth into super-natural life through a cycle of which a descent into the dark night of the soul is a recurring preliminary. This appears as a process for the common man as much as for the professed mystic, whether he recognizes it or not, and Sweeney is the common man, the average, decent, lout.

Such a man is put to torture by his soul, of whose existence he is at first but dimly aware, as a maturing man becomes aware of the upthrust of a wisdom-tooth. It hurts, and it drives him, naturally, to violence. So Sweeney, *l'homme moyen sensuel*, awakens to disgust and pain in his beloved *saeculum*, his frowzy world, and tries to cut his way out of it; the wrong surgery. But the Orestes-Crippen impulse masters him.

Mr Doone's interpretation (as I received it) was nevertheless a shock. It seemed to justify the ways of Crippen to woman, and thus to destroy my more metaphysical speculations, in that there appeared to be no alternative for Sweeney than to murder Doris. But his production was so convincing. Could it, after all, have been what Mr Eliot had really meant?

I do not remember the date on which I first met Mr Eliot. It was at lunch with Father D'Arcy. Conversation was about the Lambeth Conference, then recently terminated. As I did not know what the Bishops had been talking about I kept a tactful but ashamed silence and studied with admiration the zest of my companions in their theological discussion. Poetry was not mentioned and I had no chance to put the questions I had been nursing.

Not long after — a year maybe — I found myself once again seated at lunch next to Mr Eliot. It was at All Soul's College on Encaenia Day and there were enough Bishops about to reintroduce Lambeth topics. Cantuar himself was there. I resolved to start straight into poetry rather than expose myself in theology; but what would Mr Eliot want to talk about? Would he rather not talk at all? Would he remember me?

To my great pleasure he seemed to know me at once. And in a rush I began to talk to him about the production of *Sweeney Agonistes*. So far as I can remember this is what was said:

Myself:
> I think I saw you at Rupert Doone's production of *Sweeney Agonistes?*

Mr Eliot:
> Very likely indeed. I was there.

Myself:
> I had no idea the play meant what he made of it . . . that everyone is a Crippen. I was astonished.

Mr Eliot:
> So was I.

Myself:
> Then you had meant something very different when you wrote it?

Mr Eliot:
> Very different indeed.

Myself:
> Yet you accept Mr Doone's production?

Mr Eliot:
> Certainly.

Myself:
> But . . . but . . . can the play mean something you didn't intend it to mean, you didn't know it meant?

Mr Eliot:
> *Obviously it does.*

Myself:
> But can it then also mean what you *did* intend?

Mr Eliot:
> I hope so . . . yes, I think so.

Myself:

But if the two meanings are contradictory, is not one right and the other wrong? Must not the author be right?

Mr Eliot:

Not necessarily, do you think? Why is either wrong?

This was to me so staggering a point of view that I could only put it down to modesty. I therefore abandoned this attack for one more frontal.

Myself:

Tell me, Mr Eliot, who *is* Sweeney? How do you see him? What sort of man is he?

Mr Eliot:

I think of him as a man who in younger days was perhaps a professional pugilist, mildly successful; who then grew older and retired to keep a pub.

I do not remember any more of this conversation, but what I have written is true so far as it goes, subject to correction from Mr Eliot, should he remember it at all. I was disturbed and excited by what he said and have often since then reflected on these occasions, and on the critical implications of his remarks. They repay thought. At least they have the merit of being authentic anecdotes.

[From "Charting Eliot's Course in Drama"]

Marjorie J. Lightfoot*

T. S. Eliot's initial choice of conventions of music-hall comedy for *Sweeney Agonistes* was largely abandoned in the course of his career as a dramatist. E. Martin Browne conjectures that had Eliot followed the lead of *Sweeney Agonistes*, his plays would appear more "immediate" to the 1960's, but he recognizes that the change of "climate" found in Eliot's poetry at the time of his religious conversion was bound to be reflected in the content of the plays. This new content, rather than a change of attitude toward music-hall comedy, presumably led the author to seek a more suitable medium for his material.

But a religious conversion was not the only factor relevant to the significant changes of form and content in Eliot's plays. The very nature of the poet's dramatic theory saw an apparent reversal over the years, a reversal of tremendous significance to Eliot's experimentation. Early, he held that verse drama should emphasize its differences from the naturalistic prose drama then popular; later he tried to adapt naturalistic conventions to his own ends and to keep the audience from being conscious — or at least self-

*Reprinted with permission, from *Educational Theatre Journal*, 22 (1968), 186–97.

conscious—that it was listening to verse drama. Accordingly, the early experimental plays, *Sweeney Agonistes*, *The Rock*, *Murder in the Cathedral*, and the transitional *The Family Reunion* exhibit such attention-getting devices as a chorus, caricature, soliloquy, lyric duets, elevated rhetoric, and formal ritual, while the later plays, *The Cocktail Party*, *The Confidential Clerk*, and *The Elder Statesman*, avoid devices which focus special attention on the poetry. They employ instead a conventional setting in a picture-frame stage, the language of modern speech, and either realistic situation or one which points up plot in the tradition of farce—but maintain a naturalistic surface.

It is noteworthy, however, that from first to last, from *Sweeney Agonistes* to *The Elder Statesman*, use of *some* convention remained Eliot's basis of appeal. Using it, he hoped to create immediate rapport with the audience, although he continued to vary his form and content. Charting the dramatist's shifts in course from "over-statement" to "understatement" of verse drama reveals that Eliot's experiments in diction and prosody correspond to the change of conventions he employed, reflecting not only the religious conversion but the poet's remarkable reversal in dramatic theory. Helen Gardner recently praised the "speakability" of the later plays.[2] It is surely relevant in evaluating Eliot's theatrical career to remember that in adapting himself to the demands of the contemporary theatre, one of his major goals was the creation of a verse form which could carry a transparent poetry in the language of common speech.

Eliot turned his interest to verse drama, following "The Hollow Men," in a need to stimulate his own creativity, as his criticism during the 1920's reveals. A glance at some of his essays shows his dramatic theory at the time. In " 'Rhetoric' and Poetic Drama" (originally published as "Whether Rostand had Something about Him," 1919) the critic pointed out the value of rhetoric as an indication of dramatic self-awareness, self-consciousness which might involve the presence of a sense of humor. He expressed his belief that poetic drama should give artistic form to typical human emotions, and that the dramatic and poetic elements should be fused. The article "Prose and Verse," 1921, indicated the suitability of relaxed, almost prosaic verse for less intense moments of poetry; his introduction to *Savonarola*, 1926, a verse drama largely in iambic pentameter heroic couplets, written by the poet's mother, revealed that the common idiom was a source of suitable dramatic language in a modern world where rhythm had been affected by the internal combustion engine; and "The Poetic Drama" offered convention as a device to permit the audience a habit of response. Eliot's first essay for *The Dial*, 1920, "The Possibility of a Poetic Drama," suggested the drama should be a simplification and universalizing of the world as seen by the author, and the critic proposed the music-hall comedian as a guide to reaching an audience.[3]

In "The Beating of a Drum," 1923, the author spoke of drama as originally a ritual set of movements, repeated as in a dance, arising in primitive art from an impulse both tragic and comic. He regretted the absence of such stylized rhythm in contemporary theatre, and he preferred the rhythm of Rastelli's juggling and the acting of Chaplin and Massine to the naturalistic rhythms and acting of Ibsen's *A Doll's House*. While we retained comedy and tragedy as causes for the ritual and rhythm of drama, we had lost the drum. (He wrote later in *The Use of Poetry and the Use of Criticism*, "Poetry begins, I dare say, with a savage beating a drum in a jungle.") He also observed that all art arose from and was nourished by ritual. In "Four Elizabethan Dramatists," 1924, he reaffirmed his belief in the need for conventions of form and content as successfully achieved in *Everyman*, although some sacrifice of realism might be demanded for the sake of form.[4] His beliefs indicate a desire for a formal, ritualistic drama of conventions — a desire anticipated in thought and practice by William Butler Yeats, among others.

In 1924 Eliot began *Sweeney Agonistes*, a stylized drama dealing with characters from furnished flat society. When Hallie Flanagan prepared to present the drama at Vassar in 1933, Eliot wrote her that the play should be stylized as was the Japanese Noh play — of current interest in the literary world to such men as Ezra Pound and W. B. Yeats. The characters should wear masks and speak without much expression. Light drum taps should accompany the rhythms of the verse for accentuation and give the choruses an emphatic street drill rhythm.[5] In this work the formal conventions, including the verse, should be emphasized rather than minimized, in accord with the dramatist's desire to set his verse drama apart from the realistic or naturalistic prose theatre of William Archer and Ibsen.

The author uses music-hall devices, dealing with low-life, employing minstrel-show caricatures and a stylized chorus, parodying jazz rhythms and such songs as "Under the Bamboo Tree," "Ain't We Got Fun," and the Lord Chancellor's nightmare song from Gilbert and Sullivan's *Iolanthe*. Drunkenness, a routine of the music-hall, was used for satire and criticism, as it had been used for centuries in comedy. The play has been called a jazz operetta,[6] with 4-stress syncopated jazz rhythm insulating the characters from reality in a jazz world where individuals cannot communicate.

The jazz rhythms, stylized language, and caricatures create a speech that is tense and symbolic. The condensation is so great the conversation is pointless, as Sweeney indicates when he says, "I gotta use words when I talk to you / But if you understand or if you dont / That's nothing to me and nothing to you."[7]

Helen Gardner believes Eliot returned, consciously or unconsciously, to the medieval tradition of accentual verse, based on the Old English 4-stress line with the number of syllables not fixed.[8] Here is an example:

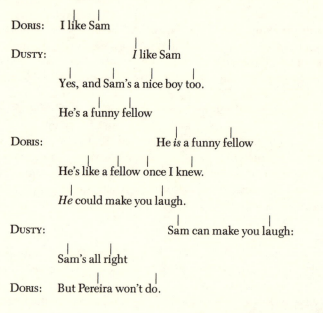

DORIS: I like Sam

DUSTY: *I* like Sam

Yes, and Sam's a nice boy too.

He's a funny fellow

DORIS: He *is* a funny fellow

He's like a fellow once I knew.

He could make you laugh.

DUSTY: Sam can make you laugh:

Sam's all right

DORIS: But Pereira won't do.

(*Sweeney Agonistes*, p. 75)

The 4-stress line appears in *The Rock* and *Murder in the Cathedral*, as in well as in "Four Quartets," together with *many other* verse forms.[9] But it is the *basic* line in *The Family Reunion, The Cocktail Party, The Confidential Clerk*, and *The Elder Statesman*. Eliot first identified the line as 3-stress, in "Poetry and Drama," 1951, but later admitted W. H. Auden might be right in calling it 4-stress. Eliot's director, E. Martin Browne, called it 4-stress too. The issue is prosodic *description*, not performance, since the author approved the direction of his plays. Justification for describing the line as 4-stress is founded on the predominance of lines with four metrical stresses, i.e. "that sound (normally accented) or silence which attains prominence through appearing at apparently or approximately isochronous intervals, establishing a pattern of expectation" across the line.[10] Analysis of the Decca recording of *The Cocktail Party* demonstrates the applicability of such a 4-stress description.

The dramatist experimented with this line, from play to play, through changes in diction, style, syntax, and characterization, in his growing desire to find a verse form which would contain the rhythms of contemporary speech, but would *not* call attention to itself as verse as it does in *Sweeney Agonistes*. Such experimentation in the treatment of the 4-stress line and the extent of its use reflects the poet's changes in dramatic theory as well as subject matter.

Notes

1. E. Martin Brown, "T. S. Eliot in the Theatre," *T. S. Eliot: The Man and His Work*, ed. Allen Tate (New York, 1966), p. 118.

2. Helen Gardner, "The Comedies of T. S. Eliot," *T. S. Eliot: The Man and His Work*, ed. Allen Tate (New York, 1966), p. 181.

3. T. S. Eliot, " 'Rhetoric' and Poetic Drama," *The Sacred Wood: Essays on Poetry and Criticism* (New York, 1960), pp. 81, 83, 84; T. S. Eliot, Introduction to Charlotte's Eliot's *Savonarola: A Dramatic Poem* (London, n.d.), p. ix; Leo Hamalian, "The Voice of This Calling: A Study in the Plays of T. S. Eliot," unpublished Ph.D. dissertation, Columbia University, 1955, pp. 52–54; T. S. Eliot, "The Possibility of a Poetic Drama," *The Sacred Wood: Essays on Poetry and Criticism* (New York, 1960), pp. 68–70.

4. T. S. Eliot, "The Beating of a Drum," *The Nation and The Athenaeum*, XXXIV (Oct. 6, 1923), 11. T. S. Eliot, *The Use of Poetry And The Use of Criticism* (London, 1933), p. 155. T. S. Eliot, "Marianne Moore," *The Dial*, LXXV (1923), 597. T. S. Eliot, "Four Elizabethan Dramatists," *Selected Essays* (New York, 1950), p. 93.

5. Hallie Flanagan, *Dynamo* (New York, 1943), p. 83.

6. Hamalian, p. 3.

7. *Sweeney Agonistes*, p. 84. Since all references from *Sweeney Agonistes, Murder in The Cathedral, The Family Reunion*, and *The Cocktail Party* are in *The Complete Poems and Plays: 1909–1950* (New York, 1952), page reference only will be given in the text of the paper hereafter. Scansion is mine.

8. Helen Gardner, *The Art of T. S. Eliot* (London, 1949), pp. 26–27.

9. Ibid., p. 32. Grover Smith, Jr., *T. S. Eliot's Poetry and Plays: A Study in Sources and Meaning* (Chicago, 1956), pp. 172, 193–197.

10. This description is supported at length in my article, "The Uncommon Cocktail Party," to be published by *MD*.

[From "Eliot and the Living Theatre"]

Katharine Worth[*]

I

No playwright of our time has been more difficult to "see" than Eliot. The poetry and the piety have worked a potent spell, obscuring both dramatic weaknesses and actual or potential strengths. The argument of this essay is that to be seen in perspective Eliot's plays must be seen in the context of the living theatre, not as an extension of the poetry and the dramatic theory, nor as a special kind of activity called "religious drama."

We know that Eliot desperately wanted to elude the kind of audiences who attended his early plays expecting "to be patiently bored and to satisfy themselves with the feeling that they have done something meritorious."[1]

[*]Reprinted, by permission of the publishers, from *Eliot in Perspective*, edited with an introduction by Graham Martin, New York, Humanities Press, 1970.

His anxiety to make contact with "real" audiences was an important factor in the evolution of his post-war style. He put the poetry on a thin diet and overlaid his symbols with a conventionally seductive façade.

Yet the plays seem to keep their place in the not very jolly corner labelled "verse and religious drama." Is the reason for this simply their inadequacy as plays? Must they always be performed in what Ivor Brown jocularly called "the crypt of St. Eliot's" and have they no relevance to the development of the modern theatre? Are they quite out of the main stream, as far out as the plays of Masefield, Drinkwater and Stephen Phillips are now seen to have been?

I do not believe that we have to answer "yes" to these questions, though much of the existing criticism of the drama, no doubt against its intention, forces us to do so by emphasising so heavily moral patterns, Christian solutions and thematic progressions. What in my view emerges as theatrically interesting, and what gives Eliot a place, however tentative, in the main stream, is his feeling for alienation and violence, his gift for suggesting metaphysical possibilities in the trivial or absurd and his exploration of new dramatic means for working upon the nerves and pulses of an audience.

Of course these potentialities are imperfectly realised. Again and again he seems to be on the verge of striking out an entirely new line, of creating, even, the modern theatre. Then he abandons the promising experiment, conceals the real experience. *Sweeney Agonistes* must be one of the most exciting beginnings ever made by a poet turning towards the theatre, a Yeatsian concept of total theatre, full of primitive power. *The Family Reunion* showed that the impulse of the fragments could be sustained in a full-length piece and opened out still new vistas; even in *The Cocktail Party*, though not acknowledged for what it is, sounds the note of Beckett and Pinter; not irrelevantly, as M. C. Bradbrook has noted,[2] do the title and situation of the play bring into mind *The Birthday Party*.

What these experiments grew from, why they were not followed up and Eliot's dramatic powers fully realised, are the questions we might expect criticism to be asking. But, on the contrary, critics tend to accept the idea of painful self-improvement from *The Rock* to *The Cocktail Party* which Eliot offers in *Poetry and Drama*. Few would be found, of course, to place the last plays, *The Confidential Clerk* and *The Elder Statesman*, at the summit of his achievement. These are fairly generally admitted to show a falling away of power, though even here, to some minds, the edification in the subject-matter is more than compensation for thinness of texture.[3] And there will, no doubt, always be some for whom *Murder in the Cathedral* has no need to abide our questions: "Of the greatness of *Murder in the Cathedral*, there can be no doubt — it may even be the greatest religious play ever written — and the other plays will survive if only as parts of the unity of which it is the finest element."[4] But setting aside these acts of homage to the subject-matter, it has still been common form for Eliot's own chart of his progress to be taken as a basis for study, for *The Cocktail Party* to be seen, as he presents it, as a dramatic advance upon *The Family Reunion*, and for *Sweeney Agonistes* to be totally ignored.

Eliot is, then, not without responsibility for a situation in which his real theatrical powers are not recognised. In small ways, too, he has encouraged an untheatrical view, by allowing recordings of the choruses detached from their dramatic context; indeed, by making them himself, in a voice admirably suited to *Four Quartets* but hardly likely to increase our belief in the real existence of the Women of Canterbury. The early publication of *Sweeney Agonistes* in *Collected Poems* (1936) and its subsequent omission from *Collected Plays* (1962) has also served to misdirect. Even critics such as Northrop Frye and G. S. Frazer here referred to this most exciting theatrical piece as a 'poem'.

Criticism of poetic drama in our time has often taken untheatrical directions for want of a theatrical context, but there is no need for this in Eliot's case. A wealth of theatrical material exists, from reviews and actors' accounts of their roles to records of the growth of the texts under the pressure of stage requirements.

Two kinds of interest attach to this material. It has, in the first place, the interest which first-hand accounts of plays in preparation and production must always have for students of drama, offering a perspective which can never be quite the same as that from the study.[5] In the second place, it raises questions about Eliot's special kind of relationship with the theatre world. Some of those involved in production of his plays were deeply committed to the idea of a "religious drama"; their commentaries often combine shrewd stage judgements with a tendency, common in non-theatrical criticism, to look through what is there in the play to what ought to be there.

How important was the influence from within the theatrical milieu in turning Eliot towards the morality patterns of the late plays is, indeed, one of the as yet unanswerable questions with which future criticism must be concerned. It is already clear from E. Martin Browne's illuminating accounts of his share in the plays (especially from *The Making of a Play* (1966)) that his own influence was of the greatest importance. In giving Eliot much needed advice on stage necessity, he was also moving him towards a less ambiguous and equivocal expression of theme; suggesting such changes as the replacement of the word "daimon," by "guardian" in Edward's analysis of his own condition and requiring an exact account of Celia's fate, which Eliot, we are told, had in the first draft left "as vague as, at the end of *The Family Reunion*, he had at first left Harry's" (p. 22). Whether this last change really was an improvement is a question to which different answers have been and will be given, according to whether the play is seen as the Christian morality it purports to be, or as an abortive attempt at a less easily defined structure, in which the word "daimon" is in fact the right one.

The many critics, in and out of the theatre, who are in sympathy with

Eliot's doctrinal intentions, will hardly recognise the existence of such alternatives, or will at least have no hesitation in emphasising the orthodox interpretation of any play under discussion. But even the criticism uncommitted to a religious viewpoint sometimes seems slightly out of focus with what is happening in the plays, perhaps because critical argument is so often conducted in a context composed almost exclusively of Eliot's own theory and practice. Much light has been thrown on the plays by studies of the relation of theory and practice and of the plays to the poems, of sources and meaning, ritual and symbolic patterns. Yet the separation of the play from the theatrical context has its dangers, not least the danger of over-interpretation. A critic, like C. H. Smith, who tells us that she is "not primarily concerned with an evaluation of Eliot's work by current theatrical standards" may have, and, indeed, has many valuable insights to offer about the ritualistic overtones, but she is also liable to move a long way from stage or any other kind of reality, as she does in her account of Harcourt Reilly: "Sir Henry's ritual identity is suggested by his continual drink of gin with a drop of water (he is adulterating his spiritual nature with a drop of water, representing time, flux, and humanity)."[6]

II

Eliot has, of course, invited symbol-hunting of the Thurberish kind by his ubiquitous dropping of clues, followed up by the answer in his next lecture.

The critical reception given to *Sweeney Agonistes* is a case in point. This piece has attracted much scholarly attention as a source of theme and symbol. But its stage inventiveness was scarcely given credit until the production of 1965 in the memorial programme, "Homage to T. S. Eliot," at the Globe Theatre, with jazz accompaniment by John Dankworth, Cleo Laine as Doris and Nicol Williamson as Sweeney. Audience and reviewers were astonished on this occasion by the force and freshness of the piece; far from seeming a precious literary experiment, it was felt to be as alive as the sculpture by Henry Moore which preceded it on the stage. To one reviewer it seemed "in the same class as the Berlin classics of Brecht and Weill," to another it "uncannily" foreshadowed the British *avant garde* drama of the fifties.[7]

Literary critics, on the other hand, have tended to see it as a dead end, an experiment of limited interest, or even as the wrong turning which it seems to Grover Smith: ". . . the farcical music hall style, without any indication that Sweeney is deliberately talking down, is an improper vehicle for this serious theme."[8]

The selection of a "farcical music hall style" for the serious theme is in fact the best evidence of the acute theatrical sense with which Eliot was endowed at the start of his dramatic career. Nothing in his later development is more impressive than the instinct he showed then for recognising potentialities in popular and vulgar forms. In the waifs and strays of *Swee-ney Agonistes* he hit upon just those types, derived from music hall and min-strel show, which thirty years later, in *Waiting for Godot*, were to be seen as the seed around which a modern drama could crystallise.

Fascination with music hall, circus, revue, and the ritualistic interpre-tations of them offered by scholars like F. M. Cornford, was of course, a feature of *avant garde* movements in the 1920s. Paris was then, as later, a breeding-ground. e. e. cummings, another young American, like Eliot at home in literary Paris, produced his own highly original blend of ritual and burlesque, *Him*, in New York, only two years after Eliot's Aristophanic fragments had appeared in the *Criterion*, and Cocteau's voice was fre-quently heard in that journal, prophesying the future role of "le cirque, le music hall, le cinématographic." The ideas were in the air, but no one saw further into them than Eliot.

The ambiguity of his attitude towards the music hall experience largely accounts for the originality of the form he drew out of it. He was greatly struck by the possibilities it offered for a ritualistic drama: "Little Tich, George Robey, Nellie Wallace, Marie Lloyd . . . provide fragments of a possible English myth. They effect the Comic Purgation."[9] These possibil-ities are no doubt uppermost in his mind when he emphasises what might to most people seem the quality least characteristic of music hall, the "pure and defiled detachment" which he found in performers of the supreme class. It sometimes seems that Eliot was attending the Islington Empire with a cold eye, seeing in the grotesqueness of some of the turns an approxi-mation to that ideal, inhuman drama of masked beings which visited his imagination as it did that of Yeats.

Yet if we see for ourselves, even in the imperfect record of early film, a performance by one of Eliot's favourite artists, Little Tich, it becomes ap-parent that in stressing the detachment and impersonality of the great per-formers Eliot was making a profoundly imaginative judgement. It is easy enough now, after *Waiting for Godot* and *The Caretaker*, to see how the figure of Little Tich, a solitary, inscrutable dwarf, patiently manipulating his Brobdingnagian boots, was pointing the way for the modern theatre. But in the 1920s it took an Eliot to see it, to recognise in Little Tich the qualities he found in Massine, of whom he said, "Massine, the most com-pletely inhuman, impersonal, abstract, belongs to the future stage."[10]

Yet his awareness of the impersonal quality in the art of music hall did not prevent him from responding to its human warmth, as his loving essay in the first number of the *Criterion* on the occasion of Marie Lloyd's death shows very clearly. He admired the unselfconsciousness, the proletarian vi-tality and, above all, the sense of human solidarity felt in the close collabo-ration between artist and audience. Some of this "normal" human warmth comes through in *Sweeney Agonistes*, giving the fragments a quality which none of the later plays capture, even when Eliot is trying hard for it. The unsentimental, matter-of-fact relationship between Doris and Dusty projects a real sense of human closeness, a closing of the ranks against Pereira and the other menacing facts of their existence.

The special quality of the piece, however, springs from the skillful turning of elements derived from a warm, popular art to effects of isolation and disorientation. It is an exercise in black comedy whose success depends upon the sustaining of the popular note just long enough for the distortion to register. Heavily syncopated rhythms suggest sexual excitement passing into a state of hysteria and spiritual panic. The jovial nightmare song from Gilbert and Sullivan takes a sickening lurch into real nightmare, conveying in musical terms the experience Sweeney cannot find words for, the swallowing up of the known by an unknown world:

> You dreamt you waked up at seven o'clock and it's
>   foggy and it's damp and it's dawn and it's dark
> And you wait for a knock and the turning of a lock
>   for you know the hangman's waiting for you.
> And perhaps you're alive
> And perhaps you're dead
> Hoo ha ha
> Hoo ha ha
> Hoo
> Hoo
> Hoo

This is "physical" theatre, where the poetry combines with the actors' bodily movements to draw primitive responses from the audience. Eliot may have been encouraged in his experiment by seeing the performance of Yeats's *At the Hawk's Well*, in Lady Cunard's drawing-room, to which Ezra Pound had taken him in 1916. Although he later dismissed the *Plays for Dancers* as more decorative than dramatic, he was at the time of that performance struck by a modern quality in Yeats which he had not perceived before. It took an acute sense of theatrical possibilities to recognise this "modernity" in *At the Hawk's Well*, with its legendary hero, hawk goddess for heroine, and choral interludes from a group of musicians on the stage. But Eliot may well have had in mind Yeats's use of drum, gong and zither when, in 1924, he outlined to Arnold Bennett a project for a drama of modern life, "perhaps with certain things in it accentuated by drum beats."[11]

In *Sweeney Agonistes* he catches the drum beat in the verse: it plays upon the nerves, assaults the audience physically, suggesting meanings below the line which can only be apprehended in the beat. The play offers an experience of almost total alienation. The borrowings from music hall "turns" like the soft-shoe number, heighten the sense of isolation: as characters go into their routines, they convey the essential solitariness of the music-hall performer before he makes contact with his audience, an idea later to be taken up by John Osborne in *The Entertainer*. There is a sustained threat in the verse rhythms, balanced as they are, and as the Dankworth production well brought out, on the edge of a great jazz explosion, which power-fully suggests the emotional explosion to which the action must move. That this explosion was to take the form of murder, real or "acted out" is shown in early drafts of the play.[12] As the action stands, all the detail points to a slow moving together of Doris, the predestined victim, who has already turned up the coffin card, and Sweeney, the man obsessed with the thought of vio-lence: "Any man has to, needs to, wants to / Once in a lifetime, do a girl in."

A play about spiritual "lostness," expressed in the vocabulary of the jazz age, moving towards a symbolic act of violence, *Sweeney Agonistes*, even in its fragmentary state, was a very long step in a new theatrical direc-tion. That it remained unfinished because, as Hugh Kenner says,[13] "there was nowhere for it to go" has been disproved by the whole course of post-war theatre. Eliot's abandonment of the fragments may have been due to something in the subject-matter which he was not yet able to get under ar-tistic control, or it may have been, as C. H. Smith suggests, the result of his conversion and reception into the Church of England which followed shortly after the publication of the piece.

The effect of this change in his life on his dramatic writing was great and in some ways damaging. From *The Rock* onwards, much of his energy went into an effort to extend his range, so as to accommodate, within the drama of alienation natural to him, the opposite experience of communion. The strain involved in this attempt creates the "second voice," the voice of "myself addressing, even haranguing an audience," which dominates the choruses for *The Rock* and is strong in *Murder in the Cathedral*.

Religious influences may have been reinforced by the didactic drama of Auden and Isherwood, who, perhaps inspired by the printed version of *Sweeney Agonistes*, were pursuing the direction indicated in it during the years when *The Rock*, *Murder in the Cathedral* and *The Family Reunion* were being written. The Group Theatre who produced their plays were dedicated to the exploration of popular techniques; they envisaged a new drama, "analogous to modern musical comedy or the pre-medieval folk play," and in pursuit of this curious-sounding goal they explored the possi-bilities in dance, jazz effects and visual shock tactics such as masks.

Notes

1. T. S. Eliot, 'Poetry and Drama', in *PP* p. 79.

2. M. C. Bradbrook, *English Dramatic Form* (1965) p. 173.

3. C. H. Smith, *T. S. Eliot's Dramatic Theory and Practice* (1963) p. 214.

4. D. E. Jones, *The Plays of T. S. Eliot* (1960) p. 215. The most thoroughly documented account of the plays: an indispensable work of reference.

5. K. Tynan, *Tynan on Theatre* (Penguin, 1964). Kenneth Tynan's reviews, for in-stance, call attention to the stage effectiveness of the "chilly scenes," and suggest new ways of looking at the plays.

6. C. H. Smith, *Eliot's Dramatic Theory*, pp. ix, 179.

7. A recording of this production is available in "Homage to T. S. Eliot," produced by Vera Lindsay (E.M.I. Records). Reviews in the *Guardian* and *The Times*, 14 June 1965.

8. Grover Smith, *T. S. Eliot's Poetry and Plays: a study in sources and meaning* (1956) p. 118.

9. Cited in J. Isaacs, *An Assessment of Twentieth-Century Literature* (1951) p. 146.

10. T. S. Eliot, "Dramatis Personae," in *Criterion*, I (1923) iii 305.

11. The relevant passage from *The Journals of Arnold Bennett* is quoted in Jones, *Plays of Eliot*, p. 27.

12. A manuscript draft, reproduced in the programme of "Homage to T. S. Eliot," has stage direction for the entry of Mrs. Porter after the chorus "The Terrors of the Night"; a debate with Sweeney; her murder and, finally, the "Return of Mrs. Porter."

13. H. Kenner, *The Invisible Poet: T. S. Eliot* (1960) p. 186.

On Structure and *Sweeney Agonistes*

Charles Lloyd Holt*

Mr. Eliot's curious modesty leads him to describe the two scenes of *Sweeney Agonistes* as, respectively, the "Fragment of a Prologue" and the "Fragment of an Agon." Too many critics, unfortunately, have been content to let it go at that, to hurry apologetically through the "fragmentary super-fluities" of the opening scene in Doris Dorrance's flat to Sweeney's "broad-bottomed" appearance in the second scene and the subsequent thickenings of the plot.

I daresay this procedure proves adequate enough if (like Mr. T. H. Thompson in his essay "The Bloody Wood")[1] the critic is interested primarily in tracing the life and times of a man "who in younger days was perhaps a professional pugilist, mildly successful; who then grew older and retired to keep a pub."[2] Obviously, *Sweeney Agonistes* gives us another view of the animal who stood erect, watched Mrs. Porter wash her feet, and busied himself among the nightingales.

I suspect, however, that *Sweeney Agonistes* is more than an addendum to a character study. And to ignore the highly organized structure of the two very complex scenes is to obscure the ultimate meaning of what is perhaps one of the least fragmentary of modern one-act plays.

The title page of this "Aristophanic melodrama" provides us with several clues that open the way to a realization of the structural complexity of the play. In the first place, the title itself indicates not only the obvious comparison but takes us back through the Greek structure of *Samson Agonistes* to the biblical story of the man who was unable to sublimate, save in death, his appetite for women (Judges 13–16).

We read, for instance, that ". . . Samson went down to Timnath, and

*Reprinted, with permission, from *Modern Drama*, 10 (1967), 43–47.

saw a woman in Timnath of the daughters of the Philistines. And he came up, and told his father and mother, and said, I have seen a woman in Timnath of the daughters of the Philistines: now therefore get her for me to wife . . ." (14, i–ii); and that "then went Samson to Gaza, and saw there an harlot, and went in unto her. . . ." (16, i); and that Delilah ". . . made him sleep upon her knees; and she called for a man, and she caused him to shave off the seven locks of his head; and she began to afflict him, and his strength went from him . . ." (16, xix).

At the same time, however, Milton reminds us that "Samson . . . quit himself / like Samson, and heroically . . . finished / a life heroic, on his enemies fully revenged . . ." (11. 1709–1712). He nowhere suggests that Samson waked up at seven o'clock to the rhythms of W. S. Gilbert or to the hoo-ha's of a traditional fear.[3]

In a similar manner, the epigraph of the *Choephoroi* of Aeschylus presents another vital structure for comparison. "You don't see them . . . but I see them," Orestes screams, and we remember the Eumenides and the retribution they represent. We remember at the same time the KNOCK KNOCK KNOCK and the door that must be opened. With all this, however, we fail to recall that Orestes' action proceeded from a sense of honor and loyalty, from a realization of an ordered universe wherein good and evil each had its place: ". . . but he whose eye is judge of all things, the all-seeing Sun! let him behold my mother's damned deed, and let him stand . . . witness that justly I have sought and slain my mother" (11. 986–91).

Neither Samson nor Orestes appears — nor is either even mentioned by name — in *Sweeney Agonistes*. The myths of which they are representative, however, the one Hebraic and the other Greek, seem to function as over-souls to the action of the play. One of Eliot's notes to *The Waste Land* shows this method in operation in only a slightly different manner: "Tiresias," Eliot suggests, "although a mere spectator and not indeed a 'character,' is yet the most important personage in the poem, uniting all the rest."[4]

In much the same way, the figures of Samson and Orestes serve as frames of reference for the story of Sweeney. Like fixed spheres about a point (the one within the other) they circle *Sweeney Agonistes*, never intruding but always present.

Finally, the structure of the play seems to have foundation in the irony of the title-page epigraph from the writings of the 16th-century mystic, St. John of the Cross: ". . . the soul cannot be possessed of the divine union, until it has divested itself of the love of created beings." The irony exists in that although such a warning might well have reached the soul of a Samson or an Orestes, it can only be the epigraph — perhaps "epitaph" would be a better word — for Sweeney and his story.

I must turn to simile to describe what I believe to be the structure proper of *Sweeney Agonistes*. In the same way that a square piece of paper may be folded to produce a double thickness and be opened to produce a single thickness of twice the width, so may *Sweeney Agonistes* be read as a single-scene play of double thickness or a double-scene play of single thickness that is twice as long.

In other words, the two scenes are actually the same scene repeated in different ways; at the same time, however, the two scenes are so constructed that the plot may be opened up, as it were, to form a plot that is twice the length of the plot of either scene.

Eric Bentley, who has staged the show, asks, "Should a director indicate any sort of connection between the two fragments?"[5] It seems to me that the director has little or no choice in the matter, since the scenes — as I prefer to call them — are absolutely dependent each upon the other, and the second follows the first logically and inevitably. An examination of the "plot line," i.e., the double width, shows the basic coherence of the two scenes.

As the first scene (the Prologue) opens, Doris and Dusty, prostitutes, wait in Doris' flat — paid for by a Mr. Pereira — for the gentlemen friends who are to pay their respects and their money that evening. As they wait, Doris and Dusty, having commented definitively on Mr. Pereira's character, indulge in fortune-telling with a deck of playing cards. Eventually the "callers" arrive and, after a few preliminaries, everyone settles down to the business of lust. (The clever actor could build himself a pleasure-dome complete with the final line of the scene: "And he's promised to show us around.") For the sake of convention, the first scene ends here with convention's curtain or a tactful blackout.

The second scene (the Agon) opens some hours later. Sweeney has made his physical appearance, vaguely drunk, and, as the curtain rises, is sounding Doris on her views pertaining to birth, copulation, and death, with particular emphasis on copulation.

Because Sweeney is drunk or, perhaps, simply because Sweeney is Sweeney, Doris plays hard to get. Even after the songs of the gentlemen friends — songs carefully selected for their high aphrodisiac potential — Doris remains unmoved and claims that she is remarkably disinterested in life for two on a desert isle: "That's not life, that's no life / Why I'd just as soon be dead." Her choice of words gives Sweeney the opportunity for his famous pitch on to be or not to be and for his infamous story of a fellow who "once did a girl in." The KNOCK KNOCK KNOCK that ends the scene is, on this level of reading, the hand of some external force — a force that has come to listen attentively to the details of a murder and to claim the tax payable on such a luxury.

This "double width" of the plot — the literal reading of the play — seems clear enough and is consistent with the usual interpretation of *Sweeney Agonistes* as a play that shows the appearance of a spiritual reality in the ultimately unreal world of cheap slang, vulgar superstitions, and heightened sensuality.

This reading alone, however, tends to reduce the first scene to a simple background of multiple and comparatively unrelated details. It seems to me that the full impact of the play depends upon the evaluation of the Prologue as a dumb show for the Agon that follows, a reheasal that is at the same time the performance itself. "Time present and time past are both present in time future." What is, is to be; what is, has been.

There are at least three incidents that seem to indicate that the Prologue may be read as a pre-statement of the Agon, as a document of time fused within time, as a suggestion that the waste land of which Sweeney is a product is a cycle without movement.

At the beginning of the Prologue we are given Mr. Pereira: a) "he pays the rent," b) "he's no gentleman," c) "you can't trust him," and d) although "Sam's a nice boy . . . a funny fellow [who] could make you laugh," Mr. Pereira "won't do . . . we can't have Pereira." And so this gentleman with the foreign name, who exists only on the other end of a telephone, is characterized for the audience. Then the cards are brought out, and the following dialogue is enacted:

> DORIS.   . . . Oh guess what the first is.
> DUSTY.   First is. What is?
> DORIS.   The King of Clubs
> DUSTY.   That's Pereira
> DORIS.   It might be Sweeney
> DUSTY.   It's Pereira
> DORIS.   It might *just* as well be Sweeney.

The implication, I think, is plain enough. The parallelism of Sweeney and Pereira at this point makes obvious the fact that those character traits which were ascribed to Mr. Pereira are also Sweeney's. They are both Kings of Clubs. Neither is a gentleman nor to be trusted. Each is a symbol of sexuality. Sweeney is, in fact, Pereira or, at least, *a* Pereira. Notice how Sweeney's fierce proposition to Doris at the beginning of the second scene seems to introduce us to a Sweeney that we already know:

> I'll carry you off
> To a cannibal isle . . .
>   I'll
> Gobble you up. I'll be the cannibal.

A second incident in the Prologue that pre-states the action of the Agon is in the significant narrative to be followed in the reading of the "wicked pack of cards." Doris and Dusty make the following thoughtful evaluation as they flip through their pieces of cardboard:

The king of clubs (phallic symbol) — Mr. Pereira, Sweeney

The 4 of diamonds — money, a present, wearing apparel, a party

The 3 (of diamonds?) — news of an absent friend, Pereira (Sweeney!)

The queen of hearts — Mrs. Porter, Doris, Dusty (prostitutes)

The 6 (of hearts?) — a quarrel, an estrangement, separation of friends

The deuce of spades — a coffin

Sweeney (k of c) is among the guests who attend a party where money or presents (4 of d) are the only invitations necessary. He brings news (3 of d) of an absent friend. (Even though Dusty says when the card is turned up that the absent friend is Pereira, we remember that "it might *just* as well be Sweeney.") The absent friend, then, is Sweeney himself, who has been in seclusion for "a couple of months." Sweeney explains to Doris (q of h) that the man who'd been hiding out — and Doris says, "I know who" — had killed a woman (6 of h). Then there is the KNOCK KNOCK KNOCK at the door, and we know that the hangman's waiting" (2 of s). Notice that the knocking in the first scene follows the final use of the word "coffin"; and in the second scene it follows the reference to the hangman.

Such a reading as this of the fortune-telling incident tends to remind us when we come to the action of the second scene that all this business has gone on before.

In the same way, perhaps, the implied consummation of the lust affairs at the end of the Prologue seems to be the ironic pre-statement of the final consummation that waits for Sweeney beyond the KNOCK KNOCK KNOCK on the door at the end of the Agon. Whether a hangman, waiting to claim Sweeney's body, or St. John and Mr. Eliot, waiting to annotate Sweeney's soul, *someone* is waiting, and he has promised to show Sweeney around.

Notes

1. From *The London Mercury*, XXIX (January 1931), 233–239. The essay is included in *T. S. Eliot: A Selected Critique*, ed. Leonard Unger (New York, 1948), pp. 161–169.

2. T. S. Eliot described Sweeney in this manner to Nevill Coghill. Quoted in Eric Bentley's *From The Modern Repertoire*, Series One (Denver, 1949), p. 389.

3. Cf. Gilbert's "Headache" patter in *Iolanthe* and "Under the Bamboo Tree," an American popular song in the 1920's.

4. *Selected Poems 1925–1935* (New York, 1936), p. 94. *Sweeney Agonistes* also appears in this volume, pp. 135–154.

5. Bentley, op. cit., p. 391.

General

Sweeney, the Sties of the Irish, and
The Waste Land

Jonathan Morse*

For a poignant moment in "Sweeney Agonistes," the protagonist struggles with the fundamental incommunicability of knowledge. "I gotta use words when I talk to you," he protests; then, stoically facing the void at the heart of these words, he continues, "But if you understand or if you don't / That's nothing to me and nothing to you." J. Alfred Prufrock has the same problem: "It is impossible to say just what I mean!" But Prufrock's complaint fits into language in a different way from Sweeney's. Prufrock's distance from the world of experience is sartorial: the carefully dressed Prufrock yearns to sympathize, but cannot sympathize, with the lonely men in shirt-sleeves. The lonely men smoke pipes and lean out of windows: their manners place them in a different social class from Prufrock, at the far side of a chasm of incommunicability. The differences go beyond manners to physiology itself: the insignia of the lower classes which are displayed in "Preludes" (the smells of steak, at that time the cheapest meat you could buy; the beer, the dirty feet, the short square fingers stuffing pipes) are images of a bodily life fundamentally alien to consciousness. The poet's persona gazes on these images, early and late, with horrified fascination. "Sordid," he says in "Preludes" (III); "Eating and drinking. Dung and death," he says in "East Coker" (I). When a J. Alfred Prufrock utters such words, they are immediately understandable. We do not have to locate their context in the world, since we share it. But when Sweeney says, "Birth, and copulation, and death. / That's all the facts when you come to brass tacks," difficult ironies come into play. Suddenly the words become elliptical, hard to understand, almost a private code. We readers of poetry are at home in Prufrock's world; we are uneasy tourists in Sweeney's.

Which means that some homework in social history has to be done before we can read the Sweeney poems. The people in Sweeney's world, for example, are physically strange, and that strangeness has a value in the emotional economics of our poetic transaction. It will pay us to think of the degree to which, for example, the phrase "short square fingers stuffing

*This essay was written specifically for publication in this volume and is included here by permission of the author. © Jonathan Morse, 1984.

pipes" serves our class as a synecdoche for a complete image of a laborer, rich in connotations — say, the laborer described in Emerson's "Fate": "Let him value his hands and feet, he has but one pair. So he has but one future, and that is already predetermined in his lobes, and described in that little fatty face, pig-eye, and squat form." And when we move on to Sweeney's own words, we will discover that they serve an analogous social function. They have a poetic value which extends beyond the limits of the text and takes in the library in which the text is being read. This value has to do with the idea of Sweeney as a subject of contemplation. It can be expressed in sociological terms, but at its fundamental level it is psychological. The particular way in which it affects us is conditioned by a historical association between spoken language and body language, modified in this case by phrenology, physiognomy, the doctrine of racial superiority, and other nineteenth-century attempts to find a short solution to the mind-body problem. Since this positivist way of looking at people does originate in the nineteenth century, we need not be surprised to see its verbal traces running, virtually unchanged, from the first of Eliot's poems to the last. It is a social attitude but a ubiquitous one, and it is therefore not even present to consciousness until society has changed. When that happens we perceive its strangeness, and with that perception the literary history of its embodying texts begins.

Perhaps viewing history from this angle can help us understand why so much of the older social criticism of Eliot now seems shallow and trivial. Prejudice and class thinking are there to be criticized and defended in Eliot's writing, but discussion of these things has almost inevitably tended to shift our attention from the poems to the social consciousness of their readers — that is, from the history of words fixed in a text to the fluctuating human history surrounding the text. The two histories have been subject to related but different vicissitudes, and we have to be clear at all times about which history we are reading. One way to do that is to read the two histories at the locus where they meet: in the life of the poet. Considering that life, we may be able to say something like this:

Like most people, Eliot had prejudices. He grew up in a milieu — Harvard University in the early twentieth century — in which it was socially acceptable to speak one's prejudices aloud. He worked in another milieu — the London literary world dominated by Virginia Woolf — in which snobbery and exclusiveness were almost de rigueur. Under these circumstances, the prejudice observable in some of Eliot's lines is not historically interesting. And once we have decided that Eliot's poems are worth reading, the poet's human failings will have little literary interest either. The critics of the 1940s who deplored the anti-semitism of "Gerontion" and "Burbank with a Baedeker" were humanly right, no doubt, but most of their arguments only boil down to the fact that Eliot was a poet working at a bad time for the human race. Poets are more articulate than the rest of us, and one of the things they have always done is to tell us what we were thinking. If they wind up saying evil things, so much the worse for us.

To put the matter this way, though, is to make the poet nothing but the mouthpiece for his age. Some good poets, it is true, have seen themselves in precisely those editorial terms; that is why England has a poet laureate. But to read Eliot as a representative man is to overlook the obvious fact that he was an original, both as a revolutionary poetic technician and as a highly idiosyncratic social thinker. His social vision bears a significant epistemological similarity to his poetic technique: both the vision and the technique operated by reassembling and reconstituting fragments of previously articulated thought. (For how many other poets is an essay in history — I am thinking of "Tradition and the Individual Talent" — also a poetic manifesto?) This unity in Eliot's technique allows us to read Eliot fragment by fragment, more analytically than we read other poets, closer to the surface of the mosaic. To see where certain key words fit in is to see how their functions in a poem differ from their functions in the general lexicon from which the poem has been precipitated. And, seeing that, we will be seeing how and why the poem yields us our certainty that it is not an anonymous historical artifact but a subject in itself, a recombination of words with the power of reshaping history around it. We will be looking at the first signs of the poem's historical trace.

So I want to examine a few words from the Sweeney poems, demonstrate how they function in the vocabulary of social belief, and then make a generalization about those words which may apply to *The Waste Land*. The object will be to establish part of the uniqueness of the poems' textual history.

I

A man will not need to study history to find out what is best for his own culture. But alas! the culture of an Irishman is an enterprise to be undertaken with a sort of moral bog hoe.
                    — Henry David Thoreau, *Walden*, ch. 10

The key phrase is the Homeric epithet which begins "Sweeney among the Nightingales": "Apeneck Sweeney." Sweeney is not just a generalized animal with zebra stripes; his name identifies him as an Irishman, one of the monsters who shambled through the nightmares of literary America during the second and third quarters of the nineteenth century. Sweeney is physically and morally repulsive, but his repulsiveness is generic, not individual. In evoking this repulsiveness, the Sweeney poems are not so much elliptical as allusive.

One convenient source for recovering the significance of the allusion is the graphic art of Thomas Nast. Nast, the greatest American editorial cartoonist of the nineteenth century, owes his enduring reputation primarily to his menagerie of beastly caricatures: the Republican elephant, the Democratic donkey, the Tammany tiger, and the vultures of the Tweed Ring. The Nast Irishman, a squat, barrel-chested Celt dressed in boots and a leprechaun hat, is very much a part of this Aesopian tradition. He is usually carrying either a shillelagh, a rosary, a policeman's club, or a bottle; he is always pug-nosed, beetle-browed, and unshaven, with tiny, deep-set eyes and a wide, lipless mouth full of pointed teeth. He is, in short, an ape. And his moral nature is as menacing as his physical appearance: once admitted to the American body politic, he corrupts it. As an ordinary citizen in the streets, he riots (against Orangeman, against blacks, against Chinese, against the police); in office, he violates the sanctity of the ballot; in office or out, he is a tool of the priests who are attempting to destroy America's public schools.[1] In the plan of things, the caricature Irishman of the nineteenth century serves a cautionary function: he represents all that is less than human in humanity.

Generalized this way, Nast's Irishman shares a room in the heart of darkness with hundreds of other stereotypes. These stereotypes differ from one another in matters of costume and complexion, but the differences are only superficial. Under their clothing, the creatures whom we have selected for this purpose are all Calibans, fresh-and-blood realizations of our own words of horror and disgust. They body forth the id, and we think of them with the aid of images brought forth from our nightmares: metaphors of invasion and pollution.

The metaphors retain their psychological power as history changes around them; only the vehicles change from era to era. In Eliot's time the Irishman was immediately accessible as a vehicle, and Eliot used his Sweeney accordingly. (Warner Berthoff: "[T]he grounding of [Eliot's] thought in polite opinion of the '80s and '90s is always worth noting."[2]) But the metaphor itself is a general one, and Eliot himself was able to generalize it politically as well as poetically. Consider, for example, Eliot's lamentation, in a well-known passage near the beginning of *After Strange Gods*, over "the sordor of the half-dead mill towns of southern New Hampshire and Massachusetts." This decay of a native region ("I speak as a New Englander") is not just a matter of economics, or even of culture; the word *sordor*, its connotations and its etymology, bring the discussion to bear on the primitive psychology at the heart of our economic thinking. The economic decay of New England originates in an act of immorality: an opening of the body of the land to uncleanness. New England has glutted itself with filth, and its punishment has been sterility. The South, by contrast, is unpolluted and still fertile. ". . . I think that the chances for the re-establishment of a native culture are perhaps better here [in Virginia] than in New England. You are farther away from New York; you have been less industrialised and less invaded by foreign races; and you have a more opulent soil."[3]

What is at work here is something like an image of virgin motherhood — an image which originates less with Eliot than with his culture. We

The Ignorant Vote—Honors Are Easy.

December 9, 1876

Reprinted, with permission, from Morton Keller, The Art and Politics of Thomas Nast *(New York: Oxford University Press, 1968), plate 155.*

can trace it, if we wish, all the way back to *Oedipus Rex* and the beginnings of Christianity, but in a specifically New England document, chapter 9 of *Walden*, we can see it in the specific terms which Eliot was later to employ in the Sweeney poems: ". . . of all the characters I have known, perhaps Walden wears best, and best preserves its purity. Many men have been likened to it, but few deserve that honor. Though the woodchoppers have laid bare first this shore and then that, and the Irish have built their sties by it, and the railroad has infringed on its border, and the ice-men have skimmed it once, it is itself unchanged; all the change is in me." In a characteristic Transcendentalist maneuver, Thoreau has psychologized the landscape here, abolishing all distinctions between the phenomenal world and the universe brought into ideal being by metaphor. Everything at Walden becomes a metaphor of a spiritual maternity whose function is to help the utterer of physical words grow out of his body and into the wordless, disembodied illumination toward which the chapter titled "Higher Laws" yearns.[4] But metaphor takes on a different maternal function when it comes into contact with the uncleanness of the world beyond Walden.[5] There, metaphor must protect the psyche by isolating, derealizing, and turning the literal into the figurative. We need its help to make the phenomenal keep its distance. The Irishmen who lived on the far side of Walden Pond in Thoreau's time were laborers, not farmers; their sties were not occupied by swine but by human beings.

A technical objection arises at this point. Much of Thomas Nast's anti-Irish prejudice is simply an expression of anti-Catholicism — a quite conventional attitude among American liberals during the papacy of the reactionary Pius IX (1846–78), but not thereafter. Similarly, the worst of the anti-Irish sentiment in Thoreau's Massachusetts (as represented, for example, by the Know-Nothing party) was over by the end of the Civil War. In terms of its political content, therefore, Nast's and Thoreau's prejudice was obsolete long before Eliot was born.[6] But the phrase "apeneck Sweeney" demonstrates that Nast's Irishman remains psychologically alive for Eliot, as part of a symbol system — the same system that led another Harvard poet, William Vaughn Moody, to image *his* id in 1901 as "an old chimpanzee with an Irish chin" ("The Menagerie," line 134). Precisely how this symbol system worked for Eliot is in question in this article, but at its fundamental level it has only one psychic task to perform for anyone: the task of rationalizing the irruption of the id into consciousness. In the case of the Sweeney poems, history has shown us a little of how the symbol of the Irishman works toward that end.

II

We are approaching the terrain which Eliot was later (at the end of "The Dry Salvages") to refer to as "significant soil": a soil bearing signs, a land made out of words, not out of the decay of our dumb bodies. One more example will bring us closer to *The Waste Land*. Grishkin in "Whispers of Immortality" is specifically a Russian because Russians, for the Eliot who was reading Hermann Hesse in the early 1920s, represented life lived on the boundary where exoticism shades into savagery. Like Sweeney, Grishkin expresses a state of mind shared by the members of a readership. She is a psychic allusion.

Consider the way a French audience would read Gautier's "Carmen," the model for Eliot's nice Grishkin. This poem was first published in 1861, but its antecedents in exoticism are of course much older. France has regarded Spain since at least the days of Louis XIV as a wild, seductive cousin, Latin in spirit but also mysteriously Moorish, and Gautier takes the history of his Carmen farther back still:

> Elle a, dans sa laideur piquante,
> Un grain de sel de cette mer
> D'où jaillit, nue et provocante,
> L'âcre Vénus du gouffre amer.

And the context for this exoticism has been specifically literary. When Mozart or Scarlatti or Boccherini or Rimsky-Korsakov borrows Spanish harmonies and rhythms, we think of exercises in musicology; when a French composer (Bizet, Debussy, Chabrier, Ravel) sets down Spanish notes in the same way, we think of dark eyes behind the shutters and daggers in the moonlight. The difference in our perception has to do with certain texts written by Beaumarchais and Hugo and Merimée — texts which have established permanent connotations of voluptuousness and mystery around the French word *Espagne*. For the original audience of "Whispers of Immortality," the word "Russian" would have generated an analogous but more sinister *frisson*. We can instance four texts from *The Criterion* for evidence.

The first is the note to lines 367–77 of *The Waste Land*, a quotation from Hermann Hesse's *Blick ins Chaos* which may be translated, "Half of Europe, or at least half of eastern Europe, is now on the road to chaos. As it moves, drunk with a holy madness, to the brink of the abyss, it sings, sings songs like drunken hymns as Dmitri Karamazov sang. The ordinary man laughs indignantly at these songs; the holy man and the prophet hear them with tears." This quotation is probably the only part of *Blick ins Chaos* with which American readers of Eliot are likely to be familiar; Hesse's 48-page pamphlet is scarce in the United States, only two libraries in the OCLC system showing holdings. It is worth searching out, however, if only for a connection to Eliot which may be inferred from its Swiss title page. The first edition of *Blick ins Chaos* (Bern: Seldwyla) was published in 1920; at least 7,000 copies of the book were in print by 1922;[7] and it seems at least possible that Eliot encountered Hesse's ideas at Dr. Vittoz's sanatorium in Lausanne, where he assembled *The Waste Land* during the fall of 1921.

At any rate, the three essays which comprise *Blick ins Chaos* have at least one other connection with *The Waste Land*. Eliot's German quotation comes from the end of the first essay, "Die Brüder Karamasoff oder der Untergang Europas: Einfälle bei der Lektüre Dostojewskis." The substance of the third essay, "Gespräch über die Neutöner," appears in translation as "Recent German Poetry" in Vol. 1, No. 1 of the *Criterion*, just 25 pages after the end of *The Waste Land*. If we ever misread Hesse during the 1960s, this essay will serve to remind us that Hesse was just as authoritarian as Eliot. Here Hesse echoes a theme which is central to Eliot's thought; the theme of the insignificance and even perniciousness of the individual who fails to acknowledge his subordinate place in his culture. After arguing that the two most important influences on recent German poetry have been psychoanalysis and the war, Hesse concludes (p. 93):

> The war will, sooner or later, bring home to those who have returned from it the lesson that nothing is done by violence and gunplay, that war and violence are attempts to solve complicated and delicate problems in far too savage, far too stupid, and far too brutal a fashion.
>
> And the new psychology, whose harbingers were Dostoievski and Nietzsche, and whose first architect is Freud, will teach these young men that the emancipation of the personality, the canonisation of the natural instincts, are only the first step on the way, and that this personal freedom is a poor thing and of no account in comparison with that highest of all freedoms of the individual: the freedom to regard oneself consciously and joyously as a part of humanity, and to serve it with liberated powers.

The "murmur of maternal lamentation" of *The Waste Land*, line 368, is therefore not merely the voice of Mother Russia lamenting the Bolshevik Revolution; it is the sound of culture itself ("Jerusalem Athens Alexandria") laid open to the "hooded hordes" of the newly liberated unconscious mind. And it is easy to demonstrate that the hooded hordes of *The Waste Land* are specifically Russian for the same psychological reason that Grishkin is: they are Sweeney updated and Europeanized. Our text will be one more article from the *Criterion*: "Defence of the West," by Henri Massis, trans. F. S. Flint (*New Criterion*, 4 [1926], 224–43, 476–93).

"*Défense de l'Occident*," the *Larousse du XXe Siècle* (1928 ff.) tells us s.v. "Massis," ". . . combat l'engouement pour l'Orient," combats infatuation with the Orient. The military metaphors — defense, combat — are strictly appropriate, for Massis's vision is one of a Darwinian struggle to the death:

> It is the soul of the West that the East wishes to attack, that soul, divided, uncertain of its principles, confusedly eager for spiritual liberation, and all the more ready to destroy itself, to allow itself to be broken up by Oriental anarchy, because it has of itself departed from its historical civilising order and its tradition. On the pretext of bringing us what we need, a certain kind of Asiaticism is disposing us to the final dispersal of the heritage of our culture and of all that which enables the man of the West still to keep himself upright on his feet. Personality, unity, stability, authority, continuity — these are the root-ideas of the West. We are asked to

break these to pieces for the sake of a doubtful Asiaticism in which all the forces of the human personality dissolve and return to nothingness. (p. 231)

That is, specifically, there is a deadly portent in the faseination with Oriental culture and the obsession with the *Untergang des Abendlandes* which can be seen in defeated Germany. This portent signifies that Germany is abandoning the West — an abandonment which will be irreversible because World War I has completed the historical disaster inaugurated by Martin Luther's *attentat*, and "The Greco-Latin culture is not a fundamental asset of civilisation for the German, since he has not shared its past to the point of becoming identified with it" (p. 237). Still farther east of the Rhine (pp. 237–38),

> The same phenomenon — in a more acute form in so far as its connection with the West was still more fortuitous and savage — may be observed in that Russia which, after two centuries of forced Europeanisation, is returning to its Asiatic destinies, and rousing itself and all the Asiatic races against the civilisation it endured only under compulsion and in a spirit of bitter resistance. The Marxian or Western elements which the Russian revolution offers to the gaze of those who remain on the surface of things, should not prevent us from perceiving what is fundamental in the Bolshevic upheaval: the end of the epoch of Peter the Great, which was captivated by Western liberalism, the end of the European epoch in Russia, which, with this evolution, is again turning its face towards the East.

A war has been carried to us on these two fronts — a "spiritual war that it ['the Russo-Bolshevist idea'] has declared on the human race. . . . Germanism, Slavism; it is at these common sources that all that is in revolt against the eternal order takes its strength" (p. 479). Grishkin is at one with Sir Ferdinand Klein of "Burbank with a Baedeker": both are enemies of the human, deadly precisely in that they are fascinating exotics.

In fact, deadliness is an indispensable part of their exoticism. A harmless Grishkin would be a solecism. ". . . I was prepared to find in Mr. Trotsky's book [*Problems of Life*] an exposition of a culture repellent to my own disposition," Eliot complains in 1925; "but I hoped that it would be distinct and interesting. A revolution staged on such a vast scale, amongst a picturesque, violent, and romantic people; involving such disorder, rapine, assassination, starvation, and plague should have something to show for the expense: a new culture horrible at the worst, but in any event fascinating. Such a cataclysm . . . is not justified by the dreary picture of Montessori schools, playing fields, plasticene, club-houses, communal kitchens, crèches, abstinence from swearing and alcohol, a population warmly clad (or soon to be warmly clad), and with its mind filled (or in the process of being filled) with nineteenth-century superstitions about Nature and her forces."[8]

Notice the difference here, however, between Massis's exoticism and Eliot's. For Massis, the mediating conceptuality between the writer's consciousness and his fear is metaphysical; for Eliot, it is aesthetic. And it is an aesthetic reaction that is expressed in the first person. It is less a formal idea, perhaps, than a rhetoric whose object is to express as many feelings as possible about the nature of menace. These feelings cover an astonishing emotional range, from horrified disgust to genial humor, but they are unified by a psychological intentionality which drives through diverse rhetorical strategies to a single emotional goal. In Eliot, politics and history subordinate themselves to psychology, just as they do in *Walden* and the most powerful of Thomas Nast's cartoons. We do not need to establish direct literary-historical connections between Eliot and these older texts, though the connections probably do exist; all we really need to know is that textualized states of mind have a decipherable social history. That history can help us read the animal images that constitute Grishkin and Sweeney. It is also involved in the textuality of *The Waste Land*.

III

For what dominates the psychic landscape of that poem, uniting all of the poem's many moods in itself, is a sense of nameless and unnameable dread. In the lesser poems, it has been possible to associate mental states with their external correlatives and label them with names. One kind of fear is associated with violation and called Sweeney; another is associated with a devouring sexuality and called Grishkin. The names serve to categorize and control; they limit the distressing things they describe to certain neighborhoods in the psyche. Insofar as there is a reader to understand the social allusion, there can be an assurance that Sweeney and Grishkin and the estaminet of Antwerp do not stand for any universality of experience. They are slums of the lyrical; they attract our shocked attention precisely because they are extraordinary. But in *The Waste Land* the decay of feeling is everywhere, undifferentiated. In "A Game of Chess," sterility drains the life from the enervated upper class and the exhausted lower class alike; in "Death by Water," Phlebas the Phoenician becomes a memento mori both for the unsaved and for the saved.[9] When Sweeney comes to Mrs. Porter, we need not send to know for whom the bell tolls.

So the Bradleyan isolation of the poem's characters and voices from one another (". . . my experience falls within my own circle, a circle closed on the outside; and, with all its elements alike, every sphere is opaque to the others which surround it" — note to line 412) is only half of the hell of *The Waste Land*. The other half is represented by the narrator's cry at the end of "The Burial of the Dead": "You! hypocrite lecteur! — mon semblable, — mon frère!" All through *The Waste Land* the boundaries separating soul from soul are deliquescing; Sweeney passes over London Bridge, flowing with the crowd of living dead, but he is now Everyman. Sweeney, whose friend keeps a corpse in a bathtub with a gallon of Lysol, and the narrator, whose friend has planted a corpse in his garden, are one.

If we could bring ourselves to believe that Eliot assembled *The Waste Land*, notes and all, with a conscious intention and a single thesis in mind, this coalescence of sensibility might help to resolve one of the poem's cardinal difficulties: the role of Tiresias as "the most important personage in the poem, uniting all the rest."[10] Tiresias, in this view, would be the poem's center of sensibility, presiding in himself over an agonized alternation between yearning and disgust. Lonely and dissociated, unable to think or feel in sympathy with any human being, he is suspended between regret and serenity by the thought of the two human types he unites in his own body: the hyacinth girl, say, and Sweeney. But given the sprawl and disorder of the manuscripts, this neat intentionalism is probably too simple to stand as a historically valid reading. It is more plausible to assume that the disunities we perceive in the poem really are there, simply because Eliot's feelings about his poem must have changed during the long course of its composition.[11] Nevertheless, *The Waste Land is* unified by the emotions evoked by its images, and those images are also present, as we have seen, in the Sweeney poems. The forms they take there will show us that for Eliot a bringing together of image and image, human feeling and human feeling, is an irreversible act whose consequences can be frightening. To a degree we all share this fear with Eliot; that is one reason we respond to lines like "The awful daring of a moment's surrender." But when we leave the vicarious world of our reading, our tendency is to deal with our fears simply by denying them a form. We categorize certain emotions as alien, then separate ourselves from them on our own side of Walden Pond. In *The Waste Land* Eliot chose the harder course. He looked at Sweeney in himself: not dismissively, but in an effort to see Sweeney as he was. The result was a poem whose personal horrors take on a universal relevance.

There are two specific reasons for this. The first is that we share with Eliot a social frame of reference within which the image of Sweeney can be seen in its full range of connotations. But beyond this ability to share an allusion within a restricted range of social history there lies the second reason: the image of Sweeney himself. He is one of the great id monsters of modern literature, and it seems possible that he will live on for as long as people have nightmares. In creating Sweeney, Eliot mobilized the energy of his prejudices and used it to force open the gate of horn. Behind that gate there lay the waste land: a forbidden territory to which a great poem now gives us access. On its terrain, Sweeney and J. Alfred Prufrock, the terror of energy and the terror of paralysis, fight and die and come back to life again, forever. We once thought that that struggle took place in a particular locale, in the terms of a particular social history, under banners marked with slogans of the day: Respect the Inner Check; Get in Touch with Your Feelings. After reading *The Waste Land*, we can realize that the struggle will always have to be fought once again. Art has given us that knowledge — art taking the shape of Sweeney.

Notes

1. Morton Keller, *The Art and Politics of Thomas Nast* (New York: Oxford University Press, 1968), offers a representative selection of Nast's cartoons.

2. *The Ferment of Realism: American Literature, 1884–1919* (1965; rpt. New York: Cambridge University Press, 1981), p. 10, n. 2.

3. *After Strange Gods: A Primer of Modern Heresy* (New York: Harcourt, Brace, 1934, pp. 16, 17.

4. See, for instance, the last paragraph of the chapter, in which an eponymous "John Farmer" hears in "the notes of [a] flute . . . out of a different sphere from that he worked in. . . . [a] voice [which] said to him, — Why do you stay here and live this mean moiling life, when a glorious existence is possible for you? Those same stars twinkle over other fields than these. — But how to come out of this condition and actually migrate thither? All that he could think of was to practise some new austerity, to let his mind descend into his body and redeem it, and treat himself with ever increasing respect." (*The Variorum Walden and "Civil Disobedience,"* ed. Walter Harding [New York: Washington Square Press, 1968], p. 169. My other citations of *Walden* are from this edition.)

5. In "Scatology and Eschatology: The Heroic Dimensions of Thoreau's Wordplay," *PMLA*, 89 (1974), 1043–64, Michael West discusses the creative value of Thoreau's anal imagery.

6. Shortly before Nast died, aged 62, in 1902, the journal for which he had done his most memorable work commented, "He belongs so much to the past that the impression has naturally spread that he is an old man" (Keller, p. 327).

7. The verso of the title page of the Reed College Library copy (third printing, 1922) reads "7. Tausend."

8. "A Commentary," *Criterion*, 3 (1925), 163.

9. And also, as Robert Langbaum points out in his comparison of "Death by Water" with "Dans le Restaurant," yet another metaphor of sexual failure ("New Modes of Characterization in *The Waste Land*," in *Eliot in His Time: Essays on the Occasion of the Fiftieth Anniversary of* The Waste Land, ed. A. Walton Litz [Princeton: Princeton University Press, 1973], pp. 113–14).

10. In *T. S. Eliot: The Poet and His Critics* (Chicago: American Library Association, 1982), pp. 96–103, Robert H. Canary discusses the discomfort that this note of Eliot's has caused the critics over the years.

11. Helen Gardner has made the point that Eliot "invented a form that allowed him to compose in the jets and spurts of inspiration that came naturally to him, and, like a worker in mosaic, to find a place in his pattern for lines and even passages that had been composed at very different times" ("*The Waste Land*: Paris 1922," in Litz, p. 92). If Eliot did work this way, the only compositional unity he could have achieved would appear to be psychological: a unity of affect.

The Symbolism of Sweeney in the
Works of T. S. Eliot
Nancy D. Hargrove*

For a period of nine years (1918–27), T. S. Eliot employed as one of his major symbols the figure of Sweeney. He appears in four early poems ("Sweeney Erect," "Mr. Eliot's Sunday Morning Service," "Sweeney among the Nightingales," all written in 1918–19 and published in *Ara Vos Prec* in 1920, and Section III of *The Waste Land*, written largely in 1921 and published in 1922) and in Eliot's first attempt at drama (*Sweeney Agonistes*, probably begun in 1923 or 1924 and published in 1926–27). After 1927 Eliot never again uses him in either his poetry or his drama. Yet perhaps because he is the only character, with the exception of the minor figures of Doris and Mrs. Porter, ever to appear in more than one of Eliot's works, he has been the subject of much critical attention. The interpretations of him are numerous and varied. He is most commonly described as the ordinary man, the modern man, the sensual man, or some combination of these. Often his vulgarity or his primitive, animalistic nature is stressed. While many critics suggest either explicitly or implicitly that he is a negative, unpleasant, and/ or disgusting figure, yet others assert that he evokes a more positive response. Headings, for example, says cautiously that Sweeney is "not wholly objectionable," that he "figure[s] engagingly" in several poems, and that he elicits sympathy from the reader.[1] Matthiessen, too, indicates that one has a "sympathetic feeling for [him]" in at least one poem and hypothesizes that Eliot himself had "a double feeling of . . . revulsion from vulgarity, and yet [a] shy attraction to the coarse earthiness of common life" represented by Sweeney.[2] David Ward goes so far as to call him an "amiable figure" and "a hero comparable with Agamemnon or Theseus, sharing something of the divine."[3]

These conflicting interpretations have come about, I think, for two very specific reasons beyond the normal variances expected from different readers. First, Sweeney is a complex symbol with multiple meanings, as is often the case in Eliot; some critics, however, see only one of these meanings, to the exclusion of others which are equally valid or significant. Second, the Sweeney of the dramatic piece is a substantially, though not a totally, different character from the Sweeney of the four poems, and even in the poems he has slightly differing functions as a symbol; thus, general definitions of his character or symbolism which do not take these differences into account are often limited or distorted. Accordingly, in the hopes of producing a more valid analysis of Sweeney and his symbolism, in this essay I propose to consider him in the larger context of his place in Eliot's early work as a whole, looking first at the Sweeney of the four poems and then at the Sweeney of *Sweeney Agonistes*.

*This essay was written specifically for publication in this volume and is included here by permission of the author. © Nancy D. Hargrove, 1984.

In the literature of Eliot's early career, from about 1910 to the mid-twenties, his foremost concern is to present a view of the modern world as sterile, meaningless, and chaotic. As he sees it, contemporary civilization, having rejected both human and divine love, is consequently physically, emotionally, morally, and spiritually barren, and no possibility of redemption seems to exist. Crass materialism has replaced spiritual values; bestial or indifferent sex has replaced passionate love. The early work portrays what Eliot in his 1923 *Dial* review of Joyce's *Ulysses* calls "the immense panorama of futility and anarchy which is contemporary history,"[4] and thus his "sense of his own age," like Blake's, reveals that "peculiar honesty, which, in a world too frightened to be honest, is peculiarly terrifying. It is an honesty against which the whole world conspires."[5]

Eliot employs two main symbols in communicating this terrifying vision of the modern age: urban settings and various characters. Both lower-class settings such as the backstreet slum scenes depicted in "Preludes" and in the opening passages of "The Love Song of J. Alfred Prufrock" and upper-class settings such as the elegantly furnished rooms of the Lady in "Portrait of a Lady," of Miss Helen Slingsby in "Aunt Helen," and of the anti-Cleopatra in *The Waste Land* function symbolically to convey the sterility and futility of the lives of their inhabitants.[6] Likewise, Eliot uses characters from all levels of the social scale to suggest the pervasiveness, the universality of this vacuity of modern human beings and their civilization. On the upper levels of society, Prufrock, the Lady, and Marie in *The Waste Land*, among others, lead trivial lives of quiet desperation, to greater or lesser degrees aware of the meaningless quality of their individual existences. The middle class, though not appearing often, is represented by such characters as the disillusioned narrator of "A Cooking Egg" and the businessman Mr. Eugenides. The lower levels of society, however, perhaps most forcefully suggest the sordidness, the meanness, and the emptiness of modern life. Women who are prostitutes or who are crudely sexual appear often — the women of "Rhapsody on a Windy Night" and of "Preludes," Grishkin, the epileptic, the lady in the Spanish cape, Rachel *née* Rabinovitch, Mrs. Porter, Doris, and Dusty. Other lower-class women are pathetic victims of poverty or seduction, such as the third Thames daughter, or are vulgar gossips, such as Lil's friend in Part II of *The Waste Land*. The lower-class men, though fewer in number, are equally sordid or pathetic — the "lonely men in shirt-sleeves, leaning out of windows" in "one-night cheap hotels,"[7] Gerontion,[8] Albert, and the young man carbuncular.

However, Sweeney is, of course, Eliot's major symbolic character drawn from the lower class. It is important to realize that what he symbolizes is only one part, though a very large part, of Eliot's negative portrayal of modern man in the works written through the mid-1920s; he is no more ✓ *the* symbol of modern man or of man in general than is, for example, J. Alfred Prufrock. These two, who represent the opposite extremes in social class, education, and personality, when looked at together with their "supporting" cast of characters, symbolize Eliot's comprehensive, and undeniably bleak, concept of modern humanity in the early works.[9]

What then precisely does Sweeney symbolize? We will consider first, and at some length, his role in the four poems. It seems to me that Eliot intended him to represent that element of humanity, and more specifically *modern* humanity, which is vulgar, physical, uneducated, and without human or spiritual values. Because of his physicality, he represents the crass materialism which Eliot so deplored in modern civilization. Because he is uneducated, he represents that waste of the mind, that lack of a sense of culture and tradition which Eliot found equally distressing. Finally, because he has no significant relationships with either human beings or with God, he represents the emotional and spiritual sterility which seems to have disturbed Eliot most deeply about modern man and which is the major concern of the early poetry.[10] Eliot's attitude (and the reader's) would seem then to be one of disgust and dismay, perhaps even hatred and contempt as suggested by Heath-Stubbs and Spender, but surely not sympathy as Matthiessen and others have argued.[11] And, although Sweeney may be a caricature, a grotesque exaggeration in cartoon form, he is not a comic character nor a joke to be laughed at. Eliot's treatment of him is deadly serious, for he represents grave flaws, as Eliot sees it, in the contemporary human being, flaws of such magnitude as to evoke horror rather than laughter.

Sweeney's symbolic meaning in the poems is perhaps best caught up in the parenthetical, and too often overlooked, quatrain of "Sweeney Erect":

> (The lengthened shadow of a man
>   Is history, said Emerson
> Who had not seen the silhouette
>   Of Sweeney straddled in the sun.)

Here Eliot refutes Emerson's contention that the meaning of history lies solely in human beings, clearly suggesting that those elements of man represented by Sweeney are too crude, insignificant, and appalling to give history any but the most deplorable meaning. Indeed, he implies that, had Emerson seen Sweeney, he would have changed his definition of history. Taking up Emerson's own image of the shadow of a man, Eliot describes the grotesque shadow of Sweeney "straddled in the sun"; the word "straddled," meaning the physical position of sitting or standing with legs wide apart in a kind of sprawl, conveys his vulgarity, his physicality, and his apathetic attitude. It is highly significant that in the closing passage of "Little Gidding," Eliot's last serious poem, the poet offers an alternate, and obviously preferable, definition to replace Emerson's: ". . . history is a pattern / Of timeless moments." Mankind alone, particularly since it includes figures such as Sweeney, is incapable of endowing history with real significance; according to Eliot, history is only given meaning through the intervention of the timeless (spiritual or supernatural forces, and specifically Christ) in time.

In the four poems, Eliot uses a number of devices to communicate the various facets of Sweeney's symbolism. First, the name "Sweeney" not only has a sound which is common, prosaic, unmusical, perhaps even vulgar, but also it evokes the word "swine" with its connotations of bestial and gross physicality, ugliness, dirtiness, and stupidity. In addition, the name refers to one of Eliot's possible sources for the character, Sweeney Todd, the fictional London barber who butchered his customers and put their remains into meat pies.[12] This element of the name thus suggests both the violent and the sordid. (The other main source, according to Conrad Aiken, was probably Steven O'Donnell, an Irishman in Boston who gave Eliot boxing lessons, again a lower-class figure suggesting the physical and the violent.)[13]

Second, Eliot describes in some detail Sweeney's body, his physique, to emphasize his fleshly qualities. In two poems, he is naked; in "Mr. Eliot's Sunday Morning Service" he is sitting or lying on his buttocks in a bathtub, while in "Sweeney Erect" he is standing naked before a sink, preparing to shave ("Sweeney addressed full length to shave / Broadbottomed, pink from nape to base"). Further, the largeness and heaviness of his body are stressed through comparisons to an ape and through words describing his anatomy such as "Broadbottomed," "ham," and "Apeneck."

His movements, activities (or "inactivities"), and physical positions are also indicative of his heavy physicality. His movements tend to be slow and lumbering, suggesting an apathetic, laconic, and shiftless attitude. In the descriptions of his movements, verbs are extremely important. Often they suggest that he is acted upon rather than instigating action; he tends to be passive rather than active. However, even when he is active, his actions require a minimal effort or are performed slowly. In "Sweeney among the Nightingales," he "spreads his knees / Letting his arms hang down to laugh," the verbs "spreads" and "hang down" implying slow, loose action and "letting" implying a lack of force or control. In "Mr. Eliot's Sunday Morning Service," he is reclining in a tub, shifting slowly from one side of his buttocks to the other. In "Sweeney Erect," he is asleep in bed when the morning acts upon him, "Morning stirs the hands and feet," although his subsequent movements (and perhaps those of the prostitute) are described as "Ris[ing] from the sheets in steam."

Very much like his movements are his activities, which tend to require a minimum of energy and to be trivial and mundane in nature. In "Sweeney Erect," he gets up and prepares to shave, the extent of his efforts being to wipe suds on his face and to test the razor on his leg. Like shaving, his bathing in "Mr. Eliot's Sunday Morning Service" is a mundane activity, and in "Sweeney among the Nightingales" he seems to be sitting at a table where he does nothing more than to laugh laconically. In *The Waste Land* passage in which he appears, Eliot skillfully suggests that Sweeney does not come (active) to Mrs. Porter but is *brought* (passive) to her: ". . . I hear / The sounds of horns and motors, which *shall bring* / Sweeney to Mrs. Porter in the spring" (italics mine).

Finally, Eliot effectively uses Sweeney's physical positions to suggest his vulgarity and fleshiness. Typically, his positions are relaxed or reclining (implying slovenliness or laziness), often with legs or knees spread apart (a posture considered impolite, crude, or sexually suggestive at the time these works were written). In "Sweeney Erect," he is "straddled in the sun," a position in which the legs are wide apart; in "Mr. Eliot's Sunday Morning Service," he wallows in the tub, most likely with knees raised and slightly spread apart; and in "Sweeney among the Nightingales" he "spreads his knees" and lets his arms hang down like an ape's.

While the descriptions of Sweeney's appearance and his actions suggest his sheer physicality as well as a sense of inertia, Eliot's use of varied types of imagery not only conveys these elements but also other revealing traits. Images of animals, of bodily parts, of disease, decay, or death, and of sterility run throughout the poems. The animals associated with Sweeney are symbols of man's regression, of his bestial nature. The dominant animal is, of course, the ape,[14] suggesting that man as represented by Sweeney has made little if any progress in terms of evolution. The title "Sweeney Erect" evokes "Pithecanthropus Erectus," the ape on its hind legs, and this allusion is reinforced by the comparison of his movements in arising from bed to those of an orangutan and by the description of his thick neck as "Apeneck." Other animals associated with him are the zebra, the giraffe, and the hog, all suggesting the dominance of the bestial in him.[15] In addition to those animals specifically compared to Sweeney, other animal comparisons and allusions fill the poems, an indication that the world in which he lives is as animalistic as he; these include the Raven, the Dog, the hornèd gate, the "silent vertebrate in brown," Rachel's paws, the nightingales ("Sweeney among the Nightingales"), the bees and caterpillars ("Mr. Eliot's Sunday Morning Service"), and the epileptic's "clawing at the pillow slip" ("Sweeney Erect").

The poems also contain numerous examples of one of Eliot's favorite devices, the use of bodily parts (rather than the whole) to suggest not only the physicality but also the fragmentation and dehumanization of modern man. Sweeney is referred to in terms of his "feet and hands," his broad bottom, his "nape" and "base," his face, his leg ("Sweeney Erect"), his hams ("Mr. Eliot's Sunday Morning Service"), and his neck, knees, arms, and jaw ("Sweeney among the Nightingales"). The same device is employed in descriptions of those with him, extending the symbolism again to the entire segment of society of which he is a part. In "Sweeney Erect," for example, the epileptic is described wholly through parts of her body; her head is "This withered root of knots of hair / Slitted below and gashed with eyes, / This oval O cropped out with teeth," and the description of her seizure refers to her thighs, knees, heel, hip, and sides. Even the brief sketch of Doris concentrates on a part of her body, her "broad feet," the word "broad" emphasizing a heavy or dull physicality. In the Sweeney segment of *The Waste Land*, Mrs. Porter and her daughter are also described in terms of their feet:

"They wash their feet in soda water." In "Sweeney among the Nightingales," this device seems mainly to suggest the dehumanization of the characters, their anonymity and lack of personality: Rachel's paws, the stockinged leg of the woman in the cape, the "heavy eyes" and "golden grin" of the silent vertebrate (in itself a reference to a part of the body, the spine, as well as to a class of animals).

References to disease, decay, and death reflect the climate of moral and spiritual corruption that characterizes Sweeney and his world; it is interesting that in this case the images do not apply directly to Sweeney but to the surroundings and the other characters. Spiritual corruption is symbolized in "Mr. Eliot's Sunday Morning Service" by the pimpled, inflamed faces of the young and by the reference to "enervate Origen," who castrated himself at seventeen, while moral sickness or decay is conveyed by the epileptic's seizure, which dominates the action of "Sweeney Erect," and by the description of her "*withered* root of *knots* of hair" (italics mine). Decay, filth, and desecration are suggested in "Sweeney among the Nightingales" by the reference to Sweeney as "maculate giraffe" and by the image with which the poem closes, as the nightingales "let their liquid siftings fall / To stain the stiff dishonoured shroud." A death-like atmosphere broods over the setting of that poem, communicated by references to "Death and the Raven," to the gloom of an approaching storm ("the stormy moon," "Gloomy Orion," "veiled"), to Rachel's "murderous paws," and, of course, to the violent death by stabbing of Agamemnon.

Finally, several images of sterility serve to characterize Sweeney's world and its inhabitants. The best examples are found in "Mr. Eliot's Sunday Morning Service" where Eliot employs two animal images and one human image of sterility to suggest spiritual barrenness. The first occurs in the epigraph, in which the servant in *The Jew of Malta* describes two friars as caterpillars. Not only are caterpillars small and low forms of animal life, but they may technically be considered as sterile in that, being the larval stage of the developing butterfly or moth, they cannot reproduce their own kind. The second image is the worker bees, which are sexless and incapable of reproduction. Both these creatures are used to symbolize the sterility of the clergy and the learned theologians of the Church. The human image is that of Origen, an early theologian who produced voluminous works and who castrated himself; thus, he was literally sterile and was also responsible for "overfertilizing" the Word of God, thereby ironically sterilizing its meaning. Other images of sterility can be found in the description of the epileptic's mouth as an "oval O" in "Sweeney Erect" and in the "oranges / Bananas figs and hothouse grapes" of "Sweeney among the Nightingales." The latter is an example of an earlier symbol of fertility which has become sterile and its meanings reversed in the modern world; it might thus be called a "double negative" of sterility.

In addition to the imagery, Eliot also uses the technique of ironic contrast, one of his most consistent devices in the early poetry, to emphasize the pettiness and vacuity of the present world by juxtaposition with an earlier, more significant civilization, usually that of ancient Greece. However, Matthiessen's comments have since 1935 suggested that critics who see such a contrast convict Eliot as well as themselves of the charge of being simple-minded and shallow: "In Eliot's earlier work . . . it at first looked as though he was so absorbed in the splendours of the past that he was capable of expressing *only* the violent contrast between its remembered beauty and the actual dreary ugliness of contemporary existence. . . . But on closer examination it appears that . . . he is not *confining* himself to voicing anything *so essentially limited and shallow* as the inferiority of the present to the past" (italics mine).[16] Yet, as Elizabeth Drew (one critic among others who has refused to be intimidated by those remarks) perceptively points out, Eliot seems to be making precisely that type of contrast and with a great deal of depth and complexity: ". . . all the finest poems in the 1920s volume are concerned with the dramatic opposition of the world of today to the sources of vitality and order from which it is now cut off and of which it has the most urgent need. . . . The present, indeed, is uniformly stale and unsavoury . . . but interwoven with it is the continuous reminder of times when it was not so, and of works of the creative imagination in art and thought which have embodied a different reality and pictured a different vision."[17] Sweeney and his world seem incapable of meaningful action or relationships and clearly lack the possibility of rebirth, metamorphosis, or redemption, conditions made even bleaker by the painful contrast with the past.

In three of the four poems, Sweeney or his civilization is contrasted ironically to characters or situations from Greek mythology. In "Sweeney Erect," his emotional abandonment of the epileptic during her seizure is similar to Theseus' abandonment of Ariadne on the island of Naxos, but in every other way he is unlike the great hero of Attic legend, renowned for his accomplishment of spectacular feats requiring courage and prowess. Similarly, while he shares the bestial nature of the Cyclops Polyphemus, he lacks the power and ferocity of that terrifying giant. In contrast to these two, Sweeney, his actions, and his world are small and petty. Certainly included in the ironic contrast is his bed-partner, the epileptic prostitute, who is no fertility goddess, as was Ariadne, and lacks the innocence and loveliness of both Ariadne and Nausicaa. Even the settings are juxtaposed, a dramatic wind-swept shore on a Grecian island on the one hand and a seedy boarding house on the other. In "Sweeney among the Nightingales," although it has generally been assumed that Sweeney himself is being contrasted (or compared) to Agamemnon, with much critical debate about whether Agamemnon was a "good" or a "bad" person and whether Sweeney is as heroic or as unheroic as the Greek king, I would argue that it is the *world* of Sweeney which is contrasted to the *world* of Agamemnon. While the actions and characters in the Agamemnon story are of great magnitude, evoke horror or awe, and exist in a moral framework where crimes are punished, those in "Sweeney among the Nightingales" are trivial, insignificant, and ambiguous, evoking curiosity at most and existing in an amoral framework. Finally, in *The Waste Land* passage, an ironic contrast is set up between Sweeney, the vulgar customer of a prostitute, and Actaeon, the young hunter who stumbled innocently upon Diana, the goddess of chastity, in her bath. Mrs. Porter is, of course, hardly a model of chastity and her soaking her feet in soda water is a debased version of Diana's bathing.

Eliot also makes skillful use of both Sweeney's companions and his surroundings to reinforce the various elements of his symbolism. In all the poems except "Mr. Eliot's Sunday Morning Service," where Sweeney is alone, he is in the company of prostitutes: the epileptic (and perhaps the other women) in "Sweeney Erect," the woman in the Spanish cape and Rachel in "Sweeney among the Nightingales" (*nightingales* being a slang term for prostitutes), and Mrs. Porter and her daughter in *The Waste Land*. These female companions, like Sweeney, are lower class, vulgar, sexual, and apparently without any redeeming qualities. His only male companions are the anonymous and impersonal men in "Sweeney among the Nightingales"—the waiter, the host, and the "silent vertebrate in brown" who never speaks and soon leaves the room. The sex and identity of the "someone indistinct" with whom the host talks are never divulged. Many of these characters are nameless, suggesting a lack of personality, and there is little communication among them, conveying man's essential isolation as well as the indifference towards others so common in modern urban society; clearly, Sweeney's relationships with these faceless, fragmented people are transient, shallow, and without significance.

The urban settings are likewise seedy, vulgar, or trivial: "Sweeney Erect" takes place in a bedroom of either a rooming house or a brothel, "Sweeney among the Nightingales" in what is apparently a low-class dive or nightclub, the Sweeney portion of "Mr. Eliot's Sunday Morning Service" in a bathroom, and that of *The Waste Land* at Mrs. Porter's brothel.

A last, but extremely important, aspect of Eliot's treatment of Sweeney in the poems is that he is portrayed entirely from the outside by an objective, unidentified narrator who describes only his appearance and his actions. The reader is effectively distanced from him and knows virtually nothing of his thoughts, feelings, or motives. The closest one ever comes to receiving a glimpse of the internal Sweeney is in "Sweeney Erect," where the narrator's remark that he "knows the female temperament" conveys his chauvinistic, superior, and entirely unsympathetic attitude toward the epileptic. Further, as far as the reader can tell, Sweeney is totally unaware of the sterile quality of his life and his world.

Thus the Sweeney of the four poems is a complex symbol reflecting some of the most deplorable aspects of modern man and his world. A close reading of the poems will reveal that Eliot makes brilliant use of Sweeney, emphasizing a different facet of his symbolism in each.

In "Sweeney Erect," the title character symbolizes the degradation of the human capacity for love, on the sexual level as well as on the level of compassion and caring. Indeed, the poem focuses on the callous indifference of Sweeney's response to the epileptic's seizure more than on their sordid sexual relationship, although the degeneration of romantic love into loveless and bestial copulation is clearly an issue.

The poem's title has a triple meaning. On the surface level, it simply states Sweeney's physical position: he is standing before a sink preparing to shave. On a deeper level, it suggests his animalistic nature by the implied comparison to an ape standing on its hind legs. And, of course, its sexual implications evoke the meaningless copulation of Sweeney and the epileptic. The epigraph sets up the situation of abandonment which is the central action of the poem. In Beaumont and Fletcher's *The Maid's Tragedy*, Aspatia, who has been abandoned by her lover Amintor and is mourning her plight, criticizes a tapestry depicting the abandonment of Ariadne woven by one of her women; it is, she says, an inadequate portrayal of Ariadne's grief: "These colors are not dull and pale enough / To show a soul so full of misery / As this sad lady's was." She then tells her woman to use her as the model for Ariadne:

> Do it again by me, the lost Aspatia . . .
> Suppose I stand upon the sea breach now,
> Mine arms thus, and mine hair blown with the wind,
> Wild as that desert, and let all about me
> Tell that I am forsaken. Do my face . . .
> Thus, thus, Antiphila: strive to make me look
> Like Sorrow's monument; and the trees about me,
> Let them be dry and leafless; let the rocks
> Groan with continual surges; and behind me
> Make all a desolation. Look, look, wenches,
> A miserable life of this poor picture.[18]

The quotation leads directly into the first two stanzas of the poem, where a first-person narrator, who remains anonymous and impersonal, orders a dramatic painting of the classical scene of abandonment: "Paint me a cavernous waste shore / Cast in the unstilled Cyclades. . . ." Described in elevated and stirring diction ("cavernous," "cast," "unstilled," "anfractuous," "insurgent," "gales," "perjured"), the Greek setting is wildly desolate and spectacular as Theseus' ship sails away from the grief-stricken Ariadne.[19]

Having evoked two dramatic situations of abandonment from past literature, the narrator describes, in less elegant diction, a sordid contemporary situation of emotional, rather than physical, abandonment, with stanzas 3–8 focusing on the epileptic's seizure and Sweeney's indifference and stanzas 9–11 on the reactions of the ladies, Mrs. Turner, and Doris. While there are clearly parallels in the situations (a man deserts a woman), the emphasis falls on the differences. Chief among them are the settings, a "cavernous waste shore" in the Cyclades as opposed to a cheap rooming house (or perhaps a brothel), and the characters. Aspatia and Ariadne, lovely, innocent, and of the nobility (Ariadne later became the wife of Dionysus and goddess of fertility and the spring), are set against the lower class epileptic prostitute who is clearly unattractive. Her hair ("This withered root of knots of hair") is juxtaposed to Ariadne's wind-blown hair, and the details of her description imply her decay ("withered"), her sterility ("oval O"), her animalism ("clawing"), and her physicality (lines 13–18 each end with a part of her body). Even the verbs used to describe her face ("slitted," "gashed," "cropped out") convey brutality and ugliness. Although Sweeney is like Amintor and Theseus in abandoning a woman, he is quite unlike them otherwise. Amintor is "a noble gentleman" known for his honor and valor, who is forced by the king to abandon Aspatia, and Theseus is one of the great heroes of Greek mythology, renowned for his daring and courage. Both had promised to marry the women they abandoned, as opposed to Sweeney, whose one-night stand involves no commitment whatsoever.

In stanza 3, the narrator tells of the awakening of Sweeney and the prostitute, who are described in terms of their "feet and hands." In a parenthetical line, they are called "Nausicaa and Polypheme," two characters from *The Odyssey* who have no relationship in that work. Nausicaa, the innocent but spirited young princess who helps Odysseus, is clearly meant as a contrast to the epileptic. However, Polyphemus, the violent Cyclops, is like Sweeney in his crudity, size, and uncivilized nature, though he far surpasses his modern counterpart in degree. The lines "Gesture of orangoutang / Rises from the sheets in steam" seem to describe the ape-like Sweeney's getting out of bed,[20] the phrase "in steam" suggesting the heat of recent sexual activity and / or the sweat resulting from such activity, with overtones of a steamy jungle in the background.

Stanzas 4 and 5 describe first the head and face of the woman (ll. 13–15) and then, in minute detail, her epileptic seizure (ll. 16–20). While her convulsive movements evoke horror and even pity from the reader, they evoke only annoyance from Sweeney, who callously dismisses her actions as the result of "the female temperament." Stanzas 6 and 8 focus entirely on his selfishness and lack of compassion as he stands naked before the sink, directing all his efforts ("addressed") to the mundane task of shaving, waiting impatiently for the epileptic's shriek of agony to cease so that he will not cut himself.

The parenthetical stanza 7 is the most important in the poem and is central to any attempt to understand Sweeney's symbolism in the poems as a whole. Abruptly inserted in the midst of the description of him, naked, heavy, completely indifferent to the suffering of a human being with whom he has recently had sex, it catches up the worst of humanity. As mentioned earlier, the stanza refutes Emerson's definition of history, which must of necessity include such scum as Sweeney.

In the last three stanzas, the focus shifts from Sweeney's reactions (or lack of them) to those of the women who are nearby, women corresponding perhaps to Aspatia's ladies. Their three different responses suggest the shallowness, the selfishness, and the materialism of modern society. The phrase "ladies of the corridor" can be interpreted in two ways, with "of the corridor" meaning either that they live (or work) in rooms along the corridor or that they have gathered in the corridor outside Sweeney's room upon hearing the screams of the prostitute. If they are prostitutes and the setting is a brothel, the term *ladies* is used ironically; however, it seems unlikely that prostitutes would feel "disgraced" nor would they "Call witness to their principles / And deprecate the lack of taste." On the other hand, they could well be boarders in a rooming house, who might actually feel or pretend to feel shocked at illicit sex. At any rate, they are concerned, not with the epileptic's condition, but with their own reputations and with the maintenance of decorum. Mrs. Turner, who apparently is the owner of the boarding house (or perhaps the madam of the brothel), is equally lacking in compassion and is worried solely about the reputation of her establishment. Only Doris, who has come directly from the bathroom, tries to help the epileptic, bringing smelling salts and a glass of brandy. Yet, as several critics have noted, these are physical aids for a physical ailment, while the more serious emotional ailment of Sweeney's world goes unrecognized and thus untreated. Although the moral and spiritual weaknesses of that world hover around the edges of the poem, its primary focus is on the absence of emotional commitment and concern among modern human beings.

In "Mr. Eliot's Sunday Morning Service" Eliot criticizes, in a biting satirical manner, the corruption of the Church, attacking both the present-day clergy (the "sapient sutlers," the "sable presbyters") and the learned theologians of the past (Origen, the "masters of the subtle schools"), whose verbosity and excessive erudition are reflected in the poem's elevated diction ("Polyphiloprogenitive," "sapient," "Superfetation," "enervate," "gesso," "pustular," "piaculative," "staminate," "pistilate," "epicene," "polymath"). These two groups are compared and contrasted to worker bees; they are similar in that they are spiritually sterile, as the bees are sexually sterile, but they are different in that, while the bees do fertilize the flowers as they go from part to part, these representatives of the church are ineffective in carrying the Word of God to humanity and thus "fertilizing" it spiritually. Although the role Sweeney plays in this poem is small (he appears in only 2 lines out of 32), it is significant, suggesting that the Church has no meaning, no power, no influence in the lives of modern people such as Sweeney, who on Sunday morning ministers to his *physical* being, taking a bath rather than going to church.

Eliot's use of abstract and unfamiliar words, of obscure allusions, and of a complex structure produces in the poem the same ambiguous, dry, and sterile quality that characterizes the modern Church. Perhaps the risk he has taken in making his poem remote and unappealing is too great, for it is elusive and difficult even with close and careful analysis. Its structure, dictated by the mind of its highly intelligent narrator, is extremely complex and shifts quickly and abruptly from subject to subject.

The epigraph sets the satirical tone as well as introducing one of the objects of satire; in *The Jew of Malta*, Barabas and his servant ridicule the lust and materialism of the clergy, who are supposed to be devoted to chastity and poverty; when two friars approach, the servant describes them to his master as "two religious caterpillars," suggesting their lowness and their spiritual sterility (though, ironically, they are quite fertile sexually). The poem itself opens with a long and difficult word which not only establishes the erudite tone of the poem but also indicates one of its main points, the proliferation of corrupt clergy in the Church. In addition, it introduces the poem's major image pattern of sterility / fertility; while the corrupt clergy multiply at a staggering rate, they are, ironically, spiritually sterile.[21] They are characterized as "sutlers," those who follow an army to sell provisions, indicating the materialistic and self-seeking motives of these servants of God. As they drift (a word implying aimlessness) past the windows, the narrator contrasts them to the simplicity of the "Word of God," a reference both to Christ and to the Scripture.

In the second stanza, the narrator turns to a criticism of learned theologians with their erudite and voluminous exegeses of the Bible and of the meaning of Christ: "Superfetation of $\tau\grave{o}\ \ddot{\epsilon}\nu$." This superfetation eventually,[22] and logically, produced Origen, symbol of the ultimate sterility of such excessive "fertility." Literally sterile, the self-made eunuch wrote over 6,000 works of exegesis, many of which were devoted to the opening words of the book of John.

Stanzas 3 and 4 present a contrast to the corruption of both the clergy and the theologians in the simple description of a fresco of Christ being baptized.[23] In the fresco, although the world is a barren waste land ("The wilderness is cracked and browned"), Christ is portrayed at its center, associated with light ("shine") and life ("the water pale and thin") and endowing it with spiritual significance. That He is both divine and human is suggested by His "nimbus" and His "feet," while His purity is conveyed by "unoffending." Above the scene are God and the Holy Spirit, placing the world in a secure and ordered framework. (Aeolus has a similar function in the classical painting described in "Sweeney Erect.") The modern world, in contrast, seems to have no supernatural figure above.

In stanza 6, the narrator returns to the corruption of the contemporary Church as the black-robed priests arrive to hear confession (or perhaps to take up the offering) from those who will buy their expiation:

> The sable presbyters approach
> The avenue of penitence;
> The young are red and pustular
> Clutching piaculative pence.

The word "sable" may mean, in addition to "black," that the priests are somber or that their vestments are decorated with expensive fur. The physicality and materialism of the youth who have come to purchase forgiveness are stressed through their red, pimply faces (suggesting lust and / or infection) and through the coins they clutch tightly in their fists.

Contrasted to them in stanza 7 are "the souls of the devout," apparently buried beneath the church floor. While the young burn brightly and intensely with lust for sex and material gain, the burning of spiritual devotion or zeal, it is suggested, is now to be found only in the dead where it is "invisible and dim." Although the seraphim on the ornamental gates near the confessionals stare down at modern young people, they seem powerless in the present age to perform their traditional functions as the fiery purifying angels of Jehovah.

After the description of the worker bees in stanza 8, a symbolic contrast to the spiritually sterile clergy and theologians who are unable to fulfill the "Blest office of the epicene" by bringing God and his Word to man, Sweeney appears abruptly and briefly. As indicated earlier, he functions symbolically as the modern sensual man without religious values or spiritual inclinations, whom the enervated Church is incapable of reaching. His physicality is stressed by the reference to his hams, a very heavy part of the body suggesting vulgarity in its sound as well as its meaning. That he is immersed in water sets up a contrast to the painting of the Baptized Christ, indicating how far modern man is from the spiritual rebirth the latter represents. Finally, his *shifting* from ham to ham and his *stirring* of the water recalls to the mind of the narrator Origen and the "masters of the subtle schools," whose multitudes of meaningless explications muddy the waters of thought and are far too "subtle" to communicate with the common mass of humanity. The poem is from beginning to end a scathing criticism of the modern Church for its failure to bring Christ's salvation to twentieth-century man, for whom the possibility of redemption thus ceases to exist.

"Sweeney among the Nightingales" is the most difficult of the works[24] in which Sweeney appears; it raises at least five major questions that must be answered in any analysis of its meaning. First, what is going on? Is there a plot to kill Sweeney or someone else? Is Sweeney actually killed? In fact, very little is going on except for trivial actions; Sweeney laughs, the woman in the cape tries to sit in his lap but falls to the floor, the man in brown "sprawls at the window-sill" first inside and then outside, a waiter brings in fruit, Rachel greedily eats the grapes, the host talks with an unidentified person, and the nightingales sing. There is no evidence that there is a plot to murder Sweeney or that he is killed, although many critics have followed Matthiessen's lead in assuming one or both of these to be true.[25] If there is a plot of some kind, whether seduction or murder, it is indicated only by the *suspicion* that the two women are "in league" and by the host's conversation "at the door apart" and seems to be directed at "the man with heavy eyes"; at any rate, it is not carried out within the poem.

Second, does Sweeney appear solely in the first three stanzas, or is he the same person as the man in brown? There is no evidence that they are one and the same, although Williamson and Davidson assume so in their interpretations of the poem.[26] In fact, the evidence indicates that they are two separate people. Since Sweeney has a name, it seems logical that Eliot would have continued to use it for the man, if he intended him to be Sweeney; by employing the phrase "the silent man in mocha brown," he clearly means another person.

Third, is there a relationship between Sweeney and Agamemnon? Are they meant to be compared or contrasted as individuals? I would suggest, as noted earlier, that there is a relationship between them, but not as individuals; indeed, since Sweeney is not killed and there is no evidence of a plot to murder him, there is no basis for such a comparison / contrast. Rather, it is the world of Sweeney and his companions that is juxtaposed to the world of Agamemnon and Greek myth in general.

Fourth, what is the meaning of the nightingales? They have two significant meanings in the poem. In Greek mythology they were associated with the violent acts of adultery, rape, and murder as well as with the positive actions of metamorphosis or rebirth. The Philomela myth embodies both of these meanings as Philomela was raped and had her tongue cut out by King Tereus, but was later transformed into a nightingale with a beautiful voice. The legend and the double meaning of the bird are alluded to in Aeschylus' *Agamemnon*, when Cassandra is compared to a nightingale:

> CHORUS: . . . Unwearied in her tuneless song;
> As the shrill nightingale
> Unburdens her distracted breast,
> Sobbing *Itun, Itun*, remembering all her wrong.
> CASSANDRA: Bitter was her ordeal;
> Yet by the kind gods' wish
> The lovely robe she wears
> Is feathered wings; and even
> The plaint she pours to heaven,
> Note answering note with tears,
> Rings sweet.[27]

Further, in Sophocles' *Oedipus at Colonus*, the nightingales in the grove of the Furies symbolize Oedipus' purgation as a result of suffering. While the poem's allusions to Agamemnon and to nightingales in general evoke both their positive and negative connotations, a second epigraph from the anonymous "Raigne of King Edward the Third," which appeared with the poem only in the *Ara Vos Prec* volume, emphasizes the latter: "Why should I speak of the nightingale? The nightingale sings of adulterous wrong." In addition to the connotations from Greek mythology, the word "nightingales" was at the time of the poem's composition a slang term for prostitutes, so that the title can mean Sweeney among the prostitutes as well as among singing birds. In the poem, the nightingales symbolize on the one hand the corruption and degradation that do exist in the world of Sweeney and on the other the possibility of regeneration, which does not.

Fifth, what is the poem about thematically? Is it about death, or the degradation of love and sex, or the triviality and futility of modern civilization? Although oblique references to death evoke an ominous atmosphere,[28] no death occurs in the poem; in fact, the characters seem incapable of such an act. And, although the women are prostitutes, there is no sexual activity other than the unsuccessful attempt of the woman in the cape to sit on Sweeney's knees. The poem does, however, portray in some detail the vacuity of contemporary life. The characters lead a death-like existence, in which their actions are largely laconic (Sweeney spreads his knees, the lady yawns, the silent man gapes, has tired eyes, and shows fatigue) or trivial and mundane (the lady overturns a coffee cup and pulls up a stocking, the waiter brings in fruit). Rachel, the most active character, only attacks grapes.

Eliot's content and technique in this poem reflect those of surrealism, a movement just underway in Europe at the time, and anticipate those of Theatre of the Absurd. As in those works, in order to reflect a world without order, meaning, or vitality, he uses a minimum of plot, actions that lack coherence, characters without personality or significance, and a nightmarish, obscure setting. The poem seems to create in words the same type of world as that depicted in George Grosz's surrealist painting *Beauty, I Shall Praise Thee* (1920) in its nightclub setting, its ugly characters who seem isolated and without life, and its dark colors.

The poem can be divided into four parts. The first stanza describes Sweeney in animal terms, with an emphasis on the feeling of inertia, triviality, and disorder. Although he laughs, we do not know why. Part two (11. 5-10) evokes the ominous and brooding atmosphere which characterizes this sterile world. As in a nightmare, the exact location is dark and uncertain; the allusion to the River Plate, which runs between Uruguay and Argentina, may suggest a South American setting. It seems to be night, with a storm approaching. References to images of fertility which are hidden or diminished in this world convey its sterility; Orion and the Dog Star, both of which were associated with the season of fertility in the ancient world, are "veiled," and the seas, traditional symbol of life, are hushed and shrunken. Even the verbs *slide* and *drift* suggest the aimless quality of life. The line "And Sweeney guards the hornèd gate" has several possible meanings. If the gate refers to the gate of horn through which true dreams pass, then Sweeney, as materialistic and sterile modern man, guards it in the sense of blocking it and preventing true dreams from entering his world. If the hornèd gate refers either to animalism or to lechery, then Sweeney is its guard in the manner of Dante's guardians of various portions of the Inferno; that is, he is its perfect representative.

The third, and longest, part of the poem describes the trivial actions of Sweeney's companions, who are silent and uncommunicative. As mentioned earlier, they are described in terms of their bodily parts to suggest dehumanization and fragmentation, of animals to suggest their bestiality, and of clothing to suggest their lack of real identity. The verbs are especially important in communicating the apathy and triviality of their actions: "overturns," "yawns," "sprawls," "gapes," "contracts," "declines," "lean[s] in".

The last and most difficult part is the final six lines, in which Agamemnon and the nightingales are evoked. As indicated earlier, Eliot seems to intend a contrast between the mythological world where actions were great, had meaning, and were set in a moral framework that included punishment / reward and the possibility of redemption, and the modern world where actions are small, lack meaning, and are not set in any moral framework. The two most puzzling aspects about these final lines are the references to the "bloody wood" and to the nightingales defecating on Agamemnon's shroud. The former is puzzling because Agamemnon was killed in his bath, not in a wood. However, Eliot reveals in a letter to the *Sunday Times* (April 6, 1958) that "the wood I had in mind was the grove of the Furies at Colonus; I called it 'bloody' because of the blood of Agamemnon in Argos."[29] As for the meaning of the nightingales' defecation, perhaps Eliot intends to emphasize that they were real birds, defecating as well as singing, and that, by implication, the world of order, meaning, and value of which they were a part actually did exist and was not just a romantic dream.

In Part III of *The Waste Land*, the last of the four poems in which Sweeney appears, Eliot presents nine examples of the sterility and perversion of love and sex in human relationships outside marriage. The second of these examples focuses on Sweeney and his visit to the prostitute Mrs. Porter. In a brilliant display of his ability to interweave various sources for the purposes of ironic contrast, Eliot combines references to Marvell's "To His Coy Mistress," to Day's "Parliament of Bees," to a popular bawdy tune about a brothel sung by soldiers in World War I, to the Grail legend, and to the Philomela myth.

The ironic contrasts are complex and serve to reveal the debasement of innocence, love, and sex in the modern metropolis. Eliot superimposes these lines from "Parliament of Bees,"

> When of the sudden, listening, you shall hear,
> A sound of horns and hunting, which shall bring
> Actaeon to Diana in the spring,
> Where all shall see her naked skin . . . ,

on this passage from the current bawdy song,

> O the moon shone bright on Mrs. Porter
> And on the daughter of Mrs. Porter.
> They wash their feet in soda water
> And so they oughter
> To keep them clean.[30]

Thus the protagonist in *The Waste Land*, while fishing in sluggish waters in an industrial area of London, hears behind him the sounds, not of "Time's wingèd chariot" nor of a woodland hunt, but of urban traffic, which delivers Sweeney to Mrs. Porter. Like Actaeon, Sweeney is hunting, but his object is a prostitute rather than deer; and, while Actaeon stumbled by chance upon the goddess of chastity in her bath, Sweeney is not so innocent, having sought Mrs. Porter for the specific purpose of illicit sex. The association of Sweeney with Actaeon may also be a subtle implication of the former's animalistic nature in that the young hunter was transformed into a stag. As for Mrs. Porter, although associated with the moon, as was Diana, she represents the extreme opposite of sexual purity, and her foot washing is a debased version of Diana's bathing as well as of the foot-washing ceremony preceding the restoration of the Fisher King and his kingdom evoked by the line from Verlaine's *Parsifal*: "Et O ces voix d'enfants chantant dans la coupole." That the presumed copulation of the two takes place in the spring is another wry irony, for in the *The Waste Land* this season has lost its meaning of new life or rebirth. Finally, the passage is followed by four brief lines alluding to the myth of Philomela; again the irony is heavy, for Mrs. Porter is no innocent Philomela violently raped against her will, Sweeney is no powerful and terrifying king, and there is to be no transformation into nightingale or hawk. Indeed, as suggested earlier in the poem, even the nightingale has been vulgarized in the modern world, its meanings lost and its song degenerated into the sounds "twit twit twit / Jug jug jug jug jug jug."

Thus, the Sweeney of the four poems is a major symbol of the degradation of modern man; vulgar, sexual, without spiritual or human values, he leads a death-in-life existence in a world devoid of meaning, order, or the possibility of redemption. In each of the poems, however, Eliot emphasizes a particular element of his symbolism: in "Sweeney Erect," he represents primarily the lack of human solidarity, of compassion, and secondarily the debasement of romantic love and meaningful sex; in "Mr. Eliot's Sunday Morning Service," the absence of spiritual values and the dominance of the physical; in "Sweeney among the Nightingales," the triviality and chaos of modern civilization in general; and in *The Waste Land*, the desecration of love between men and women.

The Sweeney of *Sweeney Agonistes*, while sharing some of the characteristics of the earlier Sweeney, is different in several highly significant ways. Indeed, these differences are of such magnitude that Matthiessen comments: "The hero is so different a character from the 'apeneck Sweeney' of the poems that Eliot might better have given him a different name."[31] However, it seems to me that Eliot purposely gave him the same name to indicate that he is, in effect, the same person, who has undergone some essential changes. He is the lower-class, uneducated "Apeneck Sweeney" who has lived a sordid and sterile life among prostitutes and other sordid elements of society in the sleazy nightclubs, boarding houses, and brothels of seedy urban districts. In *Sweeney Agonistes*, his language reflects his lack of education and his lower-class status in its slang ("I knew a man once did a girl in"), its pronunciation ("We're gona sit here and drink this booze"), and its grammatical errors ("I tell you again it don't apply"). His vulgarity and sensuality are also evident in his sexual banter with Doris, especially in his description of himself as a cannibal who will gobble her up. His companions are still materialistic, vulgar, and of the lower class; the women seem to be prostitutes and the men, their customers; as Eliot indicated to Arnold Bennett in 1924, he "wanted to write a drama of modern life (furnished flat sort of people). . . ."[32] The setting is the urban flat of one of the prostitutes, and the plot, as in the poems, is minimal, dominated by trivial activities such as fortune telling with cards and singing and drinking at a party. A prevalent theme of the play, again echoing the poems, is the sterility, chaos, and anxiety of modern civilization. The shallow characters, the superficial chatter, and the ominous references to estrangement and death reveal an uneasy world in which nothing is certain, nothing is meaningful.

However, while these similarities exist, Eliot makes significant changes both in Sweeney's character and in the way in which he is presented. First, and most important, unlike the Sweeney of the poems, he is painfully aware of the vacuity of modern life, of the life he himself has led; indeed, *Sweeney Agonistes* can be seen as an enactment of "The Love Song of J. Alfred Prufrock" on the lower-class level, for Sweeney expresses the overwhelming question that Prufrock never dared to ask, with exactly the results that Prufrock feared—misunderstanding and rejection. Eliot indicates in the concluding essay of *The Use of Poetry and the Use of Criticism* his intention in *Sweeney Agonistes* to set a "conscious" character against a group of "unconscious" characters:

> I once designed, and drafted a couple of scenes, of a verse play. My intention was to have one character whose sensibility and intelligence should be on the plane of the most sensitive and intelligent members of the audience; his speeches should be addressed to the latter, who were to be material, literal-minded and visionless, with the consciousness of being overheard by the former. There was to be an understanding between this protagonist and a small number of the audience, while the rest of the audience would share the responses of the other characters in the play. Perhaps this is all too deliberate, but one must experiment as one can.[33]

Sweeney is, without a doubt, this "conscious" character, and he is meant to evoke the sympathy of the audience (or reader), in contrast to the earlier Sweeney. He has had an insight into the meaningless quality of modern existence and the sinful nature of man, an insight which he tries unsuccessfully to communicate to the others. He attempts to make them see that life as they are living it is nothing more than "Birth, and copulation, and death," that in fact "Life is death." The story of the man who murdered the girl reveals man's capacity for evil; it also suggests that the murderer, a symbol for man in general, in a very real sense lived a life-in-death existence. In "Eeldrop and Appleplex," a sketch published in 1917, Eliot describes a similar situation and makes clear its meaning: "In Gopsum Street a man murders his mistress. The important fact is that for the man the act is eternal, and that for the brief space he has to live, he is already dead."[34]

However, despite his attempts to take them metaphorically to a barren island where they cannot hide from "the facts" by means of telephones, gramophones, or motorcars, they do not understand. Sweeney's frustration increases until he finally gives up, resigning himself to the fact that nothing more will happen at the party (and in their lives) than drinking, singing, and aimless coming and going: "We're gona sit here and drink this booze / We're gona sit here and have a tune / We're gona stay and we're gona go."

There are other differences proceeding from this central and all-important one, most of which concern the manner in which Sweeney is presented. While in the poems Sweeney never speaks nor is presented from the inside, in "Fragment of an Agon" he has a large speaking role and directly expresses his moral and spiritual insights. Further, little emphasis is placed on his physicality. There are no references at all to his body or his physical positions and only two to his actions; although these actions appear to be wholly sexual ("I'll carry you [Doris] off to a cannibal isle," "I'll gobble you up"), they are later seen to be spiritual in nature. Likewise the imagery of animals and bodily parts, so prevalent in the poems, largely disappears. Images of death and sterility, however, are pervasive, suggesting the death-like quality of modern existence as well as man's sinful nature. They include Doris' drawing the two of spades ("THAT's THE COFFIN!!"), Sweeney's description of life as death, his story of the man who murdered the girl, and the numerous negatives used throughout the dialogue.

Finally, there is no ironic contrast of the present to the past in the play itself. However, through the title and the epigraphs Sweeney himself is specifically both compared and contrasted to two heroic figures from the past, one Biblical and the other classical. The title evokes Milton's dramatic poem *Samson Agonistes*; like Samson, Sweeney is a sinful human being who experiences conflict and is spiritually isolated from the other characters by his insights. The first epigraph ("ORESTES: You don't see them, you don't — but *I* see them: They are hunting me down, I must move on. — *Choephoroi*") links Sweeney with Aeschylus' Orestes, who realizes in the quotation that he is being pursued by the Furies for the murder of his mother. It suggests Sweeney's realization of man's sinful nature as well as his isolation from the other characters who cannot see what he sees. In conjunction with the second epigraph ("Hence the soul cannot be possessed of the divine union, until it has divested itself of the love of created beings — *St. John of the Cross*"), Sweeney's association with Orestes perhaps was meant to shed light on projected later scenes in which he would attain a state of purgation and spiritual purity. However, Eliot also seems to intend an ironic contrast between Sweeney and these two figures in that Sweeney's stature, situation, and language are considerably less heroic than those of Samson and Orestes.

An analysis of the play will reveal in more detail the significant changes, as well as the similarities, in this Sweeney. The original and the subsequent titles reflect not only Milton's dramatic poem but also the modern British music hall and Greek drama, and they convey a great deal about Eliot's complex intentions. The original overall title, "Wanna Go Home, Baby?," refers to the vacuous and superficial world portrayed in the work. The 1932 title, *Sweeney Agonistes: Fragments of an Aristophanic Melodrama*, in addition to linking Sweeney with Samson,[35] serves to emphasize connections with Aristophanes' works and with the contemporary melodrama of the British music hall. The play is Aristophanic in its satire of the present age, in its mixture of comedy and tragedy, and in its use of the structure of Old Comedy. It is a melodrama in its presentation of exaggerated emotions and situations and in its use of songs.

Heavily influenced by the British music hall, the play is composed of dialogue interspersed with popular songs. The first scene, "Fragment of a Prologue," fulfills the functions of a Greek prologue in presenting material that prepares for the action of scene 2. Doris and Dusty, who seem to be prostitutes, tell fortunes with cards while awaiting the arrival of men who are apparently their customers. Although Sweeney's name is mentioned twice in connection with the King of Clubs, he does not appear in this scene. The cards suggest strange and frightening possibilities for the evening's party, casting an ominous pall over the immediate future and preparing the audience for the morbid and bizarre conversation of scene 2. The scene ends with the arrival of four men.

The second scene, "Fragment of an Agon," takes place a little later in the evening with the party in full swing. Three additional "guests" have arrived, one of whom is Sweeney. The ominous predictions of scene 1 come true as death, ambiguity, and sterility dominate this scene. There is a conflict, as implied by the word "Agon," between Sweeney on the one hand and Doris and the rest of the group on the other. Sweeney threatens to take Doris to a "cannibal isle" where the trivialities of modern life would be stripped away to reveal the bare facts of their bleak existence:

> There's no telephones
> There's no gramophones
> There's no motor cars . . .
> Nothing at all but three things.

The insistent use of negatives (11 of them in 10 lines) reinforces life's emptiness. When Doris objects, "I'd be bored," Sweeney quickly makes his point: "You'd be bored / Birth and copulation and death. / That's all the facts when you come to brass tacks." Two songs, echoing such popular tunes as "Under the Bamboo Tree" and "Ain't We Got Fun," describe the monotony and meaninglessness of life on the island, a symbol in miniature of modern civilization without its superficial distractions: "For it won't be minutes but hours / For it won't be hours but years."

Sweeney then turns to his second major revelation, the sinful nature of man, illustrating it by the story of the man who murdered the girl. He tries to explain the frightening meanings that he sees in the story, but, as Prufrock had feared, the others do not understand and Sweeney realizes that nothing will change; their vacuous lives, their death-in-life existence will go on. The scene closes with a chorus of four of the men describing a nightmare about one's own death, and the play ends with the ominous sounds of knocking.

In his drama, one of Eliot's foremost goals was to appeal to a large and varied audience that would include the lower and middle classes as well as the elite. In his 1920 essay, "The Possibility of a Poetic Drama," for example, he suggests that contemporary dramatists should follow the lead of Elizabethan dramatists who "aimed at a public which wanted *entertainment* of a crude sort, but would *stand* a good deal of poetry."[36] Thus, in *Sweeney Agonistes*, in the hope of reaching the lower levels of society, he experiments with the use not only of the music hall format ("The working man who went to the music hall and saw Marie Lloyd and joined in the chorus was himself performing part of the act . . .")[37] but also of the common, lower-class man (Sweeney) as the sensitive, conscious character who realizes and tries to communicate to others the essential vacuity of a world and an existence without human or spiritual values as well as the sinful nature of man and his need for redemption. I would suggest that he felt the experiment with Sweeney to be a failure and abandoned it, leaving *Sweeney Agonistes* incomplete at least partially for this reason. In subsequent plays he continues to set a conscious character against others, but these major figures are always upper class, intelligent and educated, and more spiritual than physical in nature. Sweeney is Eliot's first experiment with this type of character in drama and as such is the forerunner of Thomas à Becket, Harry, and Celia.

Thus Sweeney's role as a major symbol in Eliot's early work is extremely complex and of central importance in conveying the poet's predominant themes. In the poems he functions as a symbol of the lower-class modern man who lives a sensual life without meaning or value in a materialistic, urban-centered civilization, entirely unaware of the sterility of his existence and of his world. However, in *Sweeney Agonistes*, he symbolizes the same man who not only has become conscious of the harsh reality but also attempts unsuccessfully to communicate his penetrating and painful insights to others.

Notes

1. Philip R. Headings, *T. S. Eliot* (New York: Twayne Publishers, 1964), pp. 40, 43, 44.

2. F. O. Matthiessen, *The Achievement of T. S. Eliot* (New York: Oxford University Press, 1959), pp. 129, 59.

3. David Ward, *T. S. Eliot: Between Two Worlds* (Boston: Routledge & Kegan Paul, 1973), pp. 40, 175.

4. T. S. Eliot, "Ulysses, Order, and Myth," *The Dial*, November 1923, 483.

5. Eliot, "William Blake," *Selected Essays* (New York: Harcourt, Brace and World, 1960), p. 275.

6. For a discussion of this topic, see Nancy D. Hargrove, *Landscape as Symbol in the Poetry of T. S. Eliot* (Jackson: The University Press of Mississippi, 1978).

7. Eliot, *Collected Poems: 1909–1962* (New York: Harcourt, Brace and World, 1963), p. 3. All references to Eliot's work will be to this edition.

8. Although Gerontion is at the present clearly living in poverty, and thus may be taken to be of the lower class, it is difficult to tell whether or not he has always been at this level of society. His language might indicate that he once was in a higher class.

9. Because I have restricted my discussion to the early works published in *Collected Poems*, I have not included Eliot's portrayal of humanity in the juvenilia, where the Christian saint appears occasionally. For a discussion of this more positive view of man, see Lyndall Gordon, *Eliot's Early Years* (New York: Oxford University Press, 1977). However, Gordon notes that Eliot's concept of modern man in the teens was largely negative; he speaks of Eliot's "sensitivity to human degradation in twentieth-century cities" and comments, "Whatever the city — Boston, Paris, London — he saw the same: people who were too apathetic and inarticulate and undisciplined to hope to escape their dreary fates" (pp. 38–39). Further, he points out that, in Eliot's depictions of Christian saints, they are not modern but "traditional and literary": "Eliot failed to imagine saints in an appropriate contemporary guise . . ." (p. 63).

10. While Sweeney himself seems totally unconcerned about religious issues or establishing a relationship with God / Christ, it might be argued that, since Christ's sacrifice includes such figures as Sweeney, a relationship with God / Christ is made available to him. However, as far as I can tell, the Sweeney of the *poems* never accepts nor indeed seems even to be aware of this possibility.

11. John Heath-Stubbs, "We Have Heard the Key Turn," *T. S. Eliot*, ed. by Tambimuttu and Richard March (London: Frank and Cass Co., 1965), p. 240; Stephen Spender, *T. S. Eliot* (New York: Penguin Books, 1975), pp. 50, 189; Matthiessen, p. 59.

12. Grover Smith, *T. S. Eliot's Poetry and Plays: A Study in Sources and Meaning* (Chicago: The University of Chicago Press, 1956), p. 45.

13. Conrad Aiken, "King Bolo and Others," *T. S. Eliot*, ed. by Tambimuttu and March, p. 21.

14. Eugene O'Neill also uses the ape to characterize man's bestial and crude elements, though with more sympathy, in *The Hairy Ape* (1922). Also in the choruses from "The Rock," Eliot writes of the modern period as "an age which advances progressively backwards," p. 108.

15. One other oblique association of Sweeney with an animal is the stag into which Actaeon is transformed by Diana; see Part II of *The Waste Land* in which Sweeney is compared / contrasted to Actaeon.

16. Matthiessen, p. 34.

17. Elizabeth Drew, *T. S. Eliot: The Design of His Poetry* (New York: Charles Scribner's Sons, 1949), p. 37.

18. Beaumont and Fletcher, *The Maid's Tragedy*, ed. by Howard B. Norland (Lincoln: University of Nebraska Press, 1968), II, ii, 63–66, 68–71, 73–78.

19. Theseus' sails are "perjured" because he broke his promise to marry Ariadne. I can find no justification for Maxwell's statement that the reference is to Tristan and Isolde; see D. E. S. Maxwell, *The Poetry of T. S. Eliot* (London: Routledge & Kegan Paul, 1952), p. 81.

20. The lines could also suggest the animalistic movements of Sweeney and the prostitute as they copulate beneath the sheets.

21. The word may also refer to their abstract, verbose, and overly complex explications, verbal or written, of Scripture.

22. The word *mensual* is not in the dictionary; however, it may refer to *mensural* and thus suggest a measured amount of time.

23. Two early Renaissance painters from Umbria, Perugino and Pinturicchio, collaborated on a fresco entitled "The Baptism of Christ" in the Sistine Chapel (1481–82). "Pinturicchio," *Encyclopedia Britannica*, 1967, VII, 1020. Perhaps Eliot had this particular fresco in mind.

24. Eliot notes in the *Paris Review* interview, "I think that in the early poems it was a question of not being able to—of having more to say than one knew how to say, and having something one wanted to put into words and rhythm which one didn't have the command of words and rhythm to put in a way immediately apprehensible." The *Paris Review* Interview, in Donald Hall, *Remembering Poets* (New York: Harper and Row, 1978), p. 215. This comment may help to explain the poem's obscurity, noted by Smith (p. 45) and others.

25. Matthiessen, p. 129.

26. George Williamson, *A Reader's Guide to T. S. Eliot* (New York: The Noonday Press, 1953), p. 97, and James Davidson, "The End of Sweeney," *College English*, 27 (February 1966), 400–407.

27. Aeschylus, *The Oresteian Trilogy*, trans. by Philip Vellacott (Baltimore: Penguin Books, 1956), p. 82.

28. According to Matthiessen, Eliot "once remarked that all he consciously set out to create in 'Sweeney Among the Nightingales' was a sense of foreboding," p. 129.

29. Eliot, as quoted by P. G. Mudford, " 'Sweeney Among the Nightingales,' " *Essays in Criticism*, 19 (July 1969), 291.

30. See Eliot's Notes to *The Waste Land*; and Richard Ellmann and Robert O'Clair, eds., *The Norton Anthology of Modern Poetry* (New York: W. W. Norton & Co., 1973), p. 465.

31. Matthiessen, p. 159.

32. Arnold Bennett, *The Journals of Arnold Bennett*, III, 1921–1928, ed. by Newman Flower (London: Cassell & Co., 1933), p. 52.

33. Eliot, *The Use of Poetry and the Use of Criticism* (Cambridge: Harvard University Press, 1933), pp. 153–154.

34. Eliot, "Eeldrop and Appleplex," *Little Review*, 4 (May 1917), 9.

35. The play recalls Milton's work not only in the major character but also in that both are dramatic poems based on the classical concepts of Greek tragedy, concern actions essentially internal, and contain bold metrical innovations.

36. Eliot, *The Sacred Wood* (London: Methuen & Co., 1920), p. 63.

37. Eliot, "Marie Lloyd," *Selected Essays*, p. 407.

T. S. Eliot in 1920: The Quatrain Poems and *The Sacred Wood*

Jerome Meckier*

> Subterrene laughter synchronous
> With silence from the sacred wood
> —T. S. Eliot, "Ode" (1919)

When T. S. Eliot's *The Sacred Wood* appeared in 1920, it contained thirteen pieces selected for reprinting from the large number of essays and reviews Eliot had done since 1917. In *Poems 1920*, Eliot published seven quatrain poems, all of which must have been composed or put into final

*Reprinted, with permission, from *Forum for Modern Language Studies*, 5 (1969), 350–76.

form during the period in which the essays were written. Hugh Kenner has observed that Eliot's critical essays are attempts at defining his own art[1] while Eliot himself has stimulated the reading of his poetry in light of his prose criticism by stating "that the critical writings of poets . . . owe a great deal of their interest to the fact that the poet . . . is always trying to defend the kind of poetry he is writing or to formulate the kind that he wants to write."[2] But no attempt has yet been made to relate the quatrain poems to the critical tenets advanced in *The Sacred Wood*. In this sense there has been "silence from the sacred wood."

Despite this silence, however, it can be shown that many of Eliot's major critical ideas began to operate in his poetry for the first time in 1920 and that it was in accord with those ideas that the quatrains were composed. Indeed, the view Eliot took of the quatrains provides an early indication of the way in which he came to visualize the entire corpus of his poetry.

I. Tradition and Mr. Eliot's Individual Talent

What is most striking about the 1920 quatrains as compared with Eliot's earlier poems? Clearly they are much more allusive and complex. The allusions are generally used to give the reader a strong sense of the past and of the discrepancies between then and now. The ideas about the relationship of past and present that Eliot expressed in "Tradition and the Individual Talent" begin to function in his poetry in 1920 as his satire exposes the present age as a hollow echo of the past. His concern with tradition, and its preservation, causes him to see his own poetry first as a means of keeping tradition alive and then as a tradition itself.

In the earlier poetry, allusions to the past and its literature, although numerous, are less concentrated and less frequent than in the quatrains. The contrast is generally between an individual of the present and some figure from the past. The women in "The Love Song of J. Alfred Prufrock" are airy and unstable. Although they come and go, the subject of their conversations, Michelangelo, dwarfs them not only by his reputation as compared with their anonymity, but also because of the multisyllabic quality of his name. His permanence in history and art contrasts with their coming and going. Prufrock compares himself with John the Baptist, Lazarus, and Prince Hamlet, but finds he lacks the stamina to be like any of them. He perceives the loss of vitality and meaning in his way of life and his complaints to himself make him a voice in the wilderness. But he fails to utter a sound in public and the women's apparent content with their form of existence remains unchallenged. Because he realizes that the endless round of tea-parties that constitutes his existence is a form of death, he is Lazarus returned from the dead. He could tell the others of the insight he has had about their lives and his own, but fear silences him. Because he is for a time undecided whether or not to assume the roles of Lazarus and the Baptist, he resembles Hamlet. However, he is not capable of sustained indecision and refuses this role along with the other two.

The lady's room in "Portrait of a Lady" is compared to Juliet's tomb and the lady accuses the young man who comes to tea of having no Achilles' heel. But the lady is no Juliet and the young man, though he suspects he is a heel, knows he is no Achilles. In the quatrains, Eliot satirizes the same lack of meaning and vitality that his earlier poems exposed. However, the allusions begin to compare not only present-day characters but contemporary society as a whole with times when things were otherwise and with the literature and art of those times. Eliot broadens the base of his satire and satirizes neither a particular kind of individual nor a certain class of society, but an entire age. Allusions that were previously occasional now become more central and often carry a considerable portion of the poem's meaning.

In "Burbank with a Baedeker: Bleistein with a Cigar," Burbank's introduction to Venice and its history must come through a Baedeker. The poem contains allusions to Shakespeare and Tennyson, and to Spenser and Ruskin. In Tennyson's "The Sisters," it is the girl who falls when she meets an earl, but here it is a woman, Princess Volupine, who belongs to the nobility and it is Burbank, the man, who falls when they meet. He is satirically compared to Shakespeare's Marc Antony and she is a "phthisic" or wasted Cleopatra.[3] Bleistein, in comparison with a "perspective of Canaletto," seems crudely simian. He suggests "A lustreless protrusive eye" that "Stares from the protozoic slime." Canaletto had excellent vision, but Bleistein is a throwback with a colorless eye. The line "Chicago Semite Viennese" not only informs us of Bleistein's place of residence, his religious persuasion, and his present masquerade (as a Viennese) but also suggests there is no longer any distinction between a Viennese, a Semite, or Chicago. Bleistein's lack of vision is thus symptomatic of a more universal blurring of distinctions. The fragment "On the Rialto once," hearkens back to "Semite" while also recalling *The Merchant of Venice* and the vanished commercial glory of Antonio's city. Now, however, "The rats are underneath the piles. / The Jew is underneath the lot." In the Venice and Europe of Shakespeare, Shylock was outwitted. But here his modern counterpart, the merchant Sir Ferdinand Klein, is the man Princess Volupine finally chooses.

In the last quatrain, Burbank stares at the lions of St. Mark's and wonders who clipped their wings and pared their claws. He mediates on "Time's ruins, and the seven laws." The first is possibly a reference to Spenser's "Ruins of Time" while it also summarizes what Venice and those touring it have become. The second is an allusion to Ruskin at the same time that it implies Venice no longer has laws for architecture, tradition, or anything else. In *The Seven Lamps of Architecture*, Ruskin observed that laws of growth and decay depend upon an age's morals. The entire poem is about decay and decline and the allusions that place past and present alongside each other emphasize the decline quite forcibly. By referring to two sixteenth-century authors and to a pair of nineteenth-century ones Eliot indicates that the process of decline can be measured against two prior periods, the first over four hundred years ago and the second less than a century previous. The process is something that has happened and that is still going on.

Just as "Burbank with a Baedeker: Bleistein with a Cigar" juxtaposes modern Venice and its sixteenth- and nineteenth-century counterparts, the two Sweeney poems contrast the age of Sweeney with the classical world. "Mr Eliot's Sunday Morning Service" contrasts the Word as it was in the beginning with what contemporary religion has made of it. "Whispers of Immortality" juxtaposes the unified sensibility the past of Donne and Webster possessed and the cheap sensuality of Grishkin and the present. Commercially, and in terms of religion and sensibility, the quatrain poems compare past and present.

The connection between the 1920 essays and the increased allusiveness of the quatrains is readily found in "Tradition and the Individual Talent" in which Eliot wrote that the struggle to obtain tradition and hold on to it

> involves, in the first place, the historical sense . . . and the historic sense involves a perception not only of the pastness of the past, but of its presence: the historical sense compels a man to write not merely with his own generation in his bones, but with a feeling that the whole of the literature of Europe from Homer and within it the whole of the literature of his own country has a simultaneous existence and composes a simultaneous order. This historical sense . . . is what makes a writer traditional. And it is at the same time what makes a writer most acutely conscious of his place in time, of his contemporaneity.[4]

Although Eliot was never unaware of the past in his earlier work, the 1920 poems, especially the quatrains with their increased allusiveness, first show the effect of his having consciously adopted the historical sense. He places Sweeney and Agamemnon in the same poem just as he contended the literature of Europe from Homer and the literature of one's own country must exist simultaneously with the literature of the present. "Burbank with a Baedeker: Bleistein with a Cigar" compares three centuries of Venice just as the quatrains show Sweeney, Christ, Origen, Cleopatra, Grishkin, Donne and Webster all existing simultaneously, all commenting on one another.

In 1920, Eliot began to write as — indeed he became — the historical sense. The method he recommends for evaluating a new poet is also his method of evaluating an age. One must compare a new poet with his predecessors by making "a judgment . . . in which two things are measured by each other."[5] In the quatrains, details relating to the past are interwoven with those from the present and the two comment on each other at the same time that the tension between them holds the poem together. As the historical sense, Eliot stands outside time and sees the present through the past. He functions as Tiresias does in *The Waste Land*. Elizabeth Drew calls Tiresias "a universal contemplative consciousness, almost, 'the historical sense' itself."[6] But in the quatrains, Eliot personifies the historical sense and writes as the mind of Europe. Tiresias, who watches Sappho's sailor home from the sea and the typist home at tea time, who has been both man and woman, advisor to Oedipus and rider in taxicabs, represents accumulated wisdom and universal experience. What Tiresias represents, the Eliot of the quatrains personifies. The stance Eliot was to use in *The Waste Land* is first introduced in the quatrains.

Through the use of extensive allusion Eliot found he could do two things. He could recapture tradition while making it a yardstick against which to measure his own age. In this sense, the past would be altered by the present as the past would become a standard for comparison and the object of an unemotional nostalgia. The same allusions that would point out what had been lost ("that pastness of the past") would, by their inclusion in the quatrains, accomplish a restoration ("the presence of the past"). The references used satirically to undercut the present would have their positive aspect as preservers of the past.

To write as the mind of Europe, a poet must achieve impersonality. After defining tradition and the manner in which the historical sense assures its continuance, Eliot argues that "the progress of an artist is . . . a continual extinction of personality."[7] As one who brings the present and the past to bear on one another, the mature poet does not put his undisguised personal feelings into verse but tries instead to become "a more finely perfected medium in which special, or very varied, feelings are at liberty to enter into new combinations."[8] He tries to make his mind "a receptacle for seizing and storing up numberless feelings, phrases, images, which remain there until all the particles which can unite to form a new compound are present together."[9] The poet's mind is in effect first a storehouse and then a catalyst. It is not difficult to imagine the poet storing up his impressions of the lines from Marlow about religious caterpillars ("phrases"), of a painting showing the baptized Christ, or of bees moving from flower to flower ("images"), and eventually fusing these and other impressions in "Mr. Eliot's Sunday Morning Service." Those who object to the catalyst image are in effect disagreeing with the way in which Eliot wrote much of his poetry. No single quatrain was ever the product of one inspiration. Rather Eliot accumulated fragments (an allusion that could be used ironically, a choice line or two of his own) and waited for several of the fragments to betray a pattern of cohesion which he then solidified into a new combination or compound. To some degree this method also operated in *The Waste Land*.

The pressure under which the fusion takes place, Eliot rightly notes, is more important than the greatness of the emotions involved. For the impressions must form a compact system of cross-fertilizations wherein one impression helps explain another. "An impression needs to be constantly refreshed by new impressions in order that it may persist at all; it needs to take its place in a system of impressions."[10] The quatrains, more so than the later poetry but not too much more so than *The Waste Land*, seem to exist as systems of impressions fused together by the poet's mind. The catalyst image is extremely precise: what the poet experiences in the first throes of composition is not the emotions involved in the lines and impressions he has jotted down at different times, but a sense of the compound those impressions will form when rightly fused. Sweeney, as he stirs the bath with his hams in stanza eight of "Mr. Eliot's Sunday Morning Service" is a mock version of the baptized Christ of stanzas three and four. Yet he is closer to that Christ than the polymath sutlers of stanzas one and two, who only stir up pointless controversy. If one ignores the rest of the poem and reads only the quatrains about the bees, the lines lose nearly all their power and meaning. The section derives most of its force not from its inherent value or from any personal feeling of the poet, but from the fact that the poet's mind has placed it amid surroundings that explain it as it reciprocally explains them. It draws more meaning from its position than it contains in itself.

The method Eliot used to form the epigraph for the Burbank and Bleistein poem is an exaggeration of the method of telescoping, fusing, and compressing that he uses in the poem itself and throughout the quatrains. In all seven poems, Eliot accomplishes an extinction of personality as he becomes the historical sense, a combining, compressing, catalystic force behind the poetry but never visible or present in it. Though he has never explicitly recommended compression as an ideal for the poet, his statements about fusion in *The Sacred Wood*, as well as the method behind the quatrains, show that it has always been one of his prime assumptions.

The fact that a poet must have a sense of tradition and keep that tradition alive in his own works implies that he will be borrowing from other writers and poets. In his essay on "Philip Massinger," Eliot discusses the way this borrowing should proceed. An immature poet imitates, as the later *Advocate* poems and several selections in *Prufrock and Other Observations* imitated Laforgue, but "mature poets steal." Where "bad poets deface what they take, . . . good poets make it into something different. The good poet welds his theft into a whole of feeling which is unique, utterly different from that from which it was torn."[11] Here again the stress is on compiling, welding, and fusing, concerns central to the technique of the quatrains. Though it is unwise to overlook other ways in which Eliot innovated, he himself was probably correct in implying that much of his own originality rests on his ability to create a unique whole of feeling — a good description of *The Waste Land* — out of seemingly diverse impressions seasoned with multiple thefts. The poetic process itself thus becomes symbolic of what a disintegrated age must do: combine its elements into new wholes.

The quatrain poems are the first of Eliot's works to show evidence of an extensive series of borrowings. Arthur Davidson complained that one line in every nine of *The Waste Land*'s 433 does not belong to Eliot.[12] Edmund Wilson found the poem contained "quotations from, allusions to, or imitations of, at least thirty-five different writers . . . as well as several popular songs" and that six foreign languages were used, including Sanskrit.[13] But on a proportionate basis, the 249 lines of quatrain poetry probably contain almost as many deliberate borrowings. In the Burbank and Bleistein poem there are at least five borrowings or allusions within thirty-two lines. In every case, however, Eliot makes something new of what he borrows by putting it into a context of feeling very different from its original one. This not only allows him to carry out his own advice about borrowing, but also permits him to set up a contrast between the context into which he puts what he has borrowed and the context it was drawn from.

But if the poet borrows only or largely from his contemporaries, as Massinger did, the present simply perpetuates itself and the new and the old are not brought to bear on one another. Thus good poets "usually borrow from authors remote in time, or alien in language, or diverse in interest."[14] In the quatrains, Eliot borrows from, among others, Shakespeare and Spenser (remote in time), from Gautier (alien in language), and from consistently non-satiric poets such as Tennyson (diverse in interests).

The increase in the number and frequency of allusions in the quatrain poems stems from Eliot's growing awareness of the way allusions can function as symbols. Reuben Brower notes that for Dryden and Pope "allusion, especially in ironic contexts, is a resource equivalent to symbolic metaphor and elaborate imagery."[15] When Eliot's allusion involves an ironic use of a line that previously appeared in an un-ironic context, the allusion brings with it "an ironical reminder of a lost melody or a lost ideal."[16] Brower argues that Pope's "keen responsiveness to the society about him is expressed through an equally keen responsiveness to literary modes that had imaged other societies, both human and divine."[17] Eliot realizes, as did Pope, that a line from a poem of the past or a simple reference to a title of a past work can often stand for the work as a whole. It can bring into Eliot's own verse by extension and implication the entire play or poem from which the line is drawn. Thus the allusions to Antony and Cleopatra in "Burbank with a Baedeker: Bleistein with a Cigar" incorporate Shakespeare's play into Eliot's poem as the world of Antony and Cleopatra is evoked. The atmosphere of tragic love and heroic struggles for power carries over from Shakespeare and increases our dissatisfaction with the Venice of Burbank and Princess Volupine. The mention of the "unstilled Cyclades" and of "Aeolus above / Reviewing the insurgent gales / Which tangles Ariadne's hair" stands for the corpus of Greek mythology and brings it into "Sweeney Erect" by implication.

Later, in *The Waste Land*, an allusion to Baudelaire's "Au Lecteur" or to Nerval's "El Desdichado" may cause the reader to review mentally the themes and tones of those poems and find a more extensive connection between them and *The Waste Land* than the lines from those two poems can convey by themselves. For a poet with the historical sense, an awareness of the ability of allusion to function as symbol is essential.

By writing with the historical sense and through his use of extensive and symbolic allusion, Eliot used his poetry to revive, preserve, and add to tradition. Gradually, as he went on to *The Waste Land* and the later poetry, he began to visualize his own work as a tradition in itself. From an exploration of the relationship between tradition and his own individual talent, he concluded that the latter could produce the former. In the later poems, his historical sense includes an awareness, in each poem he writes, of the presence of all his earlier poems. "Gerontion" seems to be very much in his mind as he composes "Ash Wednesday." He seems to recall Prufrock's inability to become John the Baptist when Sweeney finally delivers Prufrock's message (revised and expanded, of course) in "Fragment of an Agon." Eliot begins to borrow from himself. He alludes to himself by re-using the symbols and themes of previous poems — though never precisely for the same purpose — in his later poetry. He puts Sweeney of the quatrains into *The Waste Land* and "Sweeney Agonistes." The fire of Section III of *The Waste Land* reappears in *Four Quartets*, as does the rose of "Ash Wednesday." In *Four Quartets* the fire and the rose become one and "the still point of the turning world" in "Triumphal March" also returns. Each new poem keeps the earlier poems before one's eyes and causes the "whole existing order" those poems comprise to be "ever so slightly altered." Each new poem causes a readjustment of "the relations, proportions, values of each work of art toward the whole" of Eliot's work. Eliot's search for tradition in *The Sacred Wood* and in the quatrain poems led to a visualization of all his poetry as a tradition in which the later poems are directed by the earlier ones and the earlier poems are altered by the later ones.

In the quatrains, Eliot began to contrast his own era with periods that were not cut off from the sources of vitality and tradition. Thus it is from 1920 and not from the appearance of *Prufrock and Other Observations* that one should date the birth of Eliot as a satirist. It is with the quatrains that Eliot's satire begins to have a world view behind it, a sense of not only what was wrong with Prufrock, Aunt Helen, and Cousin Nancy, but of the many ways in which an entire age fell short of the norms and ideals previous ages had embraced. With the quatrains, Eliot began to revive satire for twentieth-century poetry. His concern with revitalizing tradition included the reviving of a traditional genre that, except for Byron, had largely remained dormant throughout the nineteenth century. What he effected was nothing less than a resurrection of wit. According to Hazlitt, wit is "founded on the detection of unexpected likeness or distinction in things, rather than in words."[18] And Eliot saw several ways in which, for example, a hippopotamus was both like and unlike the True Church. The heightening of absurdity by "some sudden and unexpected likeness or opposition of one thing to another"[19] that the compact form of the quatrain made possible, enabled Eliot's individual talent to revitalize a tradition that ran through the Metaphysical poets and that had apparently ended with Pope.

II. Prufrock and His Problems: The World of the Quatrains

In the quatrain poems, especially those dealing with Sweeney, T. S. Eliot devised a set of characters that would serve as an objective correlative for the world view that was behind his satire for the first time in 1920. He created a microcosm in which traditional values and life itself had lost their meaning, in which all the aspects of the twentieth-century that he wished to satirize could be simply and compactly presented. He constructed a world in much the same sense that he maintained Ben Jonson created one in each of his plays. The essays on Jonson, Massinger, and poetic drama in *The Sacred Wood* contain numerous statements about the worlds artists create. Since the quatrains were Eliot's first proving ground for the tenets advanced in *The Sacred Wood*, one must keep in mind the following statements while discussing these poems:

> The essential is to get upon the stage this precise statement of life which is at the same time a point of view, a world — a world which the author's mind has subjected to a complete process of simplification.[20]

> The characters of Shakespeare are such as might exist in different circumstances than those in which Shakespeare sets them . . . Volpone's life, on the other hand, is bounded by the scene in which it is played . . . the life of the character is inseparable from the life of the drama.[21]

> . . . in Shakespeare the effect is due to the way in which the characters *act upon* one another, in Jonson it is given by the way in which the characters *fit in* with each other. The artistic effect [is due] simply to their combination into a whole . . . they are constituents.[22]

> [In Jonson's case] it is not so much skill in plot as skill in doing without a plot . . . In *Bartholomew Fair* . . . it is the fair itself not anything that happens to take place in the fair.[23]

> [Jonson's work] is the creation of a world . . . the words created by artists like Jonson are like systems of non-Euclidean geometry. They are not fancy, because they have a logic of their own; and this logic illuminates the actual world, because it gives us a new point of view from which to inspect it.[24]

> But small worlds — the worlds which artists create — are complete worlds, drawn to scale in every part. . . .[25]

> But the satire like Jonson's is great in the end not by hitting off its object, but by creating it. . . .[26]

> [Jonson] did not get the third dimension, but he was not trying to get it.[27]

> [Massinger] did not, out of his own personality, build a world of art. . . .[28]

> [Massinger lacked] the ability to perform that slight distortion of all the elements in the world of a play or a story, so that this world is complete in itself.[29]

The characters in "Sweeney Among the Nightingales," like those in a play of Jonson's, fit in with each other very closely. They combine to form a whole that is, one hopes, a distortion of reality, but which one readily recognizes as something complete in itself. The poem's meaning rests not in what the characters do to each other, but in the way they form a pattern. All the characters have certain traits in common. Because Eliot has excluded everything that does not pertain to these traits and to the pattern they form, the poem becomes a simplified world in which details take on added significance.

Nearly all the characters have animal traits. Sweeney is likened to an ape, a zebra, and a blotched giraffe. The "man in mocha brown" is a "silent vertebrate," and Rachel "tears at the grapes with murderous paws." Most display a lack of vitality and animation. The "person in the Spanish cape" "yawns" after a clumsy attempt to sit on Sweeney's knees. The "man in mocha brown" "sprawls," "Declines the gambit, shows fatigue." There is an unmistakable lack of contact and communication. Sweeney prepares to laugh but one never learns why or even if he does. The "person in the Spanish Cape" attempts to make contact with Sweeney's lap but ends by falling to the floor. Whenever he appears, the "man in mocha brown" is described as "silent." Few of the characters have names. Most are identified by some aspect of their dress. The implication is that without that aspect they would be completely without personality. Any coming together is sinister and "suspect," as is the connection between Rachel and the woman in the cape. The host converses with someone, but that person remains "indistinct" and the conversation takes place "at the door apart." The characters form a miniature society which suffers greatly from in-animation and which has experienced a complete breakdown of communication and human relationships. The statements one can make about Sweeney and his friends emerge from the way the characters fit together, not from their acting upon one another.

Although twelve lines begin with active verbs or participles, the poem as a whole is a place where nothing happens. The characters' lives, like Volpone's, are bounded by the poem in which they appear. One cannot imagine them turning up under different circumstances. They are, in fact, the perfect objective correlatives for the circumstances in which they appear. When Sweeney does appear in other quatrains or in *The Waste Land*, the circumstances under which he makes his appearance are always remarkably similar. As in a Jonson play, there is little trace of plot. Some critics contend that a plot to eliminate Sweeney is in progress, but the poem provides no conclusive evidence for such conjecture. Even as late as "Fragment of an Agon" Sweeney seems in excellent health. What is clear, however, is that everything in the poem is drawn to scale so that it is the design that matters, not what happens in the poem.

The characters have no connection with each other or with the natural or spiritual world. Overhead "Death and the Raven drift," attracted by society's corpse-like quality. Sweeney "guards the horned gate" so that messages from the shades and the past cannot pass through. The "man in mocha brown" fills up the window so that the nightingales singing near the Convent of the Sacred Heart are neither seen nor heard. The seas are "hushed and shrunken." Orion and the Dog, the first a harbinger of the Egyptians' vintage season and the second a herald of the Nile's fertilizing flood, are "veiled." The world in which Aeschylus' Agamemnon was killed has been dealt a mortal blow by the world of Sweeney. The poem is in fact air-tight and all the means of ingress by which tradition and the vitality of the past could stir up Sweeney's world are blocked or stifled.

Agamemnon's death amounted to murder, but the crime occurred in a society where people at least were alive and where acts were not only performed but followed by their logical reward or retribution. Clytemnestra was unfaithful, Orestes killed for revenge, Tereus violated Philomela. But Orestes punished Clytemnestra and the Furies dealt with Orestes. Philomela's tragedy also had its resolution when the tongue Tereus had cut out was replaced by the voice of a nightingale. In Agamemnon's world, crimes were committed, but those committing them acted against a universally recognized backdrop of order. Their acceptance or rejection of an invitation to fornication did not depend on whether or not they felt fatigued. The nightingales sang for Agamemnon and they sing now, but other similarities that should connect the classical world and the present are now non-existent.

The world of Sweeney and his associates is not the real world, nor is it a fanciful one. Instead, it has a logic of its own. It enables Eliot to inspect the real world's debilitation from a new point of view. In creating this world, Eliot deliberately simplified. He left out everything except what he wished to satirize. For him, as for Jonson, the very act of creating what he wished to treat satirically constituted a large part of the satire. The characters in "Sweeney Among the Nightingales" form one design or world at the same time that the poem they appear in is part of the world the seven quatrains comprise. Where Jonson's satire created its object instead of hitting it off, Eliot does both. The world of "Sweeney Erect" is a satire on the state of the actual world but Eliot also hits off Sweeney's world by comparing it with the world of Greek mythology.

Thus quotations from three different essays in *The Sacred Wood* show how concerned Eliot was in 1920 with getting a precise statement of life that would also be a world, a point of view. He praised Jonson for creating one and blamed Massinger for failing to do so. Jonson's characters, Eliot conceded, never reached the third dimension, but Jonson was only trying for two dimensions. So too with Eliot in the quatrains. In this way he managed to avoid the problems that made Prufrock more like Hamlet than Prufrock suspected.

In "Hamlet and His Problems," Eliot announced that Shakespeare's play suffered from an acute lack of objective correlative. He defined this correlative as "a set of objects, a situation, a chain of events which shall be the formula of that particular emotion: such that when the external facts which must terminate in sensory experience, are given, the emotion is immediately evoked."[30] In "The Love Song of J. Alfred Prufrock," however and even in "Gerontion" and "Portrait of a Lady," Eliot failed to achieve a thoroughly satisfactory objective correlative. Critics persistently ignored the emotions for which the situations in these poems were supposed to be the formulas. Instead, they linked Eliot with the main male character of each poem or tried to find similarities between the poems and events in the poet's life. In 1935, F. O. Matthiessen criticized C. Day Lewis for the latter's contention that "Prufrock should be read as an allegory of Eliot's own life."[31] Yet Kristian Smidt argued, in 1949, that "as for the Prufrock figure, it can hardly be considered irrelevant to our understanding of the poem to feel that Eliot is present in this creature of his imagination."[32] An early reviewer wondered if Eliot felt prematurely antique, since Gerontion was many years his creator's senior. Even Hugh Kenner, in 1959, equated Prufrock and Eliot in the very sentence in which he tried to separate them. "It was a stroke of genius," Kenner enthusiastically states, "that separated the speaker of the monologue from the writer of the poem by the solitary device of affixing an unforgettable title."[33] For Kenner, only a solitary device keeps Eliot and Prufrock apart, a device in the title, not in the body of the poem.

No one, however, equates Burbank or Bleistein with Eliot or infers that the Sweeney poems constitute an allegory of Eliot's own life. For in the quatrains Eliot found a suitable objective correlative for his world view. He managed to project his poems into a world of persons who could not be likened to himself. By simply presenting Sweeney, Grishkin, Bleistein, and the other inhabitants of the quatrains, Eliot makes one see the world's plight, whereas Prufrock and Gerontion had to explain their difficulties. Though both of them strenuously avoided mendacity, the reader had only their opinions of what they felt was wrong with themselves and their milieu. The quatrains present an actual milieu which, by its presence, speaks for itself. Sudden contrasts that measure Sweeney against Agamemnon or Origen against Christ divulge the poet's meaning instantly. The point is made by contrast, not by the poet or his persona. The escape from personality that Eliot talked of in "Tradition and the Individual Talent" is more successfully accomplished here than in the earlier poetry. The world of the quatrains, like the world created by the god of the Deists, was obviously made by someone. But no traces of that someone's personality are in it. The poet cannot be linked to any one of the characters and it is the way of life they all represent, rather than what any one character says about himself or others, that is the core of the satire in these poems.

The complaint that Eliot treats his characters in the quatrains as mere objects is an exaggeration. However, he no doubt intended them to be closer to objects than to a three-dimensional character such as Prufrock. For part of the purpose of the quatrains is to depict a dehumanized age. Bleistein lives on a lower level than Canaletto and Sweeney's life style is bestial compared to Agamemnon's. It is to Eliot's advantage to have two-dimensional characters, just as it was an advantage for Jonson. Eliot, like Jonson, used only those details that would make his characters "conform to a particular setting." The important thing was the roundness of the setting, not of the characters. Prufrock would have been out of place in the Sweeney poems. By speaking of the Baptist and Hamlet, Prufrock appears to be an expert on tradition by comparison with Sweeney.

Thus, in the quatrains, the method of revelation through monologue yields to a more impersonal method of objective depiction. This method is also used in much of *The Waste Land*. When the first person monologue returns in "The Hollow Men" and in the Ariel and Coriolan poems, the speaker is more easily recognized as a persona. In "Ash Wednesday" and *Four Quartets*, the poet is present in the poem as an undetailed "I" and his identity is less important than the experience he undergoes.

Critics were not as eager to see Eliot in the quatrains as they were to put him in "Prufrock" and the other early poems. In fact, Kristian Smidt, who identified the poet with Prufrock, suggested the 1920 poems "may have been written in pursuance of a deliberate policy of depersonalization."[34] D. E. S. Maxwell correctly constitutes the attainment of an objective correlative.[35] But the ultimate success of such a projection depends on whether or not the character into whose person the poet projects the poem is sufficiently dissimilar from the poet. Just as Eliot felt the external events in Shakespeare's play could not account for what Hamlet was feeling and saying, some critics felt Prufrock was too close to Eliot to be a formula for anything but the poet's personal experiences. Prufrock was more like Hamlet than he himself suspected. "Prufrock" and "Gerontion" may still remain better poetry than the quatrains, since the ultimate superiority of one work over another depends on more than the relative values of their objective correlatives. But *The Sacred Wood* testifies to the importance the objective correlative had for Eliot in 1920 as the quatrains live up to the points Eliot made in his essay on *Hamlet*.

Because Eliot created a world in the quatrains, many of the observations made about other artistic worlds, such as William Faulkner's Yoknaptawpha, apply to the quatrains. Frederick Hoffman stresses Faulkner's "ability to bring his fictional world to such a level of imaginative realization that it proves to be more actual than the real."[36] Eliot's world is also more actual than the real, but he gains his effects by exclusion, whereas Faulkner prefers inclusion. Eliot selects only the details that fit his design, while Faulkner surrounds his central themes with a wealth of description and anecdote to heighten the sense of reality. Naturally there are more dissimilarities than similarities between Yoknapatawpha and the world of Sweeney. But both represent a conscious attempt to create a controllable microcosm that is more actual than the real world and that has an order, logic, and design of its own, a world that permits the writer to inspect the real world with a greater objectivity and universality than could otherwise be obtained. For Eliot's world, integration and destruction are side by side. Eliot puts together his world in an orderly fashion but the completed picture — in which the faults of the real world glare at the reader — turns out to be an anatomy.

Eliot credited Dante with creating a world in his poetry. Everything, Eliot felt, went together so that the parts could only be understood in terms of the whole. The same, Eliot maintained, was true of Jonson and Marlowe. Eliot realized that a self-created world could serve as the objective correlative for the author's world-view. After he constructed Yoknapatawpha in one novel, Faulkner recognised that "not only each book had to have a design, but the whole output or sum of an artist's work had to have a design."[37] Eliot too seems to have moved from the creation of a world in individual quatrains to a sense of all the quatrains as a microcosm and finally to the perception that his work as a whole should form a design, should stand as a world. Grishkin in "Whispers of Immortality" is certainly a member of Sweeney's world. The bored Cleopatra in *The Waste Land*, the typist home at tea time, the young man carbuncular, and the people in the pub at its closing also fit. It is from the world of "Gerontion" and the quatrains that the speaker in "Ash Wednesday" strives to escape. The themes permeating the quatrains form part of a development that starts in "Prufrock" (perhaps even in the later *Advocate* poems) and ends with *Four Quartets*.

Clearly, Shakespeare, Jonson and Massinger, as they appear in *The Sacred Wood*, are virtually symbols for Eliot. They stand for the virtues the quatrains aim at and the vices the poems try to avoid. While Shakespeare is accused of exalting characters over circumstance (in *Hamlet* the situation is inadequate for the feelings the hero experiences), Massinger is blamed for the incompleteness of his attempts at setting up a world. Only Jonson, less extravagant than Shakespeare and more thorough than Massinger, is found acceptable.

More important, however, is the similarity between the world of the quatrains and that of *The Waste Land*. If the seven quatrains are taken as a unit, it becomes clear that they constitute a sort of Ur-*Waste Land*, a trial run that Eliot was to repeat two years later at greater length, with a wider emotional range, and with sensational success. Once the quatrains receive their proper appreciation as the proving ground for the theories in *The Sacred Wood*, *The Waste Land*, though the jump to it from the quatrains is considerable, becomes a product of evolution rather than the totally new animal it seemed to the twenties.

III. T. S. Eliot and the Perilous Chapel of Form: Structural Virtuosity in the Quatrain Poems

For T. S. Eliot in 1920, form resembled a perilous chapel. As he considered the problem of form in plays and, by implication, in all poetry, he seemed to be looking out "Over the tumbled graves, about the chapel" and saw in the chapel itself "only the wind's home." As far as forms were concerned, the twentieth century was a waste land. The Elizabethan Age, Eliot wrote in the essay in *The Sacred Wood* on "The Possibility of a Poetic Drama," continually absorbed great quantities of new thoughts and images because it possessed a "great form of its own which imposed itself on everything that came to it."[38] Dante, too, enjoyed the benefit of inheriting forms that his predecessors had brought to a high stage of development. But with the exception of the dramatic monologue, whose origins are at least partially in the soliloquy, the nineteenth century did not originate any new forms or alter any of the old ones. Nineteenth-century poets either had no form in which to confine their fresh impressions or else they hammered out forms that were purely personal. Consequently, when Eliot commenced writing poetry, he found, instead of the crude form capable of indefinite development that awaited Shakespeare, only an empty chapel through which the wind blew. Traditional forms, such as the eighteenth century's couplet and the Elizabethan sonnet, were just so many "tumbled graves" and "Dry bones" from which the life had gone out.

Eliot's use of the quatrain in 1920 thus seems to be an attempt to revive a traditional form, to breathe new life into old bones. Outside of the dramatic monologue, the quatrains are virtually the only traditional form Eliot ever used. Surely the adoption of traditional quatrains in 1920 was the practical expression of Eliot's theoretical statements in *The Sacred Wood* about the value of tradition and the need for vital, developing forms within which a poet could work.

Hugh Kenner points out that the quatrains "constitute an attempt to create a satire medium for twentieth-century usage."[39] This is certainly part of the answer, but two things must be added. The attempt at devising a new satiric medium was also an effort to revive an old one. Quatrains, though by no means frequent in English poetry, have a tradition behind them. They are thus novel for modern readers and yet have a respectable pedigree, particularly in French literature. To write in quatrains is thus to allude to all the poets who have used them in the past. Possibly this form is also an allusion to the Augustans, since the quatrain, a form known for its ability to condense and juxtapose, has some resemblance to the couplet of Pope.

The second thing that must be added is this: Eliot used quatrains because he realized the advantages a traditional form would afford him and because they were most suited to what, at that time, he wanted to say. He knew that where a traditional form existed, there would be "a preparedness, a habit on the part of the public, to respond to particular stimuli."[40] When he published *The Waste Land* two years later, many were baffled by it. It was in some ways like the poetry he had written earlier, but its newness, especially its form, puzzled readers because it did not openly appeal to their preparedness or offer the accustomed stimuli. There are certain things one expects when reading quatrains or couplets. The poet can satisfy these expectations and occasionally frustrate them for a purpose. In either case, the form does part of his work for him. It prepares the audience for a certain regularity and provides a background against which deviations from regularity can be attained.

In 1920, Eliot wished to deal in contrast and juxtaposition, to measure a devitalized age against a more attractive past. He wanted to confine his impressions in such a way that their comments on one another would convey his meaning. The form of the quatrain would provide a pattern whose tightness and compression would underline the contrasts. The form would do part of his work for him. Thus, although the quatrains constitute an attempt to create a twentieth-century satiric medium, the medium was not sought before the content. The latter determined the former. Other mediums for verse satire might have been created, but the quatrain was a form particularly suited to Eliot's content. The admirable thing, Eliot noted, "is not so much the author's skill in adapting himself to the pattern as the skill and power with which he makes the pattern comply with what he has to say."[41]

Throughout the quatrains one finds a variety of styles, moods, and vocabularies. To analyze the calculation behind Eliot's use of rhyme or the alterations in tone from one poem to another might require a book. The present discussion is mainly concerned with form. It will center on the basic patterns Eliot employs throughout the quatrains, those he sets up within the individual quatrain and those that contrast one set of quatrains against another. In this way, Eliot's skill in making the pattern comply with what he has to say will become evident.

Despite some extraordinary rhymes (savannas-hosannas), "The Hippopotamus" is built around the simplest of all the patterns Eliot uses in the quatrains. This pattern involves a contrast, within each quatrain, of the first two lines with the last two. The first stanza, however, does not fall into this pattern, although the one it does fall into is related to the poem's central theme:

> The broad-backed hippopotamus
> Rests on his belly in the mud:
> Although he seems so firm to us
> He is merely flesh and blood.

The contrast here is between lines one and two and again between lines three and four. The hippo is broad-backed, but must rest on his belly. He seems firm, but is only flesh and blood. The poem as a whole will do what this stanza does. It will show that although the hippo seems to be one thing, he is in reality another. Though he appears to be a clumsy, materialistic animal, he is, by contrast with the True Church, the real representative of the Church Militant. In stanzas seven to nine, in what is not merely a flight of Eliot's fancy but also a fine piece of satire, the hippo ascends to heaven and is recognized by the Church Triumphant.

Beginning with stanza two the basic pattern of the poem asserts itself and persists through most of the remaining stanzas. Since the hippo and the True Church are being contrasted, they are appropriately made to share each quatrain, the first two lines making a point about the hippo and the last two contrasting that point with some facts about the Church. The quatrain form and within it the pattern of two lines against two lines are ideally suited to the poet's purpose. The quatrain locks the two things being contrasted firmly together and the tightness and compression are increased by the fact that Eliot rhymes lines one and three and two and four, whereas in the other quatrains, generally only two and four rhyme.

Stanza three reads:

> The hippo's feeble steps may err
> In compassing material ends,
> While the True Church need never stir
> To gather in its dividends.

Unlike the hippo, who is feeble and erring, the True Church obtains its dividends without effort. The hippo compasses or enclosed his ends while the Church sucks its profits in like a vacuum cleaner. The poem's epigraph advised the faithful to love the deacons and the presbyters, but said nothing about the obligations these officials have to love the people. All the love in the epigraph goes from the people into the Church and there is no mention of anything coming out in return. All the contrasts between the hippo and the Church show the Church effortlessly absorbing but never giving in return.

The contrasts, however, are never so complete as to preclude comparison. First, one perceives a way in which the Church seems superior to the hippo: the Church is not feeble and never errs. Then one notes a way in which the hippo and Church are the same. The hippo pursues "material ends" and the Church is after "dividends." It is as materialistically oriented as the hippo and is more successful not because its goals are higher but because it enjoys the advantages large corporations always have over the individual in business for himself. Thus one passes through three stages in an approach to the poem's full meaning: first, there is a contrast between hippo and Church that seems to favor the Church. Being based on rock seems better than being "Susceptible to nervous shock." Second, there is a way in which the contrasted things are also similar. And finally, once the hippo has made his ascension, one sees that the comparisons that initially favored the Church really support the hippo.

Thus it is beneficial to be "based upon rock," but that same rock that can serve as a stabilizing foundation can also serve as an anchor. The hippo can take wing, but the Church must remain below, "Wrapt in the old miasmal mist." The same rock that assures one "The True Church can never fail" also prevents the Church from succeeding. The rock upon which Christ built His Church was once a means of attaining permanence but is now the cause of the Church's hardness and immobility. Like all else in the world of quatrains, the True Church is part of the universal loss of vitally alive traditions. The mere far-fetched association of the True Church and a hippopotamus works to the Church's disadvantage, and the discovery that the hippo is superior is the *coup de grace*. The hippo attains union with God, whereas the Church must go on singing of its "being one with God" without ever experiencing that unity.

The basic pattern runs without interference from stanza two through stanza six. But stanzas seven and eight seem to contain a variation as both are devoted entirely to the hippo. Along with the first two lines of stanza nine, they give us the poet's vision of the hippo's ascension. As an account of the hippo's last days, they are a sort of gospel. They are also full of prophecy about what will happen to the hippo in heaven and sound like a chant or litany. In stanza nine, the basic pattern returns and seems to have acquired added force because of its absence in the two preceding stanzas. So strong is the force of this final contrast that it seems to extend backwards into stanzas seven and eight. One feels one has been reading a sort of refrain:

> I saw the 'potamus take wing
> Ascending from the damp savannas,
> While the True Church remains below
> Wrapt in the old miasmal mist.

or:

> And quiring angels round him sing
> The praise of God in loud hosannas.
> While the True Church, etc.

or:

> Blood of the Lamb shall wash him clean
> And him shall heavenly light enfold.
> While the True Church, etc.

F. O. Matthiessen maintains Eliot believed "freedom is only truly freedom when it appears against the background of artificial limitation."[42] The quatrain form, with its contrast of the first two lines and the last two, is an artificial limitation Eliot creates for himself. When this limitation is momentarily abandoned, one gets the impression of freedom. Eliot then skilfully re-introduces the pattern in such a way that one feels it was never really abandoned.

The quatrain pattern that runs through "The Hippopotamus" also appears in other quatrains, but is never again the main or controlling pattern. It occurs in the last stanza of "Mr. Eliot's Sunday Morning Service" where Sweeney stirs the water in his bath and the subtle masters only stir up controversy. It appears in the last stanza of "Whispers of Immortality" where the first two lines describe the lot of the Abstract Entities and the last two contrast their lot with ours. The pattern is excellent for making sharp contrasts in limited space. In both "Mr. Eliot's Sunday Morning Service" and

"Whispers of Immortality," where the contrasts are between whole quatrains or groups of quatrains, Eliot employs the pattern of "The Hippopotamus" in order to end with a strong contrast. He vivifies in the closing lines
the principle around which both poems are constructed.

Another pattern which Eliot uses within the individual quatrain is a
contrast of three lines against one line. The first two stanzas of "Mr. Eliot's
Sunday Morning Service" provide a good example:

> Polyphiloprogenitive
> The sapient sutlers of the Lord
> Drift across the window-panes.
> In the beginning was the Word.

> In the beginning was the Word.
> Superfetation of $\tau\grave{o}\ \overset{\epsilon\prime}{\epsilon}\nu$
> And at the mensual turn of time
> Produced enervate Origen.

In stanza one, line four contains the simple statement from St. John. But the
first three lines show what has become of the beginning. The sutlers (servers
or camp-followers) of the Lord, in their love of whatever is progenitive,
have needlessly complicated the originally monosyllabic Word. Though
they appear sure of their sapience, they, or their shadows, "Drift" across the
window-panes, very much at sea.

Stanza two reverses the process of stanza one. The first stanza describes
the present and then refers to the way the Word was in the past. The second
stanza begins with what the Word was in the past and shows what happened to it as time moved towards the present. Once the Word was simple
and direct. It was "$\tau\grave{o}\ \overset{\epsilon\prime}{\epsilon}\nu$" or "the one." But those with a fondness for the
progenitive went for superfetation, for conception on top of conception.
For them the Word's becoming flesh once was not enough. The meaning of
this Incarnation had to be made more involved. The Church has had too
many mental conceptions of the Word's conceptions so that the unity of
creed visible in the early days is no longer discoverable. Although the metaphors refer to propagation, the mental conceptions have only produced
barrenness. At the mensual turn of time, when the uterus secretes and conception is impossible, superfetation gave birth to Origen. Despite his name,
he was an end rather than a beginning. As a eunuch, he was sterile physically and that is symbolic of the barrenness allegedly in his theological
thought.

The pattern of three lines against one line enforces the poet's contention that simplicity of belief has been fruitlessly convoluted, that meaning
has been lost rather than augmented. It takes only one line to describe
the initial state of the Word, but three to relate what has been made out of
the beginning. The three lines pertaining to the work of the sutlers require
the use of a dictionary, but the words one must look up do not add to one's
understanding of the Word.

The pattern used here also reappears elsewhere in the quatrains. In "Whispers of Immortality," the first three lines of stanza six describe the activities of a Brazilian jaguar as contrasted with Grishkin, the owner of "a maisonette." The first three of stanza seven contrast the feline smell the jaguar gives off in the jungle with the one Grishkin exudes in a drawing-room. But the contrasts really aim at connecting Grishkin with the jaguar by showing she is more of a cat than the animal is. The pattern allows Eliot to make Grishkin less appealing than she would be if he described her directly.

Having seen what Eliot does within the quatrain, one can now examine the patterns he makes out of a series of quatrains. When the things being contrasted share a quatrain, the form holds them side by side to stress the contrast. But the quatrain can also be seen as a sort of self-contained capsule or building-block. When two things are put into separate quatrains or capsules, they are sharply contrasted, since the point being made about them is that their separation is absolute. They are divided formally as well as thematically. The first two stanzas of "Sweeney Erect" are effectively self-contained and separated from the rest of the poem. Sweeney and his lady friend may be a mock version of Aeolus and Ariadne, but the boarding-house world remains permanently severed from the world of Greek mythology.

In "Sweeney Among the Nightingales," the characters' loss of vitality and purposeful existence is reflected in the form as the quatrains cease to be self-contained and compact:

> The person in the Spanish cape
> Tries to sit on Sweeney's knees
>
> Slips and pulls the table cloth
> Overturns a coffee-cup —

The tightness of the quatrain slips and falls along with the lady. The last line of stanza three spills over into stanza four just as the cup spills. When Eliot keeps his quatrains tight and compressed, he can underline the complete separation between the present in one quatrain and the tradition-filled past in another. When he slackens the tightness, he can suggest, formally as well as thematically, the loss of order and regularity characteristic of Sweeney's world. The last two stanzas of "Sweeney Among the Nightingales" flow together and the pitch of the poet's voice seems to rise as he moves from stanza nine to ten. The nightingales are singing now and they sang within the bloody wood. However, Sweeney's world and Agamemnon's do not really touch. Their worlds are both connected with the nightingales but not with each other. The way the stanzas flow into one another is due to the presence of the nightingales in both worlds. But their presence stresses the fact that C is common to A and B, while A and B are as far apart as the sordid is from the heroic.

In "Whispers of Immortality," the world of Donne and Webster fills the first four quatrains and our world and Grishkin's occupies the last four. Between the two series of quatrains, Eliot inserts a dotted line. Some critics see this line as the Cartesian chasm.[43] But the point to be stressed is that both halves are in perfect formal balance and no connection between them exists. The style in the first four recalls metaphysical poetry and the last four have a fin-de-siecle smartness. The extent to which the elements in Grishkin's world are the opposite of those in the world of Donne and Webster is stressed by the two different styles. Grishkin's eye is underlined for emphasis. Her bust is friendly. She is purely physical. But Webster saw the skull beneath the skin. He saw death make creatures eyeless and breastless. Through his senses, he acquired knowledge. While Donne used his senses to penetrate beyond the sensual, all that comes from Grishkin is a rank and feline smell. An expert at "contact possible to flesh," she never suspects there is such a thing as "the fever of the bone."

The first four stanzas depict a world of unified sensibility (a subject *The Sacred Wood* also discusses),[44] and the second four present a world where the senses and the mind have lost their former unity. The skull is no longer beneath Grishkin's skin. And thought, "our metaphysics," crawls through dry ribs that are "no substitute for sense." The poem divides neatly into two halves as the self-sufficiency of the quatrains in each half emphasizes the separation between the sixteenth-century world of Donne and Webster and the twentieth-century world of Grishkin.

"A Cooking Egg" falls into three carefully organized parts. Like the speaker in the epigraph,[45] the speaker in the poem has to swallow all his illusions. The first two quatrains describe the speaker's present situation. The next four relate what he hopes to have in the future and, therefore, what he has lacked up until now. And the last two deal with what he once thought he would have. The first two are contrasted with the last two and both the first and last two are contrasted with the middle group of four quatrains. The completeness, the rounded-off effect of the first two quatrains, would serve to set them off against the middle group and the final two quatrains even if Eliot did not use a dotted line to mark the poem's divisions.

The first two stanzas give a picture of the life the speaker and Pipit have in terms of one of the rooms they occupy. Pipit appears to be the speaker's wife. Her name suggests *Great Expectations*, which is what the speaker once had, perhaps on his wedding day. There is something stiff about Pipit. She "sate upright." The impression of stiffness is reinforced by the archaic form of *sit*. Ironically, "sate" also means "Satiate" or "gratify" and it is precisely the fulfillment of his expectations in life that the speaker has never experienced. Perhaps Pipit's uprightness has been the obstacle between them and that keeps her sitting "some distance" from him. The disclosure that *Views of the Oxford Colleges* is on the table seems momentarily promising until its significance is undercut by the appearance of the knitting. The *Views* is probably a sort of photograph book that ornaments the table but is seldom opened. Pipit's real concern is for her knitting. It suggests the limits of her accomplishments.

On the mantle piece, rows of daguerreotypes and silhouettes show the room is full of ghosts. It seems to have no present life of its own. Although the presence of the pictures may seem oppressive, they are ironically in a supporting role. They give support to a painting entitled "Invitation to the Dance." But the room is not at all inviting to the speaker. None of the pictures are of his ancestors. The room has an air of boredom and ennui that no music or dance could dispel. In one way, however, the pictures do invite the speaker to a dance, but it is the dance of sameness and ennui at the end of which his picture and Pipit's will take their places among the silhouettes.

In contrast to what the first two quatrains reveal about the speaker's present circumstances, the next four record his hopes for the future. They all begin with "I shall not want" and form a sort of prayer or psalm the speaker recites to cheer himself up. "I shall not want" can be taken in two senses. The speaker may mean he shall not want or be without certain things he obviously lacks at present. Or he may mean that he shall not desire certain things in heaven because he will have something better than those things: namely people who personify them. "Honour," "Capital," "Society," and even Pipit by association are all abstractions in comparison with Sidney or Madame Blavatsky. In the next world the speaker will encounter and cultivate real people, not abstractions. He will meet Lucretia Borgia and Sidney instead of Pipit and daguerreotypes.

Each of the four stanzas in this group contrast an abstraction with real people who embody that abstraction concretely. Where there was a distance between himself and Pipit, the speaker now sees himself having actual contact with Sir Alfred Mond and Piccarda de Donati. The first and third stanzas in this middle group mention historical personages. The second is devoted to one of the speaker's contemporaries. And the fourth contains both a contemporary and a figure from the past. In heaven, the speaker will find past and present available to him simultaneously, whereas the room he and Pipit now occupy has the past only on the walls or as a ghostly presence. The past does not communicate with the present and the two figures in the present. Pipit and the speaker have no words for each other.

The speaker's definition of heaven and the people to whom he grants admittance should not surprise anyone, although the tone in this middle group is playful and ironic. The speaker has not had honor, society, capital, amusing anecdote, instruction, or guidance in this world: so he imagines the next in terms of what this one lacks. The presence of Lucretia Borgia and Madame Blavatsky in heaven is clearly not due to merit or saintliness. The criterion the speaker uses admits only those who were once really alive. They may have excelled at excellence, as Sidney did, or in wickedness, as did Lucretia Borgia. But they lived. They had the courage to either good or bad, unlike the speaker and Pipit who are neither. Pipit is apparently content to end as another daguerreotype on the wall, for she is scarcely more alive than they are. Like Ruskin, who wanted Rose La Touche in this world because there would be Pythagoras to talk to in the next, the speaker wanted Pipit and the penny world in the present, but did not have them.

The last two stanzas review what the speaker once thought life held for him. But the "penny world" he bought to eat with Pipit has gone untasted. The screen he intended to eat it behind has proved an inadequate protection against the creeping reality of the red-eyed scavengers. Kentish Town, which suggests a bygone era (perhaps Chaucer's time), and Golden's Green, a name made of the green of fertility and the gold of wealth, both succumb to the locust-like scavengers. The speaker never ate his penny world, but the scavengers are devouring these two locales.

At this point, the speaker's disillusionment, his longing for what life seemed once to promise but never brought, becomes so intense that it breaks out of the quatrain pattern. The line "Where are the eagles and the trumpets?" stands by itself in the space between two quatrains. It serves as a climax for the feelings building up in the speaker since the start of the poem. It is a one-line summary of the question the entire poem asks. As a cry of disappointment and puzzlement, it becomes more pronounced by its isolation from the pattern followed throughout the rest of the poem. That the eagles and trumpets, a shorthand for power and glory, have no place in the speaker's world is stressed by their inability to penetrate any of the quatrains. The line is also a generalization that permits the poet to suggest an overall situation of an era and not just the speaker's plight. Otherwise, the speaker could be taken as a married Prufrock who popped the overwhelming question but still measures out his life in coffee-spoons. The speaker's sense of loss has overridden the poem's form. But the variation is soon smoothed over as "Buried" reaches back to modify both the penny world and the eagles. The unexpected rhyme of "trumpets" with "crumpets" stresses what the speaker has found as compared with what he expected.

A more complex pattern of contrasts bind together the eight stanzas of "Mr. Eliot's Sunday Morning Service." The dotted line after stanza four divides the poem into two halves. The first half describes the Word as it was in the beginning and in the gesso ground of the Umbrian painter. The second half presents what the bathing Sweeney and the sable presbyters, who are like epicene bees, have made of it. The sharpest contrast is between stanzas four and eight. In place of the baptized Christ, stanza eight offers Sweeney, whose baptism is his bath. It offers the subtle masters, who stir up controversy. The sight of Christ's "unoffending feet" is replaced by the sound of Sweeney's hams. And Christ's ability to be "$\tau \grave{o} \overset{,}{\epsilon} \nu$" is replaced by the masters who are "polymath."

However, a close reading of the poem reveals a second pattern superimposed upon the first. In it, stanzas three and four contrast with one and two, five and six oppose three and four, and seven and eight contrast with five and six. The stanzas describing the simplicity of the Umbrian painters Christ contrast with those describing the Christ of the sapient sutlers and Origen. What the painter made of Christ is more alive and enduring than what the schools have produced. The souls of the supposedly devout in stanzas five and six "burn invisible and dim" in contrast with the feet of Christ that "Still shine" through the water in the painting. The water is "pale and thin" and the feet are "unoffending." But the presbyters are "red," "pustular," and dressed in sable. They have been demanding rather than unoffending and are "clutching" the "piaculative pence" collected from the faithful. The painter set the Father and the Paraclete "above" Christ, but the souls of the devout are "under the penitential gates" instead of inside them. The gates, and not the souls of the devout, are "Sustained by staring Seraphim."

The bees of stanza seven are neither male nor female, but their hairy bellies can fertilize both staminate and pistilate. Their office as go-between seems insignificant compared with Christ's mediations between God and man. But they are more in accord with Christ and perform a greater act of fertilization than the presbyters of stanza five. Thus their office is "blest." Even Sweeney in his bath is closer to the baptized Christ than are the presbyters. He stirs up the water whereas they stir up nothing at all. The masters of the schools merely excite controversy but seem less reprehensible than the presbyters who crawl up the aisle like caterpillars as they gather up one collection after another.

In the quatrain poems, then, Eliot often uses the quatrain as a self-contained capsule or building block. He sets one series of quatrains against another. But, as was briefly mentioned earlier, Eliot can allow the quatrain form to break down and thus illustrate through form as well as content the loss of order and meaning in the world the quatrain poems comprise. The best example of this breakdown can be found in the last four stanzas of "Burbank with a Baedeker: Bleistein with a Cigar" [here Meckier quotes the stanzas]. The "smoky candle end of time" is a metaphor for the present age. By contrast with the full glow of the past, the present is about to flicker out. The decline that has taken place in time, in Venice, and in the poem's diction ("Declines"), also takes place in the poem's form as the quatrain loses its customary order and compactness. The verb that goes with the smoky candle falls into the next quatrain and the fragment from Shakespeare's *Merchant of Venice* increases the sense of breakdown and loss of order. It is a prepositional phrase that is grammatically unattached, although its evocation of the world of Antonio and Shylock is particularly apt.

The declining and slipping continues in the form as the first three lines of the third stanza break up a long sentence into three uneven parts. The first three lines of the first stanza quoted above also break up a long sentence, but there all three segments are of equal size and subject, verb, and object each fit neatly into a line of their own. But here the verb's appearance in line one along with its subject ("Princess Volupine extends") emphasized the separation of verb and object. The extraordinary number of adjectives attached to the object ("hand") creates such a separation between "extends" and the infinitive in line three that the two seem disconnected. The first line of the stanza ends with "extends" and one asks "Extends what?" Will she extend the life of the flickering candle? But all she extends is her wasted hand. Again a question: Does she extend a hand to uplift the times, to raise up the arts? On the contrary, she extends it to climb a water-stair.

The cry of "Lights, lights" increases the disorder as it implies the Princess is in the dark. It refers back to the decline of time's smoky candle end. No matter how much light her attendants produce, the former brilliance of Venice cannot be recaptured. The Princess will entertain Sir Ferdinand. The way the stanza ends at first creates suspense. "Sir Ferdinand who?" is the immediate question. "Klein" is thrust out into the same position "Declines" occupied. The fact that there is a break between "time" and "Declines" and between "Ferdinand" and "Klein" indicates that Klein and decline are one and the same. He comes to symbolize the decline the poem is about and his name rhymes with the process he stands for. Formerly the nobility patronized the arts. Now it entertains Shylock. Had "Klein" been used to end stanza three, the "Who" of line one in stanza four could only have been the beginning of a question. But because of its position next to "Klein," it has some of the force of a relative pronoun. The line strongly implies it was "Klein. Who pared the lion's wings."

In "The Possibility of a Poetic Drama" in *The Sacred Wood*, Eliot discussed the advantage of working in a traditional form, and in the quatrains he actually worked in one. By so doing Eliot managed to enter the perilous chapel of form, to resurrect some of the bones scattered around it. He paid homage to a traditional form in his poetry just as he had done in his criticism. *The Waste Land*, however, could not have been written in quatrains. They would have given the sense of desolation and dryness in the poem an uncalled-for neatness and regularity that no amount of variation could nullify. They could not have contained the larger contrasts of vignette against vignette, though on a smaller scale they point towards those contrasts.

Thus Eliot used the quatrain form extensively only in 1920. But he did not abandon his ideas on form along with the particular form of the quatrain. There is a more universal sense of form which refers to the design of the whole. And Eliot's preoccupation with form in *The Sacred Wood* and in the quatrains developed into a sense of all his poetry as one living design or form. In this form can be found the sort of cross-references, the sense of continuous development, that did not exist between Wordsworth's forms and Byron's and that one finds only with difficulty between Tennyson's and Browning's. For what Eliot learns about form in one poem influences his use of form in the next. One Eliot poem interacts with all the others the way reading one Elizabethan dramatist interacts with one's reading of all the other playwrights of that period. The corpus of Eliot's poetry seems to impose itself on each poem the way the great form of the Elizabethans imposed itself on everything that came to it. Each Eliot poem becomes clearer in light of the others. Each poem extends its implications and achieves coherence because it seems to be part of a larger design.

Malcolm Cowley's statement about Faulkner also applies to Eliot: "All his books in the Yoknapatawpha saga are part of the same living pattern. It is this pattern, and not the printed volumes in which part of it is recorded, that is Faulkner's real achievement. Its existence helps to explain one feature of his work: that each novel, each long or short story, seems to reveal more than it states explicitly and to have a subject bigger than itself."[46] With the seven quatrains as a background, each individual quatrain seems to have a larger reference than it explicitly contains. With the entire corpus of his poetry as a background, each of Eliot's poems seems to possess a greater significance and a wider extension than can be justified by an analysis of its lines. The cross-references (thematic, formal, and symbolic) that exist between "Ash Wednesday" and *Four Quartets* make each of them state more than their lines contain for they encourage the reader to let what he knows about the first operate in his reading of the second. Since all of Eliot's poetry can be said to constitute one line of development, each poem is part of a pattern or form that is larger than itself. It would be unwise to label this larger pattern Eliot's real achievement, but it is clearly an important part of that achievement and one he seems to have aimed at with considerable determination.

Thus Eliot's poetry can be visualized as a tradition in itself, as a world that is an objective correlative for the poet's point of view, and as one extensive form. This visualization emerges out of two things: out of *The Sacred Wood*'s concern for tradition, for the objective correlative, and for the problem of form; and out of the way the 1920 poems handled those concerns.

The quatrains, Herbert Howarth argues, were "meant to be unlovely" and "no one will delight in them."[47] Yet they are unlovely in a very attractive way. They are especially alluring to readers who respond to good satire and who are sensitive to manoevers within a given form. Even if they are the ugly ducklings Howarth claims, they remain, as the prelude to *The Waste Land*, the origins of a swan.

Notes

1. Hugh Kenner, *The Invisible Poet* (New York, 1964), p. 102. See also F. O. Matthiessen, *The Achievement of T. S. Eliot* (New York, 1959), p. 99. First published 1937.

2. T. S. Eliot, "The Music of Poetry," *On Poetry and Poets* (New York, 1937), p. 17. First published 1943.

3. As F. W. Bateson points out in "Burbank with a Baedeker, Eliot with a Laforgue," *The Review*, No. 4 (November, 1962), 12–15, the allusions to Shakespeare are a sort of backbone for the poem. The lines ". . . the God Hercules / Had left him, that had loved him well" compare Burbank with Anthony while ". . . Her shuttered barge / Burned on the water all the day" likens Princess Volupine to Cleopatra.

4. Eliot, *The Sacred Wood* (New York, 1960), p. 49.

5. Ibid., p. 50.

6. Elizabeth Drew, T. S. Eliot: *The Design of His Poetry* (New York, 1949), p. 67.

7. Eliot: *The Sacred Wood*, p. 53.

8. Ibid., pp. 53–54.

9. Ibid., pp. 55.

10. Ibid., pp. 14.

11. Ibid., p. 125.

12. Arthur Davidson. *The Eliot England* (London, 1956), p. 110.

13. Edmund Wilson. "T. S. Eliot," *Axel's Castle* (New York, 1959), p. 110.

14. Eliot, *The Sacred Wood*, p. 125.

15. Reuben Brower, *Alexander Pope: The Poetry of Allusions* (Oxford, 1959), p. XIII.

16. Elizabeth Drew, "T. S. Eliot". *Major British Writers*, ed. G. B. Harrison (New York, 1959), II, 822.

17. Brower, p. 146.

18. William Hazlitt, "On Wit and Humour," Lecture I in *Lectures on the English Comic Writers* (London, 1819).

19. Ibid.

20. T. S. Eliot, "The Possibility of a Poetic Drama," *The Sacred Wood* (New York 1969), p. 69. It is best to list the "touchstone" passages in a group right at the start rather than struggle to weave them into the text at intervals. This way the body of knowledge to be employed throughout the essay is immediately available.

21. Eliot, "Ben Jonson," *The Sacred Wood*, p. 112.

22. Ibid., p. 113.

23. Ibid., p. 115.

24. Ibid., pp. 116–117.

25. Ibid., p. 119.

26. Ibid., p. 120.

27. Ibid., p. 121.

28. Eliot, "Phillip Massinger," *The Sacred Wood*, p. 139.

29. Ibid., p. 142.

30. Eliot, "Hamlet and His Problems," *The Sacred Wood*, p. 100.

31. F. O. Matthiessen, *The Achievement of T. S. Eliot* (New York, 1959), p. 72.

32. Kristian Smidt, *Poetry and Belief in the Work of T. S. Eliot* (New York, 1949), p. 80.

33. Hugh Kenner, *The Invisible Poet* (New York, 1964), p. 4.

34. Smidt, p. 82.

35. See the footnote on p. 39 of D. E. S. Maxwell, *The Poetry of T. S. Eliot*, (London, 1952).

36. Frederick Hoffman, *William Faulkner* (New Haven, 1961), p. 17.

37. Ibid., p. 20.

38. T. S. Eliot, *The Sacred Wood* (New York, 1960), p. 62.

39. Hugh Kenner, *The Invisible Poet* (New York, 1964), p. 88.

40. Eliot, p. 64. Once one has read several quatrains and begins to re-read, his patterns of expectation are already forming. Even one who has no prior acquaintance with the form soon learns what to expect from it.

41. T. S. Eliot, "The Music of Poetry," *On Poetry and Poets* (New York, 1959), p. 31.

42. F. O. Matthiessen, *The Achievement of T. S. Eliot* (New York, 1959), p. 87.

43. Sister M. Cleophas, "Eliot's Whispers of Immortality," *Explicator*, VIII, Item 22.

44. T. S. Eliot, *The Sacred Wood*, p. 23.

45. The epigraph also appears in *The Sacred Wood*, p. 29.

46. Malcolm Cowley, "Introduction to the Portable Faulkner," in *William Faulkner: Three Decades of Criticism*, eds. Frederick Hoffman and Olga W. Vickery (New York, 1960), p. 99.

47. Herbert Howarth, *Notes on Some Figures Behind T. S. Eliot* (Boston, 1964), p. 226.

Sweeney among the Birds and Brutes
Herbert Knust[*]

T. S. Eliot's persistent fascination with the figure Sweeney is witnessed by the fact that he deals with him in four poems and in two dramatic fragments.[1] The critics have shared this fascination. They have been puzzled and intrigued by Sweeney's frequent but noncommittal appearances in various contexts, by his suggestive and yet elusive character. Nevertheless, judgment of Sweeney is fairly unanimous and not very flattering. He has been interpreted as the "type of the vulgar bourgeois,"[2] as "the patron of adultery,"[3] as "the common man, the average, decent lout,"[4] as "some violent, coarse and disagreeable type,"[5] as a "flat" character[6], as a "debased image of humanity,"[7] and so forth. However, some critics have also argued that there is more to his glaring primitivism, that because of Sweeney's references to brutal rites, he himself is perhaps a sacrificial figure with mythical associations, and hence may be on a spiritual pilgrimage.[8]

I believe that an investigation of Sweeney's name yields further insight into his complex nature. Eliot was fond of playing with allusive names, such as Apollinax, Gerontion, Bleistein, Princess Volupine, Fräulein von Kulp, Madame Sosostris, Pereira, Doris and Dusty—or Celia. We should therefore not content ourselves with accepting the major figure Sweeney as a modern character with a common Irish name; we should not deny him any onomastic symbolism;[9] instead, I propose to examine the history, the sound and the allusiveness of this particular name.

Such an approach finds support in Eliot's own writings. He remarks, for example: "Whatever words a writer employs, he benefits by knowing as much as possible of the history of these words . . . The essential of tradition is this: in getting as much as possible of the whole history of the language behind his word."[10] In his essay on *The Music of Poetry* Eliot argues that sound and rhythm "may bring to birth the idea and the image."[11] And in his

*Reprinted, with permission, from *Arcadia*, 11 (1967), 204–17. A shorter version of this paper was presented to the Comparative Literature Section at the eightieth convention of the Modern Language Association in Chicago (1965).

discussion of the "auditory imagination" he emphasizes "the feeling for syllable and rhythm, penetrating far below the conscious levels of thought and feeling, invigorating every word, sinking to the most primitive and forgotten, returning to the origin and bringing something back, seeking the beginning and the end. It works through meanings, certainly, or not without meanings in the ordinary sense, and fuses the old and obliterated and trite, the current, and the new and surprising, the most ancient and the most civilised mentality."[12]

Let me take Eliot at his word. Sweeney is a modern name. But it is also a poetic word with musical overtones, echoing archaic sounds and suggesting various meanings. Although the etymology of *Sweeney* is not clear, it should be noted that all the MacSweeneys of Ireland and Scotland trace their name historically back to the Gaelic *Suibhne*, which is also the source of such related names as MacSween, MacEwens, MacSwine, MacSwiney and MacSwynne.[13] The most famous of all Sweeneys is the legendary Suibhne of the Middle Irish romance *Buile Suibhne*, the *Frenzy of Sweeney*. It is the story of a king who falls under a curse, goes mad, suffers bodily changes and is redeemed at his death. Together with an English translation, this Irish romance was edited in 1913,[14] a few years before Sweeney appears for the first time in Eliot's poetry. We have no documentation of Eliot's knowledge of the book. But certain striking parallels, which I shall presently discuss, point toward a connection between the Irish King Sweeney and Eliot's Sweeney.

A closer examination of the word *Sweeney* leads to rather discrepant results. Some etymologists consider the word *swayne* to be a synonym for *Sweeney*.[15] However, *swayne* (*swain*) is probably of Scandinavian origin, deriving from O. N. *sveinn* ("young man," "servant"). It is interesting to note that the word *swain* has also meant "swineherd" and "warrior," especially in the O. E. form *swān*. *Swān* and *swain* in turn, have been confused with the word *swan*, especially in names of persons and places. *Swan*, however, is derived from the O. N. *svanr* ("sound"). There exists the widespread belief that the swan got his name from "sounding" or "singing." Lastly, the word *Sweeney* has also been associated with O. E. *swīn* and has been explained as "dweller at the swine meadow."[16] And the word *sweeny or swinn(e)y* in American usage, meaning "emaciation," "atrophy," "stiffness of pride," has been thought to be related with the German word *Schweine*.[17] Such phonetic cross connections are fascinating; but scientifically they are most questionable. However, what presents a problem to etymology is not necessarily a problem to the auditory imagination, for certainly, a poet's imagination is not restricted by etymological principles, but, rather, responsive to the similarities of sounds. I suggest, therefore, that without straining phonetic relations too much, the auditory imagination — even without the help of dictionaries — can associate *Sweeney* not only with the old *Suibhne*, name of the Irish king, or with the other word *sweeney* (*sweeny*), but also with the word *swain* in its several meanings;

with *swan*, the divine bird, symbol of purity, prophecy or death; and with *swine*, symbol of animal nature. I shall proceed with the argument that the allusiveness of these words may have generated some ideas and images in Eliot's creative imagination.

A general comparison between the Irish King Sweeney and Eliot's Sweeney reveals that both are fallen heroes, that both suffer a degeneration of their bodies, and that both are to some extent in a state of frenzy. Being under a curse, King Sweeney degenerates from royal stature to the pitiful state of a restless, wandering madman. Repeatedly he bewails his dereliction:

(I am) . . .
without the title of a king,

. . .

a bitter madman in the glen,
bereft of senses and reason.
Without being on a kingly circuit,
but rushing along every path;
that is the great madness,
O King of Heaven of saints   (p. 27)

All men see that I am not shapely,

. . .

the crazy madman am I.   (p. 31)

. . . I am without strength, O Son of God,   (p. 37)

. . . a noble, emaciated madman;   (p. 89)

I have parted from my faultless shape;
O Son of God, great is the misery!   (p. 123)

That Eliot's Sweeney, too, is a fallen hero is shown by his unfavorable contrast with great heroes of antiquity; that he does not possess a faultless shape becomes glaringly obvious through his characterization in animal terms; and that he is in a frenzy — at least in *Sweeney Agonistes* — is suggested by the words of the mad and haunted Orestes, which Eliot uses as an epigraph to *Sweeney Agonistes*, and which correspond to the persecution complex of the mad King Sweeney who is constantly escaping and moving from place to place.

The degeneration of Eliot's Sweeney is further illustrated if we contrast Sweeney with a swain. The archaic *swain*, according to its most elevated meaning, refers to an "attendant knight" or a "warrior." According to Eliot's *mythical method*, by which he draws modern déclassé parallels to heroic figures of antiquity, we can see in Sweeney a degradation of "warrior," particularly in view of Eliot's remark that he pictured Sweeney as a retired boxer.[18] But *swain* also refers to a rustic character with the attributes of an admirer of ladies, a lover, wooer or sweetheart, especially in pastoral poetry. Sweeney is quite the ladies' man who "knows the female temperament" (p. 25); but he is the degenerate lover, a frequent visitor of brothels. The female counterpart of a swain, the pastoral nymph, shepherdess or lady, often has the name Doris. In antiquity she was a fertile nymph of the ocean, mother of fifty lovely daughters. It is none other than Doris who appears as Sweeney's most prominent partner. But, corresponding to Sweeney the swain in degradation, Doris is no longer the nymph or pastoral lady, but a degenerate nymph, a prostitute. *Swain*, lastly, also means "swineherd," which suggests the swine association, to which I shall turn in due course.

First, let me glance once more at the affliction of the Irish King Sweeney. He offers a great deal of evidence that during his madness he developed bird-like characteristics: he flies, grows feathers, dwells in trees among other birds, and sings melodiously.[19] To him this bird stage represents a punishment caused by a Saint's prophecy; but it also reveals the purgatorial effect of this punishment on Sweeney's soul.

Eliot's Sweeney, too, is associated with birds, especially in "Sweeney Among the Nightingales." In this context the meaning of "nightingales" is ambiguous. On the one hand, "nightingale" is a slang term for a prostitute and may well be applied to the dubious female figures in this poem.[20] On the other hand, there is reference to the pure song of the birds proper (p. 36): "The nightingales are singing near / The Convent of the Sacred Heart."

Both these meanings are merged through Eliot's allusions to the myth of Philomela, Procne and Tereus by way of his epigraph to "Sweeney Among the Nightingales." This epigraph is the death cry of Agamemnon, which, in Aeschylus' drama, is woven into a subtle texture of bird imagery alluding to the Philomela-Tereus myth: The lamenting Cassandra, mistress of Agamemnon, is compared with the ravished Philomela who was transformed into a nightingale.[21] As if to emphasize the bearing of this metamorphosis on the women and the nightingales in "Sweeney Among the Nightingales," Eliot had originally prefixed another epigraph to this poem: "Why should I speak of the nightingale? The nightingale sings of adulterous wrong."[22] In *The Waste Land*, Eliot uses the same myth more explicitly (lines 97–103), and, significantly, again in immediate connection with Sweeney (lines 196–206). An association of Sweeney and birds is also hinted at in *Sweeney Agonistes*. In a letter to Hallie Flanagan, Eliot supplied some stage directions for the performance of the play, and he sketched a conclusion to the second fragment.[23] According to this letter, the characters are to wear masks; Sweeney is to scramble eggs (the egg standing for "Birth, and copulation, and death" ["Fragment of an Agon," p. 80]); and lastly, Sweeney is to end up with puzzling allusions to birds. These notes seem to throw some light on the subtitle *Fragments of an Aristophanic Melodrama*. In the "Agon" of Aristophanes' *The Birds*, the egg — as the beginning of all life — is of supreme concern to the aspiring birds. But the breaking of the egg also serves as an obscene reference to sexual desires. This occurs in a passage where Aristophanes ridicules the legend of Philomela, Procne and Tereus.

In typical Aristophanic irony, the ravished Procne, transformed into a nightingale, appears in the gay trappings of a courtesan with the mask of a nightingale among the other masked birds. It seems to me that Eliot uses this sort of Aristophanic travesty not only in *Sweeney Agonistes*, where a masked Sweeney appears among masked prostitutes, but also in "Sweeney Among the Nightingales," where Sweeney is among prostitutes as well as among nightingales,[24] and again in *The Waste Land*, where Sweeney visits prostitutes and where the succeeding comment in bird language suggests his relation to them in terms of the Philomela-Procne-Tereus myth (lines 203–206):

> Twit twit twit
> Jug jug jug jug jug jug
> So rudely forc'd
> Tereu

I think it likely, therefore, that one of Sweeney's masks is a bird mask, that he is symbolically involved in a man-to-bird metamorphosis, similar to that of King Tereus, who became a hoopoe, and to that of the Irish King Sweeney, who became — or imagined himself to be — a bird, but who does not afford us any clear picture as to the kind of bird he was. But auditory imagination suggests linking *Sweeney* with *swan*. Certainly the swan is a favorite bird of metamorphosis, especially for royal or divine characters, in classical antiquity as well as in Norse and Celtic myths. If I may speculate for a moment on the Irish King Sweeney in his bird stage: he would seem eligible for metamorphosis into a swan, for he is of royal descent. There are, in fact, frequent allusions to King Sweeney's white appearance, which may have to do with his skin, or, more likely, with his feathers. Once he even refers to *splendid melodious swans* (p. 35), although not by way of self-identification. However, the Irish Sweeney is himself a superior singer and at his death issues a veritable swan song. In another Irish story, which is apparently based on *The Frenzy of Sweeney*, the swan metamorphosis actually occurs.[25]

There are, I think, even more definite — if more subtle — grounds for linking Eliot's Sweeney with the swan symbolism. It is noteworthy that Agamemnon's death cry is actually associated with the death song of the swan through Cassandra, the god-inspired mad seer and prophetess of Agamemnon's death and her own.[26] Aeschylus supposedly introduced into literature the folkloristic motif of the swan who sings at his death.[27] This image fits the context precisely, for Cassandra is possessed by Delphic Apollo, whose sacred bird is the prophetic swan. Eliot, who uses Agamemnon's death cry as if to foreshadow Sweeney's fate in "Sweeney Among the Nightingales," must have been aware of the dying swan image among the nightingale imagery in Aeschylus' complex elaboration of the great death scene. Eliot's parallel suggests that Sweeney in a house of ill fame is involved in the foreboding atmosphere pervading Agamemnon's ill-fated house. If we realize that this atmosphere is created mainly by the frantic prophecy of swan-like Cassandra who was mistress both of Apollo and of Agamemnon, we are struck by still another parallel, an ominous scene in *"Sweeney Erect."* Again Sweeney is among women in a house of ill repute. One of his mistresses is an epileptic, whose hysteric shriek is portentous and "does the house no sort of good" (p. 26). According to Eliot's *mythical method*, we can see her as a modern counterpart of the possessed Cassandra. Whereas the wailing Cassandra wished that she could flap her wings like an innocent bird, the raving epileptic "curves backward, clutching at her sides" (p. 26.) This gesture recalls, figuratively, the shape of Apollo's sacred bird, the swan, with neck curved backward and flapping wings. The crucial passage is the last stanza in which another of Sweeney's mates appears on the scene (p. 26):

> But Doris, towelled from the bath,
> Enters padding on broad feet
> Bringing sal volatile
> And a glass of brandy neat.

In folklore, according to Jacob Grimm, the flat feet ("platschfuβ") of women are the modern relics of the broad feet of swan maidens, indicating their connection with some higher, divine nature.[28] Eliot's nymph Doris "enters padding on broad feet," and conspicuously comes from an aquatic realm, however domestic. Grimm also points out that white coverings of women were associated with the swan garments as magic attributes.[29] Doris comes "towelled from the bath," her towel being the modern vestige of the swan cover which the swan maiden puts on again after her bath in the *svanrād*. There may also be a pun on *sal volatile*. It means "ammonium carbonate," to be sure, and is a medicine for fainting. But *volatile* also means "bird," from Lat. *volare*, "to fly." This meaning seems symbolically appropriate for the birdlike underpattern of the imagery involving the epileptic, Sweeney and Doris.

Yet, whatever the findings about Sweeney and birds, his association with swine is still more prominent than his hidden ties with *swan*. As was stated earlier, one meaning of the word *Sweeney* is actually listed as "the dweller at the swine meadow," and one meaning of *swain* is "swineherd." It is a significant coincidence that the Irish King Sweeney himself does not only go through a bird stage, but that he is also humbled as though he were a swine. At the end of his wanderings he comes to Saint Moling, who has a swineherd by the name of Muirghil. Muirghil's wife Mongan feeds Sweeney in this fashion; "she used to thrust her heel up to her ankle in the cowdung nearest her and leave the full of it of new milk there for Suibhne" (p. 143). Another woman accuses the swineherd's wife of adultery with Sweeney. The swineherd hears this, grasps a spear and kills Sweeney, who "was lying down eating his meal out of the cowdung" (p. 145):

> Sad is that, O swineherd of Moling,
> thou hast wrought a wilful, sorry deed,

> woe to him who has slain by dint of his strength
> the king, the saint, the saintly madman.

Turning to Eliot's Sweeney, we do not have to look too hard to see his general brute characteristics. Sweeney is compared with an ape, a zebra, a giraffe, an orang-outang; and then there are these suggestive lines (p. 25): "Sweeney, addressed full length to shave / Broadbottomed, pink from nape to base," and (p. 34): "Sweeney shifts from ham to ham / Stirring the water in his bath."

Critics have not minced their words about Sweeney's swinish traits: "Sweeney," remarks one, "like some 'broadbottomed' pig . . . clumsily 'shifts from ham to ham' to stir the water in his bath."[30] And another is even more to the point: "Gesture of orang-outang / Shambling, hairy, human swine."[31] A more delicate suggestion is offered by still another commentator, who feels that the Sweeney "setting reminds us of the 'Circe' chapter of James Joyce's *Ulysses* . . ."[32] We should note, too, that "broadbottomed" Sweeney has a piggish pink color "from nape to base" (p. 25). He is apparently naked, which recalls the curse on the Irish King Sweeney, who is doomed — among other punishments — to move about in nakedness.[33]

The symbolic contrast between bird and beast may be generally interpreted as the disparity between spirit and body. This contrast appears not only in the adventures of the Irish King Sweeney, but also in the situation of his namesake in Eliot's poetry. It is a theme which concerned Eliot so much that it is not at all surprising to find the juxtaposition of brute and bird imagery in other passages. I quote from "The Hippopotamus," who is a striking parallel to "broadbottomed" Sweeney (p. 30f.): "The broad-backed hippopotamus / Rests on his belly in the mud;" and later:

> I saw the 'potamus take wing
> Ascending from the damp savannas,
> And quiring angels round him sing
> The praise of God, in loud hosannas,
>
> . . .
>
> He shall be washed as white as snow

In "Burnt Norton," too, we hear an echo of the bird-brute contrast: the bird invites us into the rose garden, and in the succeeding passage occur the lines (p. 119):

> We move above the moving tree
> In light upon the figured leaf
> And hear upon the sodden floor
> Below, the boarhound and the boar.

With regard to Sweeney the brute and swine allusions are unmistakable, whereas the bird and swan allusions are concealed, pointing to mythical prototypes. Accordingly, Sweeney appears much more as a man of the body than as a man of the spirit. Yet, both characteristics are simultaneously evoked by his allusive name, and there is sufficient evidence that Eliot had both aspects in mind in his portrayals of Sweeney. Let me examine two further examples under this double aspect. The most complex Sweeney passage of all occurs in *The Waste Land*. It is the Fisher King who speaks the lines (196–206):

> But at my back from time to time I hear
> The sound of horns and motors, which shall bring
> Sweeney to Mrs. Porter in the spring.
> O the moon shone bright on Mrs. Porter
> And on her daughter
> They wash their feet in soda water
> Et O ces voix d'enfants, chantant dans la coupole!
>
> Twit twit twit
> Jug jug jug jug jug jug
> So rudely forc'd
> Tereu

Eliot has fortified this passage with several notes indicating literary parallels. The first three lines are shaped partly after the well-known lines in Marvell's "To His Coy Mistress" (see note 196): "But at my back I always hear / Time's winged chariot hurrying near;" and partly after a passage in Day's *Parliament of Bees* (see note 197);

> When of the sudden, listening, you shall hear,
> A noise of horns and hunting, which shall bring
> Actaeon to Diana in the spring,
> Where all shall see her naked skin . . .

On the one hand, the verbal borrowing emphasizes spring as a time of expectation and salvation (for the waiting Fisher King). On the other hand, the significance of these parallels lies in the obvious parody: Sweeney and Mrs. Porter are caricatures of the great huntsman Actaeon and the goddess Diana, and of Marvell and his coy and still virgin mistress. Whereas Actaeon unintentionally sees the naked skin of a virgin goddess, who is also the protectress of childbirth, Sweeney makes a customer's visit to a prostitute, to whom the line "Where all shall see her naked skin" applies with a new twist; and whereas Marvell is aware of death, Sweeney is himself a death-in-life figure. This parallelism is true to Eliot's waste-land methods and seems complete at first sight; it is a reversal of the sacredness of spring and of life.

There are, however, deeper implications. As we know, the bathing Diana splashed water into Actaeon's face and thereby changed him into a stag, who was torn into pieces by his own dogs. He thus died a sacrifice to Diana the goddess of hunting; and, since Diana is a triple goddess, we think of her in this connection also as the goddess of the dead in the underworld. Her third aspect is that of the goddess of the moon. Eliot significantly alludes to this aspect by quoting the song "O the moon shone bright on Mrs. Porter" (see note 19). It is a matter of consequent analogy to associate not only Mrs. Porter but also Sweeney with the moon symbol. Because of the parallelism between him and Actaeon, it is near at hand to think again of Sweeney's metamorphosis, of his animal mask. And, being not Actaeon but Sweeney, he is not transformed into a stag, but appears in his swine identity. The relation of a swine to the moon goddess is no riddle and explains the deeper meaning of this particular parallelism. Eliot tells us in his notes that he used especially Frazer's accounts of Adonis, Attis and Osiris. Frazer shows in detail that Adonis, Attis and Osiris were old gods, once embodied in the swine (pig, boar), and that therefore the swine was a sacred animal in the Orient. (Similar deifications are to be found in Norse and Irish mythology.) In the chapter "Osiris, the Pig and the Bull" Frazer shows that swine were sacrificed every year to Osiris and the Moon.[34] The moon is in some versions Osiris himself, but is commonly considered to be the triple goddess Isis, sister and wife of Osiris as the sun god. As such she corresponds to Diana, who is sister of the sun god Apollo.

The relation of Sweeney to the moon (Mrs. Porter-Diana) corresponds therefore to the partnership of Osiris and the moon goddess Isis. Osiris and Sweeney are both embodiments of the swine symbol, which was once a fertility symbol. In Egypt (and also in Scandinavia and Ireland) swine were used in fertility rites. The annual killing of the pig represented not only a sacrifice to the god Osiris and the moon, but was also a representation of the killing of Osiris himself, who, like Attis and Adonis, was killed by a boar. This image of the "Dying God," being simultaneously a sacrifice to the god, is a close analogy to the myths of the "Hanged God" and the "Drowned God," whose sacrificial deaths terminate and in turn originate the fertility cycle. It is therefore plausible that one aspect of Sweeney the swine is a modern equivalent of the Osiris-swine myth, and that in this disguise, degenerate and unfruitful as it is, he nevertheless belongs to the line of "Dying Gods."[35]

It appears then that on the mythical level Sweeney becomes victim to the moon, alias Diana, alias Isis, alias Mrs. Porter, alias Doris, alias Dusty, alias other feminine embodiments. It should be remembered that the Irish King Sweeney, too, died in his swinish stage and that the cause was women. And we should also keep in mind that Eliot offers quite a few suggestions which indicate that Sweeney will die a sacrificial death conjured up by women. There is the parallel with Agamemnon, who died in his bath at the hands of his wife. Sweeney is among women who are "suspect, thought to be in league," and one of them has "murderous paws" (p. 35). There are the sinister omens showing Sweeney under the spell of the moon and death goddess, whose gate he guards (p. 35) . . .

> The circles of the stormy moon
> Slide westward toward the River Plate

Death and the Raven drift above
And Sweeney guards the horned gate.

The River Plate is probably a disguise for the river of the underworld, over which Death and the Raven drift as portents to Sweeney, the victim. It looks like a clever disguise, indeed, for the River Plate, i.e., "Rio de la Plata," was originally called "Rio de Solis" after its discoverer, de Solis, who was killed there by Indians. There may possibly exist here another case of concealed name symbolism.[36] "De Solis" suggests a Latin form of *solus*, meaning "solitary," "forlorn," "forsaken," while acoustically it also calls to mind the Latin *sol (solis)*, "sun." These implications seem relevant to Sweeney's situation. He is doomed, and, in analogy to Osiris, we have again the motif of a sacrificed sun god. In *Sweeney Agonistes*, too, there occurs a hint that Sweeney is a symbolic victim. In cutting the cards, the women come upon the black card, King of Clubs, which to them signifies Sweeney just as well as Pereira. This identification of the two characters by one common card is ominous in that *Pereira* suggests *perire*, and *perire* means "to perish,""to die."[37]

The mythical component of Sweeney's swine identity thus adds archetypal meaning to his relationship with Mrs. Porter under the moon. But we still have to consider his other side, which is relevant in that it substantiates the appropriateness of the Sweeney passage within this immediate context. Apparently Sweeney and Mrs. Porter are directly linked with the Grail legend: first, through the Fisher King himself, who muses on the next of his kin, and who experiences Sweeney's noisy arrival (lines 189–192);[38] second, through the ironic line about the washing of feet in soda water (line 201), which not only recalls Diana's bath but also provides a connection with the story of the Fisher King, for it alludes to Parsifal's footwashing shortly before he is to redeem Amfortas (in Wagner's drama the king's salvation by the knight is accompanied by the voices of boys sounding from the cupola of the Grail Hall, telling of the mystery of the Grail); third, through the French quotation from Verlaine's *Parsifal* (see note 202), evoking Wagner's scene, but adding—as it does—a problem of sexual perversion. What then does Sweeney's visit to Mrs. Porter have to do with the Fisher King's disillusioned—if not perverted—state of mind? What is the significance of Sweeney's association with the Grail legend, apart from the parodistic allusion to the footwashing rite and to Sweeney's role as questor? I believe that Sweeney's bird mask answers these questions. The swan is not only a symbol of old gods—he is also the symbol of the Grail. Specifically, the swan stands for the last of the Grail kings, for Parzival's son, the swan knight, who thus, too, belongs to the Fisher King's kin.[39] However, this Grail knight did not distinguish himself by redeeming a king. On the contrary, he aids a lady in distress and then becomes her lover. The motif of a marvellous stranger visiting a lady has mythical roots. It reminds us of Amor visiting Psyche, or of Zeus visiting mortal women, and points to a precarious union of the divine with the human — which lastly ends in failure. This religio-erotic motif may be parodistically reflected in Sweeney's visit: just as Zeus, in the form of a swan, visited Leda,[40] and just as the swan knight, divine messenger of the Grail, visited a lady (or a lady and her daughter),[41] so Sweeney in his swan identity — perverted by his swine identity — visits Mrs. Porter (and her daughter) under the moon. The succeeding quotation refers, fittingly, to bird metamorphosis and to rape. Thus the ends of the swine and swan interpretations would meet not only on a phonetic but also on a mythical level.

From the double perspective of bird — relating to the spirit — and of brute — relating to the body —, Eliot's epigraphs to *Sweeney Agonistes*, in turn, may be interpreted in the following way: Sweeney is in agony, for his soul and his body, his swan and his swine identities are at war. The first epigraph, the words of Orestes: "You don't see them, you don't — but I see them: they are hunting me down, I must move on" (p. 74) refer to the Furies that are persecuting him. The Furies have the appearance of brutes, and just as Orestes is hunted by them, so Sweeney (figuratively speaking) is hunted by his brutal swine fate; or, to use the images from *Burnt Norton:* the boarhound hunts the boar. The second epigraph, a quotation from St. John of the Cross, refers on the other hand to the soul, Sweeney's swan identity: "Hence the soul cannot be possessed of the divine union, until it has divested itself of the love of created beings" (p. 74). Sweeney will find spiritual peace only if he will shake off his animal nature just as Orestes must free himself of the Furies.

The Irish King Sweeney went on a similar quest as indicated in such lines as these (p. 35):

> O Christ, O Christ, hear me!
> O Christ, O Christ, without sin!
> O Christ, O Christ, love me!
> sever me not from thy sweetness!

And the last stanza of King Sweeney's dying song reads (p. 155):

> To thee, O Christ, I give thanks
> for partaking of Thy Body;
> sincere repentance in this world
> for each evil I have ever done.

Eliot's Sweeney never gets that far. The last evidence we have of him is the fragment of a fragment with references to the angelus, and with the confrontation of a figure resembling Father Christmas, speaking about tardy souls — and Sweeney, babbling about birds.

Notes

1. "Sweeney Erect"; "Mr. Eliot's Sunday Morning Service"; "Sweeney Among The Nightingales"; *The Waste Land; Sweeney Agonistes* ("Fragment of a Prologue" and "Fragment of an Agon"). My Eliot references are to *The Compl. Poems and Plays 1909–1950,* New York

1952, and are hereafter included in the text by page numbers (for *The Waste Land* by line numbers).

2. Cleanth Brooks: *Mod. Poetry And The Tradition*, Chapel Hill, 1939, 153.

3. Leo Kirschbaum: "Eliot's 'Sweeney Among The Nightingales,' " in: *The Explicator* 2, No. 3 (December 1943), 18.

4. Nevell Coghill: *Sweeney Agonistes*, in: *T. S. Eliot — A Symposium*, ed. Richard March and Tambimuttu, London 1948, 84.

5. C. M. Bowra: *The Creative Experiment*, London 1949, 182.

6. Carol H. Smith: *T. S. Eliot's Dramatic Theory And Practice from "Sweeney Agonistes" to "The Elder Statesman,"* Princeton 1963, 60.

7. D. E. Jones: *The Plays of T. S. Eliot*, London 1960, 31.

8. See, for instance, Grover Smith's chapter on *Sweeney Agonistes* in his book *T. S. Eliot's Poetry And Plays: A St. in Sources And Meaning*, Chicago 1956, 1961 (zit. Grover Smith), 110–118. Elizabeth R. Homann, in commenting on Sweeney's composite mask, says that Sweeney, besides being a brute, also represents a priest and an intended sacrifice *("Eliot's 'Sweeney Among The Nightingales,' "* 8, in: *The Explicator* 17, No. 5 (Feb. 1959), 34. See also Carol H. Smith (Anm, 6), 32–75.

9. In his witty detective story *The Bloody Wood*, in: *The London Mercury* 29 (January 1934), 233–239, T. H. Thompson claims: "I think I have solved the Sweeney problem. . . . Sweeney is anything but a symbol" (p. 233). The article, a skilful but unsatisfactory mosaic-work compounded from Sweeney's behavior in various poems and fragments, is reprinted in *T. S. Eliot — A Selected Critique*, ed. Leonard Unger, New York 1948, 161–169.

10. In *The Tyro*, No. 3, 1922.

11. *On Poetry And Poets*, London 1957, 38.

12. *The Use of Poetry And The Use of Criticism*, London 1933, 118 f.

13. Leabhar Chlainne Suibbne — *An Account of The MacSweeney Families in Ireland, with Pedigrees*, ed. Paul Walsh, Dublin 1920.

14. *The Adventures of Suibbne Geilt*, ed. J. G. O'Keefe, *Irish Texts* Soc. XII 1910, London 1913.

15. For documentation of the following statements see, for instance, Flavell Edmunds: *Traces of Hist. in The Names of Places*, London 1869, 264; Joseph Bosworth: *An Anglo-Saxon Dict.*, ed. T. N. Toller, Oxford 1882, 943, 957; Henry Harrison: *Surnames of The United Kingdom — A Concise Etymological Dict.*, 2 vols., London 1912, 1918, II 202; James B. Johnston: *The Place-Names of England And Wales*, London 1914, 463 f.; Ernest Weekley: *The Romance of Names*, New York 1914, 10; Ernest Weekley: *Surnames*, London 1916, 1917, 1936, pp. 37, 42, 234; J. R. C. Hall: A Concise Anglo-Saxon Dict., Cambridge 1931, 329, 332; P. H. Reaney: *A Dict. of British Surnames*, London 1958, 313; Edward MacLysaght: *A Guide to Irish Surnames*, Baltimore 1964, 191 f.; Edward MacLysaght: *Supplement to Irish Families*, Baltimore 1964, 142.

16. Henry Harrison, *Surnames of The United Kingdom*, II, 203; see also Eilbert Ekwall, *The Concise Oxford Dictionary of English Place Names*, Oxford 1960, 456.

17. *A New Engl. Dict. On Hist. Principles*, ed. Sir James A. H. Murray, 10 vols., Oxford 1888–1928, IX, part II (S) 302.

18. See Nevill Coghill: *Sweeney Agonistes*, in: *T. S. Eliot* (Anm. 4), 86; See also Conrad Aiken: *King Bolo and Others*, ebd. 20–23.

19. O'Keefe states, "Throughout the story he speaks as though he imagined himself a bird" (p. 33, n. 23, 1) see also pp. 11, 13, 15, 23, 43, 45, 55, 75, 119.

20. See Grover Smith, 46.

21. There are two versions of this bird metamorphosis: in the more familiar version, Philomela is transformed into a nightingale, her sister Procne into a swallow (Ovid); in the

other version, Philomela is changed into a swallow, and Procne into a nightingale (Anacreon, Apollodorus, Aristophanes).

22. See Grover Smith, 45.

23. See Hallie Flanagan: *Dynamo*, New York 1943, 82 f.

24. Since the epigraph to this poem suggests a parallel between Agamemnon's death and Sweeney's, I take the "stiff dishonoured shroud" to mean Sweeney's shroud, stained by the "liquid siftings" of the nightingales who are "singing near / The Convent of the Sacred Heart" (p. 36). For further implications of this scene, see Grover Smith, 46; Frederic L. Gwynn — Ralph W. Condee — Arthur O. Lewis, Jr.: *The Case for Poetry*, New York, 1954, 143n.

25. See James Carney: *St. in Irish Lit. and Hist.*, Dublin 1955, 157.

26. "He lies there: and she who swanlike cried / aloud her lyric mortal lamentation out / is laid against his fond heart. . . ." (*Agamemnon*, 1144–46); quoted from *The Compl. Greek Tragedies*, ed. David Grene and Richmond Lattimore, vol. I: *Aeschylus*, Chicago 1959. For the bird imagery already mentioned, see lines 1050 f., 1140–49, 1313–17.

27. According to Friedrich Kluge, Aeschylus was the first to use the "dying swan's song" as a literary motif as derived from an older folk belief (*Etymologisches Wb. der dt. Sprache*, Berlin 1953, 704).

28. Jacob Grimm: Dt. *Mythologie Viete Ausgabe* besorgt von E. H. Meyer, 3 Bde., Berlin 1875–78, I 233.

29. Ebd. I 324, 354–357.

30. Paul Fussell, Jr.: *The Gestic Symbolism of T. S. Eliot*, in: *Engl. Lit. Hist.* 22 (September 1955), 204.

31. Myra Buttle: *The Sweeniad*, New York 1959, 32.

32. P. R. Headings: *T. S. Eliot*, New York 1964, 44.

33. The curse on King Sweeney contains the lines: "Be it my will, together with the will of the mighty Lord, that even as he came stark-naked to expel me, may it be thus that he will ever be. Naked, wandering and flying throughout the world" (O'Keeffe: *The Adventures of Suibhne Geilt*, 5). The mad Sweeney himself gives in his songs ample evidence of his nakedness.

34. Sir James Georges Frazer: *The Golden Bough — A St. in Magic and Religion*, 12 vols., London 1911–1915, v 264 f.; VIII 22–39.

35. From a different point of departure Carol H. Smith reaches similar conclusions. She traces the influence of the Cambridge School of Classical Anthropology on Eliot and finds that the ritual or sacrificial death of ancient god figures (among them Adonis, Attis and Osiris) forms a mythical underpattern for Sweeney's agony (see especially pp. 43–45, 62).

36. I owe this point to Professor J. Mitchell Morse.

37. Carol H. Smith's suggestion that Pereira is a remedy for fever (*T. S. Eliot's Dramatic Theory and Practice*, 65) can be reconciled with the semantic meaning of *perire*, for death (Pereira) may "cure" the soul of a feverish and sordid earthly life.

38. There is, furthermore, a striking similarity between the Fisher King's statement (lines 325 f.):

> Fishing, with the arid plain behind me
> Shall I at least set my lands in order?

and the Irish King Sweeney's lines (pp. 99–101):

> fishing in springtime
>
> . . . .
>
> Often do I reach
> the land I have set in order.

39. Wolfram von Eschenbach incorporated the legend of the swan knight in his *Parzival*, Wagner treated it in *Lohengrin* and included swan motifs in his *Parsifal*.

40. At the opening of the passage under discussion, Eliot quotes the refrain from Spenser's *Prothalamion* lines 175–184 (see notes 176):

> The nymphs are departed
> Sweet Thames, run softly, till I end my song.
>
> . . .
>
> The nymphs are departed.
>
> . . .
>
> Sweet Thames, run softly till I end my song,
> Sweet Thames, run softly, for I speak not loud or long.

This quotation evokes Spenser's *Nymphes of the Themmes*, but also the lengthy description of the *Swannes* with reference to Jupiter (Zeus) and Leda (lines 37–54):

> With that, I saw two Swannes of goodly hewe,
> Come softly swimming downe along the Lee:
> Two fairer Birds I yet did never see:
> The snow which doth the top of Pindus strew,
> Did neuer whiter shew,
> Nor Ioue himselfe when he a Swan would be
> For loue of Leda, whiter did appeare:
> Yet Leda was they say as white as he,
> Yet not so white as these, nor nothing neare;
> So purely white they were,
> That euen the gentle streame, the which them bare,
> Seem'd foule to them, and had his billowes spare
> To wet their silken feathers, least they might
> Soyle their fayre plumes with water not so fayre,
> And marre their beauties bright,
> That shone as heauens light,
> Against their Brydale day, which was not long:
> Sweete Themmes runne softly, till I end my Song.

Eliot's scene — including Sweeney's visit to Mrs. Porter — is a sharp contrast to Spenser's.

41. A collection of the different versions of the swan knight's visit to a lady (or a lady and her daughter) can be found in *Deutsche Sagen*, hg. v, den Brüden Grimm. Vierte Auflage von Reinhold Steig, Berlin 1905, 421–434. See also Jessie L. Weston: *The Legend of the Wagner Drama — St. in Mythology and Romance*, New York 1900, 221–286. — In this connection it should be pointed out that in his *Remembrance of Things Past* Proust, too, makes intricate use of symbolic associations suggested by Swann's name, including, significantly, allusions to the swan knight legend.

Time, Doubt and Vision: Notes on Emerson and T. S. Eliot

John Clendenning*

No one reading the poems of T. S. Eliot, particularly the early poems, would deny that they were influenced by the society around Boston and Cambridge. Suffocated by its provincialism, amused by its postures of sophistication, Eliot created a world inspired by the Boston *Evening Transcript*, peopled it with Cousin Harriet, Aunt Helen and Miss Nancy Ellicott, with the mythical Mrs. Phlaccus and Professor Channing-Cheetah at whose *soirées* Mr. Apollinax, the visiting professor from Europe, is entertained. This too is the world of J. Alfred Prufrock who sits suffering at his host's table not daring to eat a peach for fear, perhaps, of squirting its juice into someone's lap, but who also impotently yearns to squeeze "the universe into a ball / To roll it toward some overwhelming question . . ."

All this is familiar enough, but one might add that the fact, if somewhat less terrifying, was scarcely less ludicrous than the fiction. The literati of Boston and Cambridge, near the turn of the century and before the first war, often found themselves lavishly feasted and flattered in the home of some prominent lady, women like Mrs. Jack Gardner and Mrs. Molly Dorr. There a Harvard professor might read parts of his new book; there one might hear easy quips issuing from the mouth of William James or thundering erudition from the massive head of Josiah Royce. John Jay Chapman has given a penetrating account of Mrs. Dorr. "She lived," Chapman reports, "in the heart-secrets of others. She had been one of the original transcendentalists, a friend of Emerson and Margaret Fuller. She gave large dinners and caused her guests to change places in the middle of the meal, called all women by their first names and all men by their last names." Chapman adds that someone once said "that if the Virgin Mary should come to Boston, Molly Dorr would drop in at the Bell household and say . . . 'Helen, dine with me tomorrow. *Mary'll be there!*' "

> The readers of the *Boston Evening Transcript*
> Sway in the wind like a field of ripe corn.

To find this in Eliot is to be reminded of Emerson's famous sentence: "I expand and live in the warm day like corn and melons." And this is also to be reminded of Christopher Cranch's apt caricature, depicting Emerson's cheerful face swelling in an ear of corn and globed melon. I cannot resist adding that a well-known Iowa poet has given one of his volumes the daring title, *Corn*, and that Mr. Douglas of Illinois is the major sponsor of a Senate resolution that would make the corn tassel our national flower. And why not? What better symbol could be offered of America's innocence, its fecundity, its uniqueness, its isolation? I am struck by the possibility that America's main contribution to the world has been its corn. Swaying, but seldom

*Reprinted, with permission, from the *American Scholar*, 36 (1966–67), 125–32.

buffeted, seldom broken, always expanding in the warm day, the readers of Emerson and the Boston *Evening Transcript* are almost perfectly described as a field of ripe corn. Cousin Nancy, we are told, strode and rode over the New England hills; she smoked and danced, and although "her aunts were not quite sure how they felt about it, . . . they knew that it was modern."

> Upon the glazen shelves kept watch
> Matthew and Waldo, guardians of the faith.
> The army of unalterable law.

In these pages I shall consider several questions concerning the relationship between the thought of T. S. Eliot and that of Ralph Waldo Emerson. Most critics imply that there is nothing positive to say on the subject. F. O. Matthiessen discussed the matter seriously, but finished by denying that Eliot was "directly indebted" to Emerson or his contemporaries. Of course one must recognize that Eliot found certain aspects of Emerson laughable, but the matter is not so simple. We must not fail to see that they both devoted their lives to the search for answers to the same persisting questions of the deepest religious and metaphysical importance: the meaning of human experience and the possibility of knowledge. Although Eliot was never to become Emerson's disciple, they shared a similar concept of time, an insistence on the necessity of skepticism, and a religion based on faith as opposed to reason.

The year 1919 was important in the career of T. S. Eliot, as in the history of European and American civilization. The broad significance of that year has been made permanently clear by John Dos Passos in the title of his second novel in the *U.S.A.* trilogy. For Eliot it was a year of tremendous poetic and critical achievement. The number of his contributions to periodicals during 1919 nearly doubled that of any year immediately preceding or following it. In June, the Hogarth Press published his second book of verse, and during the autumn, the *Egotist* printed, in two parts, the celebrated and highly influential essay, "Tradition and the Individual Talent." Less spectacular, but still of extraordinary interest, are his many reviews published in the *Athenaeum*, reviews that go far beyond one's expectations into a realm of critical theory. Here Eliot, still a young man and nearly at the outset of his career, raised the fundamental questions concerning the nature of literature and criticism.

During this same year we find Eliot searching for his own American origins — the heritage of Boston society, of Puritanism, Unitarianism, Transcendentalism. In his first piece in the *Athenaeum*, a review of the second volume in the *Cambridge History of American Literature*, Eliot, commenting on the relationship between Hawthorne and Emerson, wrote: "Hawthorne was very much a New Englander, but he was not really a member of the Transcendentalist group which clustered round Emerson." Agreeing with John Erskine, Eliot observed that Hawthorne embodied the philosophical questioning to which the Transcendentalists paid lip service.

"Neither Emerson nor any of the others," Eliot added, "was a real observer of the moral life. Hawthorne was, and was a realist." The ability to see life firmly and coldly gives Hawthorne's work the solidity and permanence of art. Of Emerson, however, Eliot could only conclude with a now frequently quoted phrase: "The essays of Emerson are already an encumbrance." The statement is explored no further, but the complexities of the Boston literary tradition are submitted to an interesting scrutiny. Compared with their English contemporaries, Eliot insisted, American writers of the nineteenth century were products of a starved environment, a sterile tradition; deprived of an *intelligentsia*, they resorted to *originality*, a quality that might make them more immediately exciting, more refreshing, more shocking than their opposite numbers in England, but which in the long run suffered from a world too thin, incorrupt, secondhand and shallow. If these remarks show that Eliot was well on the way toward his distinction between tradition and individual talent, they suggest further that his dissatisfaction with American literature grew out of his belief that great art is possible only through a reverence for the past and a conscious suppression of originality. Hawthorne, Emerson and the rest drew little from the soil of American life that could nourish a lasting greatness. Products of a shallow tradition, American letters are superficial; lacking corruption, the intuition of evil, American writers, only seemingly original and self-dependent, too often expound a pale optimism, see through a glass rosily. Reading such criticisms, we cannot fail to remember a stanza from "Sweeney Erect," also published in 1919, in the magazine *Art and Letters:*

> (The lengthened shadow of a man
>   Is history, said Emerson
> Who had not seen the silhouette
>   Of Sweeney straddled in the sun.)

This stanza refers to, even condemns with irony, two ideas that are fundamental in Emerson's thought, both of which are expressed with greatest emphasis in the first two chapters of his *Essays* (First Series), "History" and "Self-Reliance"; these ideas are, first, his concept of the self in time, and second, his belief in the purity of human conscience. Emerson frequently insisted that there was no past at his back. By this he meant to deny that history is a study of fixed events standing, as it were, independently behind us in a block, that the past can ever be understood in detachment or with objectivity. He admired and repeated the famous example of Heraclitus: "You cannot bathe twice in the same river." The notion that time is a flowing stream of experiences, that any past moment is retrievable only through human memory — this notion he found repeatedly in Plutarch and Montaigne. It seemed to show that time is illusion: all time is present; and if one moment, at the next moment, is history, the succession itself is unreal, for the past, as a collection of objective events, is never present in any single moment. And further, since each moment is known only through human experience, our knowledge of the past is merely a vague recollection of those experiences. "All history," he said, "becomes subjective; in other words there is properly no history, only biography."

Emerson's application of this principle to the field of morals led him to his beliefs in self-trust and nonconformity: a man should conduct his life as if everything in experience were ephemeral except himself. The only good, Emerson believed, is self-reliance, obedience to conscience or the moral sentiments, and the only evil is violation of these sentiments. The difficulties involved in making conscience the basis of moral discrimination are complex, but they are not especially relevant to the present discussion. I cite only the well-used, if not well-worn, instance of Hitler's self-reliance, the implications of which are, to say the least, terrifying. This suggests what every reader of Emerson already knows, that his moral outlook was a consequence of his assumption that human nature is essentially pure, healthy and good.

From Eliot's viewpoint, then, Emerson had never seen the brute soul of Sweeney, had never known the reality of evil or examined the limitations of an uncritical humanism. One is not surprised, therefore, to find F. O. Matthiessen reporting that Eliot had privately expressed his long-standing distaste for Emerson. With little respect for traditions and institutions, Emerson was willing to deny history and to lift the originality of self-reliance to a point of religious consecration; with a conscience limited by its sweetness, he became the prophet of a pale moral optimism. But again from Eliot's viewpoint, Emerson's deficiencies were those of America. "The narrowness of the Boston horizon," to use another of Eliot's phrases, is reflected in the creatures of his early poems; Emerson is merely a revealing emblem of that narrowness. Along with Matthew Arnold, he guards the faith from his glassed-in bookcase; outwardly pristine and triumphant, inwardly he is dusty and confined. It is Emersonianism, then, not merely Emerson, that is the target of Eliot's criticism — Emersonianism as we find an instance of it in the world of Molly Dorr, at whose dinner parties the same spirit, provincial, ageless and pure, seemed inevitably to reign, where the innocence of bad manners might express one's habitual self-reliance, and where the Blessed Virgin was just one of the girls. For Eliot, such a world was mildly, not even profoundly, distasteful — overly sweet and slightly bitter:

> Of dowager Mrs. Phalccus, and Professor and Mrs. Cheetah
> I remember a slice of lemon, and a bitten macaroon.

This might seem to close the matter of the relationship between Emerson and Eliot. Indeed on moral grounds, one could hardly cite more different views or more different poems than, for example, "May-Day" and "The Waste Land." In one we find:

> April cold with dropping rain
> Willows and lilacs brings again . . .

while in the other:

> April is the cruellest month, breeding
> Lilacs out of the dead land . . .

One is a pastoral celebration of God in nature; the other is a descent into an inferno of sterility and despair. But we should remember that this is basically a moral difference, a difference emphasized by Eliot's remark: "Neither Emerson nor any of the others was a real observer of the moral life."

There was another aspect of Emerson's outlook that Eliot readily admired. This was his tendency toward skepticism. In another piece printed by the *Athenaeum* in 1919, a review of *The Education of Henry Adams*, Eliot focused attention on what he called "the Boston doubt," a doubt that he believed to be a fundamental and unique characteristic of the American mind. Finding it admittedly difficult to explain this skepticism to an Anglo-European audience, Eliot chose Emerson as his example. He retold the story of Emerson's resignation from his pulpit, of his sermon on "The Lord's Supper" in which he announced his doubts about the validity and the usefulness of the sacrament, announced that he did not believe in it, that he was not interested in it and would not continue to administer it. Emphasizing the importance of these doubts, Eliot added: "That is an instance of the point of view of several thousands of well-bred people in a provincial American town; and, arrested at the point of ecclesiastical procedure, it is not without an austere grandeur."

This "Boston doubt" with its "austere grandeur" deserves a moment's consideration. We have already seen one of its aspects as it appears in Emerson's writings. In questioning the reality of time, he was proposing, and this he frequently repeated, that experience is so hopelessly divorced from reality that one can never answer with certainty the huge questions that faith presses upon us. Time, he readily admitted, is part of experience; indeed it is the necessary structure of experience — that is, necessarily limited and limiting. Our difficulty arises from the fact that time is never encountered as a continuous whole, but rather as an aggregate of successive moments. There is, in other words, no continuity of experience, no real duration. "We live in succession, in division, in parts, in particles," he said in a fairly typical passage. "Meantime within man is the soul of the whole; the wise silence; the universal beauty, to which every part and particle is equally related; the eternal ONE." Like his Puritan forebears, and like most believers who lean toward mysticism, Emerson believed that God is infinitely incomprehensible. This God exists, Emerson would affirm, but He exists in a realm beyond ordinary experience, a timeless realm; consequently, we must question all philosophies, all dogmatisms that would seek to justify claims concerning God's existence and nature. Thus far, Emerson was a skeptic, and like the skeptics that he knew — principally Montaigne and Hume — he emphasized the futility and imprecision of language that attempts to explain or define the doctrines of faith. Words, he said, cannot span or define the dimensions of truth: "They break, chop, and impoverish it." His striking phrase, "the wise silence," suggests both his doubts of rational religions, such as Unitarianism, and his longing for the irrational vision of the mystic. In silent suspension of judgment he refused to engage in polemics concerning questions of faith, but with the wordless knowledge of religious insight he gave himself fully to "the eternal ONE." Like Saint Peter, Emerson felt himself called upon to take the absurd step onto the waters of faith. He willingly took that step, yet afterward found that experience, with its successions, divisions, parts and particles, was still unredeemed. Doubt returned, and accepting this, he could only await a renewal of insight. This is the central drama of Emerson's religious quest, the major theme of his writings, enacted and reenacted in nearly all of his essays.

We may recognize this theme clearly with a close reading of his mature and perhaps his finest poem, "Days." It concerns his lifelong desire to find permanent value in the day-to-day succession of experiences. Each day, he would often remark, offers richly all that a man could wish, but skeptics had taught him to doubt, to hesitate, taught him that the day is delusive, that there is no simple way of finding the riches behind the delusions. "What does this saying of some mean," asked his old gossip Montaigne, "that the heavens in growing old bow themselves down nearer towards us, and put us into an uncertainty even of hours and days?"

> Daughters of Time, the hypocritic Days,
> Muffled and dumb like barefoot dervishes,
> And marching single in an endless file,
> Bring diadems and fagots in their hands.
> To each they offer gifts after his will,
> Bread, kingdom, stars, and sky that holds them all.

A persisting controversy has centered on the meaning of "hypocritic" in the first line. Joseph Jones, refusing to accept the obvious meaning of the word, argued that "Nature as a deceiver is quite out of tone with Emerson's fundamental thought . . ." This position fails to account for an important fact, that for Emerson it is not nature, but experience that deceives. Perfectly neutral in itself, nature became important for Emerson only when it entered consciousness, when it wore the colors of the human spirit. The "hypocritic Days" personify the succession of experience that continually blocks the poet's discovery of the permanent wholeness of reality. They are hypocrites or dissemblers because they are children of Time: the illusion of Time being the father of each doubtful moment or day in experience. It is further significant that the "Days" are "Daughters"; distinctly feminine, they are alluring, enticing, apparently offering boundless gifts, but muffled, hidden, virginal and dumb. An endless file of contradictions, the "Days" reveal only their exotic, but false appearances; they stir desire yet hide the means of fulfillment. This is not to say that a hoax is deliberately perpetrated; as children of Time, the "Days" cannot be otherwise, for temporal experience is an inevitable, but not a willful limitation. As Seymour L. Gross has read the poem, the "Days" offer the lowest and the highest of life's opportunities; "diadems" and "fagots," he has suggested, are metaphors for "glory" and "utility." We should recognize, however, that the gifts are not metaphors, but metonymies or literally examples of whatever mere experience offers. The "Days" deceive because they seem to offer, but cannot actually offer, reality itself. "Bread, kingdoms, stars, and sky" — each has its own apparent and limited value. We have been seduced if we accept any of them, believing it to be real. Here the march of the "Days" is a mere pomp, a frenzied dance. Some will accept the useful fagots, the bread, or strive for kingdoms; others, desiring the richer gifts, will seek reality in diadems, in stars and sky. But regardless of the choice, experience still deceives. The utilitarian thinks he has grasped reality in his bundle of twigs; the idealist, reaching for the sky, gains only a glossy piece of metamorphic rock.

In the last five lines, the focus of the poem shifts from the "Days" to the persona and to his response to experience:

> I, in my pleachèd garden, watched the pomp,
> Forgot my morning wishes, hastily
> Took a few herbs and apples, and the Day
> Turned and departed silent. I, too late,
> Under her solemn fillet saw the scorn.

The "pleachèd garden" symbolizes the poet's temperament, his reticence, his desire to give some practical order and meaning to the dumb succession. He does not, perhaps cannot, name his "morning wishes"; they are forgotten as he stands fascinated by the pomp, but still they are the only hint of a transcendent reality in the poem. His lost wish is to accept none of the gifts, but rather to fly beyond the limits of time. But instead of seeing the "Day" for what she is, he commits a hasty error; taking "a few herbs and apples," he is seduced. The lady's scorn, seen at the last moment, should have been recognized at first. Relatively his choice is a bad one, but absolutely it is no better or worse than any, for whatever he chooses, the poet is a victim of experience. The poem describes, then, a pathetic reenactment of the Fall of Man. Standing in his garden, the doubting Adam is reticent, forgetful, hasty — always at the wrong moments. Like his Biblical father, he too is beguiled by feminine charms, he too accepts the false gift, the apple, his "few herbs and apples." A much sadder story than Genesis or *Paradise Lost*, "Days" depicts that impotent creature, modern man, depicts the failure of his poetic and religious vision.

T. S. Eliot spoke to a different generation, to different issues, spoke with a much deeper tragic sense than we ever find in Emerson. Yet the "Boston doubt," to which Eliot was connected by family and by education, which he clearly recognized at the beginning of his career, was and remained his doubt. Once, discussing Pascal, he said: "For every man who thinks and lives by thought must have his own skepticism, that which stops at the question, that which ends in denial, or that which leads to faith and which is somehow integrated into the faith which transcends it." This sentence, I would submit, might equally describe the doubts and faith of Emerson or of T. S. Eliot himself.

"The Love Song of J. Alfred Prufrock" suggests most clearly the similarities and differences between their views. Like Emerson's persona of "Days," Prufrock is also a modern antihero, one who retains a bit of the Romantic hero's stature; but mixed with a fundamental impotence, he is only half Prometheus, half prude. He is indeed crippled, yet not by any tragic encounter, rather by his own foolishness and that of his society. As Prufrock himself suggests, he is a kind of Charlie Chaplin playing Hamlet. Worried, reticent, forgetful, impulsive — again like the persona of "Days," he is troubled by unnamed longings, overwhelming questions, yet always retreats to a pleached garden of propriety:

> Oh, do not ask, "What is it?"
> Let us go and make our visit.

Thus, Emerson's "herbs and apples" become Prufrock's "toast and tea." Nor can he escape the problem of time. "There will be time, there will be time," he cannot forget. If to the defective side of Prufrock time is merely the irresistible coming of old age, another side of him sees a succession of detached moments, filled with visions and revisions, each different, each unclear, yet requiring some ultimate act, some final confrontation:

> There will be time to murder and create
> And time for all the works and days of hands
> That lift and drop a question on your plate.

The phrase, "works and days," is usually identified as an allusion to Hesiod's famous poem, although apparently there is no similarity beyond this curious agreement in phrasing. But while it is not at all clear why Prufrock should, at this point, allude to Hesiod, there are excellent reasons why he might allude to Emerson, whose essay of the same title was published as the seventh chapter of *Society and Solitude* with, and this is the significant point, the poem "Days" as its preface. Eliot, it seems plausible to suggest, has chosen this phrase in order to underscore the fact that Prufrock is a latter-day Emersonian, one of "several thousands of well-bred people in a provincial American town" who has faced the "Boston doubt." But he is not Emerson himself. Indeed, Prufrock, quite unlike Emerson, has very definitely seen Sweeney's straddled silhouette: "For I have known them all already, known them all . . ." Important among the characteristics of Prufrock's moral vision is his loss of innocence; his world reveals no trace of the Garden of Eden. He has known, he has seen, and now he longs to return to "silent seas" where the dreadful knowledge vanishes. Here Prufrock's case is especially painful, for without the moral optimism that repeatedly saved Emerson from the tragic consequences of his skepticism, without that vigorous faith in the individual, Prufrock malingers. Take self-reliance from Emerson and you have a rather silly and very frightening view of life; you have Prufrock, the prophet, if at all, of self-obsession.

Time, doubt and vision — these are the foremost themes in nearly all of Eliot's major poems. Like Emerson, his concept of time was basically and self-consciously Heraclitean, characterized by its discontinuous succession. Divisions and particles of experience found symbolic expression through Eliot's poetry in his "heaps of broken images" of *The Waste Land*, in the decayed house in "Gerontion," in the succession of rising and falling houses of "East Coker." Again like Emerson, Eliot's skepticism proceeded directly from this view of time. "History," he said, "has many cunning passages, contrived corridors"; its issues and deceptions end in the vanities of Ecclesiastes. A single moment of ecstasy might seem to illuminate these doubts, but this is only a "partial ecstasy," for in the flowing succession of time the vision becomes a mere "recollected passion." So God remains inscrutable and incomprehensible, a "word within a word, unable to speak a word, / Swaddled with darkness." Just as Emerson saw through the shallow rationalism of the Unitarians and, in response, abandoned all hope of naming, defining or describing his God, Eliot repeatedly emphasized the poverty of language that seeks to communicate religious feelings:

> Words strain,
> Crack and sometimes break, under the burden,
> Under the tension, slip, slide, perish,
> Decay with imprecision, will not stay in place,
> Will not stay still.

Silence, stillness and humility were attitudes that they knew to be essential if one is to preserve faith in a dark, doubtful world. For both Emerson and Eliot, then, an inevitable skepticism preceded the coming to religious knowledge, a skepticism that could not be defeated on rational grounds, that rather had to be transcended by and integrated into faith:

> To arrive where you are, to get from where you
>   are not,
>   You must go by a way wherein there is no
>   ecstasy.
> In order to arrive at what you do not know
>   You must go by a way which is the way of
>   ignorance.

But here the paths that Emerson and Eliot took to faith sharply diverged. For Emerson, succession is a necessary condition of temporal experience; it is a "lord of life." There is indeed a timeless realm, but this can be known only in certain moments of great intensity and vision. Thus Emerson's view of experience remained dualistic in its distinction between the human and the divine worlds. He might hope to cross over, to transcend his limitations, but he made no attempt to integrate time on the human level; his transcendence is possible only through succession. The transcendent moment is only one among many atomic units of time—moments that must be regarded as ephemeral and therefore doubted. For Eliot, this notion of transcendence within succession is thoroughly unsatisfactory; in "Geron-tion" he implicitly denied it, in "East Coker" he made his objection clear;

> Not the intense moment
> Isolated, with no before and after,
> But a lifetime burning in every moment.

The journey to Little Gidding is a quest for a total integration of time, not simply a collection of successive moments, certainly not a denial of time, but a visionary fusion in which past and future are present in every mo-ment. "A people without history," he said, almost in answer to Emerson, "Is not redeemed from time . . ."

> So, while the light fails
> On a winter's afternoon, in a secluded chapel
> History is now and England.

Basically, the difference here between Emerson's and Eliot's concepts of time is implied in the classical distinction between *being* and *becoming*. Emerson found himself in an endless flow of unrealities, but believed that he might, at one rich point of time, rise to a vision of a timeless Being. His intellectual life began, we should remember, with his studies of Locke, Hume and the Scottish Realists; it was Hume's striking analysis of succes-sion that formed the persisting assumptions of Emerson's view of time. Al-though in later years he attempted to make room for an evolution, the new theory was never fully digested, and his empiricism prevailed. Eliot, on the other hand, was distinctly post-Darwinian in outlook. History in the *Four Quartets* is change, development, duration; vision is an intuitive grasp of a reality that is still temporal, but not discontinuous. "Only through time time is conquered." For Eliot there was no escape, only a hope for an integration of past and future. I call this an evolutionary view because it assumes that duration is reality itself; each man's history, bio-logical and social, is gathered up in the present, and the future is likewise implied in the same moment. There is but one reality and this is temporal, this is Becoming. In the chapel—"At the still point of the turning world"—time and God are one.

> Quick, now, here, now, always—
>
> .   .   .
>
> And the fire and the rose are one.

To come finally to an understanding and an estimate of the relation-ship between Emerson and Eliot, one might well keep in mind the distinc-tion between morals and mysticism. The younger Eliot was profoundly and exactingly a moralist, a critic in prose and verse who viewed Emerson as the spokesman for much that was blind and even pernicious in nine-teenth-century America. Everything implied by that "lengthened shadow" came under Eliot's scrutiny giving rise to a new morality for the twentieth century. Indeed, after *The Waste Land*, after the social horrors that brought it about and that it describes, it seems not likely that many can return to the tepid doctrines of "Compensation" and the rest. Still, Eliot recognized a tougher aspect of Emerson's thought: undergoing his own agony of skepticism, he saw that Emerson too was born to the "Boston doubt," was, to use Emerson's phrase, born with a knife in his brain. Both were unable to accept the neat dogmas offered them; but also unwilling to stop at the question or end in denial, they went toward faith and gained the mystical vision that confirmed it.

The Evolution of Sweeney in the Poetry of T. S. Eliot
Robert M. DeGraaff*

The characters of effete Prufrock and earthy Sweeney have often been seen as important polarities in the pre-conversion poetry of Eliot. Criticism has as yet failed, however, to properly recognize the gradual evolution by which Sweeney in his five appearances eventually triumphs over Prufrock and comes to represent Eliot himself. Instead, Sweeney has been consistently maligned, and Eliot has been identified more or less closely with Prufrock. Perhaps the prominence of the intellectual in all of Eliot's writings as well as in our academic approaches to literature has blinded us to this very real development of Eliot's poetic sympathies.

In the beginning, Prufrock dominates. "The Love Song of J. Alfred Prufrock" (1917) embodies an essentially modern quality of ennui, alienation, futility. In a world perceived as lacking a teleology, in which communication itself is impossible, Prufrock seems to stand for Eliot, the reader, or any intelligent being. The opposing polarity to Prufrock in the poem is suggested by the lines, "I should have been a pair of ragged claws / Scuttling across the floors of silent seas." Prufrock longs for the ability to act in a world without consciousness or communication. The only alternative to painful, over-refined self-consciousness which the poem offers, unfortunately, is unconsciousness.

In the same 1917 volume with "Prufrock," however, Eliot introduced the character of "Mr. Apollinax," whose "irresponsible," "submarine," and "profound" laughter tinkles among the Prufrockian teacups. Mr. Apollinax, though intelligent and self-conscious, suggests violent action and energy, the potency of "Priapus in the shrubbery" or "the beat of centaur's hoofs." He combines intelligence with the earthy qualities of Sweeney. The poem ends by gibing at the Prufrockian academicians who have incongruously played host and hostess to this volatile manifestation of Prufrock's seaweed

*Reprinted, with permission, from *Mid-Hudson Language Studies*, 2 (1979), 102–113.

world: "Of dowager Mrs. Phlaccus, and Professor and Mrs. Cheetah / I remember a slice of lemon, and a bitter macaroon."

The Prufrock-Sweeney struggle hinted at in the 1917 volume, is eventually resolved in *Sweeney Agonistes* (1926–27), not by Eliot's vitalizing Prufrock, but by his humanizing Sweeney. Eliot's preference, therefore, until his conversion to Christianity in 1927, lies with the "natural man" rather than with the over-refined intellectual.

Sweeney makes the first of his five appearances in "Sweeney Erect" (1920). Eliot's central point in this poem is generated by the juxtaposition of a heroic mythological past and a sordid rooming house (or brothel) present. As Charles Peake suggests, this juxtaposition may reflect Eliot's negative judgment on Emerson's theory of heroism as historically repetitive:

> Eliot is not merely contrasting a sordid modern scene with the glory that was Greece; but . . . he presents a satirical picture of one aspect of modern life and at the same time exposes the false ideas which are part cause and part consequence of it. Emerson's two essays ["History" and "Self-Reliance"] advocated and were expressions of that very state of anthropocentric, individualistic, self-sufficient blindness, without faith, humility or obedience, which Eliot saw as the fundamental cause of the spiritual barrenness of his times.[1]

The three characters who act in the "barren present" of the poem represent three alternative human positions. Sweeney's female consort, suffering a nightmare, an epileptic fit, or a bout of acute neurasthenia upon the bed, exhibits a perfectly Prufrockian panic. Sweeney, whose sexual potency is declared in the title, is associated with Polyphemus and an orang-outang — the second pole is animalistic. The poem is grim and frightening so long as it threatens a brutal razor attack by Sweeney upon his pathetic and helpless victim. This threat is dissipated, however, when Doris, a practical and humane third character who mediates between the first two, "enters padding on broad feet" to minister to the distraught. Her entrance, which calms the poem, subtly shifts the reader's perspective on the first two characters. Since Sweeney no longer threatens, he may now be seen as not only harmless, but even attractively simple and innocent: he stands before the mirror to shave, "broadbottomed pink from nape to base." At worst, he is perhaps understandably callous. The female on the bed, however, appears almost absurd in an atmosphere which Doris domesticates and humanizes. The "ladies of the corridor," reminiscent of those who came and went talking of Michelangelo at Prufrock's imaginary tea party, properly "tut tut" her unwarranted hysteria. Sweeney may not be a hero in the poem, but his animalism connects more closely with Doris' comfortable padding on broad feet than does the female's irrelevant terror. Sweeney and Doris, earthy but not unkind, become the humanized pair in the poem and stand in opposition to the over-refined or pseudo-refined ladies.

In his second appearance, in "Mr. Eliot's Sunday Morning Service," Sweeney is given that key position in the poem's final stanza which Doris holds in "Sweeney Erect." Again he is presented naked and broadbottomed, this time shifting from ham to ham in his bath. His innocent simplicity connects with the unified, unsophisticated, pre-theological Christian church[2] as his shifting buttocks reduce to absurdity the proliferating subtleties of scholastic debate. The poem's purpose is to satirize the modern church in its gross materialism and over-refined, sterile theology. Since Sweeney is introduced in pointed contrast to this corrupt church, he occupies an extremely favorable position in the poem's value-structure. As Grover Smith has pointed out, "through Sweeney . . . the poem contrives . . . a kind of vindication of the brawny natural man, with his carnal appetites, against duplicity and asceticism."[3]

The position of Sweeney in "Sweeney Among the Nightingales" is more difficult to evaluate. F. O. Matthiessen finds that Eliot is trying, in this poem, for "a paradoxical precision in vagueness":

> That is to say, he . . . wants to make as accurate a description of the object as he can and then let its indefinite associations unfold variously in different readers' minds.[4]

If this is indeed what Eliot wanted, he succeeded only too well: there are almost as many ingenious interpretations of this poem as there are critics of it. Elizabeth Drew sees the poem as a dramatization of the disparity between a glorious past, which connects itself through the ordering of its myth to archetypal human patterns, and a shabby, disordered, and meaningless present (which features Sweeney as its chief representative).[5] George Williamson sees Sweeney being threatened in the poem (as indeed almost everyone does), but refers all the actions of both the man in brown and the man with heavy eyes to Sweeney, and so has him sitting, standing, withdrawing, laughing, yawning, and at the same time grinning through the window.[6] Everett Gillis reads the poem as a parable of the degeneration of ritual life (more specifically, religious life) in the modern world. He regards Sweeney as "Eliot's most familiar symbol of the gross materialism and vulgarity of contemporary civilization . . . modern man in all his grossness and spiritual ineptitude."[7]

The extreme ambiguity of this poem makes it a happy hunting ground for explicators, and puzzling controversies over many of its details and images are numerous; however, almost everyone who has attempted an interpretation has begun with a totally negative view of Sweeney and has thus been forced into reading the poem as an indictment of contemporary society. As Babette Deutsch writes, for example, "we may observe that the poet, with a romanticism he has denied, is exalting the past and sneering at the present scene, harking back with bitterness to the glory that was Greece, to crime dignified by passion and terrible retribution."[8]

The romanticism, one suspects, is really in the eye of the critic. As Mr. Smith points out, Agamemnon, with whom Sweeney is identified, "was at

the peak of form when adulterous, murderous, and proud," and any interpretation based on his "untarnished grandeur" is misleading.[9]

As for the character of Sweeney in the poem, there is little justification
for viewing him as an incarnate demon. Like Lear he is a man more sinned
against than sinning. His association with animals is inconclusive: though
usually taken negatively, as an index to his "low bestiality," it might as easily
be read as a positive vindication of his "animal vitality." At least the ape,
zebra, and giraffe are comparatively innocuous, unlike the disquieting
Raven, who consorts with death. In the sinister silence of the setting there is
something almost appealing in the way Apeneck Sweeney spreads his knees
and lets his arms hang down to laugh — laughs so vigorously as to contort his
features (he obviously cannot be identified with the man with the heavy
eyes). There is nothing objectionable either in Sweeney's treatment of "the
person in the Spanish cape," evidently an extremely bored and slightly tipsy
prostitute, who tries to sit on his lap. He neither pushes her away, which
would be unkind, nor grasps her to him, which would be absurd (though
perhaps bestial enough to suit many critics). He does not even seem to resent
her spilling of his coffee — it is coffee, not liquor, he is drinking. As in "Mr.
Eliot's Sunday Morning Service," Sweeney possesses the dignity of uncom-
plicated innocence. Though associated with animals, he seems sympatheti-
cally human in a setting in which all other humanity has been distorted. As
F. O. Matthiessen points out, "The contrast that seems at first to be mocking
a debased present as it juxtaposes Sweeney with the hero of antiquity, ends
in establishing also an undercurrent of moving drama: for a sympathetic
feeling for Sweeney is set up by the realization that he is a man as well as
Agamemnon, and that his plotted death is therefore likewise a human tragedy, as the end of Agamemnon's career was also sordid."[10] Eliot indicts society on the same grounds that he had attacked the church in "Sunday
Morning Service" — for a sophisticated corruption which abuses or threatens the innocent natural man.

The fourth appearance of Sweeney occurs early in "Part III: The Fire
Sermon" of Eliot's *The Waste Land* (1922). Here he seems to partake of the
universal corruption; he and Mrs. Porter (and / or daughter?) make up the
first pair in the series of "unholy loves" which sing about the ears of the
Fisher King — surely a reprobate position.[11] However, Eliot generates a degree of ambivalence by his juxtaposition of a sordid present with a mythological or historical past. Again, this past (e.g., the forcing of Philomel) is
not uniformly glorious or ideal; it cannot be sustained as a satiric norm. The
purpose of the juxtapositions throughout the poem, whether or not one
reads it as totally pessimistic, resembles Joyce's in *Ulysses* — a recognition of
the Viconian cyclic nature of history. From this point of view, while the
contrasts between pairs of characters may initially seem humorous, the
identifications between them are seriously intended. We may laugh at
the notion of a Leopold Bloom as a reincarnation of Odysseus, but *Ulysses*
ratifies Bloom's heroic stature.

The major problem with this Sweeney passage is that the three love episodes to which it is allusively connected, in lines 196–206, reveal important differences in what they suggest about Sweeney. As the ditty about Mrs. Porter establishes beyond question,[12] there would be no forcible or cruel rape involved in this particular love affair; at worst, it would be strictly business. Marvell's "To His Coy Mistress" echoed in the lines "But at my back from time to time I hear / The sound of horns and motors . . . ," initially seems to place Sweeney in the position of lecher, threatening rape. The coyness of Marvell's mistress, however, is really only a foolish hesitation since her "willing soul transpires / At every pore with instant fires." The rape proposed here is not the forcing of Philomel, but the ravishing of life itself, in which the lovers would be partners. If Grover Smith is right in seeing "O the moon shone bright on Mrs. Porter" as Eliot's parody of John Day's description of Diana in the Diana-Actaeon myth, then this third referent is even less apt than the first two as a counterpart for the "ravager Sweeney."[13] Diana's virginity is not even threatened, and the merely mortal Actaeon is surely punished far beyond his deserts.

It remains for each reader to respond to Sweeney in terms of the referent that strikes him most clearly, and needless to say, for most readers Sweeney is the Tereus of lines 203–206. Still, while there is little about Sweeney that is consistent with the intellectual ingenuity of Marvell's persona (until *Sweeney Agonistes*), his threatened position in "Sweeney Among the Nightingales" is at least vaguely similar to Actaeon's. Though Sweeney's reputation is consistently blighted by the company he keeps, I believe that even in this poem he is entitled to a more lenient view than is generally taken. Certainly the lines in which he appears are the only comic relief in this rather heavy sermon.

In Sweeney's final appearance, *Sweeney Agonistes*, he comes into his own as the central figure of the piece. The work is fragmentary and certainly not compelling either as poetry or drama, but as usual a wide variety of interpretation has emerged. Some critics have been induced by Mr. Thompson's detective story hoax to read the play as a kind of suspenseful revelation of the criminal actions of Sweeney, either already performed, perhaps upon Mrs. Porter, or plotted against Doris. Others see Sweeney as a heroic figure among shallow hedonists.[14] I am not concerned here with adding any further speculations on the plot or its significance, but only with the significance of Sweeney's role.

Concerning the character of Sweeney, we do have some clues from Eliot himself:

My intention was to have one character whose sensibility and intelligence should be on the plane of the most sensitive and intelligent members of the audience; his speeches should be addressed to them as much as to the other personages in the play — or rather, should be addressed to the latter, who were to be material, literal-minded and visionless, with the consciousness of being overheard by the former. There was to be an understanding between this protagonist and a small number of the audience, while the rest of the audience would share the responses of the other characters in the play.[15]

The only character who can assume this central role is Sweeney. In his awareness of the essential emptiness of a nonspiritual world and the difficulties of human communication, he becomes the direct spokesman for Eliot himself, as Sears Jayne has pointed out:

> Sweeney . . . has a good deal of the poet about him. He alone perceives the truth about the modern situation and tries hopelessly to communicate to his fellows that the life they are living, on a human plane of sex and misunderstanding, is death. Mr. Eliot explores Sweeney's difficulties with a subtlety born of personal experience. Sweeney, the poet-philosopher, is in a real sense Eliot himself agonizing with the problem of communicating an idea.[16]

In explaining Eliot's motivation for the music-hall rhythms used in the poem-play, Mr. Matthiessen quotes another interesting remark of Eliot's, "that any hope for a popular drama would spring from the robust entertainment of the lower class."[17] The presence of Sweeney as protagonist in the work accords with this idea.

It should now be apparent that Sweeney does indeed undergo a remarkable evolution in the course of these five poems: from dumb "a gesture of orang-outang" to "Well here again that dont apply / But I've gotta use words when I talk to you." Only his animal vitality remains constant. It is no use to complain, as Matthiessen does, that the final Sweeney should really have a different name; name-conscious Eliot has chosen to retain the distinctive "Sweeney." The poetry insists on the development of this specific character.

The contrasting masks of Eliot in the early poetry are those of Prufrock and Sweeney; most of the poetic characters can by subsumed under one or the other of these two poses. At first the two personae are diametrically opposed: Prufrock is the old-young man, thin-armed, thin-legged, upper-class, fastidious, virgin, morbidly sensitive, and losing his hair; Sweeney is the pair of ragged claws, young, virile, lower-class, insensitive and imperturbable, gross, hirsute, perhaps bestial. Eliot's respect for the animal in man is shown by the fact that in establishing a human position between these two poles he chooses to add an intellectual dimension to Sweeney rather than attempt to vitalize Prufrock. The decisive factor in their conflict may be that Prufrock is intrinsically stagnant: it is difficult to sustain a literature of inaction (that "Prufrock," "Gerontion," *The Waste Land*, and "The Hollow Men" should all have been written by Eliot is remarkable). Simple bodily functions may occasionally disrupt the effete, adolescent languors of Prufrock, but Sweeney comes to represent more than mere physical animality. His humanized vitality is both sympathetic and durable — until

Eliot's Christian asceticism shifts the polarities in the post-1927 poetry and renders the Prufrock-Sweeney dichotomy irrelevant.

Notes

1. Charles Peake, " 'Sweeney Erect' and the Emersonian Hero," *Neophilologus*, XLIV (January 1960), 54–61. The quote is from p. 61.

2. See Ernest Schanzer, " 'Mr. Eliot's Sunday Morning Service,' " *Essays in Criticism*, V (April 1955), 154.

3. Grover Smith, *T. S. Eliot's Poetry and Plays: A Study in Sources and Meaning* (Chicago and London: University of Chicago Press, 1956), p. 45.

4. F. O. Matthiessen, *The Achievement of T. S. Eliot* (New York: Oxford University Press, 1959), p. 116.

5. Elizabeth Drew, *T. S. Eliot: The Design of His Poetry* (New York: The Noonday Press, 1966), pp. 42–46.

6. George Williamson, *A Reader's Guide to T. S. Eliot* (New York: The Noonday Press, 1966), pp. 98–99.

7. Everett A. Gillis, "Religion in a Sweeney World," *Arizona Quarterly*, XX (Spring 1964), 57.

8. Babette Deutsch, "T. S. Eliot and the Laodiceans," *American Scholar*, IX (Winter 1939–40), 24.

9. Smith, pp. 46–47.

10. Matthiessen, p. 129.

11. Drew, p. 78.

12. See Smith, p. 86.

13. *Ibid.*, p. 85.

14. See, for example, Charles L. Holt, "On Structure and *Sweeney Agonistes*," *Modern Drama*, X (May 1967), 46–47.

15. T. S. Eliot, *The Use of Poetry and the Use of Criticism* (London: Faber and Faber, 1933), p. 153.

16. Sears Jayne, "Mr. Eliot's Agon," *Philological Quarterly*, XXXIV (October 1955), 411–12.

17. Matthiessen, p. 159.

Religion in a Sweeney World   Everett A. Gillis*

The devotional and mystical aspects of T. S. Eliot's later poems and plays have proclaimed him formally as a religious poet. A number of the early poems which offer as their chief substance a devastating indictment of modern civilization may also be placed in the category of religious verse if we consider that their central focus in each instance is the decline of traditional religious values. The best known of these is *The Waste Land*, but with it may be placed others: for example, "The Hippopotamus," "Mr.

*Reprinted, with permission, from *Arizona Quarterly*, 20 (1964), 55–63

Eliot's Sunday Morning Service," "The Hollow Men," and the poem which furnishes the title of our discussion, "Sweeney Among the Nightingales." Associated very closely with Eliot's earliest, mordantly satiric inventions in the mode of Jules Laforgue, these earlier poems expose with brilliance and finesse the death of religion as part of the ruin to which modern culture has come. In intent and effect they are totally negative, since they offer neither hope nor remedy for the problem raised, merely exposing the tumor without attempting to excise it. It is only with "Ash Wednesday" in 1930 that Eliot begins to suggest his own solution: a return to traditional Christian belief and ritual.

Critics have not recognized the special religious emphasis in "Sweeney Among the Nightingales" partially, perhaps, because of the obscurity inherent in the grotesque nightclub facade comprising the foreground of the piece, partially because of Eliot's own modest deprecation of the poem as an effort merely at creating a mood of foreboding. A sense of foreboding is certainly present, but the poem has a profounder meaning as well. The chief clue to the religious values represented in the poem is the presence of the nightingales in the title and concluding stanzas, as they sing, first, near a typical Catholic institution, the Convent of the Sacred Heart, and, then, within the "bloody wood" where Agamemnon met his death. The wood may be taken in a religious sense when we remember the grove of the Eumenides near Athens in Sophocles' play *Oedipus at Colonus*, described by Antigone to her blind father as "filled with the voices of many nightingales." If the two woods are the same, as seems likely, the grove in Agememnon's day is "bloody" because it is still occupied, in effect, by the Erinyes, not yet changed from Furies to Kindly Ones.

The transformation of the Furies in Aeschylus' trilogy, the *Oresteia*, from which Eliot's epigraph is taken (specifically from the *Agamemnon*, line 1343), into the Eumenides suggests an ameliorative progression. Originally dark agents of a justice untouched by any trace of pity or mercy — representing in Greek tradition a primitive notion of conscience or remorse troubling the heart of the guilty — the Furies are changed after their pursuit of Orestes for his sin of matricide, and after his final acquittal in the temple of Athena, into beneficent forces. But at the time of Agamemnon's death the old dispensation is still in force; the curse — the chain reaction of monstrous deeds and equally monstrous vengeance characterizing the successive generations of the House of Atreus — still looms darkly above. Functioning as an objective correlative, Agamemnon's death cry prefixed to the poem — "Alas, I am smitten with a mortal blow!" — brings into the poem's context both the past history of Agamemnon's family, including the grisly banquet upon Thyestes' children and Agamemnon's own heartless sacrifice of his daughter Iphigenia, and the future torment of Orestes by the Furies and his final exculpation. The events of the *Choephoroe* and the *Eumenides*, the plays which complete Aeschylus' trilogy, effect after many years an expiation of the ancient curse. The trilogy as a whole thus reveals an ethical progression from a concept of implacable justice based upon an eye for an eye and a tooth for a tooth to a concept of purification through suffering and the beneficial role of the conscience in the human heart. In the light of this ethical development, Agamemnon's death takes on spiritual importance itself as a necessary step in the expiation of the curse and the ultimate salvation of his house; and, since his death initiates the process, it is in a sense sacrificial. In the same fashion that the Catholic convent recalls the ritual and theological implications of Catholic Christianity, including the sacrificial role of Christ represented in the Mass and the sexual symbolism implicit in the deification of the Virgin, so Eliot's epigraph evokes Agamemnon's heroic career, and suggests the ethical role which his death must play in the final saving of his house.

The juxtaposition of Sweeney and the nightingales in the title of the poem now provides a significant index to the poem's essential meaning: Sweeney, Eliot's most familiar symbol of the gross materialism and vulgarity of contemporary civilization, is modern man among the nightingales: modern man in all his grossness and spiritual ineptitude in the presence of religion as it is represented in two of the major religio-ethical traditions of western civilization, the Classical and the Christian. In a world characterized by this situation, obviously, spiritual truth and its concrete manifestations in religious ritual must of necessity be garbled, and religious vision inadequate and misleading. And this is true of the poem: Sweeney's first reaction in the midst of the nightingales, in the presence of sacred things, is a vulgar laugh, and it is he who guards the portal of religious vision – the Gate of Horn through which in more remote but spiritually effective times issued forth true dreams.

As is true of other of Eliot's poems, "Sweeney Among the Nightingales" proceeds on two levels of meaning. On the surface, against a background of gloom and foreboding, it depicts life in the modern world as a nightclub universe in which a curious aggregation of lost souls engage in meaningless and grotesque activity: a nightmare world marked by ambiguity and illogical shifts of scene and containing a confusing welter of impressionistic detail: Apeneck Sweeney, with his animal-like posture and raucous laughter, the mordant cabaret scene, the brutal mob-murder of Agamemnon. At its deeper level the poem is concerned with the theme of the impotency of sacrificial death, which is developed through the middle portion of the poem by a thinly-disguised travesty of the Catholic Mass and generally throughout the piece by references to Agamemnon's tragic assassination.

At the surface level of the poem Sweeney's presence projects us immediately into the ambivalent *bête-noire* universe which forms the larger foreground of the poem and introduces us to the brute-like character of all the inhabitants of his world soon to be introduced. Sweeney is ape necked: i.e., thick and stolid like one of the great primates; his arms hang down gorilla fashion, and the laughter that creases the flesh along his jaws is described in terms of zebra stripes that swell into giraffe-like blotches. The passage that follows, replete with signs of ominous foreboding, projects before us a vast immensity of dark heavens in the midst of which the encircled moon, death and its carrion bird the raven, Sweeney guarding the "hornèd gate," and Orion and the Dog star Sirius brood like dim constellations above a somber sea. Orion and Sirius, and the Raven (*Corvos*), are the only actual constellations in this list, although the "hornèd gate" might conceivably be taken as the moon in one of its phases. The others are of Eliot's own invention for this particular context, and his representation of Sweeney among the glittering constellations is one of his most ironic touches. Each of these connotes some dread omen or dark portent.

The nightclub passage which now follows encompasses three important features: the attempted seduction of Sweeney by the lady in the Spanish cape; the serving of food and the reactions of various characters to it; and an abortive conspiracy against some unknown person plotted by the host and a mysterious assailant. The lady's overtures toward Sweeney, little more than those of a common streetwalker, are rebuffed by him, and as she slides from his knees to the floor, she clutches at the table, overturning a coffee cup and pulling the cloth awry. The characters respond variously to the food (oranges, bananas, figs, and grapes) — fare traditionally associated with feeding time at the zoo, particularly at the cages of the monkeys and primates. The response of the "silent vertebrate in brown" (who is also the "silent man in mocha brown" and the "man with heavy eyes") is a sort of sullen indifference. He refuses not only to eat but betakes himself from the room, though a moment later he reappears at the window leaning in, like some gross Bacchus, with a garland of wistaria around his head. His companion, Rachel *née* Rabinovitch, however, shows a vigorous reaction, tearing at the grapes with "murderous paws."

It is now apparent as the air grows thick with ominous implications that Rachel and the lady in the cape are in league in some evil design, and, furthermore, that a nefarious plot is going forward near the door, where the nightclub host can be seen in intimate tête-à-tête with "someone indistinct." Yet before the outcome of this fateful conspiracy can be ascertained, the whole scene mysteriously vanishes, and in the abrupt fashion of a dream the disreputable nightclub has become a convent haunted by singing nightingales. Equally as suddenly the scene is once more shifted, from the sordid night life of the modern world to the realm of Classical tragedy, where we observe with astonishment and horror the bloody corpse of the hero Agamemnon, slain by his wife and her paramour, tossed upon the garbage heap and grossly stained by the careless droppings of the singing nightingales.

Superficially, then, the poem gives us little more than the sense of foreboding mentioned by Eliot, against a backdrop of enigmatic detail which obscures as much as it reveals the plot that robs the hero of his life. The world of modern man, it implies, is a nightmare, a zoo-like universe peopled by animalistic creatures, in which the most representative institution is a nightclub characterized by ennui, rampant sensualism, and crime: truly a Sweeney world!

At the deeper level of the poem the details just described take on more cogent meaning. As already implied, religion in the Sweeney world is a cheap travesty. Its source is not a church but a low cafe; its rubrics are twisted and distorted and its ministers displayed as negativistic and vulgar; and the typical lay participant in its worship service is Sweeney himself. The ribald parody of the Mass which occupies the central portion of the poem is already hinted at earlier, in the astronomical passage of the poem, in the reference to the River Plate, an estuary lying between Argentina and Uruguay, discovered by the Spaniards in their religious and economic conquest of the New World. As an objective correlative it recalls the fact that Spanish Catholicism at the time of the conquest was notable for its fervor (epitomized in the institution of the Inquisition), and that Spanish plate is traditionally the symbol of the Spanish exploitation of the New World's natural resources, and thus it helps in association with the Spanish cape (a word which may also mean a geographical location) to identify the lady as the Church. The silent vertebrate in brown is her priest (one of his aliases, "The silent man in mocha brown," connects him via the coffee cup, since Mocha is a variety of coffee, with the lady in the Spanish cape). The presence of Rachel *née* Rabinovitch at the service, her tearing at the grapes — the source of the Communion wine — reminds us of the historical role of the Jews in Christ's passion and death which the Mass commemorates. The hint of seduction which opens the scene may be interpreted as the effort of the Church to woo the materialistic Sweeney into her fold — an effort which Sweeney, considering his nature, appropriately and summarily rejects.

As we peruse the stanzas devoted to the cabaret scene we seem to be present at a bizarre charade through which, dimly observed, the ritual of the Mass may be perceived. The coffee cup and tablecloth now assume deeper significance as macabre representations of the Holy Chalice containing the sacramental wine and the richly adorned table furnishings of the Catholic altar during Mass. The lady's indifference to the fate of the sacred vessel, suggested by her actions in upsetting it, is matched by that of her priest, who yawns ("gapes") and sprawls awkwardly at the window like an animal, his eyes heavy with sleep. Both animalism and sleep are, of course, traditional symbols of spiritual sluggishness. The food served by the waiter is quite obviously a parody of the sacred meal of the Communion, especially the hothouse grapes (i.e., grapes grown artificially rather than naturally in the fields). Furthermore, since the wine of the Communion, of which the grapes are the source, symbolizes Christ's blood, Rachel's violence against them — her tearing them "with murderous paws" — suggests the historical slaying of Christ. The fact that the lady in the cape is in league with her is understandable on the grounds that the Church itself slays Christ in each reenactment of the Mass, which, as Catholic devotional manuals note, is not only a sacramental meal but a sacrifice as well. The priest's withdrawal at this moment is a striking instance of his total disregard of the special spiritual role which as chief celebrant of the service he plays in the Eucharistic ceremony. The fact is further highlighted by the phrase "declines the gambit," since the gambit is a chess term for a sacrificial play made to obtain strategic position on the board. Both by his indifference and his departure the priest "declines" to perform the sacrifice demanded by the rite.

We are now arrived at the most solemn moment of the Mass, the moment of the consecration of the bread and wine: the point at which the elements are miraculously transformed, as Catholic dogma states, into the actual body and blood of the Lord. The profundity of the mystery surrounding this act in the Catholic ritual is paralleled in the poem by the section at which it, in turn, reaches its greatest obscurity and difficulty of meaning: the point at which its details — the purple racemes of the wistaria, the golden grin, the host's shadowy figure at the door — become most dense, most impressionistic. The picture evoked is that of the actual priest as he stands immediately in front of the tabernacle containing the bread and wine, in the act of consecration. The purple hue of the wistaria appropriately hints at the wine within the Chalice and the "golden grin" at its circular rim glinting within the semi-darkness of the tabernacle's interior. A grin, being circular, suggests itself as a natural epithet in the gross nightmare realm of contemporary society (like the coffee cup earlier) for the precious Cup. The sacred wafer is likewise scurrilously parodied. The word "host" is of course the technical name of the sacred bread, and the impression of a private conversation between it and someone indistinct — the priest in the act of consecrating the bread — is a grotesque detail. Yet when we realize that the priest's prayer at this point is conventionally recited in a low, almost inaudible tone, we recognize Eliot's intent: the theological truth implicit in the sacred bread at the moment of its consecration, of the literal transformation of the wafer into Christ's broken body, *is*, for the Sweeney world, as dim and indistinct as a whispered message in a half-obscured doorway of a sordid cabaret!

In many respects the theme of Agamemnon's death is the central one in the poem. His cry of anguish provides Eliot with his epigraph. His death, climaxing the poem, brings him into central focus and throws into perspective around him the manifold details contained in it. Many of the dark portents of the early portion of the poem refer directly to him. Even the attempt at seduction on Sweeney, and the memorial meal in which Christ's flesh and blood are eaten and drunk, echo as well the seduction of Atreus' wife by Thyestes and the horrible banquet in which Thyestes dines upon his own children.

As suggested, Agamemnon's fate is clearly reflected in the astronomical phenomena in the poem if we consider them in the light of Greek mythology. The stormy moon suggests the wrath of Artemis, goddess of the moon, at the slaying of her sacred stag at Aulis while the Greeks impatiently awaited a wind for Troy, and the propitiation of the crime by Agamemnon's sacrifice of his daughter. The horned gate recalls the gates of sleep, one of ivory, one of horn, through which, respectively, false and true dreams emerged. Orion and the Dog also evoke the Artemis myth. Beloved of the moon goddess and accidentally slain by her arrow, Orion — followed by his dog — was placed by her among the stars and thus became a symbol of immortality glittering forever in the heavens. The reference to the "shrunken seas" which concludes the portent passage surely reflects, by ironic contrast, the resounding, wine-dark seas of Greek epic poetry. These are truly awesome portents in Agamemnon's fateful heavens: the wrath of Artemis predicts his death at Clytemnestra's hand avenging her daughter slain to placate the goddess; the veiling of Orion, symbol of immortality, implies the failure of his own death to assume its symbolic function. Sweeney's guardianship of the portal of true visions and the ebbing of the splendor of Greek epic seas suggests the inefficacy of any myth in the modern world to fulfill its normal function as a valid groundwork of belief.

Agamemnon's death, when it actually occurs, takes place as in any good Greek tragedy off stage, and we observe only the accomplished fact in the final stanza of the poem. But Agamemnon's death, no more than Christ's, in the modern world has no validity. Agamemnon's death cry suggests merely an instinctive reaction, not any awareness on his part that his death has any special value. Salvation in the Greek sense of a spiritualization of human life and a deepening of ethical truth is equally impotent with Christian regeneration in Sweeney's calloused world; like the Greek classical tradition as a whole, it has come to have no meaning in the modern culture.

The end of the poem thus suggests the world of the Erinyes rather than that of the Eumenides. The ethnical progression signaled by the song of the nightingales at Colonus in Sophocles' play fails to materialize. The Erinyes still pursue the guilty with undiminished hatred; their wood is still bloody; Agamemnon's death is merely a death. In the final analysis, then, it is not the music of the nightingales that has the greater meaning in the poem, but their "liquid siftings," which by their stains but deepen the shame of the fallen hero's dishonored shroud stiffening beneath its encrustations of blood and excrement within the indifferent wood.

The Epigraphs to the Poetry
of T. S. Eliot
Jane Worthington*

When the title of one of Eliot's poems is mentioned in conversation, it often elicits a quotation, not from the poem, but from the epigraph to the poem. "Mistah Kurtz—he dead," or "but that was in another country . . ." are two quotations frequently offered in token of the genuine article. Apparently readers of Eliot's poetry sense a peculiar fitness in the quotations which head his poems; they recognize that the quotation, no less than the title, belongs inherently to the text which it serves. Even when the aptness of the quotation is not perfectly understood, its authority is clearly felt.

Because Eliot's epigraphs are occasionally obscure, it is not always easy for a reader to grasp the relationship between the epigraph and the poem. Yet, as Mr. Matthiessen remarks in *The Achievement of T. S. Eliot,* an epigraph may illuminate a whole poem, and is itself "designed to form an integral part of the effect of the poem."[1] In this study my primary aim is to indicate by simple, yet specific, references the sources for Eliot's epigraphs. Wherever the original context of the epigraph seems to bear closely upon the whole poem, I shall summarize that context. Always, I shall attempt to show what connection the epigraph has with the poem, and hence what part it plays in an interpretation, or criticism, of the whole poem. I shall take up the poems in the order in which they are arranged in the *Collected Poems 1909–1935.*

"THE LOVE SONG OF J. ALFRED PRUFROCK"

> S'io credesse che mia risposta fosse
> A persona che mai tornasse al mondo,
> Questa fiamma staria senza piu scosse.
> Ma perciocche giammai di questo fondo
> Non torno vivo alcun, s'i'odo il vero,
> Senza tema d'infamia ti rispondo.[2]
>   (Dante, *Inferno*, Canto XXVII, ll. 61–66)

In the twenty-seventh canto of the *Inferno* Dante describes one of the flames that appeared to him in the eighth circle of hell. He saw the point of the flame shake, and he heard a voice issuing forth and asking for news of Romagna. In reply Dante described briefly the unhappy condition of that land, and in turn asked the flame to tell his name and why he was thus being punished. The spirit, later identified as Count Guido da Montefeltro, prefaced his reply with the words which Eliot has used as the epigraph to "Prufrock." In effect his reply was: "If I thought you were alive, I would not speak; but since you are dead and cannot repeat my story to the living, I have no fear and I shall answer you." Thus did fear of the world's judgment

*Reprinted, with permission, from *American Literature*, 21 (1949), 5–13.

and utter disregard for the judgment of the dead condition the response of Guido da Montefeltro.

Prufrock too was afraid to speak; he was afraid of comments, of snickers, of not being understood. The irony, of course, lies in the fact that Prufrock fears the comments, not of the living, but of the dead. The women who come and go, talking of Michelangelo, the women whom he sits beside after tea and cakes and ices — they are the ones who would comment upon his words, and they are all dead. We sympathize with, and yet smile at, his predicament. Irony and pathos are both intensified by Prufrock's own realization that the women to whom he would speak of love, of the differences between life and death, are themselves all dead. By placing Guido's fear of infamy among the living against Prufrock's fear of a snicker from among the dead, Eliot has underscored the irony of the poem.[3]

"PORTRAIT OF A LADY"

> Thou has committed —
> Fornication: but that was in another country,
> And besides, the wench is dead.[4]
>   (Marlowe, *The Jew of Malta*, Act IV, scene i, ll. 41–43)

Here is one of Eliot's simplest and most brilliant epigraphs. The striking contrast between the tone of the epigraph and that of the poem produces a fine irony and makes possible a clearer perception of the whole poem.

In the scene from which the epigraph is drawn, Barabas comically defeats the friars who are vainly trying to denounce his crimes. Whenever either of the friars approaches anything like a direct accusation, Barabas interrupts and supplies one for them. Lightly he assumes a multitude of crimes. He is a Jew, a usurer; he has committed fornication — but what of that? "That was in another country, and besides, the wench is dead."

At the end of "Portrait of a Lady" the hero wonders what would be his attitude if the lady were to die while he is in another country. To her restless, yet timid, advances he had dared no response. His sins have all been sins of omission, and yet he feels that if she should die, he could not take her death lightly. Confused, worried, tangled in his own timidity, the hero concerns himself over a situation that has not even arisen. If she should die, would he "have the right to smile?" Inevitably one contrasts this sickly and pale cast of thought with the rough language and callous attitude of Barabas; one is left with an obvious irony and a sharper perception of two extremes.

"MR. APOLLINAX"

> Ω τῆς καινότητος. Ἡράκλεις, τῆς παραδολογίας. εὐμήχανος. ἄνθρωπος.[5]
>   (Lucian, *Zeuxis or Antiochus*, I)

In *Zeuxis or Antiochus* Lucian delivered a gentle, yet telling, reproof to the art critics of his day. He recorded the praise that people awarded him, and thus, with apparent fortuity, revealed the shallowness of their understanding. They had praised him for the novelty of his work; wherever they found anything new or unusual, there they applauded loudest. His own experience reminded him of a story about Zeuxis and the admirable contempt which Zeuxis had shown to people who dealt him foolish compliments on his picture of the centaurs. Zeuxis, like Lucian, was praised for the novelty of his work, whereas his technique—traditional, full of grace and skill—his imagination, and his harmony of colors went unobserved.

The quotation which Eliot chose for the epigraph to "Mr. Apollinax" is a remark made by one of Lucian's admirers. It was as pertinent to Lucian as were the remarks made of Mr. Apollinax. " 'He is a charming man'—'But after all what did he mean?' " Actually, Mr. Apollinax was as old as the satyrs and centaurs of Zeuxis, but his novel behavior at tea was all that attracted attention. Mrs. Phlaccus, Professor Cheetah, and their friends ignored the variety of expression, the imaginative life of Mr. Apollinax, and instead fixed their regard upon his pointed ears.

It is quite likely that Charles Whibley, whom Eliot so much admired, was to a large degree responsible for the quotation from Lucian. In one of his essays Whibley criticized at length the *Zeuxis* of Lucian. It is worth noting that in his essay the only Greek quotation from Lucian is the one that later served as epigraph to "Mr. Apollinax." Whibley introduced the quotation by remarking that "The shouts of the people were as fatuous then as today."[6] There, indeed, is the theme of "Mr. Apollinax."

"LA FIGLIA CHE PIANGE"

O quam te memorem virgo . . .[7]
(Virgil, *Aeneid*, Book I, l. 327)

The loveliness of "La Figlia che Piange" is made more lovely by the quotation which prefaces the poem. The question was originally asked of Venus, loveliest of all goddesses. She was met by Aeneas for a few moments on the Libyan shore; she spoke briefly to him, and he asked her her name, even though he at once believed her to be a goddess. Like Aeneas's meeting with Venus, the momentary vision of the girl who mourns was beautiful, disturbing, and long remembered. The epigraph, therefore, enhances the already lovely vision.

The epigraph may also suggest, though obliquely, the passionate parting of Aeneas and Dido. Such a suggestion would make even more pitiable the speaker's way of parting, a way "incomparably light and deft . . . Simple and faithless as a smile and shake of the hand."[8] The poem mocks the overcultured, the palely aesthetic, those who know the passions in art but turn from them in life. Similar poems, "Prufrock" and "Portrait of a Lady," Eliot prefaces with ironic, mocking epigraphs.

"GERONTION"

> Thou hast nor youth nor age
> But as it were an after dinner sleep
> Dreaming of both.
>
> (Shakespeare, *Measure for Measure*,
> Act III, scene i, ll. 32–34)

The theme of "Gerontion" is given in the first half line of the epigraph, whereas the tone and atmosphere of the poem are suggested in the following line and a half. Such completeness is rare in Eliot's epigraphs. Usually they gain in value when they summon up in one's memory their whole context.

The quotation comes from the Duke's long speech to Claudio in which he urges Claudio to "Reason thus with life." To get the theme into the epigraph Eliot might have chosen other lines from the same speech:

> Happy thou art not;
> For what thou hast not, still thou strivest to get,
> And what thou hast, forget'st.

"Gerontion" makes specific that truth: we would see a sign, and when it is given, we neither see nor understand. But nowhere could Eliot have found in so brief a space both the theme and tone of his poem. The mind of Gerontion moves over history with just that broken, sudden kind of movement that the mind follows in a half-waking dream. Sustained passages of reasoning are broken by peculiar, fragmentary glimpses of personal history. The dream state, suggested by the epigraph, directs the movement of the poem, and is, I think, consciously emphasized in the conclusion. Consider the epigraph as a part of the poem, and then observe the symmetry achieved by the poem's last one and a half lines.

> Tenants of the house,
> Thoughts of a dry brain in a dry season.

"BURBANK WITH A BAEDEKER: BLEISTEIN WITH A CIGAR"

Tra-la-la-la-la-la-laire
> (Théophile Gautier, "Sur Les Lagunes," *Variations sur Le Carnaval de Venise*, in *Émaux et Camées*.)
— nil nidi divinum stabile est; caetera fumus
> (An inscription on a late painting of St. Sebastian by Mantegna which is in a house on the Grand Canal. An illustration of the painting may be seen in Paul Kristener, *Andrea Mantegna*, London, 1901, p. 329.
> The inscription — "Only the divine is permanent; the rest is smoke" — appears on the flag of an emblematic candle at the lower right hand corner of the picture.)

— the gondola stopped, the old palace was there, how charming its grey
and pink

> (Henry James, *The Aspern Papers*, in *The Novels and Tales of Henry
> James*, New York Edition, XII, 9. Mr. Eliot has slightly altered the
> quotation.)

— goats and monkeys

> (Shakespeare, *Othello*, Act IV, scene i, 1. 294)

— with such hair too!

> (Robert Browning, "A Toccata of Galuppi's")

— so the countess passed on until she came through the little park, where
Niobe presented her with a cabinet, and so departed.

> (John Marston, "Entertainment of Alice, Dowager-Countess of
> Derby," in *The Works of Marston*, ed. A. H. Bullen, London, 1888,
> III, 383–404. The lines are the concluding directions of the masque.)

The epigraph to "Burbank with a Baedeker: Bleistein with a Cigar" is a
patchwork of quotations, all but one being connected with Venice in one
way or another. Three of these quotations were identified and commented
upon by Mr. Matthiessen in *The Achievement of T. S. Eliot*.[9] Mr. Eliot
kindly identified for me the sources of the three remaining.

Taken together, the quotations remind one of the glorious past of Venice. Individually they remind one of the particular glories of an older Venice: its music and dances, its religious faith reflected in its religious art, the
color and design of its handsome buildings, the poetry and passion of its
dramatic past. Finally, they remind one of a way of life not limited to Venice, but common to all Renaissance societies — as they are now ideally imagined — societies where all was gracious, ceremonious, elegant, where
countesses were entertained by poets celebrating their worth and beauty in
songs and masques. A far remove from the Venice where Princess Volupine
prepared to entertain Sir Ferdinand Klein!

The epigraph adds to the many contrasts between past and present
upon which the whole poem turns. Since the poem makes explicit enough
the death that has overtaken Venice, and since the epigraph adds nothing
new, merely increasing the number of contrasts, I am inclined to believe
Mr. Matthiessen that it is less successful than most of Eliot's epigraphs.

"SWEENEY ERECT"

> And the trees about me,
> Let them be dry and leafless; let the rocks
> Groan with continual surges; and behind me
> Make all a desolation. Look, look wenches!
>
> (Beaumont and Fletcher, *The Maid's Tragedy*
> Act II, scene ii, ll. 74–77)

The scene in *The Maid's Tragedy* from which Eliot chose the epigraph
for "Sweeney Erect" is a scene of lamentation. Aspatia, forsaken by her
lover, calls her women about her and bids them "be sad." With an almost

voluptuous delight in grief, she lingers over the sorrows of the lovelorn. She examines a tapestry of Ariadne which one of her ladies has worked, and finding the colors "not dull and pale enough," she offers herself as a model.

> Suppose I stand upon the sea-beach now,
> Mine arms thus, and mine hair blown with the wind,
> Wild as that desert; and let all about me
> Tell that I am forsaken. Do my face
> (If thou had'st ever feeling of a sorrow)
> Thus, thus, Antiphilia: strive to make me look
> . Like Sorrow's monument: *and the trees about me,*
> *Let them be dry and leafless; let the rocks*
> *Groan with continual surges; and behind me*
> *Make all a desolation. Look, look, wenches!*

When this scene from *The Maid's Tragedy* is set against "Sweeney Erect," the effect is at first shocking. In the opening lines Eliot forces an immediate connection. He orders a scene of wild desolation where the winds shall "tangle Ariadne's hair / And swell with haste the perjured sails." Suddenly the poem shifts to the sordid bedroom scene—Sweeney standing erect in the morning sun, the epileptic, stretched out upon the bed, "clawing at the pillow slip." The epigraph and the introductory lines of the poem have recalled to the reader the familiar, poetic laments of the forsaken; now he hears the forsaken one cry out in epileptic screams. The effect of such violent juxtaposition is shocking, but at the same time it suggests a new criticism of both past and present societies.

The central problem in *The Maid's Tragedy* lies in the conflict between love and honor. The drama ought to be a noble and exalted one, dealing as it does with such high matters of ethics. Actually, the play has a kind of mustiness; for all its splendid passages of poetry, it leaves a bad taste. The moral tone of *The Maid's Tragedy* is debased because the poets consider the conflict not in terms of the individual (his character and action), but in terms of an artificial society. The same criticism can be made of "Sweeney Erect"—with one important reservation. It is not the poet who regards the affairs of Sweeney from the point of view of society; instead, the "ladies of the corridor" speak for society.

> The ladies of the corridor
> Find themselves involved, disgraced,
> Call witness to their principles
> And deprecate the lack of taste.
>
> Observing that hysteria
> Might easily be misunderstood;
> Mrs. Turner intimates
> It does the house no sort of good.

In the end, Eliot's clear criticism of such values paradoxically raises his poem to a higher moral level than that reached by *The Maid's Tragedy*.

Surely his brilliant, yet indirect, attack upon the evaluation of honor made by a large section of modern society is superior to the easy acceptance given by Beaumont and Fletcher to the standards of a degraded court society. . . .

"MR. ELIOT'S SUNDAY MORNING SERVICE"

Look, look, master, here comes two religious caterpillars.
(Marlowe, *The Jew of Malta*, Act IV, scene i, l. 21)

Eliot's volume of *Poems* (1920) contains three poems on the paradoxical nature of the flesh: "The Hippopotamus," "Whispers of Immortality," and "Mr. Eliot's Sunday Morning Service." In "The Hippopotamus" the church, no longer flesh and blood, is left behind as the fleshly hippopotamus takes wings and soars to heaven. In "Whispers of Immortality" the modern metaphysician, profiting nothing from the teaching of Webster and Donne, fails to grasp the Abstract Entities—end of all metaphysics—because he denies, as Webster and Donne did not, experience of the flesh. In "Mr. Eliot's Sunday Morning Service" the sable presbyters do penance for the flesh, even as they prepare to take for their salvation the body and blood of Christ. Eliot contemns the fleshly of past and present as vigorously as he contemns the fleshless. The epigraph to "Mr. Eliot's Sunday Morning Service" should help to make this point clear.

In *The Jew of Malta*, from which the epigraph is taken, the Church of the Renaissance is attacked for its fleshly indulgences, especially for its polyphiloprogenitive ways. In the scene from which the quotation comes, the Jew and his servant are found jesting at the falsely celibate life of the nuns and friars. The Jew remarks that for a while he was half-afraid the poison they had fed the nuns had failed to do its work, "Or, though it wrought, it would have done no good, / For every year they swell, and yet they live." But at last assured the nuns have this time swelled with poison and so died, he rejoices with his servant. The latter, delighted with this exciting new occupation, suddenly spies a monastery and eagerly asks permission to "poison all the monks." Barabas, always economical, denies him the pleasure; there is no need, he says, "for now the nuns are dead, / They'll die with grief." At that moment two friars approach, and the servant calls out, "Look, look, master, here come two religious caterpillars."

The paradox of the flesh, emphasized by the poet's injecting this line from Marlowe into "Mr. Eliot's Sunday Morning Service" is a cunning one: Christ incarnate—the Word, or Intellect made Flesh—brought salvation (in an Umbrian painting "Still shine the unoffending feet"), but since then the saving harmony of flesh and intellect has rarely been achieved. Almost always there have been two extremes, and both exist today: Sweeney in his bath—descended probably from a long line of religious caterpillars, and related to the fleshly presbyters of today, who "red and pustular" bear to the altar their "piaculative pence"; and, on the other hand, the modern metaphysician, controversial master of the subtle schools — descended from enervate Origen. The division once repaired by Webster and Donne, who experienced the flesh in a way that brought knowledge of death to the flesh and hence whispers of immortality, remains to plague Mr. Eliot at his Sunday Morning Service.

"SWEENEY AMONG THE NIGHTINGALES"

ωμοι, πεπληγμαι καιωριαν πληγὴν ἔσω.[12]
(Aeschylus, Agamemnon, 1, 1343)

Eliot has said of this poem that he intended to convey merely "a sense of foreboding."[13] The epigraph, a single line from Aeschylus's *Agamemnon*, immediately establishes the sense of foreboding, for it is the cry of Agamemnon as he is struck the mortal blow. The action and atmosphere of Eliot's poem portend a similarly treacherous attack upon Sweeney, and in view of the poem's last lines, the epigraph is correct and striking.

I suspect that other parallels may exist between the poem and the drama. Thus a case may be made out for Aegisthus, who withdrew from the action because he felt it was "The woman's part" (*Agamemnon*, ll. 1636 ff.), and the man in mocha brown, who "Leaves the room and reappears / Outside the window leaning in." Also in the drama could be found parallels for the trampled cloth (*Agamemnon*, ll. 944 ff.), the Dog star veiled (*Agamemnon*, ll. 958 ff.), and the foreign woman — Rachel *née* Rabinovitch — who, tearing at the grapes with murderous paws, prophesies the coming doom, as did Cassandra with her "barbarian hand" (*Agamemnon*, ll. 1050 ff.). The parallels do not stand in perfect order, but they are sufficient to increase the tragic overtones.

Notes

1. F. O. Matthiessen, *The Achievement of T. S. Eliot* (London, 1935), p. 52.

2. Translated by J. S. Carlyle, *The Inferno*, Temple Classics, p. 303: "If I thought my answer were to one who ever could return to the world, this flame would shake no more; but since none ever did return alive from this depth, if what I hear be true, without fear of infamy I answer thee."

3. My reading of "Prufrock" has been influenced by the analysis which Cleanth Brooks, Jr. and Robert Penn Warren have made of the poem in *Understanding Poetry* (New York, 1938), pp. 589–596. Roberta Morgan and Albert Wohlstetter in "Observation on 'Prufrock,' " *Harvard Advocate*, CXXV, 27–40 (Dec., 1938) present a slightly different interpretation, putting more emphasis upon the confessional nature of "The Love Song." According to their interpretation, the epigraph increases the irony of the poem because it prefaces a poem wherein the speaker confesses "to himself as someone who will never return to the world and therefore in confidence." Mr. Matthiessen (op. cit., p. 52) likewise emphasizes the confessional nature of the poem, and sees the epigraph as underlining "the closed circle of Prufrock's frightened isolation."

4. The first half line is spoken by Friar Barnardine; the rest by Barabas, the Jew.

5. Lucian, *Opera*, ed. Carolus Jacobitz (Leipzig, 1864), I, 395. The line may be translated: "O the novelty! Hercules, what a tale of wonder! [or, what use of paradox?] An ingenious man!" The Lucian text has been rearranged, and this essay has not yet appeared in either the Loeb Library or the new Teubner edition.

6. "Lucian—II," *Studies in Frankness* (London, 1898), p. 217.

7. Translated by H. R. Fairclough, *Virgil*, Loeb Classical Library, I, 265: "by what name should I call thee, O maiden?"

8. As opposed to a scene which the speaker can only imagine, a scene wherein the lover would leave, "As the soul leaves the body torn and bruised."

9. p. 53.

10. Matthiessen (op. cit., p. 53) identifies the epigraph and explains the connection between the title and the epigraph.

11. For Eliot's version, see Migne's *Patrologia Graeca*, V (1857), 779, nn. 28–29: "And likewise let all the deacons be reverenced, as commanded by Jesus Christ, the living son of the Father; also let the presbyters be reverenced, as the council of God and the assembly of the apostles. Without these there can be no church; of these things I persuade you as I can."

12. Translated by H. W. Smyth, *Aechylus*, Loeb Classical Library, II, 119: "Ay me! I am smitten deep with a mortal blow!"

13. Matthiessen, *op. cit.*, p. 129.

INDEX